Made in the USA
San Bernardino, CA
12 May 2020

The Kalevala
The Epic Poem of Finland
By Lönnrot
Translated into English by John Martin Crawford (1888)

Devoted Publishing
Woodstock, Ontario, 2016

The Kalevala

The Kalevala
The Epic Poem of Finland
By Lönnrot
Translated into English by John Martin Crawford (1888)
Edited by Anthony Uyl

The text of The Kalevala is all in the Public Domain. The layout is not in the Public Domain and is Copyright 2016© Devoted Publishing a division of 2165467 Ontario Inc.

Let us hear your stories and thoughts!

Contact us at: devotedpub@hotmail.com
Visit us on Facebook: www.facebook.com/DevotedPublishing
Visit our gaming division website: www.solacegames.ca
Published in Woodstock, Ontario, Canada 2016.

ISBN: 978-1-365-35308-6

Table of Contents

PREFACE	4
THE KALEVALA	15
PROEM	15
RUNE I	18
RUNE II	23
RUNE III	30
RUNE IV	41
RUNE V	51
RUNE VI	56
RUNE VII	61
RUNE VIII	68
RUNE IX	73
RUNE X	83
RUNE XI	93
RUNE XII	101
RUNE XIII	110
RUNE XIV	115
RUNE XV	124
RUNE XVI	136
RUNE XVII	144
RUNE XVIII	154
RUNE XIX	166
RUNE XX	175
RUNE XXI	186
RUNE XXII	194
RUNE XXIII	203
RUNE XXIV	217
BOOK II	226
RUNE XXV	226
RUNE XXVI	237
RUNE XXVII	250
RUNE XXVIII	257
RUNE XXIX	262
RUNE XXX	272
RUNE XXXI	281
RUNE XXXII	288
RUNE XXXIII	296
RUNE XXXIV	301
RUNE XXXV	306
RUNE XXXVI	312
RUNE XXXVII	318
RUNE XXXVIII	322
RUNE XXXIX	327
RUNE XL	334
RUNE XLI	340
RUNE XLII	345
RUNE XLIII	354
RUNE XLIV	361
RUNE XLV	366
RUNE XLVI	371
RUNE XLVII	381
RUNE XLVIII	387
RUNE XLIX	393
RUNE L	401
EPILOGUE	410
GLOSSARY	412

PREFACE

The following translation was undertaken from a desire to lay before the English-speaking people the full treasury of epical beauty, folklore, and mythology comprised in The Kalevala, the national epic of the Finns. A brief description of this peculiar people, and of their ethical, linguistic, social, and religious life, seems to be called for here in order that the following poem may be the better understood.

Finland (Finnish, Suomi or Suomenmaa, the swampy region, of which Finland, or Fen-land is said to be a Swedish translation,) is at present a Grand-Duchy in the north-western part of the Russian empire, bordering on Olenetz, Archangel, Sweden, Norway, and the Baltic Sea, its area being more than 144,000 square miles, and inhabited by some 2,000,000 of people, the last remnants of a race driven back from the East, at a very early day, by advancing tribes. The Finlanders live in a land of marshes and mountains, lakes and rivers, seas, gulfs, islands, and inlets, and they call themselves Suomilainen, Fen-dwellers. The climate is more severe than that of Sweden. The mean yearly temperature in the north is about 27°F., and about 38°F., at Helsingfors, the capital of Finland. In the southern districts the winter is seven months long, and in the northern provinces the sun disappears entirely during the months of December and January.

The inhabitants are strong and hardy, with bright, intelligent faces, high cheek-bones, yellow hair in early life, and with brown hair in mature age. With regard to their social habits, morals, and manners, all travellers are unanimous in speaking well of them. Their temper is universally mild; they are slow to anger, and when angry they keep silence. They are happy-hearted, affectionate to one another, and honorable and honest in their dealings with strangers. They are a cleanly people, being much given to the use of vapor-baths. This trait is a conspicuous note of their character from their earliest history to the present day. Often in the runes of The Kalevala reference is made to the "cleansing and healing virtues of the vapors of the heated bathroom."

The skull of the Finn belongs to the brachycephalic (short-headed) class of Retzius. Indeed the Finn-organization has generally been regarded as Mongol, though Mongol of a modified type. His color is swarthy, and his eyes are gray. He is not inhospitable, but not over-easy of access; nor is he a friend of new fashions. Steady, careful, laborious, he is valuable in the mine, valuable in the field, valuable oil shipboard, and, withal, a brave soldier on land.

The Finns are a very ancient people. It is claimed, too, that they began earlier than any other European nation to collect and preserve their ancient folk-lore. Tacitus, writing in the very beginning of the second century of the Christian era, mentions the Fenni, as he calls them, in the 46th chapter of his De Moribus Germanoram. He says of them: "The Finns are extremely wild, and live in abject poverty. They have no arms, no horses, no dwellings; they live on herbs, they clothe themselves in skins, and they sleep on the ground. Their only resources are their arrows, which for the lack of iron are tipped with bone." Strabo and the great geographer, Ptolemy, also mention this curious people. There is evidence that at one time they were spread over large portions of Europe and western Asia.

Perhaps it should be stated here that the copper, so often mentioned in The Kalevala, when taken literally, was probably bronze, or "hardened copper," the amount and quality of the alloy used being not now known. The prehistoric races of Europe were acquainted with bronze implements.

It may be interesting to note in this connection that Canon Isaac Taylor, and Professor Sayce have but very recently awakened great interest in this question, in Europe especially, by the reading of papers before the British Philological Association, in which they argue in favor of the Finnic origin of the Aryans. For this new theory these scholars present exceedingly strong evidence, and they conclude that the time of the separation of the Aryan from the Finnic stock must have been more than five thousand years ago.

The Finnish nation has one of the most sonorous and flexible of languages. Of the cultivated tongues of Europe, the Magyar, or Hungarian, bears the most positive signs of a deep-rooted similarity to the Finnish. Both belong to the Ugrian stock of agglutinative languages, i.e., those which preserve the root most carefully, and effect all changes of grammar by suffixes attached to the original stein. Grimin has shown that both Gothic and Icelandic present traces of Finnish influence.

The musical element of a language, the vowels, are well developed in Finnish, and their due sequence is subject to strict rules of euphony. The dotted o; (equivalent to the French eu) of the first syllable must be followed by an e or an i. The Finnish, like all Ugrian tongues, admits rhyme, but with reluctance, and prefers alliteration. Their alphabet consists of but nineteen letters, and of these, b, c, d, f, g, are found only in a few foreign words, and many others are never found initial.

One of the characteristic features of this language, and one that is likewise characteristic of the Magyar, Turkish, Mordvin, and other kindred tongues, consists in the frequent use of endearing diminutives. By a series of suffixes to the names of human beings, birds, fishes, trees, plants, stones, metals, and even actions, events, and feelings, diminutives are obtained, which by their form, present the names so made in different colors; they become more naive, more childlike, eventually more roguish, or humorous, or pungent. These traits can scarcely be rendered in English; for, as Robert Ferguson remarks: "The English language is not strong in diminutives, and therefore it lacks some of the most effective means for the expression of affectionate, tender, and familiar relations." In this respect all translations from the Finnish into English necessarily must fall short of the original. The same might be said of the many emotional interjections in which the Finnish, in common with all Ugrian dialects, abounds. With the exception of these two characteristics of the Ugrian languages, the chief beauties of the Finnish verse admit of an apt rendering into English. The structure of the sentences is very simple indeed, and adverbs and adjectives are used sparingly.

Finnish is the language of a people who live pre-eminently close to nature, and are at home amongst the animals of the wilderness, beasts and birds, winds, and woods, and waters, falling snows, and flying sands, and rolling rocks, and these are carefully distinguished by corresponding verbs of ever-changing acoustic import. Conscious of the fact that, in a people like the Finns where nature and nature-worship form the centre of all their life, every word connected with the powers and elements of nature must be given its fall value, great care has been taken in rendering these finely shaded verbs. A glance at the mythology of this interesting people will place the import of this remark in better view.

In the earliest age of Suomi, it appears that the people worshiped the conspicuous objects in nature under their respective, sensible forms. All beings were persons. The Sun, Moon, Stars, the Earth, the Air, and the Sea, were to the ancient Finns, living, self-conscious beings. Gradually the existence of invisible agencies and energies was recognized, and these were attributed to superior persons who lived independent of these visible entities, but at the same time were connected with them. The basic idea in Finnish mythology seems to lie in this: that all objects in nature are governed by invisible deities, termed haltiat, regents or genii. These haltiat, like members of the human family, have distinctive bodies and spirits; but the minor ones are somewhat immaterial and formless, and their existences are entirely independent of the objects in which they are particularly interested. They are all immortal, but they rank according to the relative importance of their respective charges. The lower grades of the Finnish gods are sometimes subservient to the deities of greater powers, especially to those who rule respectively the air, the water, the field, and the forest. Thus, Pilajatar, the daughter of the aspen, although as divine as Tapio, the god of the woodlands, is necessarily his servant.

One of the most notable characteristics of the Finnish mythology is the interdependence among the gods. "Every deity", says Castren, "however petty he may be, rules in his own sphere as a substantial, independent power, or, to speak in the spirit of The Kalevala, as a self-ruling householder. The god of the Polar-star only governs an insignificant spot in the vault of the sky, but on this spot he knows no master."

The Finnish deities, like the ancient gods of Italy and Greece, are generally represented in pairs, and all the gods are probably wedded. They have their individual abodes and are surrounded by their respective families. The Primary object of worship among the early Finns was most probably the visible sky with its sun, moon, and stars, its aurora-lights, its thunders and its lightnings. The heavens themselves were thought divine. Then a personal deity of the heavens, coupled with the name of his abode, was the next conception; finally this sky-god was chosen to represent the supreme Ruler. To the sky, the sky-god, and the supreme God, the term Jumala (thunder-home) was given.

In course of time, however, when the Finns came to have more purified ideas about religion, they called the sky Taivas and the sky-god Ukko. The word, Ukko, seems related to the Magyar Agg, old, and meant, therefore, an old being, a grandfather; but ultimately it came to be used exclusively as the name of the highest of the Finnish deities. Frost, snow, hail, ice, wind and rain, sunshine and shadow, are thought to come from the hands of Ukko. He controls the clouds; he is called in The Kalevala, "The Leader of the Clouds," "The Shepherd of the Lamb-Clouds," "The God of the Breezes," "The Golden King," "The Silvern Ruler of the Air," and "The Father of the Heavens." He wields the thunder-bolts, striking down the spirits of evil on the mountains, and is therefore termed, "The Thunderer," like the Greek Zeus, and his abode is called, "The Thunder-Home." Ukko is often represented as sitting upon a cloud in the vault of the sky, and bearing on his shoulders the firmament, and therefore he is termed, "The Pivot of the Heavens." He is armed as an omnipotent warrior; his fiery arrows are forged from copper, the lightning is his sword, and the rainbow his bow, still called Ukkon Kaari. Like the German god, Thor, Ukko swings a hammer; and, finally, we find, in a vein of familiar symbolism, that his skirt sparkles with fire, that his stockings are blue, and his shoes, crimson colored.

In the following runes, Ukko here and there interposes. Thus, when the Sun and Moon were stolen from the heavens, and hidden away in a cave of the copper-bearing mountain, by the wicked

The Kalevala

hostess of the dismal Sariola, he, like Atlas in the mythology of Greece, relinquishes the support of the heavens, thunders along the borders of the darkened clouds, and strikes fire from his sword to kindle a new sun and a new moon. Again, when Lemminkainen is hunting the fire-breathing horse of Piru, Ukko, invoked by the reckless hero, checks the speed of the mighty courser by opening the windows of heaven, and showering upon him flakes of snow, balls of ice, and hailstones of iron. Usually, however, Ukko prefers to encourage a spirit of independence among his worshipers. Often we find him, in the runes, refusing to heed the call of his people for help, as when Ilmatar, the daughter of the air, vainly invoked him to her aid, that Wainamoinen, already seven hundred years unborn, might be delivered. So also Wainamoinen beseeches Ukko in vain to check the crimson streamlet flowing from his knee wounded by an axe in the hands of Hisi. Ukko, however, with all his power, is by no means superior to the Sun, Moon, and other bodies dwelling in the heavens; they are uninfluenced by him, and are considered deities in their own right. Thus, Paeivae means both sun and sun-god; Kun means moon and moon-god; and Taehti and Ottava designate the Polar-star and the Great Bear respectively, as well as the deities of these bodies.

The Sun and the Moon have each a consort, and sons, and daughters. Two sons only of Paeivae appear in The Kalevala, one comes to aid Wainamoinen in his efforts to destroy the mystic Fire-fish, by throwing from the heavens to the girdle of the hero, a "magic knife, silver-edged, and golden-handled;" the other son, Panu, the Fire-child, brings back to Kalevala the fire that bad been stolen by Louhi, the wicked hostess of Pohyola. From this myth Castren argues that the ancient Finns regarded fire as a direct emanation from the Sun. The daughters of the Sun, Moon, Great Bear, Polar-star, and of the other heavenly dignitaries, are represented as ever-young and beautiful maidens, sometimes seated on the bending branches of the forest-trees, sometimes on the crimson rims of the clouds, sometimes on the rainbow, sometimes on the dome of heaven. These daughters are believed to be skilled to perfection in the arts of spinning and weaving, accomplishments probably attributed to them from the fanciful likeness of the rays of light to the warp of the weaver's web.

The Sun's career of usefulness and beneficence in bringing light and life to Northland is seldom varied. Occasionally he steps from his accustomed path to give important information to his suffering worshipers. For example, when the Star and the Moon refuse the information, the Sun tells the Virgin Mariatta, where her golden infant lies bidden.

"Yonder is thy golden infant,
There thy holy babe lies sleeping,
Hidden to his belt in water,
Hidden in the reeds and rushes."

Again when the devoted mother of the reckless hero, Lemminkainen, (chopped to pieces by the Sons Of Nana, as in the myth of Osiris) was raking together the fragments of his body from the river of Tuoui, and fearing that the sprites of the Death-stream might resent her intrusion, the Sun, in answer to her entreaties, throws his Powerful rays upon the dreaded Shades, and sinks them into a deep sleep, while the mother gathers up the fragments of her son's body in safety. This rune of the Kalevala is particularly interesting as showing the belief that the dead can be restored to life through the blissful light of heaven.

Among the other deities of the air are the Luonnotars, mystic maidens, three of whom were created by the rubbing of Ukko's hands upon his left knee. They forthwith walk the crimson borders of the clouds, and one sprinkles white milk, one sprinkles red milk, and the third sprinkles black milk over the hills and mountains; thus they become the "mothers of iron," as related in the ninth rune of The Kalevala. In the highest regions of the heavens, Untar, or Undutar, has her abode, and presides over mists and fogs. These she passes through a silver sieve before sending them to the earth. There are also goddesses of the winds, one especially noteworthy, Suvetar (suve, south, summer), the goddess of the south-wind. She is represented as a kind-hearted deity, healing her sick and afflicted followers with honey, which she lets drop from the clouds, and she also keeps watch over the herds grazing in the fields and forests.

Second only to air, water is the element held most in reverence by the Finns and their kindred tribes. "It could hardly be otherwise," says Castren, "for as soon as the soul of the savage began to suspect that the godlike is spiritual, super-sensual, then, even though he continues to pay reverence to matter, he in general values it the more highly the less compact it is. He sees on the one hand how easy it is to lose his life on the surging waves, and on the other, he sees that from these same waters he is nurtured, and his life prolonged." Thus it is that the map of Finland is to this day full of names like Pyhojarvi (sacred lake) and Pyhajoki (sacred river). Some of the Finlanders still offer goats and calves to these sacred waters; and many of the Ugrian clans still sacrifice the reindeer to the river Ob. In Esthonia is a rivulet, Vohanda, held in such reverence that until very recently, none dared to fell a tree or cut a shrub in its immediate vicinity, lest death should overtake the offender within a year, in punishment for his sacrilege. The lake, Eim, is still held sacred by the Esthonians, and the Eim-legend is thus told by F. Thiersch, quoted also by Grimm and by Mace da Charda:

"Savage, evil men dwelt by its borders. They neither mowed the meadows which it watered, nor sowed the fields which it made fruitful, but robbed and murdered, insomuch that its clear waves grew dark with the blood of the slaughtered men. Then did the lake Him mourn, and one evening it called together all its fishes, and rose aloft with them into the air. When the robbers heard the sound, they exclaimed: 'Eim hath arisen; let us gather its fishes and treasures.' But the fishes had departed with the lake, and nothing was found on the bottom but snakes, and lizards, and toads. And Eim rose higher, and higher, and hastened through the air like a white cloud. And the hunters in the forest said: 'What bad weather is coming on!' The herdsmen said: 'What a white swan is flying above there!' For the whole night the lake hovered among the stars, and in the morning the reapers beheld it sinking. And from the swan grew a white ship, and from the ship a dark train of clouds; and a voice came from the waters: 'Get thee hence with thy harvest, for I will dwell beside thee.' Then they bade the lake welcome, if it would only bedew their fields and meadows; and it sank down and spread itself out in its home to the full limits. Then the lake made all the neighborhood fruitful, and the fields became green, and the people danced around it, so that the old men grew joyous as the youth."

The chief water-god is Ahto, on the etymology of which the Finnish language throws little light. It is curiously like Ahti, another name for the reckless Lemminkainen. This water-god, or "Wave-host," as he is called, lives with his "cold and cruel-hearted spouse," Wellamo, at the bottom of the sea, in the chasms of the Salmon-rocks, where his palace, Ahtola, is constructed. Besides the fish that swim in his dominions, particularly the salmon, the trout, the whiting, the perch, the herring, and the white-fish, he possesses a priceless treasure in the Sampo, the talisman of success, which Louhi, the hostess of Pohyola, dragged into the sea in her efforts to regain it from the heroes of Kalevala. Ever eager for the treasures of others, and generally unwilling to return any that come into his possession, Ahto is not incapable of generosity. For example, once when a shepherd lad was whittling a stick on the bank of a river, he dropped his knife into the stream. Ahto, as in the fable, "Mercury and the Woodman," moved by the tears of the unfortunate lad, swam to the scene, dived to the bottom, brought up a knife of gold, and gave it to the young shepherd. Innocent and honest, the herd-boy said the knife was not his. Then Ahto dived again, and brought up a knife of silver, which he gave to the lad, but this in turn was not accepted. Thereupon the Wave-host dived again, and the third time brought the right knife to the boy who gladly recognized his own, and received it with gratitude. To the shepherd-lad Ahto gave the three knives as a reward for his honesty.

A general term for the other water-hosts living not only in the sea, but also in the rivers, lakes, cataracts, and fountains, is Ahtolaiset (inhabitants of Ahtola), "Water-people," "People of the Foam and Billow," "Wellamo's Eternal People." Of these, some have specific names; as Allotar (wave-goddess), Koskenneiti (cataract-maiden), Melatar (goddess of the helm), and in The Kalevala these are sometimes personally invoked. Of these minor deities, Pikku Mies (the Pigmy) is the most noteworthy. Once when the far-outspreading branches of the primitive oak-tree shut out the light of the sun from Northland, Pikku Mies, moved by the entreaties of Wainamoinen, emerged from the sea in a suit of copper, with a copper hatchet in his belt, quickly grew from a pigmy to a gigantic hero, and felled the mighty oak with the third stroke of his axe. In general the water-deities are helpful and full of kindness; some, however, as Wetehilien and Iku-Turso, find their greatest pleasure in annoying and destroying their fellow-beings.

Originally the Finlanders regarded the earth as a godlike existence with personal powers, and represented as a beneficent mother bestowing peace and plenty on all her worthy worshipers. In evidence of this we find the names, Maa-emae (mother-earth), and Maan-emo (mother of the earth), given to the Finnish Demeter. She is always represented as a goddess of great powers, and, after suitable invocation, is ever willing and able to help her helpless sufferers. She is according to some mythologists espoused to Ukko, who bestows upon her children the blessings of sunshine and rain, as Ge is wedded to Ouranos, Jordh to Odhin, and Papa to Rangi.

Of the minor deities of the earth, who severally govern the plants, such as trees, rye, flax, and barley, Wirokannas only is mentioned in The Kalevala. Once, for example, this "green robed Priest of the Forest" abandoned for a time his presidency over the cereals in order to baptize the infant-son of the Virgin Mariatta. Once again Wirokannas left his native sphere of action, this time making a most miserable and ludicrous failure, when he emerged from the wilderness and attempted to slay the Finnish Taurus, as described in the runes that follow. The agricultural deities, however, receive but little attention from the Finns, who, with their cold and cruel winters, and their short but delightful summers, naturally neglect the cultivation of the fields, for cattle-raising, fishing, and hunting.

The Kalevala

The forest deities proper, however, are held in high veneration. Of these the chief is Tapio, "The Forest-Friend," "The Gracious God of the Woodlands." He is represented as a very tall and slender divinity, wearing a long, brown board, a coat of tree-moss, and a high-crowned hat of fir-leaves. His consort is Mielikki, "The Honey-rich Mother of the Woodland," "The Hostess of the Glen and Forest." When the hunters were successful she was represented as beautiful and benignant, her hands glittering with gold and silver ornaments, wearing ear-rings and garlands of gold, with hair-bands silver-tinseled, on her forehead strings of pearls, and with blue stockings on her feet, and red strings in her shoes. But if the game-bag came back empty, she was described as a hateful, hideous thing, robed in untidy rags, and shod with straw. She carries the keys to the treasury of Metsola, her husband's abode, and her bountiful chest of honey, the food of all the forest-deities, is earnestly sought for by all the weary hunters of Suomi. These deities are invariably described as gracious and tender-hearted, probably because they are all females with the exception of Tapio and his son, Nyrikki, a tall and stately youth who is engaged in building bridges over marshes and forest-streams, through which the herds must pass on their way to the woodland-pastures. Nyrikki also busies himself in blazing the rocks and the trees to guide the heroes to their favorite hunting-grounds. Sima-suu (honey-mouth), one of the tiny daughters of Tapio, by playing on her Sima-pilli (honey-flute), also acts as guide to the deserving hunters.

Hiisi, the Finnish devil, bearing also the epithets, Juntas, Piru, and Lempo, is the chief of the forest-demons, and is inconceivably wicked. He was brought into the world consentaneously with Suoyatar, from whose spittle, as sung in The Kalevala, he formed the serpent. This demon is described as cruel, horrible, hideous, and bloodthirsty, and all the most painful diseases and misfortunes that ever afflict mortals are supposed to emanate from him. This demon, too, is thought by the Finlanders to have a hand in all the evil done in the world.

Turning from the outer world to man, we find deities whose energies are used only in the domain of human existence. "These deities," says Castren, "have no dealings with the higher, spiritual nature of man. All that they do concerns man solely as an object in nature. Wisdom and law, virtue and justice, find in Finnish mythology no protector among the gods, who trouble themselves only about the temporal wants of humanity." The Love-goddess was Sukkamieli (stocking-lover). "Stockings," says Castren gravely, "are soft and tender things, and the goddess of love was so called because she interests herself in the softest and tenderest feelings of the heart." This conception, however, is as farfetched as it is modern. The Love-deity of the ancient Finns was Lempo, the evil-demon. It is more reasonable therefore to suppose that the Finns chose the son of Evil to look after the feelings of the human heart, because they regarded love as an insufferable passion, or frenzy, that bordered on insanity, and incited in some mysterious manner by an evil enchanter.

Uni is the god of sleep, and is described as a kind-hearted and welcome deity. Untamo is the god of dreams, and is always spoken of as the personification of indolence. Munu tenderly looks after the welfare of the human eye. This deity, to say the least is an oculist of long and varied experience, in all probability often consulted in Finland because of the blinding snows and piercing winds of the north. Lemmas is a goddess in the mythology of the Finns who dresses the wounds of her faithful sufferers, and subdues their pains. Suonetar is another goddess of the human frame, and plays a curious and important part in the restoration to life of the reckless Lemminkainen, as described in the following runes. She busies herself in spinning veins, and in sewing up the wounded tissues of such deserving worshipers as need her surgical skill.

Other deities associated with the welfare of mankind are the Sinettaret and Kankahattaret, the goddesses respectively of dyeing and weaving. Matka-Teppo is their road-god, and busies himself in caring for horses that are over-worked, and in looking after the interests of weary travellers. Aarni is the guardian of hidden treasures. This important office is also filled by a hideous old deity named Mammelainen, whom Renwall, the Finnish lexicographer, describes as "femina maligna, matrix serpentis, divitiarum subterranearum custos," a malignant woman, the mother of the snake, and the guardian of subterranean treasures. From this conception it is evident that the idea of a kinship between serpents and hidden treasures frequently met with in the myths of the Hungarians, Germans, and Slavs, is not foreign to the Finns.

Nowhere are the inconsistencies of human theory and practice more curiously and forcibly shown than in the custom in vogue among the clans of Finland who are not believers in a future life, but, notwithstanding, perform such funereal ceremonies as the burying in the graves of the dead, knives, hatchets, spears, bows, and arrows, kettles, food, clothing, sledges and snow-shoes, thus bearing witness to their practical recognition of some form of life beyond the grave. The ancient Finns occasionally craved advice and assistance from the dead. Thus, as described in The Kalevala, when the hero of Wainola needed three words of master-magic wherewith to finish the boat in which he was to sail to win the mystic maiden of Sariola, he first looked in the brain of the white squirrel, then in the mouth of the white-swan when dying, but all in vain; then he journeyed to the kingdom of Tuoni, and failing there, he "struggled over the points of needles, over the blades of swords, over the edges of hatchets" to the grave of the ancient wisdom-bard, Antero Wipunen, where he "found the lost-words of the Master." In this legend of The Kalevala, exceedingly interesting, instructive, and curious, are found, apparently, the remote vestiges of ancient Masonry.

It would seem that the earliest beliefs of the Finns regarding the dead centred in this: that their spirits remained in their graves until after the complete disintegration of their bodies, over which Kalma, the god of the tombs, with his black and evil daughter, presided. After their spirits had been fully purified, they were then admitted to the Kingdom of Manala in the under world. Those journeying to Tuonela were required to voyage over nine seas, and over one river, the Finnish Styx, black, deep, and violent, and filled with hungry whirlpools, and angry waterfalls.

Like Helheim of Scandinavian mythology, Manala, or Tuonela, was considered as corresponding to the upper world. The Sun and the Moon visited there; fen and forest gave a home to the wolf, the bear, the elk, the serpent, and the songbird; the salmon, the whiting, the perch, and the pike were sheltered in the "coal-black waters of Manala." From the seed-grains of the death-land fields and forests, the Tuoni-worm (the serpent) had taken its teeth. Tuoui, or Mana, the god of the under world, is represented as a hard-hearted, and frightful, old personage with three iron-pointed fingers on each hand, and wearing a hat drawn down to his shoulders. As in the original conception of Hades, Tuoni was thought to be the leader of the dead to their subterranean home, as well as their counsellor, guardian, and ruler. In the capacity of ruler he was assisted by his wife, a hideous, horrible, old witch with "crooked, copper-fingers iron-pointed," with deformed head and distorted features, and uniformly spoken of in irony in the Kalevala as "hyva emanta," the good hostess; she feasted her guests on lizards, worms, toads, and writhing serpents. Tuouen Poika, "The God of the Red Cheeks," so called because of his bloodthirstiness and constant cruelties, is the son and accomplice of this merciless and hideous pair.

Three daughters of Tuoni are mentioned in the runes, the first of whom, a tiny, black maiden, but great in wickedness, once at least showed a touch of human kindness when she vainly urged Wainamoinen not to cross the river of Tuoui, assuring the hero that while many visit Manala, few return, because of their inability to brave her father's wrath. Finally, after much entreaty, she ferried him over the Finnish Styx, like Charon, the son of Erebus and Nox, in the mythology of Greece. The second daughter of Tuoni is Lowyatar, black and blind, and is described as still more malignant and loathsome than the first. Through the East-wind's impregnation she brought forth the spirits of the nine diseases most dreaded by mankind, as described in the 45th Rune of the Kalevala:

"Colic, Pleurisy, and Fever.
Ulcer, Plague, and dread Consumption,
Gout, Sterility, and Cancer."

The third daughter of Tuoni combines the malevolent and repugnant attributes of her two sisters, and is represented as the mother and hostess of the impersonal diseases of mankind. The Finns regarded all human ailments as evil spirits or indwelling devils, some formless, others taking the shapes of the most odious forms of animal life, as worms and mites; the nine, however, described above, were conceived to have human forms.

Where the three arms of the Tuoni river meet a frightful rock arises, called Kipu-Kivi, or Kipuvuori, in a dungeon beneath which the spirits of all diseases are imprisoned. On this rock the third daughter of Tuoui sits, constantly whirling it round like a millstone, grinding her subjects until they escape and go forth to torture and slay the children of men; as in Hindu mythology, Kali (black) sits in judgment on the dead.

Various other spiritual powers than gods and goddesses are held in high reverence by the Finns. Tontu is represented as a kind-hearted house-spirit, a sort of diminutive Cyclops, and offerings of bread and broth are made to him every morning. Putting a mare's collar on one's neck and walking nine times around a church is thought to be a certain means of attracting one to the place desired. Para is a mystical, three-legged being, constructed in many ways, and which, according to Castren, attains life and action when its possessor, cutting the little finger of his left hand, lets three drops of blood fall upon it, and at the same time pronouncing the proper magic word. The possessor, by whatever means, of this mystic being, is always supplied with abundance of milk and cheese. The Maahiset are the dwarfs of Finnish mythology. Their abode is under stumps, trees, blocks, thresholds and hearth-stones. Though exceedingly minute and invisible to man they have human forms. They are irritable and resentful, and they punish with ulcers, tetter, ringworms, pimples, and other cutaneous affections, all those who neglect them at brewings, bakings, and feastings. They punish in a similar manner those who enter new houses without making obeisance to the four corners, and paying them other kindly attentions; those who live in untidy houses are also likewise punished. The Kirkonwaeki (church-folk) are little deformed beings living under the altars of churches. These misshapen things are supposed to be able to aid their sorrowing and suffering worshipers.

The Kalevala

Certain beasts, and birds, and trees, are held sacred in Finland. In the Kalevala are evident traces of arctolatry, bear-worship, once very common among the tribes of the north, Otso, the bear, according to Finnish mythology, was born on the shoulders of Otava, in the regions of the sun and moon, and "nursed by a goddess of the woodlands in a cradle swung by bands of gold between the bending branches of budding fir-trees." His nurse would not give him teeth and claws until he had promised never to engage in bloody strife, or deeds of violence. Otso, however, does not always keep his pledge, and accordingly the hunters of Finland find it comparatively easy to reconcile their consciences to his destruction. Otso is called in the runes by many endearing titles as "The Honey-Eater," "Golden Light-Foot," "The Forest-Apple," "Honey-Paw of the Mountains," "ThePride of the Thicket," "The Fur-robed Forest-Friend." Ahava, the West-wind, and Penitar, a blind old witch of Sariola, are the parents of the swift dogs of Finland, just as the horses of Achilles, Xanthos and Belios, sprang from Zephyros and the harpy Podarge.

As to birds, the duck, according to the Kalevala, the eagle, according to other traditions, lays the mundane egg, thus taking part in the creation of the world. Puhuri, the north-wind, the father of Pakkanen (frost) is sometimes personified as a gigantic eagle. The didapper is reverenced because it foretells the approach of rain. Linnunrata (bird-path) is the name given to the Milky-way, due probably to a myth like those of the Swedes and Slavs, in which liberated songs take the form of snow-white dovelets. The cuckoo to this day is sacred, and is believed to have fertilized the earth with his songs. As to insects, honey-bees, called by the Finns, Mehilainen, are especially sacred, as in the mythologies of many other nations. Ukkon-koiva (Ukko's dog) is the Finnish name for the butterfly, and is looked upon as a messenger of the Supreme Deity. It may be interesting to observe here that the Bretons in reverence called butterflies, "feathers from the wings of God."

As to inanimate nature, certain lakes, rivers, springs, and fountains, are held in high reverence. In the Kalevala the oak is called Pun Jumalan (God's tree). The mountain-ash even to this day, and the birch-tree, are held sacred, and peasants plant them by their cottages with reverence.

Respecting the giants of Finnish mythology, Castren is silent, and the following notes are gleaned from the Kalevala, and from Grimm's Teutonic Mythology. "The giants," says Grimm, "are distinguished by their cunning and ferocity from the stupid, good-natured monsters of Germany and Scandinavia." Soini, for example a synonym of Kullervo, the here of the saddest episode of the Kalevala when only three days old, tore his swaddling clothes to tatters. When sold to a forgeman of Karelia, he was ordered to nurse an infant, but he dug out the eyes of the child, killed it, and burned its cradle. Ordered to fence the fields, he built a fence from earth to heaven, using entire pine-trees for fencing materials, and interweaving their branches with venomous serpents. Ordered to tend the herds in the woodlands, he changed the cattle to wolves and bears, and drove them home to destroy his mistress because she had baked a stone in the centre of his oat-loaf, causing him to break his knife, the only keepsake of his people.

Regarding the heroes of the Kalevala, much discussion has arisen as to their place in Finnish mythology. The Finns proper regard the chief heroes of the Suomi epic, Wainamoinen, Ilmarinen, and Lemminkainen, as descendants of the Celestial Virgin, Ilmatar, impregnated by the winds when Ilma (air), Light, and Water were the only material existences. In harmony with this conception we find in the Kalevala, a description of the birth of Wainamoinen, or Vaino, as he is sometimes called in the original, a word probably akin to the Magyar Ven, old. The Esthonians regard these heroes as sons of the Great Spirit, begotten before the earth was created, and dwelling with their Supreme Ruler in Jumala.

The poetry of a people with such an elaborate mythology and with such a keen and appreciative sense of nature and of her various phenomena, was certain, sooner or later, to attract the attention of scholars. And, in fact, as early as the seventeenth century, we meet men of literary tastes who tried to collect and interpret the various national songs of the Finns. Among these were Palmskold and Peter Bang. They collected portions of the national poetry, consisting chiefly of wizard-incantations, and all kinds of pagan folk-lore. Gabriel Maxenius, however, was the first to publish a work on Finnish national poetry, which brought to light the beauties of the Kalevala. It appeared in 1733, and bore the title: De Effectibus Naturalibus. The book contains a quaint collection of Finnish poems in lyric forms, chiefly incantations; but the author was entirely at a loss how to account for them, or how to appreciate them. He failed to see their intimate connection with the religious worship of the Finns in paganism.

The next to study the Finnish poetry and language was Daniel Juslenius, a celebrated bishop, and a highly-gifted scholar. In a dissertation, published as early as 1700, entitled, Aboa vetus et nova, he discussed the origin and nature of the Finnish language; and in another work of his, printed in 1745, he treated of Finnish incantations, displaying withal a thorough understanding of the Finnish folk-lore, and of the importance of the Finnish language and national poetry. With great care he began to collect the songs of Suomi, but this precious collection was unfortunately burned.

Porthan, a Finnish scholar of great attainments, born in 1766, continuing the work of Juslenius, accumulated a great number of national songs and poems, and by his profound enthusiasm for the promotion of Finnish literature, succeeded in founding the Society of the Fennophils, which to the present day, forms the literary centre of Finland. Among his pupils were E. Lenquist, and Chr. Ganander, whose works on Finnish mythology are among the references used in preparing this preface. These indefatigable scholars were joined by Reinhold Becker and others, who were industriously searching for more and more fragments of what evidently was a great epic of the Finns. For certainly neither of the scholars just mentioned, nor earlier investigators, could fail to see that the runes they collected, gathered round two or three chief heroes, but more especially around the central figure of Wainamoinen, the hero of the following epic.

The Kalevala proper was collected by two great Finnish scholars, Zacharias Topelius and Elias Lonnrot. Both were practicing physicians, and in this capacity came into frequent contact with the people of Finland. Topelius, who collected eighty epical fragments of the Kalevala, spent the last eleven years of his life in bed, afflicted with a fatal disease. But this sad and trying circumstance did not dampen his enthusiasm. His manner of collecting these songs was as follows: Knowing that the Finns of Russia preserved most of the national poetry, and that they came annually to Finland proper, which at that time did not belong to Russia, he invited these itinerant Finnish merchants to his bedside, and induced them to sing their heroic poems, which he copied as they were uttered. And, when he heard of a renowned Finnish singer, or minstrel, he did all in his power to bring the song-man to his house, in order that he might gather new fragments of the national epic. Thus the first glory of collecting the fragments of the Kalevala and of rescuing it from literary oblivion, belongs to Topelius. In 1822 he published his first collections, and in 1831 7 his last.

Elias Lonnrot, who brought the whole work to a glorious completion, was born April 9, 1802. He entered the University of Abo in 1822, and in 1832, received the degree of Doctor of Medicine from the University of Helsingfors. After the death of Castren in 1850, Lonnrot was appointed professor of the Suomi (Finnish) language and literature in the University, where he remained until 1862, at which time he withdrew from his academical activity and devoted himself exclusively to the study of his native language, and its epical productions. Dr. Lonnrot had already published a scholarly treatise, in 1827, on the chief hero of the Kalevala, before he went to Sava and Karjala to glean the songs and parts of songs front the lips of the people. This work was entitled: De Wainainoine priscorum Fennorum numine. In the year 1828, he travelled as far as Kajan, collecting poems and songs of the Finnish people, sitting by the fireside of the aged, rowing on the lakes with the fishermen, and following the flocks with the shepherds. In 1829 he published at Helsingfors a work under the following title: Kantele taikka Suomee Kansan sek vazhoja etta nykysempia Runoja ja Lauluja (Lyre, or Old and New Songs and Lays of the Finnish Nation). In another work edited in 1832, written in Swedish, entitled: Om Finnarues Magiska Medicin (On the Magic Medicine of the Finns), he dwells on the incantations so frequent in Finnish poetry, notably in the Kalevala. A few years later he travelled in the province of Archangel, and so ingratiated himself into the hearts of the simple-minded people that they most willingly aided him in collecting these songs. These journeys were made through wild fens, forests, marshes, and ice-plains, on horseback, in sledges drawn by the reindeer, in canoes, or in some other forms of primitive conveyance. The enthusiastic physician described his journeyings and difficulties faithfully in a paper published at Helsingfors in Swedish in 1834. He had the peculiar good luck to meet an old peasant, one of the oldest of the runolainen in the Russian province of Wuokiniem, who was by far the most renowned minstrel of the country, and with whose closely impending death, numerous very precious runes would have been irrevocably lost.

The happy result of his travels throughout Finland, Dr. Lonnrot now commenced to arrange under the central idea of a great epic, called Kalevala, and in February, 1835, the manuscript was transmitted to the Finnish Literary Society, which had it published in two parts. Lonnrot, however, did not stop here; he went on searching and collecting, and, in 1840, had brought together more than one thousand fragments of epical poetry, national ballads, and proverbs. These he published in two works, respectively entitled, Kanteletar (Lyre-charm), and The Proverbs of the Suomi People, the latter containing over 1700 proverbs, adages, gnomic sentences, and songs.

His example was followed by many of his enthusiastic countrymen, the more prominent of whom are Castren, Europaeus, Polen and Reniholm. Through the collections of these scholars so many additional parts of the epical treasure of Finland were made public that a new edition of the Kalevala soon became an imperative necessity. The task of sifting, arranging, and organizing the extensive material, was again allotted to Dr. Lonnrot, and in his second editions of the Kalevala, which appeared in 1849, the epic, embracing fifty runes and 22,793 lines, had reached its mature form. The Kalevala was no sooner published than it attracted the attention of the leading scholars of Europe. Men of such world-wide fame as Jacob Grimm, Steinthal, Uhland, Carrière and Max Müller hastened to acknowledge its surpassing value and intrinsic beauty. Jacob Grimm, in a separate treatise, published in his Kleinere Schriften, said that the genuineness and extraordinary value of the Kalevala is easily

The Kalevala

proved by the fact that from its mythological ideas we can frequently interpret the mythological conceptions of the ancient Germans, whereas the poems of Ossian manifest their modern origin by their inability to clear up questions of old Saxon or German mythology. Grimm, furthermore, shows that both the Gothic and Icelandic literatures display unmistakable features of Finnish influence.

Max Müller places the Kalevala on a level with the greatest epics of the world. These are his words:

"From the mouths of the aged an epic poem has been collected equalling the Iliad in length and completeness; nay, if we can forget for a moment, all that we in our youth learned to call beautiful, not less beautiful. A Finn is not a Greek, and Wainamoinen was not a Homer [Achilles?]; but if the poet may take his colors from that nature by which he is surrounded, if he may depict the men with whom he lives, the Kalevala possesses merits not dissimilar from those of the Illiad, and will claim its place as the fifth national epic of the world, side by side with the Ionian Songs, with the Mahabharata, the Shalinameth, and the Nibelunge."

Steinthal recognizes but four great national epics, viz., the Iliad, Kalevala, Nibelunge and the Roland Songs.

The Kalevala describes Finnish nature very minutely and very beautifully. Grimm says that no poem is to be compared with it in this respect, unless it be some of the epics of India. It has been translated into several European languages; into Swedish by Alex. Castren, in 1844; into French prose by L. LeDuc, in 1845; into German by Anton Schiefuer, in 1852; into Hungarian by Ferdinand Barna, in 1871; and a very small portion of it--the legend of Aino--into English, in 1868, by the late Prof. John A. Porter, of Yale College. It must remain a matter of universal regret to the English-speaking people that Prof. Porter's life could not have been spared to finish the great work he had so beautifully begun.

Some of the most convincing evidences of the genuineness and great age of the Kalevala have been supplied by the Hungarian translator. The Hungarians, as is well known, are closely related to the Finns, and their language, the Magyar dialect, has the same characteristic features as the Finnish tongue. Barna's translation, accordingly, is the best rendering of the original. In order to show the genuineness and antiquity of the Kalevala, Barna adduces a Hungarian book written by a certain Peter Bornemissza, in 1578, entitled ordogi Kisertetekrol (on Satanic Specters), the unique copy of which he found in the library of the University of Budapest. In this book Bornemissza collected all the incantations (raolvasasok) in use among Hungarian country-people of his day for the expulsion of diseases and misfortunes. These incantations, forming the common stock of all Ugrian peoples, of which the Finns and Hungarians are branches, display a most satisfactory sameness with the numerous incantations of the Kalevala used for the same purpose. Barna published an elaborate treatise on this subject; it appeared in the, Transactions of the Hungarian Academy of Sciences, Philological Department, for 1870. Again, in 1868, twenty-two Hungarian deeds, dating from 1616-1660, were sent to the Hungarian Academy of Sciences, as having been found in the Hegyalja, where the celebrated wine of Tokay is made. These deeds contained several contracts for the sale of vineyards, and at the end of each deed the customary cup of wine was said to have been emptied by both parties to the contract. This cup of wine, in the deeds, was termed, "Ukkon's cup." Ukko, however, is the chief God according to Finnish mythology, and thus the coincidence of the Magyar Ukkon and the Finnish Ukko was placed beyond doubt.

The Kalevala (the Land of Heroes) relates the ever-varying contests between the Finns and the "darksome Laplanders", just as the Iliad relates the contests between the Greeks and the Trojans. Castren is of the opinion that the enmity between the Finns and the Lapps was sung long before the Finns had left their Asiatic birth-place.

A deeper and more esoteric meaning of the Kalevala, however, points to a contest between Light and Darkness, Good and Evil; the Finns representing the Light and the Good, and the Lapps, the Darkness and the Evil. Like the Niebelungs, the heroes of the Finns woo for brides the beauteous maidens of the North; and the similarity is rendered still more striking by their frequent inroads into the country of the Lapps, in order to possess themselves of the envied treasure of Lapland, the mysterious Sampo, evidently the Golden Fleece of the Argonautic expedition. Curiously enough public opinion is often expressed in the runes, in the words of an infant; often too the unexpected is introduced after the manner of the Greek dramas, by a young child, or an old man.

The whole poem is replete with the most fascinating folk-lore about the mysteries of nature, the origin of things, the enigmas of human tears, and, true to the character of a national epic, it represents not only the poetry, but the entire wisdom and accumulated experience of a nation. Among others, there is a profoundly philosophical trait in the poem, indicative of a deep insight into the workings of the human mind, and into the forces of nature. Whenever one of the heroes of the Kalevala wishes to overcome the aggressive power of an evil force, as a wound, a disease, a ferocious beast, or a venomous serpent, he achieves his purpose by chanting the origin of the inimical force. The thought underlying this idea evidently is that all evil could be obviated had we but the knowledge of whence and how it came.

The numerous myths of the poem are likewise full of significance and beauty, and the Kalevala should be read between the lines, in order that the fall meaning of this great epic may be comprehended. Even such a hideous impersonation as that of Kullerwoinen, is rich with pointed meaning, showing as it does, the incorrigibility of ingrained evil. This legend, like all others of the poem, has its deep-running stream of esoteric interpretation. The Kalevala, perhaps, more than any other, uses its lines on the surface in symbolism to point the human mind to the brighter gems of truth beneath.

The three main personages, Wainamoinen, the ancient singer, Ilmarinen, the eternal forgeman, and Lemminkainen, the reckless wizard, as mentioned above, are conceived as being of divine origin. In fact, the acting characters of the Kalevala are mostly superhuman, magic beings. Even the female actors are powerful sorceresses, and the hostess of Pohyola, especially, braves the might of all the enchanters of Wainola combined. The power of magic is a striking feature of the poem. Here, as in the legends of no other people, do the heroes and demi-gods accomplish nearly everything by magic. The songs of Wainamoinen disarm his opponents; they quiet the angry sea; they give warmth to the new sun and the new moon which his brother, Ilmarinen, forges from the magic metals; they give life to the spouse of Ilmarinen, which the "eternal metal-artist" forges from gold, silver, and copper. In fact we are among a people that endows everything with life, and with human and divine attributes. Birds, and beasts, and fishes, and serpents, as well as the Sun, the Moon, the Great Bear, and the stars, are either kind or unkind. Drops of blood find speech; men and maidens transform themselves into other shapes and resume again their native forms at will; ships, and trees, and waters, have magic powers; in short, all nature speaks in human tongues.

The Kalevala dates back to an enormous antiquity. One reason for believing this, lies in the silence of the Kalevala about Russians, Germans, or Swedes, their neighbors. This evidently shows that the poem must have been composed at a time when these nations had but very little or no intercourse with the Finns. The coincidence between the incantations adduced above, proves that these witch-songs date from a time when the Hungarians and the Finns were still united as one people; in other words, to a time at least 3000 years ago. The whole poem betrays no important signs of foreign influence, and in its entire tenor is a thoroughly pagan epic. There are excellent reasons for believing that the story of Mariatta, recited in the 50th Rune, is an ante-Christian legend.

An additional proof of the originality and independent rise of the Kalevala is to be found in its metre. All genuine poetry must have its peculiar verse, just as snow-flakes cannot exist without their peculiar crystalizations. It is thus that the Iliad is inseparably united, and, as it were, immersed in the stately hexametre, and the French epics, in the graceful Alexandrine verse. The metre of the Kalevala is the "eight-syllabled trochaic, with the part-line echo," and is the characteristic verse of the Finns. The natural speech of this people is poetry. The young men and maidens, the old men and matrons, in their interchange of ideas, unwittingly fall into verse. The genius of their language aids to this end, inasmuch as their words are strongly trochaic.

This wonderfully versatile metre admits of keeping the right medium between the dignified, almost prancing hexameter, and the shorter metres of the lyrics. Its feet are nimble and fleet, but yet full of vigor and expressiveness. In addition, the Kalevala uses alliteration, and thus varies the rhythm of time with the rhythm of sound. This metre is especially fit for the numerous expressions of endearment in which the Finnish epic abounds. It is more especially the love of the mother for her children, and the love of the children for their mother, that find frequent and ever-tender expression in the sonorous lines of the Kalevala. The Swedish translation by Castren, the German, by Schiefner, and the Hungarian, by Barna, as well as the following English translation, are in the original metre of the Kalevala.

To prove that this peculiar and fascinating style of verse is of very ancient origin, the following lines have been accurately copied from the first edition in Finnish of the Kalevala, collated by Dr. Lonnrot, and published in 1835 at Helsingfors, the quotation beginning with the 150th line of the 2nd Rune:

Louhi Pohjolan emanta
Sanan wirkko, noin nimesi:
"Niin mita minulleannat,
Kun saatan omille maille,
Oman pellon pientarelle,
Oman pihan rikkasille?"
Sano wanha Wainamoinen:
"Mitapa kysyt minulta,
Kun saatat omille maille,

The Kalevala

>Oman kaën kukkumille,
>Oman kukon kukkluwille,
>Oman saunan lampimille?"
>Sano Pohjolan emanta:
>"Ohoh wiisas Wainamoinen!
>Taiatko takoa sammon,
>Kirjokannen kirjaëlla,
>Yhen joukkosen sulasta,
>Yhen willan kylkyesta,
>Yhen otrasen jywasta,
>Yhen warttinan muruista."

As to the architecture of the Kalevala, it stands midway between the epical ballads of the Servians and the purely epical structure of the Iliad. Though a continuous whole, it contains several almost independent parts, as the contest of Youkahainen, the Kullervo episode, and the legend of Mariatta.

By language-masters this epic of Suomi, descending unwritten from the mythical age to the present day, kept alive from generation to generation by minstrels, or song-men, is regarded as one of the most precious contributions to the literature of the world, made since the time of Milton and the German classics.

Acknowledgment is hereby made to the following sources of information used in the preparation of this work: to E. Lenquist's De Superstitione veterum Fennorum theoretica et practica; to Chr. Ganander's Mythologia Fennica; to Becker's De Vainamoine; to Max Müller's Oxford Essays; to Prof. John A. Porter's Selections from the Kalevala; to the writings of the two Grimms; to Latham's Native Races of the Russian Empire; to the translations of the Kalevala by Alex. Castren, Anton Schieffier, L. LeDuc and Ferdinand Barna; and especially to the excellent treatises on the Kalevala, and on the Mythology of the Finns, by Mace Da Charda and Alex. Castren; to Prof. Helena Klingner, of Cincinnati, a linguist of high rank, and who has compared very conscientiously the manuscript of the following pages with the German translation of the Kalevala by Anton Schiefner; to Dr. Emil Reich, a native Hungarian, a close student of the Ugrian tongues, who, in a most thorough manner, has compared this translation with the Hungarian by Ferdinand Barna, and who, familiar with the habits, customs, and religious notions of the Finns, has furnished much valuable material used in the preparation of this preface; and, finally, to Prof. Thomas C. Porter, D.D., LL.D., of Lafayette College, who has become an authority on the Kalevala through his own researches for many years, aided by a long and intimate acquaintance with Prof. A. F. Soldan, a Finn by birth, an enthusiastic lover of his country, a scholar of great attainments, acquainted with many languages, and once at the head of the Imperial Mint at Helsingfors, the capital of Finland. Prof. Porter has very kindly placed in the hands of the author of these pages, all the literature on this subject at his command, including his own writings; he has watched the growth of this translation with unusual interest; and, with the eye of a gifted poet and scholar, he has made two careful and critical examinations of the entire manuscript, making annotations, emendations, and corrections, by which this work has been greatly improved.

With this prolonged introduction, this, the first English translation of the Kalevala, with its many imperfections, is hesitatingly given to the public.

JOHN MARTIN CRAWFORD.
October 1, 1887.

Lönnrot

THE KALEVALA

PROEM

MASTERED by desire impulsive,
By a mighty inward urging,
I am ready now for singing,
Ready to begin the chanting
Of our nation's ancient folk-song
Handed down from by-gone ages.
In my mouth the words are melting,
From my lips the tones are gliding,
From my tongue they wish to hasten;
When my willing teeth are parted,
When my ready mouth is opened,
Songs of ancient wit and wisdom
Hasten from me not unwilling.
Golden friend, and dearest brother,
Brother dear of mine in childhood,
Come and sing with me the stories,
Come and chant with me the legends,
Legends of the times forgotten,
Since we now are here together,
Come together from our roamings.
Seldom do we come for singing,
Seldom to the one, the other,
O'er this cold and cruel country,
O'er the poor soil of the Northland.
Let us clasp our hands together
That we thus may best remember.
Join we now in merry singing,
Chant we now the oldest folk-lore,
That the dear ones all may hear them,
That the well-inclined may hear them,
Of this rising generation.
These are words in childhood taught me,
Songs preserved from distant ages,
Legends they that once were taken
From the belt of Wainamoinen,
From the forge of Ilmarinen,
From the sword of Kaukomieli,
From the bow of Youkahainen,
From the pastures of the Northland,
From the meads of Kalevala.
These my dear old father sang me
When at work with knife and hatchet
These my tender mother taught me
When she twirled the flying spindle,
When a child upon the matting
By her feet I rolled and tumbled.
Incantations were not wanting
Over Sampo and o'er Louhi,
Sampo growing old in singing,
Louhi ceasing her enchantment.
In the songs died wise Wipunen,

The Kalevala
At the games died Lemminkainen.
There are many other legends,
Incantations that were taught me,
That I found along the wayside,
Gathered in the fragrant copses,
Blown me from the forest branches,
Culled among the plumes of pine-trees,
Scented from the vines and flowers,
Whispered to me as I followed
Flocks in land of honeyed meadows,
Over hillocks green and golden,
After sable-haired Murikki,
And the many-colored Kimmo.
Many runes the cold has told me,
Many lays the rain has brought me,
Other songs the winds have sung me;
Many birds from many forests,
Oft have sung me lays n concord
Waves of sea, and ocean billows,
Music from the many waters,
Music from the whole creation,
Oft have been my guide and master.
Sentences the trees created,
Rolled together into bundles,
Moved them to my ancient dwelling,
On the sledges to my cottage,
Tied them to my garret rafters,
Hung them on my dwelling-portals,
Laid them in a chest of boxes,
Boxes lined with shining copper.
Long they lay within my dwelling
Through the chilling winds of winter,
In my dwelling-place for ages.
Shall I bring these songs together
From the cold and frost collect them?
Shall I bring this nest of boxes,
Keepers of these golden legends,
To the table in my cabin,
Underneath the painted rafters,
In this house renowned and ancient?
Shall I now these boxes open,
Boxes filled with wondrous stories?
Shall I now the end unfasten
Of this ball of ancient wisdom,
These ancestral lays unravel?
Let me sing an old-time legend,
That shall echo forth the praises
Of the beer that I have tasted,
Of the sparkling beer of barley.
Bring to me a foaming goblet
Of the barley of my fathers,
Lest my singing grow too weary,
Singing from the water only.
Bring me too a cup of strong-beer,
It will add to our enchantment,
To the pleasure of the evening,
Northland's long and dreary evening,
For the beauty of the day-dawn,
For the pleasure of the morning,
The beginning of the new-day.
Often I have heard them chanting,

Lönnrot

Often I have heard them singing,
That the nights come to us singly,
That the Moon beams on us singly,
That the Sun shines on us singly;
Singly also, Wainamoinen,
The renowned and wise enchanter,
Born from everlasting Ether
Of his mother, Ether's daughter.

RUNE I
BIRTH OF WAINAMOINEN

In primeval times, a maiden,
Beauteous Daughter of the Ether,
Passed for ages her existence
In the great expanse of heaven,
O'er the prairies yet enfolded.
Wearisome the maiden growing,
Her existence sad and hopeless,
Thus alone to live for ages
In the infinite expanses
Of the air above the sea-foam,
In the far outstretching spaces,
In a solitude of ether,
She descended to the ocean,
Waves her coach, and waves her pillow.
Thereupon the rising storm-wind
Flying from the East in fierceness,
Whips the ocean into surges,
Strikes the stars with sprays of ocean
Till the waves are white with fervor.
To and fro they toss the maiden,
Storm-encircled, hapless maiden;
With her sport the rolling billows,
With her play the storm-wind forces,
On the blue back of the waters;
On the white-wreathed waves of ocean,
Play the forces of the salt-sea,
With the lone and helpless maiden;
Till at last in full conception,
Union now of force and beauty,
Sink the storm-winds into slumber;
Overburdened now the maiden
Cannot rise above the surface;
Seven hundred years she wandered,
Ages nine of man's existence,
Swam the ocean hither, thither,
Could not rise above the waters,
Conscious only of her travail;
Seven hundred years she labored
Ere her first-born was delivered.
Thus she swam as water-mother,
Toward the east, and also southward,
Toward the west, and also northward;
Swam the sea in all directions,
Frightened at the strife of storm-winds,
Swam in travail, swam unceasing,
Ere her first-born was delivered.
Then began she gently weeping,
Spake these measures, heavy-hearted:
"Woe is me, my life hard-fated!
Woe is me, in this my travail!
Into what have I now fallen?
Woe is me, that I unhappy,
Left my home in subtle ether,

Lönnrot

Came to dwell amid the sea-foam,
To be tossed by rolling billows,
To be rocked by winds and waters,
On the far outstretching waters,
In the salt-sea's vast expanses,
Knowing only pain and trouble!
Better far for me, O Ukko!
Were I maiden in the Ether,
Than within these ocean-spaces,
To become a water-mother!
All this life is cold and dreary,
Painful here is every motion,
As I linger in the waters,
As I wander through the ocean.
Ukko, thou O God, up yonder,
Thou the ruler of the heavens,
Come thou hither, thou art needed,
Come thou hither, I implore thee,
To deliver me from trouble,
To deliver me in travail.
Come I pray thee, hither hasten,
Hasten more that thou art needed,
Haste and help this helpless maiden!"
When she ceased her supplications,
Scarce a moment onward passes,
Ere a beauteous duck descending,
Hastens toward the water-mother,
Comes a-flying hither, thither,
Seeks herself a place for nesting.
Flies she eastward, flies she westward,
Circles northward, circles southward,
Cannot find a grassy hillock,
Not the smallest bit of verdure;
Cannot find a spot protected,
Cannot find a place befitting,
Where to make her nest in safety.
Flying slowly, looking round her,
She descries no place for resting,
Thinking loud and long debating,
And her words are such as follow:
"Build I in the winds my dwelling,
On the floods my place of nesting?
Surely would the winds destroy it,
Far away the waves would wash it."
Then the daughter of the Ether,
Now the hapless water-mother,
Raised her shoulders out of water,
Raised her knees above the ocean,
That the duck might build her dwelling,
Build her nesting-place in safety.
Thereupon the duck in beauty,
Flying slowly, looking round her,
Spies the shoulders of the maiden,
Sees the knees of Ether's daughter,
Now the hapless water-mother,
Thinks them to be grassy hillocks,
On the blue back of the ocean.
Thence she flies and hovers slowly,
Lightly on the knee she settles,
Finds a nesting-place befitting,
Where to lay her eggs in safety.

The Kalevala
Here she builds her humble dwelling,
Lays her eggs within, at pleasure,
Six, the golden eggs she lays there,
Then a seventh, an egg of iron;
Sits upon her eggs to hatch them,
Quickly warms them on the knee-cap
Of the hapless water-mother;
Hatches one day, then a second,
Then a third day sits and hatches.
Warmer grows the water round her,
Warmer is her bed in ocean,
While her knee with fire is kindled,
And her shoulders too are burning,
Fire in every vein is coursing.
Quick the maiden moves her shoulders,
Shakes her members in succession,
Shakes the nest from its foundation,
And the eggs fall into ocean,
Dash in pieces on the bottom
Of the deep and boundless waters.
In the sand they do not perish,
Not the pieces in the ocean;
But transformed, in wondrous beauty
All the fragments come together
Forming pieces two in number,
One the upper, one the lower,
Equal to the one, the other.
From one half the egg, the lower,
Grows the nether vault of Terra:
From the upper half remaining,
Grows the upper vault of Heaven;
From the white part come the moonbeams,
From the yellow part the sunshine,
From the motley part the starlight,
From the dark part grows the cloudage;
And the days speed onward swiftly,
Quickly do the years fly over,
From the shining of the new sun
From the lighting of the full moon.
Still the daughter of the Ether,
Swims the sea as water-mother,
With the floods outstretched before her,
And behind her sky and ocean.
Finally about the ninth year,
In the summer of the tenth year,
Lifts her head above the surface,
Lifts her forehead from the waters,
And begins at last her workings,
Now commences her creations,
On the azure water-ridges,
On the mighty waste before her.
Where her hand she turned in water,
There arose a fertile hillock;
Wheresoe'er her foot she rested,
There she made a hole for fishes;
Where she dived beneath the waters,
Fell the many deeps of ocean;
Where upon her side she turned her,
There the level banks have risen;
Where her head was pointed landward,
There appeared wide bays and inlets;

Lönnrot

When from shore she swam a distance,
And upon her back she rested,
There the rocks she made and fashioned,
And the hidden reefs created,
Where the ships are wrecked so often,
Where so many lives have perished.
Thus created were the islands,
Rocks were fastened in the ocean,
Pillars of the sky were planted,
Fields and forests were created,
Checkered stones of many colors,
Gleaming in the silver sunlight,
All the rocks stood well established;
But the singer, Wainamoinen,
Had not yet beheld the sunshine,
Had not seen the golden moonlight,
Still remaining undelivered.
Wainamoinen, old and trusty,
Lingering within his dungeon
Thirty summers altogether,
And of winters, also thirty,
Peaceful on the waste of waters,
On the broad-sea's yielding bosom,
Well reflected, long considered,
How unborn to live and flourish
In the spaces wrapped in darkness,
In uncomfortable limits,
Where he had not seen the moonlight,
Had not seen the silver sunshine.
Thereupon these words be uttered,
Let himself be heard in this wise:
"Take, O Moon, I pray thee, take me,
Take me, thou, O Sun above me,
Take me, thou O Bear of heaven,
From this dark and dreary prison,
From these unbefitting portals,
From this narrow place of resting,
From this dark and gloomy dwelling,
Hence to wander from the ocean,
Hence to walk upon the islands,
On the dry land walk and wander,
Like an ancient hero wander,
Walk in open air and breathe it,
Thus to see the moon at evening,
Thus to see the silver sunlight,
Thus to see the Bear in heaven,
That the stars I may consider."
Since the Moon refused to free him,
And the Sun would not deliver,
Nor the Great Bear give assistance,
His existence growing weary,
And his life but an annoyance,
Bursts he then the outer portals
Of his dark and dismal fortress;
With his strong, but unnamed finger,
Opens he the lock resisting;
With the toes upon his left foot,
With the fingers of his right hand,
Creeps he through the yielding portals
To the threshold of his dwelling;
On his knees across the threshold,

The Kalevala
Throws himself head foremost, forward
Plunges into deeps of ocean,
Plunges hither, plunges thither,
Turning with his hands the water;
Swims he northward, swims he southward,
Swims he eastward, swims he westward,
Studying his new surroundings.
Thus our hero reached the water,
Rested five years in the ocean,
Six long years, and even seven years,
Till the autumn of the eighth year,
When at last he leaves the waters,
Stops upon a promontory,
On a coast bereft of verdure;
On his knees he leaves the ocean,
On the land he plants his right foot,
On the solid ground his left foot,
Quickly turns his hands about him,
Stands erect to see the sunshine,
Stands to see the golden moonlight,
That he may behold the Great Bear,
That he may the stars consider.
Thus our hero, Wainamoinen,
Thus the wonderful enchanter
Was delivered from his mother,
Ilmatar, the Ether's daughter.

RUNE II
WAINAMOINEN'S SOWING

Then arose old Wainamoinen,
With his feet upon the island,
On the island washed by ocean,
Broad expanse devoid of verdure;
There remained be many summers,
There he lived as many winters,
On the island vast and vacant,
well considered, long reflected,
Who for him should sow the island,
Who for him the seeds should scatter;
Thought at last of Pellerwoinen,
First-born of the plains and prairies,
When a slender boy, called Sampsa,
Who should sow the vacant island,
Who the forest seeds should scatter.
Pellerwoinen, thus consenting,
Sows with diligence the island,
Seeds upon the lands he scatters,
Seeds in every swamp and lowland,
Forest seeds upon the loose earth,
On the firm soil sows the acorns,
Fir-trees sows he on the mountains,
Pine-trees also on the hill-tops,
Many shrubs in every valley,
Birches sows he in the marshes,
In the loose soil sows the alders,
In the lowlands sows the lindens,
In the moist earth sows the willow,
Mountain-ash in virgin places,
On the banks of streams the hawthorn,
Junipers in hilly regions;
This the work of Pellerwoinen,
Slender Sampsa, in his childhood.
Soon the fertile seeds were sprouting,
Soon the forest trees were growing,
Soon appeared the tops of fir-trees,
And the pines were far outspreading;
Birches rose from all the marshes,
In the loose soil grew the alders,
In the mellow soil the lindens;
Junipers were also growing,
Junipers with clustered berries,
Berries on the hawthorn branches.
Now the hero, Wainamoinen,
Stands aloft to look about him,
How the Sampsa-seeds are growing,
How the crop of Pellerwoinen;
Sees the young trees thickly spreading,
Sees the forest rise in beauty;
But the oak-tree has not sprouted,
Tree of heaven is not growing,
Still within the acorn sleeping,
Its own happiness enjoying.

The Kalevala
Then he waited three nights longer,
And as many days he waited,
Waited till a week had vanished,
Then again the work examined;
But the oak-tree was not growing,
Had not left her acorn-dwelling.
Wainamoinen, ancient hero,
Spies four maidens in the distance,
Water-brides, he spies a fifth-one,
On the soft and sandy sea-shore,
In the dewy grass and flowers,
On a point extending seaward,
Near the forests of the island.
Some were mowing, some were raking,
Raking what was mown together,
In a windrow on the meadow.
From the ocean rose a giant,
Mighty Tursas, tall and hardy,
Pressed compactly all the grasses,
That the maidens had been raking,
When a fire within them kindles,
And the flames shot up to heaven,
Till the windrows burned to ashes,
Only ashes now remaining
Of the grasses raked together.
In the ashes of the windrows,
Tender leaves the giant places,
In the leaves he plants an acorn,
From the acorn, quickly sprouting,
Grows the oak-tree, tall and stately,
From the ground enriched by ashes,
Newly raked by water-maidens;
Spread the oak-tree's many branches,
Rounds itself a broad corona,
Raises it above the storm-clouds;
Far it stretches out its branches,
Stops the white-clouds in their courses,
With its branches hides the sunlight,
With its many leaves, the moonbeams,
And the starlight dies in heaven.
Wainamoinen, old and trusty,
Thought awhile, and well considered,
How to kill the mighty oak-tree,
First created for his pleasure,
How to fell the tree majestic,
How to lop its hundred branches.
Sad the lives of man and hero,
Sad the homes of ocean-dwellers,
If the sun shines not upon them,
If the moonlight does not cheer them
Is there not some mighty hero,
Was there never born a giant,
That can fell the mighty oak-tree,
That can lop its hundred branches?
Wainamoinen, deeply thinking,
Spake these words soliloquizing:
"Kape, daughter of the Ether,
Ancient mother of my being,
Luonnotar, my nurse and helper,
Loan to me the water-forces,
Great the powers of the waters;

Lönnrot

Loan to me the strength of oceans,
To upset this mighty oak-tree,
To uproot this tree of evil,
That again may shine the sunlight,
That the moon once more may glimmer."
Straightway rose a form from oceans,
Rose a hero from the waters,
Nor belonged he to the largest,
Nor belonged he to the smallest,
Long was he as man's forefinger,
Taller than the hand of woman;
On his head a cap of copper,
Boots upon his feet were copper,
Gloves upon his hands were copper,
And its stripes were copper-colored,
Belt around him made of copper,
Hatchet in his belt was copper;
And the handle of his hatchet
Was as long as hand of woman,
Of a finger's breadth the blade was.
Then the trusty Wainamoinen
Thought awhile and well considered,
And his measures are as follow:
"Art thou, sir, divine or human?
Which of these thou only knowest;
Tell me what thy name and station.
Very like a man thou lookest,
Hast the bearing of a hero,
Though the length of man's first finger,
Scarce as tall as hoof of reindeer."
Then again spake Wainamoinen
To the form from out the ocean:
"Verily I think thee human,
Of the race of pigmy-heroes,
Might as well be dead or dying,
Fit for nothing but to perish."
Answered thus the pigmy-hero,
Spake the small one from the ocean
To the valiant Wainamoinen
"Truly am I god and hero,
From the tribes that rule the ocean;
Come I here to fell the oak-tree,
Lop its branches with my hatchet."
Wainamoinen, old and trusty,
Answers thus the sea-born hero:
"Never hast thou force sufficient,
Not to thee has strength been given,
To uproot this mighty oak-tree,
To upset this thing of evil,
Nor to lop its hundred branches."
Scarcely had he finished speaking,
Scarcely had he moved his eyelids,
Ere the pigmy full unfolding,
Quick becomes a mighty giant.
With one step he leaves the ocean,
Plants himself, a mighty hero,
On the forest-fields surrounding;
With his head the clouds he pierces,
To his knees his beard extending,
And his locks fall to his ankles;
Far apart appear his eyeballs,

The Kalevala

Far apart his feet are stationed.
Farther still his mighty shoulders.
Now begins his axe to sharpen,
Quickly to an edge he whets it,
Using six hard blocks of sandstone,
And of softer whetstones, seven.
Straightway to the oak-tree turning,
Thither stalks the mighty giant,
In his raiment long and roomy,
Flapping in the winds of heaven;
With his second step he totters
On the land of darker color;
With his third stop firmly planted,
Reaches he the oak-tree's branches,
Strikes the trunk with sharpened hatchet,
With one mighty swing he strikes it,
With a second blow he cuts it;
As his blade descends the third time,
From his axe the sparks fly upward,
From the oak-tree fire outshooting;
Ere the axe descends a fourth time,
Yields the oak with hundred branches,
Shaking earth and heaven in falling.
Eastward far the trunk extending,
Far to westward flew the tree-tops,
To the South the leaves were scattered,
To the North its hundred branches.
Whosoe'er a branch has taken,
Has obtained eternal welfare;
Who secures himself a tree-top,
He has gained the master magic;
Who the foliage has gathered,
Has delight that never ceases.
Of the chips some had been scattered,
Scattered also many splinters,
On the blue back of the ocean,
Of the ocean smooth and mirrored,
Rocked there by the winds and waters,
Like a boat upon the billows;
Storm-winds blew them to the Northland,
Some the ocean currents carried.
Northland's fair and slender maiden,
Washing on the shore a head-dress,
Beating on the rocks her garments,
Rinsing there her silken raiment,
In the waters of Pohyola,
There beheld the chips and splinters,
Carried by the winds and waters.
In a bag the chips she gathered,
Took them to the ancient court-yard,
There to make enchanted arrows,
Arrows for the great magician,
There to shape them into weapons,
Weapons for the skilful archer,
Since the mighty oak has fallen,
Now has lost its hundred branches,
That the North may see the sunshine,
See the gentle gleam of moonlight,
That the clouds may keep their courses,
May extend the vault of heaven
Over every lake and river,

Lönnrot

O'er the banks of every island.
Groves arose in varied beauty,
Beautifully grew the forests,
And again, the vines and flowers.
Birds again sang in the tree-tops,
Noisily the merry thrushes,
And the cuckoos in the birch-trees;
On the mountains grew the berries,
Golden flowers in the meadows,
And the herbs of many colors,
Many kinds of vegetation;
But the barley is not growing.
Wainamoinen, old and trusty,
Goes away and well considers,
By the borders of the waters,
On the ocean's sandy margin,
Finds six seeds of golden barley,
Even seven ripened kernels,
On the shore of upper Northland,
In the sand upon the sea-shore,
Hides them in his trusty pouches,
Fashioned from the skin of squirrel,
Some were made from skin of marten;
Hastens forth the seeds to scatter,
Quickly sows the barley kernels,
On the brinks of Kalew-waters,
On the Osma-hills and lowlands.
Hark! the titmouse wildly crying,
From the aspen, words as follow:
"Osma's barley will not flourish,
Not the barley of Wainola,
If the soil be not made ready,
If the forest be not levelled,
And the branches burned to ashes."
Wainamoinen, wise and ancient,
Made himself an axe for chopping,
Then began to clear the forest,
Then began the trees to level,
Felled the trees of all descriptions,
Only left the birch-tree standing
For the birds a place of resting,
Where might sing the sweet-voiced cuckoo,
Sacred bird in sacred branches.
Down from heaven came the eagle,
Through the air be came a-flying,
That he might this thing consider;
And he spake the words that follow:
"Wherefore, ancient Wainamoinen,
Hast thou left the slender birch-tree,
Left the birch-tree only standing?"
Wainamoinen thus made answer:
"Therefore is the birch left standing,
That the birds may liest within it,
That the eagle there may rest him,
There may sing the sacred cuckoo."
Spake the eagle, thus replying:
Good indeed, thy hero-judgment,
That the birch-tree thou hast left us,
Left the sacred birch-tree standing,
As a resting-place for eagles,
And for birds of every feather,

The Kalevala
Even I may rest upon it."
Quickly then this bird of heaven,
Kindled fire among the branches;
Soon the flames are fanned by north-winds,
And the east-winds lend their forces,
Burn the trees of all descriptions,
Burn them all to dust and ashes,
Only is the birch left standing.
Wainamoinen, wise and ancient,
Brings his magic grains of barley,
Brings he forth his seven seed-grains,
Brings them from his trusty pouches,
Fashioned from the skin of squirrel,
Some were made from skin of marten.
Thence to sow his seeds he hastens,
Hastes the barley-grains to scatter,
Speaks unto himself these measures:
"I the seeds of life am sowing,
Sowing through my open fingers,
From the hand of my Creator,
In this soil enriched with ashes,
In this soil to sprout and flourish.
Ancient mother, thou that livest
Far below the earth and ocean,
Mother of the fields and forests,
Bring the rich soil to producing,
Bring the seed-grains to the sprouting,
That the barley well may flourish.
Never will the earth unaided,
Yield the ripe nutritious barley;
Never will her force be wanting,
If the givers give assistance,
If the givers grace the sowing,
Grace the daughters of creation.
Rise, O earth, from out thy slumber,
From the slumber-land of ages,
Let the barley-grains be sprouting,
Let the blades themselves be starting,
Let the verdant stalks be rising,
Let the ears themselves be growing,
And a hundredfold producing,
From my plowing and my sowing,
From my skilled and honest labor.
Ukko, thou O God, up yonder,
Thou O Father of the heavens,
Thou that livest high in Ether,
Curbest all the clouds of heaven,
Holdest in the air thy counsel,
Holdest in the clouds good counsel,
From the East dispatch a cloudlet,
From the North-east send a rain-cloud,
From the West another send us,
From the North-west, still another,
Quickly from the South a warm-cloud,
That the rain may fall from heaven,
That the clouds may drop their honey,
That the ears may fill and ripen,
That the barley-fields may rustle."
Thereupon benignant Ukko,
Ukko, father of the heavens,
Held his counsel in the cloud-space,

Lönnrot

Held good counsel in the Ether;
From the East, he sent a cloudlet,
From the North-east, sent a rain-cloud,
From the West another sent he,
From the North-west, still another,
Quickly from the South a warm-cloud;
Joined in seams the clouds together,
Sewed together all their edges,
Grasped the cloud, and hurled it earthward.
Quick the rain-cloud drops her honey,
Quick the rain-drops fall from heaven,
That the ears may quickly ripen,
That the barley crop may rustle.
Straightway grow the seeds of barley,
From the germ the blade unfolding,
Richly colored ears arising,
From the rich soil of the fallow,
From the work of Wainamoinen.
Here a few days pass unnoted
And as many nights fly over.
When the seventh day had journeyed,
On the morning of the eighth day,
Wainamoinen, wise and ancient,
Went to view his crop of barley,
How his plowing, how his sowing,
How his labors were resulting;
Found his crop of barley growing,
Found the blades were triple-knotted,
And the ears he found six-sided.
Wainamoinen, old and trusty,
Turned his face, and looked about him,
Lo! there comes a spring-time cuckoo,
Spying out the slender birch-tree,
Rests upon it, sweetly singing:
"Wherefore is the silver birch-tree
Left unharmed of all the forest?"
Spake the ancient Wainamoinen:
"Therefore I have left the birch-tree,
Left the birch-tree only growing,
Home for thee for joyful singing.
Call thou here, O sweet-voiced cuckoo,
Sing thou here from throat of velvet,
Sing thou here with voice of silver,
Sing the cuckoo's golden flute-notes;
Call at morning, call at evening,
Call within the hour of noontide,
For the better growth of forests,
For the ripening of the barley,
For the richness of, the Northland,
For the joy of Kalevala."

RUNE III
WAINAMOINEN AND YOUKAHAINEN

Wainamoinen, ancient minstrel,
Passed his years in full contentment,
On the meadows of Wainola,
On the plains of Kalevala,
Singing ever wondrous legends,
Songs of ancient wit and wisdom,
Chanting one day, then a second,
Singing in the dusk of evening,
Singing till the dawn of morning,
Now the tales of old-time heroes,
Tales of ages long forgotten,
Now the legends of creation,
Once familiar to the children,
By our children sung no longer,
Sung in part by many heroes,
In these mournful days of evil,
Evil days our race befallen.
Far and wide the story travelled,
Far away men spread the knowledge
Of the chanting of the hero,
Of the song of Wainamoinen;
To the South were heard the echoes,
All of Northland heard the story.
Far away in dismal Northland,
Lived the singer, Youkahainen,
Lapland's young and reckless minstrel,
Once upon a time when feasting,
Dining with his friends and fellows,
Came upon his ears the story
That there lived a sweeter singer,
On the meadows of Wainola,
On the plains of Kalevala,
Better skilled in chanting legends,
Better skilled than Youkahainen,
Better than the one that taught him.
Straightway then the bard grew angry,
Envy rose within his bosom,
Envy of this Wainamoinen,
Famed to be a sweeter singer;
Hastes he angry to his mother,
To his mother, full of wisdom,
Vows that he will southward hasten,
Hie him southward and betake him
To the dwellings of Wainola,
To the cabins of the Northland,
There as bard to vie in battle,
With the famous Wainamoinen.
"Nay," replies the anxious father,
"Do not go to Kalevala."
"Nay," replies the fearful mother,
"Go not hence to Wainamoinen,
There with him to offer battle;
He will charm thee with his singing

Lönnrot

Will bewitch thee in his anger,
He will drive thee back dishonored,
Sink thee in the fatal snow-drift,
Turn to ice thy pliant fingers,
Turn to ice thy feet and ankles."
These the words of Youkahainen:
Good the judgement of a father,
Better still, a mother's counsel,
Best of all one's own decision.
I will go and face the minstrel,
Challenge him to sing in contest,
Challenge him as bard to battle,
Sing to him my sweet-toned measures,
Chant to him my oldest legends,
Chant to him my garnered wisdom,
That this best of boasted singers,
That this famous bard of Suomi,
Shall be worsted in the contest,
Shall become a hapless minstrel;
By my songs shall I transform him,
That his feet shall be as flint-stone,
And as oak his nether raiment;
And this famous, best of singers,
Thus bewitched, shall carry ever,
In his heart a stony burden,
On his shoulder bow of marble,
On his hand a flint-stone gauntlet,
On his brow a stony visor."
Then the wizard, Youkahainen,
Heeding not advice paternal,
Heeding not his mother's counsel,
Leads his courser from his stable,
Fire outstreaming from his nostrils,
From his hoofs, the sparks outshooting,
Hitches to his sledge, the fleet-foot,
To his golden sledge, the courser,
Mounts impetuous his snow-sledge,
Leaps upon the hindmost cross-bench,
Strikes his courser with his birch-whip,
With his birch-whip, pearl-enamelled.
Instantly the prancing racer
Springs away upon his journey;
On he, restless, plunges northward,
All day long be onward gallops,
All the next day, onward, onward,
So the third from morn till evening,
Till the third day twilight brings him
To the meadows of Wainola,
To the plains of Kalevala.
As it happened, Wainamoinen,
Wainamoinen, the magician,
Rode that sunset on the highway,
Silently for pleasure driving
Down Wainola's peaceful meadows,
O'er the plains of Kalevala.
Youkahainen, young and fiery,
Urging still his foaming courser,
Dashes down upon the singer,
Does not turn aside in meeting,
Meeting thus in full collision;
Shafts are driven tight together,

The Kalevala

Hames and collars wedged and tangled,
Tangled are the reins and traces.
Thus perforce they make a stand-still,
Thus remain and well consider;
Water drips from hame and collar,
Vapors rise from both their horses.
Speaks the minstrel, Wainamoinen:
"Who art thou, and whence? Thou comest
Driving like a stupid stripling,
Wainamoinen and Youkahainen.
Careless, dashing down upon me.
Thou hast ruined shafts and traces;
And the collar of my racer
Thou hast shattered into ruin,
And my golden sleigh is broken,
Box and runners dashed to pieces."
Youkahainen then make answer,
Spake at last the words that follow:
"I am youthful Youkahainen,
But make answer first, who thou art,
Whence thou comest, where thou goest,
From what lowly tribe descended?"
Wainamolinen, wise and ancient,
Answered thus the youthful minstrel:
"If thou art but Youkahainen,
Thou shouldst give me all the highway;
I am many years thy senior."
Then the boastful Youkahainen
Spake again to Wainamoinen:
"Young or ancient, little matter,
Little consequence the age is;
He that higher stands in wisdom,
He whose knowledge is the greater,
He that is the sweeter singer,
He alone shall keep the highway,
And the other take the roadside.
Art thou ancient Wainamoinen,
Famous sorcerer and minstrel?
Let us then begin our singing,
Let us sing our ancient legends,
Let us chant our garnered wisdom,
That the one may hear the other,
That the one may judge the other,
In a war of wizard sayings."
Wainamoinen, wise and ancient,
Thus replied in modest accents:
"What I know is very little,
Hardly is it worth the singing,
Neither is my singing wondrous:
All my days I have resided
In the cold and dreary Northland,
In a desert land enchanted,
In my cottage home for ayes;
All the songs that I have gathered,
Are the cuckoo's simple measures,
Some of these I may remember;
But since thou perforce demandest,
I accept thy boastful challenge.
Tell me now, my golden youngster,
What thou knowest more than others,
Open now thy store of wisdom."

Lönnrot

Thus made answer Youkahainen,
Lapland's young and fiery minstrel:
"Know I many bits of learning
This I know in perfect clearness:
Every roof must have a chimney,
Every fire-place have a hearth-stone;
Lives of seal are free and merry,
Merry is the life of walrus,
Feeding on incautious salmon,
Daily eating perch and whiting;
Whitings live in quiet shallows,
Salmon love the level bottoms;
Spawns the pike in coldest weather,
And defies the storms of winter.
Slowly perches swim in Autumn,
Wry-backed, hunting deeper water,
Spawn in shallows in the summer,
Bounding on the shore of ocean.
Should this wisdom seem too little,
I can tell thee other matters,
Sing thee other wizard sayings:
All the Northmen plow with reindeer,
Mother-horses plow the Southland,
Inner Lapland plows with oxen;
All the trees on Pisa-mountain,
Know I well in all their grandeur;
On the Horna-rock are fir-trees,
Fir-trees growing tall and slender;
Slender grow the trees on mountains.
Three, the water-falls in number,
Three in number, inland oceans,
Three in number, lofty mountains,
Shooting to the vault of heaven.
Hallapyora's near to Yaemen,
Katrakoski in Karyala;
Imatra, the falling water,
Tumbles, roaring, into Wuoksi."
Then the ancient Wainimoinen:
"Women's tales and children's wisdom
Do not please a bearded hero,
Hero, old enough for wedlock;
Tell the story of creation,
Tell me of the world's beginning,
Tell me of the creatures in it,
And philosophize a little."
Then the youthful Youkahainen
Thus replied to Wainamoinen:
"Know I well the titmouse-fountains,
Pretty birdling is the titmouse;
And the viper, green, a serpent;
Whitings live in brackish waters;
Perches swim in every river;
Iron rusts, and rusting weakens;
Bitter is the taste of umber;
Boiling water is malicious;
Fire is ever full of danger;
First physician, the Creator;
Remedy the oldest, water;
Magic is the child of sea-foam;
God the first and best adviser;
Waters gush from every mountain;

The Kalevala

Fire descended first from heaven;
Iron from the rust was fashioned;
Copper from the rocks created;
Marshes are of lands the oldest;
First of all the trees, the willow;
Fir-trees were the first of houses;
Hollowed stones the first of kettles."
Now the ancient Wainamoinen
Thus addresses Youkahainen:
"Canst thou give me now some wisdom,
Is this nonsense all thou knowest?"
Youkahainen thus made answer:
"I can tell thee still a trifle,
Tell thee of the times primeval,
When I plowed the salt-sea's bosom,
When I raked the sea-girt islands,
When I dug the salmon-grottoes,
Hollowed out the deepest caverns,
When I all the lakes created,
When I heaped the mountains round them,
When I piled the rocks about them.
I was present as a hero,
Sixth of wise and ancient heroes,
Seventh of all primeval heroes,
When the heavens were created,
When were formed the ether-spaces,
When the sky was crystal-pillared,
When was arched the beauteous rainbow,
When the Moon was placed in orbit,
When the silver Sun was planted,
When the Bear was firmly stationed,
And with stars the heavens were sprinkled."
Spake the ancient Wainamoinen:
"Thou art surely prince of liars,
Lord of all the host of liars;
Never wert thou in existence,
Surely wert thou never present,
When was plowed the salt-sea's bosom,
When were raked the sea-girt islands,
When were dug the salmon-grottoes,
When were hollowed out the caverns,
When the lakes were all created,
When were heaped the mountains round them,
When the rocks were piled about them.
Thou wert never seen or heard of
When the earth was first created,
When were made the ether-spaces,
When the air was crystal-pillared,
When the Moon was placed in orbit,
When the silver Sun was planted,
When the Bear was firmly stationed,
When the skies with stars were sprinkled."
Then in anger Youkahainen
Answered ancient Wainamoinen:
"Then, sir, since I fail in wisdom,
With the sword I offer battle;
Come thou, famous bard and minstrel,
Thou the ancient wonder-singer,
Let us try our strength with broadswords,
let our blades be fully tested."
Spake the ancient Wainamoinen:

Lönnrot

"Not thy sword and not thy wisdom,
Not thy prudence, nor thy cunning,
Do I fear a single moment.
Let who may accept thy challenge,
Not with thee, a puny braggart,
Not with one so vain and paltry,
Will I ever measure broadswords."
Then the youthful Youkahainen,
Mouth awry and visage sneering,
Shook his golden locks and answered:
"Whoso fears his blade to measure,
Fears to test his strength at broadswords,
Into wild-boar of the forest,
Swine at heart and swine in visage,
Singing I will thus transform him;
I will hurl such hero-cowards,
This one hither, that one thither,
Stamp him in the mire and bedding,
In the rubbish of the stable."
Angry then grew Wainamoinen,
Wrathful waxed, and fiercely frowning,
Self-composed he broke his silence,
And began his wondrous singing.
Sang he not the tales of childhood,
Children's nonsense, wit of women,
Sang he rather bearded heroes,
That the children never heard of,
That the boys and maidens knew not
Known but half by bride and bridegroom,
Known in part by many heroes,
In these mournful days of evil,
Evil times our race befallen.
Grandly sang wise Wainamoinen,
Till the copper-bearing mountains,
And the flinty rocks and ledges
Heard his magic tones and trembled;
Mountain cliffs were torn to pieces,
All the ocean heaved and tumbled;
And the distant hills re-echoed.
Lo! the boastful Youkahainen
Is transfixed in silent wonder,
And his sledge with golden trimmings
Floats like brushwood on the billows;
Sings his braces into reed-grass,
Sings his reins to twigs of willow,
And to shrubs his golden cross-bench.
Lo! his birch-whip, pearl-enameled,
Floats a reed upon the border;
Lo! his steed with golden forehead,
Stands a statue on the waters;
Hames and traces are as fir-boughs,
And his collar, straw and sea-grass.
Still the minstrel sings enchantment,
Sings his sword with golden handle,
Sings it into gleam of lightning,
Hangs it in the sky above him;
Sings his cross-bow, gaily painted,
To a rainbow o'er the ocean;
Sings his quick and feathered arrows
Into hawks and screaming eagles;
Sings his dog with bended muzzle,

The Kalevala
Into block of stone beside him;
Sings his cap from off his forehead,
Sings it into wreaths of vapor;
From his hands he sings his gauntlets
Into rushes on the waters;
Sings his vesture, purple-colored,
Into white clouds in the heavens;
Sings his girdle, set with jewels,
Into twinkling stars around him;
And alas! for Youkahainen,
Sings him into deeps of quick-sand;
Ever deeper, deeper, deeper,
In his torture, sinks the wizard,
To his belt in mud and water.
Now it was that Youkahainen
Comprehended but too clearly
What his folly, what the end was,
Of the journey he had ventured,
Vainly he had undertaken
For the glory of a contest
With the grand, old Wainamoinen.
When at last young Youkahainen,
Pohyola's old and sorry stripling,
Strives his best to move his right foot,
But alas! the foot obeys not;
When he strives to move his left foot,
Lo! he finds it turned to flint-stone.
Thereupon sad Youkahainen,
In the deeps of desperation,
And in earnest supplication,
Thus addresses Wainamoinen:
"O thou wise and worthy minstrel,
Thou the only true, magician,
Cease I pray thee thine enchantment,.
Only turn away thy magic,
Let me leave this slough of horror,
Loose me from this stony prison,
Free me from this killing torment,
I will pay a golden ransom."
Spake the ancient Wainamoinen:
"What the ransom thou wilt give me
If I cease from mine enchantment,
If I turn away my magic,
Lift thee from thy slough of horror,
Loose thee from thy stony prison,
Free thee from thy killing torment?"
Answered youthful Youkahainen:
"Have at home two magic cross-bows,
Pair of bows of wondrous power,
One so light a child can bend it,
Only strength can bend the other,
Take of these the one that pleases."
Then the ancient Wainamoinen:
"Do not wish thy magic cross-bows,
Have a few of such already,
Thine to me are worse than useless
I have bows in great abundance,
Bows on every nail and rafter,
Bows that laugh at all the hunters,
Bows that go themselves a-hunting."
Then the ancient Wainamoinen

Lönnrot

Sang alas! poor Youkahainen
Deeper into mud and water,
Deeper in the slough of torment.
Youkahainen thus made answer:
"Have at home two magic shallops,
Beautiful the boats and wondrous;
One rides light upon the ocean,
One is made for heavy burdens;
Take of these the one that pleases."
Spake the ancient Wainamoinen:
"Do not wish thy magic shallops,
Have enough of such already;
All my bays are full of shallops,
All my shores are lined with shallops,
Some before the winds are sailors,
Some were built to sail against them."
Still the Wainola bard and minstrel
Sings again poor Youkahainen
Deeper, deeper into torment,
Into quicksand to his girdle,
Till the Lapland bard in anguish
Speaks again to Wainamoinen:
"Have at home two magic stallions,
One a racer, fleet as lightning,
One was born for heavy burdens;
Take of these the one that pleases."
Spake the ancient Wainamoinen:
"Neither do I wish thy stallions,
Do not need thy hawk-limbed stallions,
Have enough of these already;
Magic stallions swarm my stables,
Eating corn at every manger,
Broad of back to hold the water,
Water on each croup in lakelets."
Still the bard of Kalevala
Sings the hapless Lapland minstrel
Deeper, deeper into torment,
To his shoulders into water.
Spake again young Youkahainen:
"O thou ancient Wainamoinen,
Thou the only true magician,
Cease I pray thee thine enchantment,
Only turn away thy magic,
I will give thee gold abundant,
Countless stores of shining silver;
From the wars my father brought it,
Brought it from the hard-fought battles."
Spake the wise, old Wainamoinen:
"For thy gold I have no longing,
Neither do I wish thy silver,
Have enough of each already;
Gold abundant fills my chambers,
On each nail hang bags of silver,
Gold that glitters in the sunshine,
Silver shining in the moonlight."
Sank the braggart, Youkahainen,
Deeper in his slough of torment,
To his chin in mud and water,
Ever praying, thus beseeching:
"O thou ancient Wainamoinen,
Greatest of the old magicians,

The Kalevala
Lift me from this pit of horror,
From this prison-house of torture;
I will give thee all my corn-fields,
Give thee all my corn in garners,
Thus my hapless life to ransom,
Thus to gain eternal freedom."
Wainamoinen thus made answer:
"Take thy corn to other markets,
Give thy garners to the needy;
I have corn in great abundance,
Fields have I in every quarter,
Corn in all my fields is growing;
One's own fields are always richer,
One's own grain is much the sweeter."
Lapland's young and reckless minstrel,
Sorrow-laden, thus enchanted,
Deeper sinks in mud and water,
Fear-enchained and full of anguish,
In the mire, his beard bedrabbled,
Mouth once boastful filled with sea-weed,
In the grass his teeth entangled,
Youkahainen thus beseeches:
"O thou ancient Wainamoinen,
Wisest of the wisdom-singers,
Cease at last thine incantations,
Only turn away thy magic,
And my former life restore me,
Lift me from this stifling torment,
Free mine eyes from sand and water,
I will give thee sister, Aino,
Fairest daughter of my mother,
Bride of thine to be forever,
Bride of thine to do thy pleasure,
Sweep the rooms within thy cottage,
Keep thy dwelling-place in order,
Rinse for thee the golden platters,
Spread thy couch with finest linens,
For thy bed, weave golden covers,
Bake for thee the honey-biscuit."
Wainamoinen, old and truthful,
Finds at last the wished-for ransom,
Lapland's young and fairest daughter,
Sister dear of Youkahainen;
Happy he, that he has won him,
In his age a beauteous maiden,
Bride of his to be forever,
Pride and joy of Kalevala.
Now the happy Wainamoinen,
Sits upon the rock of gladness,
Joyful on the rock of music,
Sings a little, sings and ceases,
Sings again, and sings a third time,
Thus to break the spell of magic,
Thus to lessen the enchantment,
Thus the potent charm to banish.
As the magic spell is broken,
Youkahainen, sad, but wiser,
Drags his feet from out the quicksand,
Lifts his beard from out the water,
From the rocks leads forth his courser,
Brings his sledge back from the rushes,

Lönnrot

Calls his whip back from the ocean,
Sets his golden sledge in order,
Throws himself upon the cross-bench,
Snaps his whip and hies him homeward,
Hastens homeward, heavy-hearted,
Sad indeed to meet his mother,
Aino's mother, gray and aged.
Careless thus he hastens homeward,
Nears his home with noise and bustle,
Reckless drives against the pent-house,
Breaks the shafts against the portals,
Breaks his handsome sledge in pieces.
Then his mother, quickly guessing,
Would have chided him for rashness,
But the father interrupted:
"Wherefore dost thou break thy snow-sledge,
Wherefore dash thy thills in fragments,
Wherefore comest home so strangely,
Why this rude and wild behavior?"
Now alas! poor Youkahainen,
Cap awry upon his forehead,
Falls to weeping, broken-hearted,
Head depressed and mind dejected,
Eyes and lips expressing sadness,
Answers not his anxious father.
Then the mother quickly asked him,
Sought to find his cause for sorrow:
"Tell me, first-born, why thou weepest,
Why thou weepest, heavy-hearted,
Why thy mind is so dejected,
Why thine eyes express such sadness."
Youkahainen then made answer:
"Golden mother, ever faithful,
Cause there is to me sufficient,
Cause enough in what has happened,
Bitter cause for this my sorrow,
Cause for bitter tears and murmurs:
All my days will pass unhappy,
Since, O mother of my being,
I have promised beauteous Aino,
Aino, thy beloved daughter,
Aino, my devoted sister,
To decrepit Wainamoinen,
Bride to be to him forever,
Roof above him, prop beneath him,
Fair companion at his fire-side."
Joyful then arose the mother,
Clapped her hands in glee together,
Thus addressing Youkahainen:
"Weep no more, my son beloved,
Thou hast naught to cause thy weeping,
Hast no reason for thy sorrow,
Often I this hope have cherished;
Many years have I been praying
That this mighty bard and hero,
Wise and valiant Wainamoinen,
Spouse should be to beauteous Aino,
Son-in-law to me, her mother."
But the fair and lovely maiden,
Sister dear of Youkahainen,
Straightway fell to bitter weeping,

The Kalevala
On the threshold wept and lingered,
Wept all day and all the night long,
Wept a second, then a third day,
Wept because a bitter sorrow
On her youthful heart had fallen.
Then the gray-haired mother asked her:
"Why this weeping, lovely Aino?
Thou hast found a noble suitor,
Thou wilt rule his spacious dwelling,
At his window sit and rest thee,
Rinse betimes his golden platters,
Walk a queen within his dwelling."
Thus replied the tearful Aino:
"Mother dear, and all-forgiving,
Cause enough for this my sorrow,
Cause enough for bitter weeping:
I must loose my sunny tresses,
Tresses beautiful and golden,
Cannot deck my hair with jewels,
Cannot bind my head with ribbons,
All to be hereafter hidden
Underneath the linen bonnet
That the wife. must wear forever;
Weep at morning, weep at evening,
Weep alas! for waning beauty,
Childhood vanished, youth departed,
Silver sunshine, golden moonlight,
Hope and pleasure of my childhood,
Taken from me now forever,
And so soon to be forgotten
At the tool-bench of my brother,
At the window of my sister,
In the cottage of my father."
Spake again the gray-haired mother
To her wailing daughter Aino:
"Cease thy sorrow, foolish maiden,
By thy tears thou art ungrateful,
Reason none for thy repining,
Not the slightest cause for weeping;
Everywhere the silver sunshine
Falls as bright on other households;
Not alone the moonlight glimmers
Through thy father's open windows,
On the work-bench of thy brother;
Flowers bloom in every meadow,
Berries grow on every mountain;
Thou canst go thyself and find them,
All the day long go and find them;
Not alone thy brother's meadows
Grow the beauteous vines and flowers;
Not alone thy father's mountains
Yield the ripe, nutritious berries;
Flowers bloom in other meadows,
Berries grow on other mountains,
There as here, my lovely Aino."

RUNE IV
THE FATE OF AINO

When the night had passed, the maiden,
Sister fair of Youkahainen,
Hastened early to the forest,
Birchen shoots for brooms to gather,
Went to gather birchen tassels;
Bound a bundle for her father,
Bound a birch-broom for her mother,
Silken tassels for her sister.
Straightway then she hastened homeward,
By a foot-path left the forest;
As she neared the woodland border,
Lo! the ancient Wainamoinen,
Quickly spying out the maiden,
As she left the birchen woodland,
Trimly dressed in costly raiment,
And the minstrel thus addressed her:
"Aino, beauty of the Northland,
Wear not, lovely maid, for others,
Only wear for me, sweet maiden,
Golden cross upon thy bosom,
Shining pearls upon thy shoulders;
Bind for me thine auburn tresses,
Wear for me thy golden braidlets."
Thus the maiden quickly answered:
"Not for thee and not for others,
Hang I from my neck the crosslet,
Deck my hair with silken ribbons;
Need no more the many trinkets
Brought to me by ship or shallop;
Sooner wear the simplest raiment,
Feed upon the barley bread-crust,
Dwell forever with my mother
In the cabin with my father."
Then she threw the gold cross from her,
Tore the jewels from her fingers,
Quickly loosed her shining necklace,
Quick untied her silken ribbons,
Cast them all away indignant
Into forest ferns and flowers.
Thereupon the maiden, Aino,
Hastened to her mother's cottage.
At the window sat her father
Whittling on an oaken ax-helve:
"Wherefore weepest, beauteous Aino,
Aino, my beloved daughter?"
"Cause enough for weeping, father,
Good the reasons for my mourning,
This, the reason for my weeping,
This, the cause of all my sorrow:
From my breast I tore the crosslet,
From my belt, the clasp of copper,
From my waist, the belt of silver,
Golden was my pretty crosslet."

The Kalevala
Near the door-way sat her brother,
Carving out a birchen ox-bow:
"Why art weeping, lovely Aino,
Aino, my devoted sister?"
"Cause enough for weeping, brother,
Good the reasons for my mourning
Therefore come I as thou seest,
Rings no longer on my fingers,
On my neck no pretty necklace;
Golden were the rings thou gavest,
And the necklace, pearls and silver!"
On the threshold sat her sister,
Weaving her a golden girdle:
"Why art weeping, beauteous Aino,
Aino, my beloved sister?"
"Cause enough for weeping, sister,
Good the reasons for my sorrow:
Therefore come I as thou seest,
On my head no scarlet fillet,
In my hair no braids of silver,
On mine arms no purple ribbons,
Round my neck no shining necklace,
On my breast no golden crosslet,
In mine ears no golden ear-rings."
Near the door-way of the dairy,
Skimming cream, sat Aino's mother.
"Why art weeping, lovely Aino,
Aino, my devoted daughter?"
Thus the sobbing maiden answered;
"Loving mother, all-forgiving,
Cause enough for this my weeping,
Good the reasons for my sorrow,
Therefore do I weep, dear mother:
I have been within the forest,
Brooms to bind and shoots to gather,
There to pluck some birchen tassels;
Bound a bundle for my father,
Bound a second for my mother,
Bound a third one for my brother,
For my sister silken tassels.
Straightway then I hastened homeward,
By a foot-path left the forest;
As I reached the woodland border
Spake Osmoinen from the cornfield,
Spake the ancient Wainamoinen:
'Wear not, beauteous maid, for others,
Only wear for me, sweet maiden,
On thy breast a golden crosslet,
Shining pearls upon thy shoulders,
Bind for me thine auburn tresses,
Weave for me thy silver braidlets.'
Then I threw the gold-cross from me,
Tore the jewels from my fingers,
Quickly loosed my shining necklace,
Quick untied my silken ribbons,
Cast them all away indignant,
Into forest ferns and flowers.
Then I thus addressed the singer:
'Not for thee and not for others,
Hang I from my neck the crosslet,
Deck my hair with silken ribbons;

Lönnrot

Need no more the many trinkets,
Brought to me by ship and shallop;
Sooner wear the simplest raiment,
Feed upon the barley bread-crust,
Dwell forever with my mother
In the cabin with my father.'"
Thus the gray-haired mother answered
Aino, her beloved daughter:
"Weep no more, my lovely maiden,
Waste no more of thy sweet young-life;
One year eat thou my sweet butter,
It will make thee strong and ruddy;
Eat another year fresh bacon,
It will make thee tall and queenly;
Eat a third year only dainties,
It will make thee fair and lovely.
Now make haste to yonder hill-top,
To the store-house on the mountain,
Open there the large compartment,
Thou will find it filled with boxes,
Chests and cases, trunks and boxes;
Open thou the box, the largest,
Lift away the gaudy cover,
Thou will find six golden girdles,
Seven rainbow-tinted dresses,
Woven by the Moon's fair daughters,
Fashioned by the Sun's sweet virgins.
In my young years once I wandered,
As a maiden on the mountains,
In the happy days of childhood,
Hunting berries in the coppice;
There by chance I heard the daughters
Of the Moon as they were weaving;
There I also heard the daughters
Of the Sun as they were spinning
On the red rims of the cloudlets,
O'er the blue edge of the forest,
On the border of the pine-wood,
On a high and distant mountain.
I approached them, drawing nearer,
Stole myself within their hearing,
Then began I to entreat them,
Thus besought them, gently pleading:
'Give thy silver, Moon's fair daughters,
To a poor, but worthy maiden;
Give thy gold, O Sun's sweet virgins,
To this maiden, young and needy.'
Thereupon the Moon's fair daughters
Gave me silver from their coffers;
And the Sun's sweet shining virgins
Gave me gold from their abundance,
Gold to deck my throbbing temples,
For my hair the shining silver.
Then I hastened joyful homeward,
Richly laden with my treasures,
Happy to my mother's cottage;
Wore them one day, than a second,
Then a third day also wore them,
Took the gold then from my temples,
From my hair I took the silver,
Careful laid them in their boxes,

The Kalevala
Many seasons have they lain there,
Have not seen them since my childhood.
Deck thy brow with silken ribbon,
Trim with gold thy throbbing temples,
And thy neck with pearly necklace,
Hang the gold-cross on thy bosom,
Robe thyself in pure, white linen
Spun from flax of finest fiber;
Wear withal the richest short-frock,
Fasten it with golden girdle;
On thy feet, put silken stockings,
With the shoes of finest leather;
Deck thy hair with golden braidlets,
Bind it well with threads of silver;
Trim with rings thy fairy fingers,
And thy hands with dainty ruffles;
Come bedecked then to thy chamber,
Thus return to this thy household,
To the greeting of thy kindred,
To the joy of all that know thee,
Flushed thy cheeks as ruddy berries,
Coming as thy father's sunbeam,
Walking beautiful and queenly,
Far more beautiful than moonlight."
Thus she spake to weeping Aino,
Thus the mother to her daughter;
But the maiden, little bearing,
Does not heed her mother's wishes;
Straightway hastens to the court-yard,
There to weep in bitter sorrow,
All alone to weep in anguish.
Waiting long the wailing Aino
Thus at last soliloquizes:
"Unto what can I now liken
Happy homes and joys of fortune?
Like the waters in the river,
Like the waves in yonder lakelet,
Like the crystal waters flowing.
Unto what, the biting sorrow
Of the child of cold misfortune?
Like the spirit of the sea-duck,
Like the icicle in winter,
Water in the well imprisoned.
Often roamed my mind in childhood,
When a maiden free and merry,
Happily through fen and fallow,
Gamboled on the meads with lambkins,
Lingered with the ferns and flowers,
Knowing neither pain nor trouble;
Now my mind is filled with sorrow,
Wanders though the bog and stubble,
Wanders weary through the brambles,
Roams throughout the dismal forest,
Till my life is filled with darkness,
And my spirit white with anguish.
Better had it been for Aino
Had she never seen the sunlight,
Or if born had died an infant,
Had not lived to be a maiden
In these days of sin and sorrow,
Underneath a star so luckless.

Lönnrot

Better had it been for Aino,
Had she died upon the eighth day
After seven nights had vanished;
Needed then but little linen,
Needed but a little coffin,
And a grave of smallest measure;
Mother would have mourned a little,
Father too perhaps a trifle,
Sister would have wept the day through,
Brother might have shed a tear-drop,
Thus had ended all the mourning."
Thus poor Aino wept and murmured,
Wept one day, and then a second,
Wept a third from morn till even,
When again her mother asked her:
"Why this weeping, fairest daughter,
Darling daughter, why this grieving?
Thus the tearful maiden answered:
Therefore do I weep and sorrow,
Wretched maiden all my life long,
Since poor Aino, thou hast given,
Since thy daughter thou hast promised
To the aged Wainamoinen,
Comfort to his years declining
Prop to stay him when he totters,
In the storm a roof above him,
In his home a cloak around him;
Better far if thou hadst sent me
Far below the salt-sea surges,
To become the whiting's sister,
And the friend of perch and salmon;
Better far to ride the billows,
Swim the sea-foam as a mermaid,
And the friend of nimble fishes,
Than to be an old man's solace,
Prop to stay him when be totters,
Hand to aid him when he trembles,
Arm to guide him when he falters,
Strength to give him when he weakens;
Better be the whiting's sister
And the friend of perch and salmon,
Than an old man's slave and darling."
Ending thus she left her mother,
Straightway hastened to the mountain?
To the store-house on the summit,
Opened there the box the largest,
From the box six lids she lifted,
Found therein six golden girdles,
Silken dresses seven in number.
Choosing such as pleased her fancy,
She adorned herself as bidden,
Robed herself to look her fairest,
Gold upon her throbbing temples,
In her hair the shining silver,
On her shoulders purple ribbons,
Band of blue around her forehead,
Golden cross, and rings, and jewels,
Fitting ornaments to beauty.
Now she leaves her many treasures,
Leaves the store-house on the mountain,
Filled with gold and silver trinkets,

The Kalevala
Wanders over field and meadow,
Over stone-fields waste and barren,
Wanders on through fen and forest,
Through the forest vast and cheerless,
Wanders hither, wanders thither,
Singing careless as she wanders,
This her mournful song and echo:
"Woe is me, my life hard-fated!
Woe to Aino, broken-hearted!
Torture racks my heart and temples,
Yet the sting would not be deeper,
Nor the pain and anguish greater,
If beneath this weight of sorrow,
In my saddened heart's dejection,
I should yield my life forever,
Now unhappy, I should perish!
Lo! the time has come for Aino
From this cruel world to hasten,
To the kingdom of Tuoni,
To the realm of the departed,
To the isle of the hereafter.
Weep no more for me, O Father,
Mother dear, withhold thy censure,
Lovely sister, dry thine eyelids,
Do not mourn me, dearest brother,
When I sink beneath the sea-foam,
Make my home in salmon-grottoes,
Make my bed in crystal waters,
Water-ferns my couch and pillow."
All day long poor Aino wandered,
All the next day, sad and weary,
So the third from morn till evening,
Till the cruel night enwrapped her,
As she reached the sandy margin,
Reached the cold and dismal sea-shore,
Sat upon the rock of sorrow,
Sat alone in cold and darkness,
Listened only to the music
Of the winds and rolling billows,
Singing all the dirge of Aino.
All that night the weary maiden
Wept and wandered on the border
Through the sand and sea-washed pebbles.
As the day dawns, looking round her,
She beholds three water-maidens,
On a headland jutting seaward,
Water-maidens four in number,
Sitting on the wave-lashed ledges,
Swimming now upon the billows,
Now upon the rocks reposing.
Quick the weeping maiden, Aino,
Hastens there to join the mermaids,
Fairy maidens of the waters.
Weeping Aino, now disrobing,
Lays aside with care her garments,
Hangs her silk robes on the alders,
Drops her gold-cross on the sea-shore,
On the aspen hangs her ribbons,
On the rocks her silken stockings,
On the grass her shoes of deer-skin,
In the sand her shining necklace,

Lönnrot

With her rings and other jewels.
Out at sea a goodly distance,
Stood a rock of rainbow colors,
Glittering in silver sunlight.
Toward it springs the hapless maiden,
Thither swims the lovely Aino,
Up the standing-stone has clambered,
Wishing there to rest a moment,
Rest upon the rock of beauty;
When upon a sudden swaying
To and fro among the billows,
With a crash and roar of waters
Falls the stone of many colors,
Falls upon the very bottom
Of the deep and boundless blue-sea.
With the stone of rainbow colors,
Falls the weeping maiden, Aino,
Clinging to its craggy edges,
Sinking far below the surface,
To the bottom of the blue-sea.
Thus the weeping maiden vanished.
Thus poor Aino sank and perished,
Singing as the stone descended,
Chanting thus as she departed:
Once to swim I sought the sea-side,
There to sport among the billows;
With the stone or many colors
Sank poor Aino to the bottom
Of the deep and boundless blue-sea,
Like a pretty son-bird. perished.
Never come a-fishing, father,
To the borders of these waters,
Never during all thy life-time,
As thou lovest daughter Aino.
"Mother dear, I sought the sea-side,
There to sport among the billows;
With the stone of many colors,
Sank poor Aino to the bottom
Of the deep and boundless blue-sea,
Like a pretty song-bird perished.
Never mix thy bread, dear mother,
With the blue-sea's foam and waters,
Never during all thy life-time,
As thou lovest daughter Aino.
Brother dear, I sought the sea-side,
There to sport among the billows;
With the stone of many colors
Sank poor Aino to the bottom
Of the deep and boundless blue-sea,
Like a pretty song-bird perished.
Never bring thy prancing war-horse,
Never bring thy royal racer,
Never bring thy steeds to water,
To the borders of the blue-sea,
Never during all thy life-time,
As thou lovest sister Aino.
"Sister dear, I sought the sea-side,
There to sport among the billows;
With the stone of many colors
Sank poor Aino to the bottom
Of the deep and boundless blue-sea,

The Kalevala
Like a pretty song-bird perished.
Never come to lave thine eyelids
In this rolling wave and sea-foam,
Never during all thy life-time,
As thou lovest sister Aino.
All the waters in the blue-sea
Shall be blood of Aino's body;
All the fish that swim these waters
Shall be Aino's flesh forever;
All the willows on the sea-side
Shall be Aino's ribs hereafter;
All the sea-grass on the margin
Will have grown from Aino's tresses."
Thus at last the maiden vanished,
Thus the lovely Aino perished.
Who will tell the cruel story,
Who will bear the evil tidings
To the cottage of her mother,
Once the home of lovely Aino?
Will the bear repeat the story,
Tell the tidings to her mother?
Nay, the bear must not be herald,
He would slay the herds of cattle.
Who then tell the cruel story,
Who will bear the evil tidings
To the cottage of her father,
Once the home of lovely Aino?
Shall the wolf repeat the story,
Tell the sad news to her father?
Nay, the wolf must not be herald,
He would eat the gentle lambkins.
Who then tell the cruel story,
Who will bear the evil tidings.
To the cottage of her sister?
'Will the fox repeat the story
Tell the tidings to her sister?
Nay, the fox must not be herald,
He would eat the ducks and chickens.
Who then tell the cruel story,
Who will bear the evil tidings
To the cottage of her brother,
Once the home of lovely Aino?
Shall the hare repeat the story,
Bear the sad news to her brother?
Yea, the hare shall be the herald,
Tell to all the cruel story.
Thus the harmless hare makes answer:
"I will bear the evil tidings
To the former home of Aino,
Tell the story to her kindred."
Swiftly flew the long-eared herald,
Like the winds be hastened onward,
Galloped swift as flight of eagles;
Neck awry he bounded forward
Till he gained the wished-for cottage,
Once the home of lovely Aino.
Silent was the home, and vacant;
So he hastened to the bath-house,
Found therein a group of maidens,
Working each upon a birch-broom.
Sat the hare upon the threshold,

Lönnrot

And the maidens thus addressed him:
"Hie e there, Long-legs, or we'll roast thee,
Hie there, Big-eye, or we'll stew thee,
Roast thee for our lady's breakfast,
Stew thee for our master's dinner,
Make of thee a meal for Aino,
And her brother, Youkahainen!
Better therefore thou shouldst gallop
To thy burrow in the mountains,
Than be roasted for our dinners."
Then the haughty hare made answer,
Chanting thus the fate of Aino:
"Think ye not I journey hither,
To be roasted in the skillet,
To be stewed in yonder kettle
Let fell Lempo fill thy tables!
I have come with evil tidings,
Come to tell the cruel story
Of the flight and death of Aino,
Sister dear of Youkahainen.
With the stone of many colors
Sank poor Aino to the bottom
Of the deep and boundless waters,
Like a pretty song-bird perished;
Hung her ribbons on the aspen,
Left her gold-cross on the sea-shore,
Silken robes upon the alders,
On the rocks her silken stockings,
On the grass her shoes of deer-skin,
In the sand her shining necklace,
In the sand her rings and jewels;
In the waves, the lovely Aino,
Sleeping on the very bottom
Of the deep and boundless blue-sea,
In the caverns of the salmon,
There to be the whiting's sister
And the friend of nimble fishes."
Sadly weeps the ancient mother
From her blue-eyes bitter tear-drops,
As in sad and wailing measures,
Broken-hearted thus she answers:
"Listen, all ye mothers, listen,
Learn from me a tale of wisdom:
Never urge unwilling daughters
From the dwellings of their fathers,
To the bridegrooms that they love not,
Not as I, inhuman mother,
Drove away my lovely Aino,
Fairest daughter of the Northland."
Sadly weeps the gray-haired mother,
And the tears that fall are bitter,
Flowing down her wrinkled visage,
Till they trickle on her bosom;
Then across her heaving bosom,
Till they reach her garment's border;
Then adown her silken stockings,
Till they touch her shoes of deer-skin;
Then beneath her shoes of deer-skin,
Flowing on and flowing ever,
Part to earth as its possession,
Part to water as its portion.

The Kalevala

As the tear-drops fall and mingle,
Form they streamlets three in number,
And their source, the mother's eyelids,
Streamlets formed from pearly tear-drops,
Flowing on like little rivers,
And each streamlet larger growing,
Soon becomes a rushing torrent
In each rushing, roaring torrent
There a cataract is foaming,
Foaming in the silver sunlight;
From the cataract's commotion
Rise three pillared rocks in grandeur;
From each rock, upon the summit,
Grow three hillocks clothed in verdure;
From each hillock, speckled birches,
Three in number, struggle skyward;
On the summit of each birch-tree
Sits a golden cuckoo calling,
And the three sing, all in concord:
"Love! O Love! the first one calleth;
Sings the second, Suitor! Suitor!
And the third one calls and echoes,
"Consolation! Consolation!"
He that "Love! O Love!" is calling,
Calls three moons and calls unceasing,
For the love-rejecting maiden
Sleeping in the deep sea-castles.
He that "Suitor! Suitor!" singeth,
Sings six moons and sings unceasing
For the suitor that forever
Sings and sues without a hearing.
He that sadly sings and echoes,
"Consolation! Consolation!"
Sings unceasing all his life long
For the broken-hearted mother
That must mourn and weep forever.
When the lone and wretched mother
Heard the sacred cuckoo singing,
Spake she thus, and sorely weeping:
"When I hear the cuckoo calling,
Then my heart is filled with sorrow;
Tears unlock my heavy eyelids,
Flow adown my, furrowed visage,
Tears as large as silver sea pearls;
Older grow my wearied elbows,
Weaker ply my aged fingers,
Wearily, in all its members,
Does my body shake in palsy,
When I hear the cuckoo singing,
Hear the sacred cuckoo calling."

RUNE V
WAINAVOINEN'S LAMENTATION

Far and wide the tidings travelled,
Far away men heard the story
Of the flight and death of Aino,
Sister dear of Youkahainen,
Fairest daughter of creation.
Wainamoinen, brave and truthful,
Straightway fell to bitter weeping,
Wept at morning, wept at evening,
Sleepless, wept the dreary night long,
That his Aino had departed,
That the maiden thus had vanished,
Thus had sunk upon the bottom
Of the blue-sea, deep and boundless.
Filled with grief, the ancient singer,
Wainamoinen of the Northland,
Heavy-hearted, sorely weeping,
Hastened to the restless waters,
This the suitor's prayer and question:
"Tell, Untamo, tell me, dreamer,
Tell me, Indolence, thy visions,
Where the water-gods may linger,
Where may rest Wellamo's maidens?"
Then Untamo, thus made answer,
Lazily he told his dreamings:
"Over there, the mermaid-dwellings,
Yonder live Wellamo's maidens,
On the headland robed in verdure,
On the forest-covered island,
In the deep, pellucid waters,
On the purple-colored sea-shore;
Yonder is the home or sea-maids,
There the maidens of Wellamo,
Live there in their sea-side chambers,
Rest within their water-caverns,
On the rocks of rainbow colors,
On the juttings of the sea-cliffs."
Straightway hastens Wainamoinen
To a boat-house on the sea-shore,
Looks with care upon the fish-hooks,
And the lines he well considers;
Lines, and hooks, and poles, arid fish-nets,
Places in a boat of copper,
Then begins he swiftly rowing
To the forest-covered island,
To the point enrobed In verdure,
To the purple-colored headland,
Where the sea-nymphs live and linger.
Hardly does he reach the island
Ere the minstrel starts to angle;
Far away he throws his fish-hook,
Trolls it quickly through the waters,
Turning on a copper swivel
Dangling from a silver fish-line,

The Kalevala

Golden is the hook he uses.
Now he tries his silken fish-net,
Angles long, and angles longer,
Angles one day, then a second,
In the morning, in the evening,
Angles at the hour of noontide,
Many days and nights he angles,
Till at last, one sunny morning,
Strikes a fish of magic powers,
Plays like salmon on his fish-line,
Lashing waves across the waters,
Till at length the fish exhausted
Falls a victim to the angler,
Safely landed in the bottom
Of the hero's boat of copper.
Wainamoinen, proudly viewing,
Speaks these words in wonder guessing:
"This the fairest of all sea-fish,
Never have I seen its equal,
Smoother surely than the salmon,
Brighter-spotted than the trout is,
Grayer than the pike of Suomi,
Has less fins than any female,
Not the fins of any male fish,
Not the stripes of sea-born maidens,
Not the belt of any mermaid,
Not the ears of any song-bird,
Somewhat like our Northland salmon
From the blue-sea's deepest caverns."
In his belt the ancient hero
Wore a knife insheathed with silver;
From its case he drew the fish-knife,
Thus to carve the fish in pieces,
Dress the nameless fish for roasting,
Make of it a dainty breakfast,
Make of it a meal at noon-day,
Make for him a toothsome supper,
Make the later meal at evening.
Straightway as the fish he touches,
Touches with his knife of silver,
Quick it leaps upon the waters,
Dives beneath the sea's smooth surface,
From the boat with copper bottom,
From the skiff of Wainamoinen.
In the waves at goodly distance,
Quickly from the sea it rises
On the sixth and seventh billows,
Lifts its head above the waters,
Out of reach of fishing-tackle,
Then addresses Wainamoinen,
Chiding thus the ancient hero:
"Wainamoinen, ancient minstrel,
Do not think that I came hither
To be fished for as a salmon,
Only to be chopped in pieces,
Dressed and eaten like a whiting
Make for thee a dainty breakfast,
Make for thee a meal at midday,
Make for thee a toothsome supper,
Make the fourth meal of the Northland."
Spake the ancient Wainamoinen:

Lönnrot

"Wherefore didst thou then come hither,
If it be not for my dinner?"
Thus the nameless fish made answer:
"Hither have I come, O minstrel,
In thine arms to rest and linger,
And thyself to love and cherish,
At thy side a life-companion,
And thy wife to be forever;
Deck thy couch with snowy linen,
Smooth thy head upon the pillow,
Sweep thy rooms and make them cheery,
Keep thy dwelling-place in order,
Build a fire for thee when needed,
Bake for thee the honey-biscuit,
Fill thy cup with barley-water,
Do for thee whatever pleases.
"I am not a scaly sea-fish,
Not a trout of Northland rivers,
Not a whiting from the waters,
Not a salmon of the North-seas,
I, a young and merry maiden,
Friend and sister of the fishes,
Youkahainen's youngest sister,
I, the one that thou dost fish for,
I am Aino whom thou lovest.
"Once thou wert the wise-tongued hero,
Now the foolish Wainamoinen,
Scant of insight, scant of judgment,
Didst not know enough to keep me,
Cruel-hearted, bloody-handed,
Tried to kill me with thy fish-knife,
So to roast me for thy dinner;
I, a mermaid of Wellamo,
Once the fair and lovely Aino,
Sister dear of Youkahainen."
Spake the ancient Wainamoinen,
Filled with sorrow, much regretting:
"Since thou'rt Youkahainen's sister,
Beauteous Aino of Pohyola,
Come to me again I pray thee!"
Thus the mermaid wisely answered;
Nevermore will Aino's spirit
Fly to thee and be ill-treated."
Quickly dived the water-maiden
From the surface of the billow
To the many-colored pebbles,
To the rainbow-tinted grottoes
Where the mermaids live and linger.
Wainamoinen, not discouraged,
Thought afresh and well reflected,
How to live, and work, and win her;
Drew with care his silken fish-net,
To and fro through foam and billow,
Through the bays and winding channels,
Drew it through the placid waters,
Drew it through the salmon-dwellings,
Through the homes of water-maidens,
Through the waters of Wainola,
Through the blue-back of the ocean,
Through the lakes of distant Lapland,
Through the rivers of Youkola,

The Kalevala

Through the seas of Kalevala,
Hoping thus to find his Aino.
Many were the fish be landed,
Every form of fish-like creatures,
But be did not catch the sea-maid,
Not Wellamo's water-maiden,
Fairest daughter of the Northland.
Finally the ancient minstrel,
Mind depressed, and heart discouraged,
Spake these words, immersed in sorrow:
"Fool am I, and great my folly,
Having neither wit nor judgment;
Surely once I had some knowledge,
Had some insight into wisdom,
Had at least a bit of instinct;
But my virtues all have left me
In these mournful days of evil,
Vanished with my youth and vigor,
Insight gone, and sense departed,
All my prudence gone to others!
Aino, whom I love and cherish,
All these years have sought to honor,
Aino, now Wellamo's maiden,
Promised friend of mine when needed,
Promised bride of mine forever,
Once I had within my power,
Caught her in Wellamo's grottoes,
Led her to my boat of copper,
With my fish-line made of silver;
But alas! I could not keep her,
Did not know that I had caught her
Till too late to woo and win her;
Let her slip between my fingers
To the home of water-maidens,
To the kingdom of Wellamo."
Wainamoinen then departed,
Empty-handed, heavy-hearted,
Straightway hastened to his country,
To his home in Kalevala,
Spake these words upon his journey:
"What has happened to the cuckoo,
Once the cuckoo bringing gladness,
In the morning, in the evening,
Often bringing joy at noontide?
What has stilled the cuckoo's singing,
What has changed the cuckoo's calling?
Sorrow must have stilled his singing,
And compassion changed his calling,
As I hear him sing no longer,
For my pleasure in the morning,
For my happiness at evening.
Never shall I learn the secret,
How to live and how to prosper,
How upon the earth to rest me,
How upon the seas to wander!
Only were my ancient mother
Living on the face of Northland,
Surely she would well advise me,
What my thought and what my action,
That this cup of grief might pass me,
That this sorrow might escape me,

Lönnrot

And this darkened cloud pass over."
In the deep awoke his mother,
From her tomb she spake as follows:
"Only sleeping was thy mother,
Now awakes to give thee answer,
What thy thought and what thine action,
That this cup of grief may pass thee,
That this sorrow may escape thee,
And this darkened cloud pass over.
Hie thee straightway to the Northland,
Visit thou the Suomi daughters;
Thou wilt find them wise and lovely,
Far more beautiful than Aino,
Far more worthy of a husband,
Not such silly chatter-boxes,
As the fickle Lapland maidens.
Take for thee a life-companion,
From the honest homes of Suomi,
One of Northland's honest daughters;
She will charm thee with her sweetness,
Make thee happy through her goodness,
Form perfection, manners easy,
Every step and movement graceful,
Full of wit and good behavior,
Honor to thy home and kindred."

RUNE VI
WAINAMOINEN'S HAPLESS JOURNEY

Wainamoinen, old and truthful,
Now arranges for a journey
To the village of the Northland,
To the land of cruel winters,
To the land of little sunshine,
To the land of worthy women;
Takes his light-foot, royal racer,
Then adjusts the golden bridle,
Lays upon his back the saddle,
Silver-buckled, copper-stirruped,
Seats himself upon his courser,
And begins his journey northward;
Plunges onward, onward, onward,
Galloping along the highway,
In his saddle, gaily fashioned,
On his dappled steed of magic,
Plunging through Wainola's meadows,
O'er the plains of Kalevala.
Fast and far he galloped onward,
Galloped far beyond Wainola,
Bounded o'er the waste of waters,
Till he reached the blue-sea's margin,
Wetting not the hoofs in running.
But the evil Youkahainen
Nursed a grudge within his bosom,
In his heart the worm of envy,
Envy of this Wainamoinen,
Of this wonderful enchanter.
He prepares a cruel cross-bow,
Made of steel and other metals,
Paints the bow in many colors,
Molds the top-piece out or copper,
Trims his bow with snowy silver,
Gold he uses too in trimming,
Then he hunts for strongest sinews,
Finds them in the stag of Hisi,
Interweaves the flax of Lempo.
Ready is the cruel cross-bow,
String, and shaft, and ends are finished,
Beautiful the bow and mighty,
Surely cost it not a trifle;
On the back a painted courser,
On each end a colt of beauty,
Near the curve a maiden sleeping
Near the notch a hare is bounding,
Wonderful the bow thus fashioned;
Cuts some arrows for his quiver,
Covers them with finest feathers,
From the oak the shafts be fashions,
Makes the tips of keenest metal.
As the rods and points are finished,
Then he feathers well his arrows
From the plumage of the swallow,

Lönnrot

From the wing-quills of the sparrow;
Hardens well his feathered arrows,
And imparts to each new virtues,
Steeps them in the blood of serpents,
In the virus of the adder.
Ready now are all his arrows,
Ready strung, his cruel cross-bow.
Waiting for wise Wainamoinen.
Youkahainen, Lapland's minstrel,
Waits a long time, is not weary,
Hopes to spy the ancient singer;
Spies at day-dawn, spies at evening,
Spies he ceaselessly at noontide,
Lies in wait for the magician,
Waits, and watches, as in envy;
Sits he at the open window,
Stands behind the hedge, and watches
In the foot-path waits, and listens,
Spies along the balks of meadows;
On his back he hangs his quiver,
In his quiver, feathered arrows
Dipped in virus of the viper,
On his arm the mighty cross-bow,
Waits, and watches, and unwearied,
Listens from the boat-house window,
Lingers at the end of Fog-point,
By the river flowing seaward,
Near the holy stream and whirlpool,
Near the sacred river's fire-fall.
Finally the Lapland minstrel,
Youkahainen of Pohyola,
At the breaking of the day-dawn,
At the early hour of morning,
Fixed his gaze upon the North-east,
Turned his eyes upon the sunrise,
Saw a black cloud on the ocean,
Something blue upon the waters,
And soliloquized as follows:
"Are those clouds on the horizon,
Or perchance the dawn of morning?
Neither clouds on the horizon,
Nor the dawning of the morning;
It is ancient Wainamoinen,
The renowned and wise enchanter,
Riding on his way to Northland;
On his steed, the royal racer,
Magic courser of Wainola."
Quickly now young Youkahainen,
Lapland's vain and evil minstrel,
Filled with envy, grasps his cross-bow,
Makes his bow and arrows ready
For the death of Wainamoinen.
Quick his aged mother asked him,
Spake these words to Youkahainen:
"For whose slaughter is thy cross-bow,
For whose heart thy poisoned arrows?"
Youkahainen thus made answer:
"I have made this mighty cross-bow,
Fashioned bow and poisoned arrows
For the death of Wainamoinen,
Thus to slay the friend of waters;

The Kalevala
I must shoot the old magician,
The eternal bard and hero,
Through the heart, and through the liver,
Through the head, and through the shoulders,
With this bow and feathered arrows
Thus destroy my rival minstrel."
Then the aged mother answered,
Thus reproving, thus forbidding.
Do not slay good Wainamoinen,
Ancient hero of the Northland,
From a noble tribe descended,
He, my sister's son, my nephew.
If thou slayest Wainamoinen,
Ancient son of Kalevala,
Then alas! all joy will vanish,
Perish all our wondrous singing;
Better on the earth the gladness,
Better here the magic music,
Than within the nether regions,
In the kingdom of Tuoni,
In the realm of the departed,
In the land of the hereafter."
Then the youthful Youkahainen
Thought awhile and well considered,
Ere he made a final answer.
With one hand he raised the cross-bow
But the other seemed to weaken,
As he drew the cruel bow-string.
Finally these words he uttered
As his bosom swelled with envy:
"Let all joy forever vanish,
Let earth's pleasures quickly perish,
Disappear earth's sweetest music,
Happiness depart forever;
Shoot I will this rival minstrel,
Little heeding what the end is."
Quickly now he bends his fire-bow,
On his left knee rests the weapon,
With his right foot firmly planted,
Thus he strings his bow of envy;
Takes three arrows from his quiver,
Choosing well the best among them,
Carefully adjusts the bow-string,
Sets with care the feathered arrow,
To the flaxen string he lays it,
Holds the cross-bow to his shoulder,
Aiming well along the margin,
At the heart of Wainamoinen,
Waiting till he gallops nearer;
In the shadow of a thicket,
Speaks these words while he is waiting
"Be thou, flaxen string, elastic;
Swiftly fly, thou feathered ash-wood,
Swiftly speed, thou deadly missile,
Quick as light, thou poisoned arrow,
To the heart of Wainamoinen.
If my hand too low should hold thee,
May the gods direct thee higher;
If too high mine eye should aim thee,
May the gods direct thee lower."
Steady now he pulls the trigger;

Like the lightning flies the arrow
O'er the head of Wainamoinen;
To the upper sky it darteth,
And the highest clouds it pierces,
Scatters all the flock of lamb-clouds,
On its rapid journey skyward.
Not discouraged, quick selecting,
Quick adjusting, Youkahainen,
Quickly aiming shoots a second.
Speeds the arrow swift as lightning;
Much too low he aimed the missile,
Into earth the arrow plunges,
Pierces to the lower regions,
Splits in two the old Sand Mountain.
Nothing daunted, Youkahainen,
Quick adjusting shoots a third one.
Swift as light it speeds its journey,
Strikes the steed of Wainamoinen,
Strikes the light-foot, ocean-swimmer,
Strikes him near his golden girdle,
Through the shoulder of the racer.
Thereupon wise Wainamoinen
Headlong fell upon the waters,
Plunged beneath the rolling billows,
From the saddle of the courser,
From his dappled steed of magic.
Then arose a mighty storm-wind,
Roaring wildly on the waters,
Bore away old Wainamoinen
Far from land upon the billows,
On the high and rolling billows,
On the broad sea's great expanses.
Boasted then young Youkahainen,
Thinking Waino dead and buried,
These the boastful words be uttered:
"Nevermore, old Wainamoinen,
Nevermore in all thy life-time,
While the golden moonlight glistens,
Nevermore wilt fix thy vision
On the meadows of Wainola,
On the plains of Kalevala;
Full six years must swim the ocean,
Tread the waves for seven summers,
Eight years ride the foamy billows,
In the broad expanse of water;
Six long autumns as a fir-tree,
Seven winters as a pebble;
Eight long summers as an aspen."
Thereupon the Lapland minstrel
Hastened to his room delighting,
When his mother thus addressed him
"Hast thou slain good Wainamoinen,
Slain the son of Kalevala?"
Youkahainen thus made answer:
"I have slain old Wainamoinen,
Slain the son of Kalevala,
That he now may plow the ocean,
That he now may sweep the waters,
On the billows rock and slumber.
In the salt-sea plunged he headlong,
In the deep sank the magician,

The Kalevala
Sidewise turned he to the sea-shore
On his back to rock forever,
Thus the boundless sea to travel,
Thus to ride the rolling billows."
This the answer of the mother:
"Woe to earth for this thine action,
Gone forever, joy and singing,
Vanished is the wit of ages!
Thou hast slain good Wainamoinen.
Slain the ancient wisdom-singer,
Slain the pride of Suwantala,
Slain the hero of Wainola,
Slain the joy of Kalevala."

RUNE VII
WAINIOINEN'S RESCUE

Wainamoinen, old and truthful,
Swam through all the deep-sea waters,
Floating like a branch of aspen,
Like a withered twig of willow;
Swam six days in summer weather,
Swam six nights in golden moonlight;
Still before him rose the billows,
And behind him sky and ocean.
Two days more he swam undaunted,
Two long nights be struggled onward.
On the evening of the eighth day,
Wainamoinen grew disheartened,
Felt a very great discomfort,
For his feet had lost their toe-nails,
And his fingers dead and dying.
Wainamoinen, ancient minstrel,
Sad and weary, spake as follows:
"Woe is me, my old life fated!
Woe is me, misfortune's offspring!
Fool was I when fortune, favored,
To forsake my home and kindred,
For a maiden fair and lovely,
Here beneath the starry heavens,
In this cruel waste of waters,
Days and nights to swim and wander,
Here to struggle with the storm-winds,
To be tossed by heaving billows,
In this broad sea's great expanses,
In this ocean vast and boundless.
"Cold my life and sad and dreary,
Painful too for me to linger
Evermore within these waters,
Thus to struggle for existence!
Cannot know how I can prosper,
How to find me food and shelter,
In these cold and lifeless waters,
In these days of dire misfortune.
Build I in the winds my dwelling?
It will find no sure foundation.
Build my home upon the billows?
Surely would the waves destroy it."
Comes a bird from far Pohyola,
From the occident, an eagle,
Is not classed among the largest,
Nor belongs he to the smallest;
One wing touches on the waters,
While the other sweeps the heavens;
O'er the waves he wings his body,
Strikes his beak upon the sea-cliffs,
Flies about, then safely perches,
Looks before him, looks behind him,
There beholds brave Wainamoinen,
On the blue-back of the ocean,

The Kalevala
And the eagle thus accosts him:
"Wherefore art thou, ancient hero,
Swimming in the deep-sea billows?
Thus the water-minstrel answered:
"I am ancient Wainamoinen,
Friend and fellow of the waters
I, the famous wisdom-singer;
Went to woo a Northland maiden,
Maiden from the dismal Darkland,
Quickly galloped on my journey,
Riding on the plain of ocean.
I arrived one morning early,
At the breaking of the day-dawn.
At the bay of Luotola,
Near Youkola's foaming river,
Where the evil Youkahainen
Slew my steed with bow and arrow,
Tried to slay me with his weapons.
On the waters fell I headlong,
Plunged beneath the salt-sea's surface,
From the saddle of the courser,
From my dappled steed of magic.
"Then arose a mighty storm-wind,
From the East and West a whirlwind,
Washed me seaward on the surges,
Seaward, seaward, further, further,
Where for many days I wandered,
Swam and rocked upon the billows,
Where as many nights I struggled,
In the dashing waves and sea-foam,
With the angry winds and waters.
"Woe is me, my life hard-fated!
Cannot solve this heavy problem,
How to live nor how to perish
In this cruel salt-sea water.
Build I in the winds my dwelling?
It will find no sure foundation.
Build my home upon the waters?
Surely will the waves destroy it.
Must I swim the sea forever,
Must I live, or must I perish?
What will happen if I perish,
If I sink below the billows,
Perish here from cold and hunger?"
Thus the bird of Ether answered
"Be not in the least disheartened,
Place thyself between my shoulders,
On my back be firmly seated,
I will lift thee from the waters,
Bear thee with my pinions upward,
Bear thee wheresoe'er thou willest.
Well do I the day remember
Where thou didst the eagle service,
When thou didst the birds a favor.
Thou didst leave the birch-tree standing,
When were cleared the Osmo-forests,
From the lands of Kalevala,
As a home for weary song-birds,
As a resting-place for eagles."
Then arises Wainamoinen,
Lifts his head above the waters,

Lönnrot

Boldly rises from the sea-waves,
Lifts his body from the billows,
Seats himself upon the eagle,
On the eagle's feathered shoulders.
Quick aloft the huge bird bears him,
Bears the ancient Wainamoinen,
Bears him on the path of zephyrs,
Floating on the vernal breezes,
To the distant shore of Northland,
To the dismal Sariola,
Where the eagle leaves his burden,
Flies away to join his fellows.
Wainamoinen, lone and weary,
Straightway fell to bitter weeping,
Wept and moaned in heavy accents,
On the border of the blue-sea.
On a cheerless promontory,
With a hundred wounds tormented,
Made by cruel winds and waters,
With his hair and beard dishevelled
By the surging of the billows.
Three long days he wept disheartened
Wept as many nights in anguish,
Did not know what way to journey,
Could not find a woodland foot-print,
That would point him to the highway,
To his home in Kalevala,
To his much-loved home and kindred.
Northland's young and slender maiden,
With complexion fair and lovely,
With the Sun had laid a wager,
With the Sun and Moon a wager,
Which should rise before the other,
On the morning of the morrow.
And the maiden rose in beauty,
Long before the Sun had risen,
Long before the Moon bad wakened,
From their beds beneath the ocean.
Ere the cock had crowed the day-break,
Ere the Sun had broken slumber
She had sheared six gentle lambkins,
Gathered from them six white fleeces,
Hence to make the rolls for spinning,
Hence to form the threads for weaving,
Hence to make the softest raiment,
Ere the morning dawn had broken,
Ere the sleeping Sun had risen.
When this task the maid had ended,
Then she scrubbed the birchen tables,
Sweeps the ground-floor of the stable,
With a broom of leaves and branches
From the birches of the Northland,
Scrapes the sweepings well together
On a shovel made of copper,
Carries them beyond the stable,
From the doorway to the meadow,
To the meadow's distant border,
Near the surges of the great-sea,
Listens there and looks about her,
Hears a wailing from the waters,
Hears a weeping from the sea-shore,

The Kalevala
Hears a hero-voice lamenting.
Thereupon she hastens homeward,
Hastens to her mother's dwelling,
These the words the maiden utters:
"I have heard a wail from ocean,
Heard a weeping from the sea-coast,
On the shore some one lamenting."
Louhi, hostess of Pohyola,
Ancient, toothless dame of Northland,
Hastens from her door and court-yard,
Through the meadow to the sea-shore,
Listens well for sounds of weeping,
For the wail of one in sorrow;
Hears the voice of one in trouble,
Hears a hero-cry of anguish.
Thus the ancient Louhi answers:
"This is not the wail of children,
These are not the tears of women,
In this way weep bearded heroes;
This the hero-cry of anguish."
Quick she pushed her boat to water,
To the floods her goodly vessel,
Straightway rows with lightning swiftness,
To the weeping Wainamoinen;
Gives the hero consolation,
Comfort gives she to the minstrel
Wailing in a grove of willows,
In his piteous condition,
Mid the alder-trees and aspens,
On the border of the salt-sea,
Visage trembling, locks dishevelled.
Ears, and eyes, and lips of sadness.
Louhi, hostess of Pohyola,
Thus addresses Wainamoinen:
"Tell me what has been thy folly,
That thou art in this condition."
Old and truthful Wainamoinen
Lifts aloft his bead and answers:
"Well I know that it is folly
That has brought me all this trouble,
Brought me to this land of strangers,
To these regions unbefitting
Happy was I with my kindred,
In my distant home and country,
There my name was named in honor."
Louhi, hostess of Pohyola,
Thus replied to Wainamoinen:
"I would gain the information,
Should I be allowed to ask thee,
Who thou art of ancient heroes,
Who of all the host of heroes?
This is Wainamoinen's answer:
"Formerly my name was mentioned,
Often was I heard and honored,
As a minstrel and magician,
In the long and dreary winters,
Called the 'Singer of the Northland,
In the valleys of Wainola,
On the plains of Kalevala;
No one thought that such misfortune
Could befall wise Wainamoinen."

Lönnrot

Louhi, hostess of Pohyola,
Thus replied in cheering accents
"Rise, O hero, from discomfort,
From thy bed among the willows;
Enter now upon the new-way,
Come with me to yonder dwelling,
There relate thy strange adventures,
Tell the tale of thy misfortunes."
Now she takes the hapless hero,
Lifts him from his bed of sorrow,
In her boat she safely seats him,
And begins at once her rowing,
Rows with steady hand and mighty
To her home upon the sea-shore,
To the dwellings of Pohyola.
There she feeds the starving hero,
Rests the ancient Wainamoinen,
Gives him warmth, and food, and shelter,
And the hero soon recovers.
Then the hostess of Pohyola
Questioned thus the ancient singer:
"Wherefore didst thou, Wainamoinen,
Friend and fellow of the waters,
Weep in sad and bitter accents,
On the border of the ocean,
Mid the aspens and the willows?"
This is Wainamoinen's answer:
Had good reason for my weeping,
Cause enough for all my sorrow;
Long indeed had I been swimming,
Had been buffeting the billows,
In the far outstretching waters.
This the reason for my weeping;
I have lived in toil and torture,
Since I left my home and country,
Left my native land and kindred,
Came to this the land of strangers,
To these unfamiliar portals.
All thy trees have thorns to wound me,
All thy branches, spines to pierce me,
Even birches give me trouble,
And the alders bring discomfort,
My companions, winds and waters,
Only does the Sun seem friendly,
In this cold and cruel country,
Near these unfamiliar portals."
Louhi thereupon made answer,
Weep no longer, Wainamoinen,
Grieve no more, thou friend of waters,
Good for thee, that thou shouldst linger
At our friendly homes and firesides;
Thou shalt live with us and welcome,
Thou shalt sit at all our tables,
Eat the salmon from our platters,
Eat the sweetest of our bacon,
Eat the whiting from our waters."
Answers thus old Wainamoinen,
Grateful for the invitation:
"Never do I court strange tables,
Though the food be rare and toothsome;
One's own country is the dearest,

The Kalevala
One's own table is the sweetest,
One's own home, the most attractive.
Grant, kind Ukko, God above me,
Thou Creator, full of mercy,
Grant that I again may visit
My beloved home and country.
Better dwell in one's own country,
There to drink Its healthful waters
From the simple cups of birch-wood,
Than in foreign lands to wander,
There to drink the rarest liquors
From the golden bowls of strangers."
Louhi, hostess of Pohyola,
Thus replied to the magician:
"What reward wilt thou award me,
Should I take thee where thou willest,
To thy native land and kindred,
To thy much-loved home and fireside,
To the meadows of Wainola,
To the plains of Kalevala?"
These the words of Wainamoinen:
"What would be reward sufficient,
Shouldst thou take me to my people,
To my home and distant country,
To the borders of the Northland,
There to hear the cuckoo singing,
Hear the sacred cuckoo calling?
Shall I give thee golden treasures,
Fill thy cups with finest silver?"
This is Louhi's simple answer:
"O thou ancient Wainamoinen,
Only true and wise magician,
Never will I ask for riches,
Never ask for gold nor silver;
Gold is for the children's flowers,
Silver for the stallion's jewels.
Canst thou forge for me the Sampo,
Hammer me the lid in colors,
From the tips of white-swan feathers
From the milk of greatest virtue,
From a single grain of barley,
From the finest wool of lambkins?
"I will give thee too my daughter,
Will reward thee through the maiden,
Take thee to thy much-loved home-land,
To the borders of Wainola,
There to hear the cuckoo singing,
Hear the sacred cuckoo calling."
Wainamoinen, much regretting,
Gave this answer to her question:
"Cannot forge for thee the Sampo,
Cannot make the lid in colors.
Take me to my distant country,
I will send thee Ilmarinen,
He will forge for thee the Sampo,
Hammer thee the lid in colors,
He may win thy lovely maiden;
Worthy smith is Ilmarinen,
In this art is first and master;
He, the one that forged the heavens.
Forged the air a hollow cover;

Lönnrot

Nowhere see we hammer-traces,
Nowhere find a single tongs-mark."
Thus replied the hostess, Louhi:
"Him alone I'll give my daughter,
Promise him my child in marriage,
Who for me will forge the Sampo,
Hammer me the lid in colors,
From the tips of white-swan feathers,
From the milk of greatest virtue,
From a single grain of barley,
From the finest wool of lambkins."
Thereupon the hostess Louhi,
Harnessed quick a dappled courser,
Hitched him to her sledge of birch-wood,
Placed within it Wainamoinen,
Placed the hero on the cross-bench,
Made him ready for his journey;
Then addressed the ancient minstrel,
These the words that Louhi uttered:
"Do not raise thine eyes to heaven,
Look not upward on thy journey,
While thy steed is fresh and frisky,
While the day-star lights thy pathway,
Ere the evening star has risen;
If thine eyes be lifted upward,
While the day-star lights thy pathway,
Dire misfortune will befall thee,
Some sad fate will overtake thee."
Then the ancient Wainamoinen
Fleetly drove upon his journey,
Merrily he hastened homeward,
Hastened homeward, happy-hearted
From the ever-darksome Northland
From the dismal Sariola.

RUNE VIII
MAIDEN OF THE RAINBOW

Pohyola's fair and winsome daughter,
Glory of the land and water,
Sat upon the bow of heaven,
On its highest arch resplendent,
In a gown of richest fabric,
In a gold and silver air-gown,
Weaving webs of golden texture,
Interlacing threads of silver;
Weaving with a golden shuttle,
With a weaving-comb of silver;
Merrily flies the golden shuttle,
From the maiden's nimble fingers,
Briskly swings the lathe in weaving,
Swiftly flies the comb of silver,
From the sky-born maiden's fingers,
Weaving webs of wondrous beauty.
Came the ancient Wainamoinen,
Driving down the highway homeward,
From the ever sunless Northland,
From the dismal Sariola;
Few the furlongs he had driven,
Driven but a little distance,
When he heard the sky-loom buzzing,
As the maiden plied the shuttle.
Quick the thoughtless Wainamoinen
Lifts his eyes aloft in wonder,
Looks upon the vault of heaven,
There beholds the bow of beauty,
On the bow the maiden sitting,
Beauteous Maiden of the Rainbow,
Glory of the earth and ocean,
Weaving there a golden fabric,
Working with the rustling silver.
Wainamoinen, ancient minstrel,
Quickly checks his fleet-foot racer,
Looks upon the charming maiden,
Then addresses her as follows:
"Come, fair maiden, to my snow-sledge,
By my side I wish thee seated."
Thus the Maid of Beauty answers:
"Tell me what thou wishest of me,
Should I join thee in the snow-sledge."
Speaks the ancient Wainamoinen,
Answers thus the Maid of Beauty:
"This the reason for thy coming:
Thou shalt bake me honey-biscuit,
Shalt prepare me barley-water,
Thou shalt fill my foaming beer-cups,
Thou shalt sing beside my table,
Shalt rejoice within my portals,
Walk a queen within my dwelling,
In the Wainola halls and chambers,
In the courts of Kalevala."

Lönnrot

Thus the Maid of Beauty answered
From her throne amid the heavens:
"Yesterday at hour of twilight,
Went I to the flowery meadows,
There to rock upon the common,
Where the Sun retires to slumber;
There I heard a song-bird singing,
Heard the thrush simple measures,
Singing sweetly thoughts of maidens,
And the minds of anxious mothers.
"Then I asked the pretty songster,
Asked the thrush this simple question:
'Sing to me, thou pretty song-bird,
Sing that I may understand thee,
Sing to me in truthful accents,
How to live in greatest pleasure,
And in happiness the sweetest,
As a maiden with her father,
Or as wife beside her husband.'
"Thus the song-bird gave me answer,
Sang the thrush this information:
'Bright and warm are days of summer,
Warmer still is maiden-freedom;
Cold is iron in the winter,
Thus the lives of married women;
Maidens living with their mothers
Are like ripe and ruddy berries;
Married women, far too many,
Are like dogs enchained in kennel,
Rarely do they ask for favors,
Not to wives are favors given.'"
Wainamoinen, old and truthful,
Answers thus the Maid of Beauty:
"Foolish is the thrush thus singing,
Nonsense is the song-bird's twitter;
Like to babes are maidens treated,
Wives are queens and highly honored.
Come, sweet maiden, to my snow-sledge,
I am not despised as hero,
Not the meanest of magicians;
Come with me and I will make thee
Wife and queen in Kalevala."
Thus the Maid of Beauty answered--
"Would consider thee a hero,
Mighty hero, I would call thee,
When a golden hair thou splittest,
Using knives that have no edges;
When thou snarest me a bird's egg
With a snare that I can see not."
Wainamoinen, skilled and ancient,
Split a golden hair exactly,
Using knives that had no edges;
And he snared an egg as nicely
With a snare the maiden saw not.
"Come, sweet maiden, to my snow-sledge,
I have done what thou desirest."
Thus the maiden wisely answered:
"Never enter I thy snow-sledge,
Till thou peelest me the sandstone,
Till thou cuttest me a whip-stick
From the ice, and make no splinters,

The Kalevala

Losing not the smallest fragment."
Wainamoinen, true magician,
Nothing daunted, not discouraged,
Deftly peeled the rounded sandstone,
Deftly cut from ice a whip-stick,
Cutting not the finest splinter,
Losing not the smallest fragment.
Then again be called the maiden,
To a seat within his snow-sledge.
But the Maid or Beauty answered,
Answered thus the great magician:
I will go with that one only
That will make me ship or shallop,
From the splinters of my spindle,
From the fragments of my distaff,
In the waters launch the vessel,
Set the little ship a-floating,
Using not the knee to push it,
Using not the arm to move it,
Using not the hand to touch it,
Using not the foot to turn it,
Using nothing to propel it."
Spake the skilful Wainamoinen,
These the words the hero uttered:
"There is no one in the Northland,
No one under vault of heaven,
Who like me can build a vessel,
From the fragments of the distaff,
From the splinters of the spindle."
Then he took the distaff-fragments,
Took the splinters of the spindle,
Hastened off the boat to fashion,
Hastened to an iron mountain,
There to join the many fragments.
Full of zeal be plies the hammer,
Swings the hammer and the hatchet;
Nothing daunted, builds the vessel,
Works one day and then a second,
Works with steady hand the third day;
On the evening of the third day,
Evil Hisi grasps the hatchet,
Lempo takes the crooked handle,
Turns aside the axe in falling,
Strikes the rocks and breaks to pieces;
From the rocks rebound the fragments,
Pierce the flesh of the magician,
Cut the knee of Wainamoinen.
Lempo guides the sharpened hatchet,
And the veins fell Hisi severs.
Quickly gushes forth a blood-stream,
And the stream is crimson-colored.
Wainamoinen, old and truthful,
The renowned and wise enchanter,
Thus outspeaks in measured accents:
"O thou keen and cruel hatchet,
O thou axe of sharpened metal,
Thou shouldst cut the trees to fragments,
Cut the pine-tree and the willow,
Cut the alder and the birch-tree,
Cut the juniper and aspen,
Shouldst not cut my knee to pieces,

Lönnrot

Shouldst not tear my veins asunder."
Then the ancient Wainamoinen
Thus begins his incantations,
Thus begins his magic singing,
Of the origin of evil;
Every word in perfect order,
Makes no effort to remember,
Sings the origin of iron,
That a bolt he well may fashion,
Thus prepare a look for surety,
For the wounds the axe has given,
That the hatchet has torn open.
But the stream flows like a brooklet,
Rushing like a maddened torrent,
Stains the herbs upon the meadows,
Scarcely is a bit of verdure
That the blood-stream does not cover
As it flows and rushes onward
From the knee of the magician,
From the veins of Wainamoinen.
Now the wise and ancient minstrel
Gathers lichens from the sandstone,
Picks them from the trunks of birches,
Gathers moss within the marshes,
Pulls the grasses from the meadows,
Thus to stop the crimson streamlet,
Thus to close the wounds laid open;
But his work is unsuccessful,
And the crimson stream flows onward.
Wainamoinen, ancient minstrel,
Feeling pain and fearing languor,
Falls to weeping, heavy-hearted;
Quickly now his steed he hitches,
Hitches to the sledge of birch-wood,
Climbs with pain upon the cross-bench,
Strikes his steed in quick succession,
Snaps his whip above the racer,
And the steed flies onward swiftly;
Like the winds he sweeps the highway,
Till be nears a Northland village,
Where the way is triple-parted.
Wainamoinen, old and truthful,
Takes the lowest of the highways,
Quickly nears a spacious cottage,
Quickly asks before the doorway:
"Is there any one here dwelling,
That can know the pain I suffer,
That can heal this wound of hatchet,
That can check this crimson streamlet?"
Sat a boy within a corner,
On a bench beside a baby,
And he answered thus the hero:
"There is no one in this dwelling
That can know the pain thou feelest,
That can heal the wounds of hatchet,
That can check the crimson streamlet;
Some one lives in yonder cottage,
That perchance can do thee service."
Wainamoinen, ancient minstrel,
Whips his courser to a gallop,
Dashes on along the highway;

The Kalevala
Only drives a little distance,
On the middle of the highways,
To a cabin on the road-side,
Asks one standing on the threshold,
Questions all through open windows,
These the words the hero uses:
"Is there no one in this cabin,
That can know the pain I suffer,
That can heal this wound of hatchet,
That can check this crimson streamlet?"
On the floor a witch was lying,
Near the fire-place lay the beldame,
Thus she spake to Wainamoinen,
Through her rattling teeth she answered.
"There is no one in this cabin
That can know the pain thou feelest,
That can heal the wounds of hatchets,
That can check the crimson streamlet;
Some one lives in yonder cottage,
That perchance can do thee service."
Wainamoinen, nothing daunted,
Whips his racer to a gallop,
Dashes on along the highway;
Only drives a little distance,
On the upper of the highways,
Gallops to a humble cottage,
Asks one standing near the penthouse,
Sitting on the penthouse-doorsill:
"Is there no one in this cottage,
That can know the pain I suffer,
That can heal this wound of hatchet,
That can check this crimson streamlet?"
Near the fireplace sat an old man,
On the hearthstone sat the gray-beard,
Thus he answered Wainamoinen:
"Greater things have been accomplished,
Much more wondrous things effected,
Through but three words of the master;
Through the telling of the causes,
Streams and oceans have been tempered,
River cataracts been lessened,
Bays been made of promontories,
Islands raised from deep sea-bottoms."

RUNE IX
ORIGIN OF IRON

Wainamoinen, thus encouraged,
Quickly rises in his snow-sledge,
Asking no one for assistance,
Straightway hastens to the cottage,
Takes a seat within the dwelling.
Come two maids with silver pitchers,
Bringing also golden goblets;
Dip they up a very little,
But the very smallest measure
Of the blood of the magician,
From the wounds of Wainamoinen.
From the fire-place calls the old man,
Thus the gray-beard asks the minstrel:
"Tell me who thou art of heroes,
Who of all the great magicians?
Lo! thy blood fills seven sea-boats,
Eight of largest birchen vessels,
Flowing from some hero's veinlets,
From the wounds of some magician.
Other matters I would ask thee;
Sing the cause of this thy trouble,
Sing to me the source of metals,
Sing the origin of iron,
How at first it was created."
Then the ancient Wainamoinen
Made this answer to the gray-beard:
"Know I well the source of metals,
Know the origin of iron;
If can tell bow steel is fashioned.
Of the mothers air is oldest,
Water is the oldest brother,
And the fire is second brother,
And the youngest brother, iron;
Ukko is the first creator.
Ukko, maker of the heavens,
Cut apart the air and water,
Ere was born the metal, iron.
Ukko, maker of the heavens,
Firmly rubbed his hands together,
Firmly pressed them on his knee-cap,
Then arose three lovely maidens,
Three most beautiful of daughters;
These were mothers of the iron,
And of steel of bright-blue color.
Tremblingly they walked the heavens,
Walked the clouds with silver linings,
With their bosoms overflowing
With the milk of future iron,
Flowing on and flowing ever,
From the bright rims of the cloudlets
To the earth, the valleys filling,
To the slumber-calling waters.
"Ukko's eldest daughter sprinkled

The Kalevala

Black milk over river channels
And the second daughter sprinkled
White milk over hills and mountains,
While the youngest daughter sprinkled
Red milk over seas and oceans.
Where the black milk had been sprinkled,
Grew the dark and ductile iron;
Where the white milk had been sprinkled.
Grew the iron, lighter-colored;
Where the red milk had been sprinkled,
Grew the red and brittle iron.
"After Time had gone a distance,
Iron hastened Fire to visit,
His beloved elder brother,
Thus to know his brother better.
Straightway Fire began his roarings,
Labored to consume his brother,
His beloved younger brother.
Straightway Iron sees his danger,
Saves himself by fleetly fleeing,
From the fiery flame's advances,
Fleeing hither, fleeing thither,
Fleeing still and taking shelter
In the swamps and in the valleys,
In the springs that loudly bubble,
By the rivers winding seaward,
On the broad backs of the marshes,
Where the swans their nests have builded,
Where the wild geese hatch their goslings.
"Thus is iron in the swamp-lands,
Stretching by the water-courses,
Hidden well for many ages,
Hidden in the birchen forests,
But he could not hide forever
From the searchings of his brother;
Here and there the fire has caught him,
Caught and brought him to his furnace,
That the spears, and swords, and axes,
Might be forged and duly hammered.
In the swamps ran blackened waters,
From the heath the bears came ambling,
And the wolves ran through the marshes.
Iron then made his appearance,
Where the feet of wolves had trodden,
Where the paws of bears had trampled.
"Then the blacksmith, Ilmarinen,
Came to earth to work the metal;
He was born upon the Coal-mount,
Skilled and nurtured in the coal-fields;
In one hand, a copper hammer,
In the other, tongs of iron;
In the night was born the blacksmith,
In the morn he built his smithy,
Sought with care a favored hillock,
Where the winds might fill his bellows;
Found a hillock in the swamp-lands,
Where the iron hid abundant;
There he built his smelting furnace,
There he laid his leathern bellows,
Hastened where the wolves had travelled,
Followed where the bears had trampled,

Lönnrot

Found the iron's young formations,
In the wolf-tracks of the marshes,
In the foot-prints of the gray-bear.
"Then the blacksmith, Ilmarinen,
'Thus addressed the sleeping iron:
Thou most useful of the metals,
Thou art sleeping in the marshes,
Thou art hid in low conditions,
Where the wolf treads in the swamp-lands,
Where the bear sleeps in the thickets.
Hast thou thought and well considered,
What would be thy future station,
Should I place thee in the furnace,
Thus to make thee free and useful?'
"Then was Iron sorely frightened,
Much distressed and filled with horror,
When of Fire he heard the mention,
Mention of his fell destroyer.
"Then again speaks Ilmarinen,
Thus the smith addresses Iron:
'Be not frightened, useful metal,
Surely Fire will not consume thee,
Will not burn his youngest brother,
Will not harm his nearest kindred.
Come thou to my room and furnace,
Where the fire is freely burning,
Thou wilt live, and grow, and prosper,
Wilt become the swords of heroes,
Buckles for the belts of women.'
"Ere arose the star of evening,
Iron ore had left the marshes,
From the water-beds had risen,
Had been carried to the furnace,
In the fire the smith had laid it,
Laid it in his smelting furnace.
Ilmarinen starts the bellows,
Gives three motions of the handle,
And the iron flows in streamlets
From the forge of the magician,
Soon becomes like baker's leaven,
Soft as dough for bread of barley.
Then out-screamed the metal, Iron:
'Wondrous blacksmith, Ilmarinen,
Take, O take me from thy furnace,
From this fire and cruel torture.'
"Ilmarinen thus made answer:
'I will take thee from my furnace,
Thou art but a little frightened,
Thou shalt be a mighty power,
Thou shalt slay the best of heroes,
Thou shalt wound thy dearest brother.'
"Straightway Iron made this promise,
Vowed and swore in strongest accents,
By the furnace, by the anvil,
By the tongs, and by the hammer,
These the words he vowed and uttered:
'Many trees that I shall injure,
Shall devour the hearts of mountains,
Shall not slay my nearest kindred,
Shall not kill the best of heroes,
Shall not wound my dearest brother;

The Kalevala
Better live in civil freedom,
Happier would be my life-time,
Should I serve my fellow-beings,
Serve as tools for their convenience,
Than as implements of warfare,
Slay my friends and nearest. kindred,
Wound the children of my mother.'
"Now the master, Ilmarinen,
The renowned and skilful blacksmith,
From the fire removes the iron,
Places it upon the anvil,
Hammers well until it softens,
Hammers many fine utensils,
Hammers spears, and swords, and axes,
Hammers knives, and forks, and hatchets,
Hammers tools of all descriptions.
"Many things the blacksmith needed,
Many things he could not fashion,
Could not make the tongue of iron,
Could not hammer steel from iron,
Could not make the iron harden.
Well considered Ilmarinen,
Deeply thought and long reflected.
Then he gathered birchen ashes,
Steeped the ashes in the water,
Made a lye to harden iron,
Thus to form the steel most needful.
With his tongue he tests the mixture,
Weighs it long and well considers,
And the blacksmith speaks as follows:
'All this labor is for nothing,
Will not fashion steel from iron,
Will not make the soft ore harden.'
"Now a bee flies from the meadow,
Blue-wing coming from the flowers,
Flies about, then safely settles
Near the furnace of the smithy.
"'Thus the smith the bee addresses,
These the words of Ilmarinen:
'Little bee, thou tiny birdling,
Bring me honey on thy winglets,
On thy tongue, I pray thee, bring me
Sweetness from the fragrant meadows,
From the little cups of flowers,
From the tips of seven petals,
That we thus may aid the water
To produce the steel from iron.'
"Evil Hisi's bird, the hornet,
Heard these words of Ilmarinen,
Looking from the cottage gable,
Flying to the bark of birch-trees,
While the iron bars were heating
While the steel was being tempered;
Swiftly flew the stinging hornet,
Scattered all the Hisi horrors,
Brought the blessing of the serpent,
Brought the venom of the adder,
Brought the poison of the spider,
Brought the stings of all the insects,
Mixed them with the ore and water,
While the steel was being, tempered.

"Ilmarinen, skilful blacksmith,
First of all the iron-workers,
Thought the bee had surely brought him
Honey from the fragrant meadows,
From the little cups of flowers,
From the tips of seven petals,
And he spake the words that follow:
'Welcome, welcome, is thy coming,
Honeyed sweetness from the flowers
Thou hast brought to aid the water,
Thus to form the steel from iron!'
"Ilmarinen, ancient blacksmith,
Dipped the iron into water,
Water mixed with many poisons,
Thought it but the wild bee's honey;
Thus he formed the steel from iron.
When he plunged it into water,
Water mixed with many poisons,
When be placed it in the furnace,
Angry grew the hardened iron,
Broke the vow that he had taken,
Ate his words like dogs and devils,
Mercilessly cut his brother,
Madly raged against his kindred,
Caused the blood to flow in streamlets
From the wounds of man and hero.
This, the origin of iron,
And of steel of light blue color."
From the hearth arose the gray-beard,
Shook his heavy looks and answered:
"Now I know the source of iron,
Whence the steel and whence its evils;
Curses on thee, cruel iron,
Curses on the steel thou givest,
Curses on thee, tongue of evil,
Cursed be thy life forever!
Once thou wert of little value,
Having neither form nor beauty,
Neither strength nor great importance,
When in form of milk thou rested,
When for ages thou wert hidden
In the breasts of God's three daughters,
Hidden in their heaving bosoms,
On the borders of the cloudlets,
In the blue vault of the heavens.
"Thou wert once of little value,
Having neither form nor beauty,
Neither strength nor great importance,
When like water thou wert resting
On the broad back of the marshes,
On the steep declines of mountains,
When thou wert but formless matter,
Only dust of rusty color.
"Surely thou wert void of greatness,
Having neither strength nor beauty,
When the moose was trampling on thee,
When the roebuck trod upon thee,
When the tracks of wolves were in thee,
And the bear-paws scratched thy body.
Surely thou hadst little value
When the skilful Ilmarinen,

The Kalevala
First of all the iron-workers,
Brought thee from the blackened swamp-lands,
Took thee to his ancient smithy,
Placed thee in his fiery furnace.
Truly thou hadst little vigor,
Little strength, and little danger,
When thou in the fire wert hissing,
Rolling forth like seething water,
From the furnace of the smithy,
When thou gavest oath the strongest,
By the furnace, by the anvil,
By the tongs, and by the hammer,
By the dwelling of the blacksmith,
By the fire within the furnace.
"Now forsooth thou hast grown mighty,
Thou canst rage in wildest fury;
Thou hast broken all thy pledges,
All thy solemn vows hast broken,
Like the dogs thou shamest honor,
Shamest both thyself and kindred,
Tainted all with breath of evil.
Tell who drove thee to this mischief,
Tell who taught thee all thy malice,
Tell who gavest thee thine evil!
Did thy father, or thy mother,
Did the eldest of thy brothers,
Did the youngest of thy sisters,
Did the worst of all thy kindred
Give to thee thine evil nature?
Not thy father, nor thy mother,
Not the eldest of thy brothers,
Not the youngest of thy sisters,
Not the worst of all thy kindred,
But thyself hast done this mischief,
Thou the cause of all our trouble.
Come and view thine evil doings,
And amend this flood of damage,
Ere I tell thy gray-haired mother,
Ere I tell thine aged father.
Great indeed a mother's anguish,
Great indeed a father's sorrow,
When a son does something evil,
When a child runs wild and lawless.
"Crimson streamlet, cease thy flowing
From the wounds of Wainamoinen;
Blood of ages, stop thy coursing
From the veins of the magician;
Stand like heaven's crystal pillars,
Stand like columns in the ocean,
Stand like birch-trees in the forest,
Like the tall reeds in the marshes,
Like the high-rocks on the sea-coast,
Stand by power of mighty magic!
"Should perforce thy will impel thee,
Flow thou on thine endless circuit,
Through the veins of Wainamoinen,
Through the bones, and through the muscles,
Through the lungs, and heart, and liver,
Of the mighty sage and singer;
Better be the food of heroes,
Than to waste thy strength and virtue

Lönnrot

On the meadows and the woodlands,
And be lost in dust and ashes.
Flow forever in thy circle;
Thou must cease this crimson out-flow;
Stain no more the grass and flowers,
Stain no more these golden hill-tops,
Pride and beauty of our heroes.
In the veins of the magician,
In the heart of Wainamoinen,
Is thy rightful home and storehouse.
Thither now withdraw thy forces,
Thither hasten, swiftly flowing;
Flow no more as crimson currents,
Fill no longer crimson lakelets,
Must not rush like brooks in spring-tide,
Nor meander like the rivers.
"Cease thy flow, by word of magic,
Cease as did the falls of Tyrya,
As the rivers of Tuoni,
When the sky withheld her rain-drops,
When the sea gave up her waters,
In the famine of the seasons,
In the years of fire and torture.
If thou heedest not this order,
I shall offer other measures,
Know I well of other forces;
I shall call the Hisi irons,
In them I shall boil and roast thee,
Thus to check thy crimson flowing,
Thus to save the wounded hero.
"If these means be inefficient,
Should these measures prove unworthy,
I shall call omniscient Ukko,
Mightiest of the creators,
Stronger than all ancient heroes,
Wiser than the world-magicians;
He will check the crimson out-flow,
He will heal this wound of hatchet.
"Ukko, God of love and mercy,
God and Master Of the heavens,
Come thou hither, thou art needed,
Come thou quickly I beseech thee,
Lend thy hand to aid thy children,
Touch this wound with healing fingers,
Stop this hero's streaming life-blood,
Bind this wound with tender leaflets,
Mingle with them healing flowers,
Thus to check this crimson current,
Thus to save this great magician,
Save the life of Wainamoinen."
Thus at last the blood-stream ended,
As the magic words were spoken.
Then the gray-beard, much rejoicing,
Sent his young son to the smithy,
There to make a healing balsam,
From the herbs of tender fibre,
From the healing plants and flowers,
From the stalks secreting honey,
From the roots, and leaves, and blossoms.
On the way he meets an oak-tree,
And the oak the son addresses:

The Kalevala
"Hast thou honey in thy branches,
Does thy sap run full of sweetness?"
Thus the oak-tree wisely answers:
"Yea, but last night dripped the honey
Down upon my spreading branches,
And the clouds their fragrance sifted,
Sifted honey on my leaflets,
From their home within the heavens."
Then the son takes oak-wood splinters,
Takes the youngest oak-tree branches,
Gathers many healing grasses,
Gathers many herbs and flowers,
Rarest herbs that grow in Northland,
Places them within the furnace
In a kettle made of copper;
Lets them steep and boil together,
Bits of bark chipped from the oak-tree,
Many herbs of healing virtues;
Steeps them one day, then a second,
Three long days of summer weather,
Days and nights in quick succession;
Then he tries his magic balsam,
Looks to see if it is ready,
If his remedy is finished;
But the balsam is unworthy.
Then he added other grasses,
Herbs of every healing virtue,
That were brought from distant nations,
Many hundred leagues from Northland,
Gathered by the wisest minstrels,
Thither brought by nine enchanters.
Three days more be steeped the balsam,
Three nights more the fire be tended,
Nine the days and nights be watched it,
Then again be tried the ointment,
Viewed it carefully and tested,
Found at last that it was ready,
Found the magic balm was finished.
Near by stood a branching birch-tree,
On the border of the meadow,
Wickedly it had been broken,
Broken down by evil Hisi;
Quick he takes his balm of healing,
And anoints the broken branches,
Rubs the balsam in the fractures,
Thus addresses then the birch-tree:
"With this balsam I anoint thee,
With this salve thy wounds I cover,
Cover well thine injured places;
Now the birch-tree shall recover,
Grow more beautiful than ever."
True, the birch-tree soon recovered,
Grew more beautiful than ever,
Grew more uniform its branches,
And its bole more strong and stately.
Thus it was be tried the balsam,
Thus the magic salve he tested,
Touched with it the splintered sandstone,
Touched the broken blocks of granite,
Touched the fissures in the mountains,
And the broken parts united,

Lönnrot

All the fragments grew together.
Then the young boy quick returning
With the balsam he had finished,
To the gray-beard gave the ointment,
And the boy these measures uttered
"Here I bring the balm of healing,
Wonderful the salve I bring thee;
It will join the broken granite,
Make the fragments grow together,
Heat the fissures in the mountains,
And restore the injured birch-tree."
With his tongue the old man tested,
Tested thus the magic balsam,
Found the remedy effective,
Found the balm had magic virtues;
Then anointed he the minstrel,
Touched the wounds of Wainamoinen,
Touched them with his magic balsam,
With the balm of many virtues;
Speaking words of ancient wisdom,
These the words the gray-beard uttered:
"Do not walk in thine own virtue,
Do not work in thine own power,
Walk in strength of thy Creator;
Do not speak in thine own wisdom,
Speak with tongue of mighty Ukko.
In my mouth, if there be sweetness,
It has come from my Creator;
If my hands are filled with beauty,
All the beauty comes from Ukko."
When the wounds had been anointed,
When the magic salve had touched them,
Straightway ancient Wainamoinen
Suffered fearful pain and anguish,
Sank upon the floor in torment,
Turning one way, then another,
Sought for rest and found it nowhere,
Till his pain the gray-beard banished,
Banished by the aid of magic,
Drove away his killing torment
To the court of all our trouble,
To the highest hill of torture,
To the distant rocks and ledges,
To the evil-bearing mountains,
To the realm of wicked Hisi.
Then be took some silken fabric,
Quick he tore the silk asunder,
Making equal strips for wrapping,
Tied the ends with silken ribbons,
Making thus a healing bandage;
Then he wrapped with skilful fingers
Wainamoinen's knee and ankle,
Wrapped the wounds of the magician,
And this prayer the gray-beard uttered
"Ukko's fabric is the bandage,
Ukko's science is the surgeon,
These have served the wounded hero,
Wrapped the wounds of the magician.
Look upon us, God of mercy,
Come and guard us, kind Creator,
And protect us from all evil!

The Kalevala

Guide our feet lest they may stumble,
Guard our lives from every danger,
From the wicked wilds of Hisi."
Wainamoinen, old and truthful,
Felt the mighty aid of magic,
Felt the help of gracious Ukko,
Straightway stronger grew in body,
Straightway were the wounds united,
Quick the fearful pain departed.
Strong and hardy grew the hero,
Straightway walked in perfect freedom,
Turned his knee in all directions,
Knowing neither pain nor trouble.
Then the ancient Wainamoinen
Raised his eyes to high Jumala,
Looked with gratitude to heaven,
Looked on high, in joy and gladness,
Then addressed omniscient Ukko,
This the prayer the minstrel uttered:
"O be praised, thou God of mercy,
Let me praise thee, my Creator,
Since thou gavest me assistance,
And vouchsafed me thy protection,
Healed my wounds and stilled mine anguish,
Banished all my pain and trouble,
Caused by Iron and by Hisi.
O, ye people of Wainola,
People of this generation,
And the folk of future ages,
Fashion not in emulation,
River boat, nor ocean shallop,
Boasting of its fine appearance,
God alone can work completion,
Give to cause its perfect ending,
Never hand of man can find it,
Never can the hero give it,
Ukko is the only Master."

RUNE X
ILMARINEN FORGES THE SAMPO

Wainamoinen, the magician,
Takes his steed of copper color,
Hitches quick his fleet-foot courser,
Puts his racer to the snow-sledge,
Straightway springs upon the cross-seat,
Snaps his whip adorned with jewels.
Like the winds the steed flies onward,
Like a lightning flash, the racer
Makes the snow-sledge creak and rattle,
Makes the highway quickly vanish,
Dashes on through fen and forest,
Over hills and through the valleys,
Over marshes, over mountains,
Over fertile plains and meadows;
Journeys one day, then a second,
So a third from morn till evening,
Till the third day evening brings him
To the endless bridge of Osmo,
To the Osmo-fields and pastures,
To the plains of Kalevala;
When the hero spake as follows:
"May the wolves devour the dreamer,
Eat the Laplander for dinner,
May disease destroy the braggart,
Him who said that I should never
See again my much-loved home-land,
Nevermore behold my kindred,
Never during all my life-time,
Never while the sunshine brightens,
Never while the moonlight glimmers
On the meadows of Wainola,
On the plains of Kalevala."
Then began old Wainamoinen,
Ancient bard and famous singer,
To renew his incantations;
Sang aloft a wondrous pine-tree,
Till it pierced the clouds in growing
With its golden top and branches,
Till it touched the very heavens,
Spread its branches in the ether,
In the ever-shining sunlight.
Now he sings again enchanting,
Sings the Moon to shine forever
In the fir-tree's emerald branches;
In its top he sings the Great Bear.
Then be quickly journeys homeward,
Hastens to his golden portals,
Head awry and visage wrinkled,
Crooked cap upon his forehead,
Since as ransom he had promised
Ilmarinen, magic artist,
Thus to save his life from torture
On the distant fields of Northland

The Kalevala
In the dismal Sariola.
When his stallion he had halted
On the Osmo-field and meadow,
Quickly rising in his snow-sledge,
The magician heard one knocking,
Breaking coal within the smithy,
Beating with a heavy hammer.
Wainamoinen, famous minstrel,
Entering the smithy straightway,
Found the blacksmith, Ilmarinen,
Knocking with his copper hammer.
Ilmarinen spake as follows:
"Welcome, brother Wainamoinen,
Old and worthy Wainamoinen!
Why so long hast thou been absent,
Where hast thou so long been hiding?"
Wainamoinen then made answer,
These the words of the magician:
"Long indeed have I been living,
Many dreary days have wandered,
Many cheerless nights have lingered,
Floating on the cruel ocean,
Weeping in the fens and woodlands
Of the never-pleasant Northland,
In the dismal Sariola;
With the Laplanders I've wandered,
With the people filled with witchcraft."
Promptly answers Ilmarinen,
These the words the blacksmith uses:
"O thou ancient Wainamoinen,
Famous and eternal singer,
Tell me of thy journey northward,
Of thy wanderings in Lapland,
Of thy dismal journey homeward."
Spake the minstrel, Wainamoinen:
"I have much to tell thee, brother,
Listen to my wondrous story:
In the Northland lives a virgin,
In a village there, a maiden,
That will not accept a lover,
That a hero's hand refuses,
That a wizard's heart disdaineth;
All of Northland sings her praises,
Sings her worth and magic beauty,
Fairest maiden of Pohyola,
Daughter of the earth and ocean.
From her temples beams the moonlight,
From her breast, the gleam of sunshine,
From her forehead shines the rainbow,
On her neck, the seven starlets,
And the Great Bear from her shoulder.
"Ilmarinen, worthy brother,
Thou the only skilful blacksmith,
Go and see her wondrous beauty,
See her gold and silver garments,
See her robed in finest raiment,
See her sitting on the rainbow,
Walking on the clouds of purple.
Forge for her the magic Sampo,
Forge the lid in many colors,
Thy reward shall be the virgin,

Lönnrot

Thou shalt win this bride of beauty;
Go and bring the lovely maiden
To thy home in Kalevala."
Spake the brother, Ilmarinen:
O thou cunning Wainamoinen,
Thou hast promised me already
To the ever-darksome Northland,
Thy devoted head to ransom,
Thus to rescue thee from trouble.
I shall never visit Northland,
Shall not go to see thy maiden,
Do not love the Bride of Beauty;
Never while the moonlight glimmers,
Shall I go to dreary Pohya,
To the plains of Sariola,
Where the people eat each other,
Sink their heroes in the ocean,
Not for all the maids of Lapland."
Spake the brother, Wainamoinen:
"I can tell thee greater wonders,
Listen to my wondrous story:
I have seen the fir-tree blossom,
Seen its flowers with emerald branches,
On the Osmo-fields and woodlands,
In its top, there shines the moonlight,
And the Bear lives in its branches."
Ilmarinen thus made answer:
"I cannot believe thy story,
Cannot trust thy tale of wonder,
Till I see the blooming fir-tree,
With its many emerald branches,
With its Bear and golden moonlight."
This is Wainamoinen's answer:
"Wilt thou not believe my story?
Come with me and I will show thee
If my lips speak fact or fiction."
Quick they journey to discover,
Haste to view the wondrous fir-tree;
Wainamoinen leads the journey,
Ilmarinen closely follows.
As they near the Osmo-borders,
Ilmarinen hastens forward
That be may behold the wonder,
Spies the Bear Within the fir-top,
Sitting on its emerald branches,
Spies the gleam of golden moonlight.
Spake the ancient Wainamoinen,
These the words the singer uttered:
Climb this tree, dear Ilmarinen,
And bring down the golden moonbeams,
Bring the Moon and Bear down with thee
From the fir-tree's lofty branches."
Ilmarinen, full consenting,
Straightway climbed the golden fir-tree,
High upon the bow of heaven,
Thence to bring the golden moonbeams,
Thence to bring the Bear of heaven,
From the fir-tree's topmost branches.
Thereupon the blooming fir-tree
Spake these words to Ilmarinen:
"O thou senseless, thoughtless hero,

The Kalevala
Thou hast neither wit nor instinct;
Thou dost climb my golden branches,
Like a thing of little judgment,
Thus to get my pictured moonbeams,
Take away my silver starlight,
Steal my Bear and blooming branches."
Quick as thought old Wainamoinen
Sang again in magic accents,
Sang a storm-wind in the heavens,
Sang the wild winds into fury,
And the singer spake as follows:
'Take, O storm-wind, take the forgeman,
Carry him within thy vessel,
Quickly hence, and land the hero
On the ever-darksome Northland,
On the dismal Sariola."
Now the storm-wind quickly darkens,
Quickly piles the air together,
Makes of air a sailing vessel,
Takes the blacksmith, Ilmarinen,
Fleetly from the fir-tree branches,
Toward the never-pleasant Northland,
Toward the dismal Sariola.
Through the air sailed Ilmarinen,
Fast and far the hero travelled,
Sweeping onward, sailing northward,
Riding in the track of storm-winds,
O'er the Moon, beneath the sunshine,
On the broad back of the Great Bear,
Till he neared Pohyola's woodlands,
Neared the homes of Sariola,
And alighted undiscovered,
Was Dot noticed by the hunters,
Was not scented by the watch-dogs.
Louhi, hostess of Pohyola,
Ancient, toothless dame of Northland,
Standing in the open court-yard,
Thus addresses Ilmarinen,
As she spies the hero-stranger:
"Who art thou of ancient heroes,
Who of all the host of heroes,
Coming here upon the storm-wind,
O'er the sledge-path of the ether,
Scented not by Pohya's watch-dogs?
This is Ilmarinen's answer:
"I have surely not come hither
To be barked at by the watch-dogs,
At these unfamiliar portals,
At the gates of Sariola."
Thereupon the Northland hostess
Asks again the hero-stranger:
"Hast thou ever been acquainted
With the blacksmith of Wainola,
With the hero, Ilmarinen,
With the skilful smith and artist?
Long I've waited for his coming,
Long this one has been expected,
On the borders of the Northland,
Here to forge for me the Sampo."
Spake the hero, Ilmarinen:
"Well indeed am I acquainted

Lönnrot

With the blacksmith, Ilmarinen,
I myself am Ilmarinen,
I, the skilful smith and artist."
Louhi, hostess of the Northland,
Toothless dame of Sariola,
Straightway rushes to her dwelling,
These the words that Louhi utters:
"Come, thou youngest of my daughters,
Come, thou fairest of my maidens,
Dress thyself in finest raiment,
Deck thy hair with rarest jewels,
Pearls upon thy swelling bosom,
On thy neck, a golden necklace,
Bind thy head with silken ribbons,
Make thy cheeks look fresh and ruddy,
And thy visage fair and winsome,
Since the artist, Ilmarinen,
Hither comes from Kalevala,
Here to forge for us the Sampo,
Hammer us the lid in colors."
Now the daughter of the Northland,
Honored by the land and water,
Straightway takes her choicest raiment,
Takes her dresses rich in beauty,
Finest of her silken wardrobe,
Now adjusts her silken fillet,
On her brow a band of copper,
Round her waist a golden girdle,
Round her neck a pearly necklace,
Shining gold upon her bosom,
In her hair the threads of silver.
From her dressing-room she hastens,
To the hall she bastes and listens,
Full of beauty, full of joyance,
Ears erect and eyes bright-beaming,
Ruddy cheeks and charming visage,
Waiting for the hero-stranger.
Louhi, hostess of Pohyola,
Leads the hero, Ilmarinen,
To her dwelling-rooms in Northland,
To her home in Sariola,
Seats him at her well-filled table,
Gives to him the finest viands,
Gives him every needed comfort,
Then addresses him as follows:
"O thou blacksmith, Ilmarinen,
Master of the forge and smithy,
Canst thou forge for me the Sampo,
Hammer me the lid in colors,
From the tips of white-swan feathers,
From the milk of greatest virtue,
From a single grain of barley,
From the finest wool of lambkins?
Thou shalt have my fairest daughter,
Recompense for this thy service."
These the words of Ilmarinen:
"I will forge for thee the Sampo,
Hammer thee the lid in colors,
From the tips of white-swan feathers,
From the milk of greatest virtue,
From a single grain of barley,

The Kalevala

From the finest wool of lambkins?
Since I forged the arch of heaven,
Forged the air a concave cover,
Ere the earth had a beginning."
Thereupon the magic blacksmith
Went to forge the wondrous Sampo,
Went to find a blacksmith's workshop,
Went to find the tools to work with;
But he found no place for forging,
Found no smithy, found no bellows,
Found no chimney, found no anvil,
Found no tongs, and found no hammer.
Then the-artist, Ilmarinen.
Spake these words, soliloquizing:
"Only women grow discouraged,
Only knaves leave work unfinished,
Not the devils, nor the heroes,
Nor the Gods of greater knowledge."
Then the blacksmith, Ilmarinen,
Sought a place to build a smithy,
Sought a place to plant a bellows,
On the borders of the Northland,
On the Pohya-hills and meadows;
Searched one day, and then a second;
Ere the evening of the third day,
Came a rock within his vision,
Came a stone with rainbow-colors.
There the blacksmith, Ilmarinen,
Set at work to build his smithy,
Built a fire and raised a chimney;
On the next day laid his bellows,
On the third day built his furnace,
And began to forge the Sampo.
The eternal magic artist,
Ancient blacksmith, Ilmarinen,
First of all the iron-workers,
Mixed together certain metals,
Put the mixture in the caldron,
Laid it deep within the furnace,
Called the hirelings to the forging.
Skilfully they work the bellows,
Tend the fire and add the fuel,
Three most lovely days of summer,
Three short nights of bright midsummer,
Till the rocks begin to blossom,
In the foot-prints of the workmen,
From the magic heat and furnace.
On the first day, Ilmarinen
Downward bent and well examined,
On the bottom of his furnace,
Thus to see what might be forming
From the magic fire and metals.
From the fire arose a cross-bow,
"With the brightness of the moonbeams,
Golden bow with tips of silver;
On the shaft was shining copper,
And the bow was strong and wondrous,
But alas! it was ill-natured,
Asking for a hero daily,
Two the heads it asked on feast-days.
Ilmarinen, skilful artist,

Was not pleased with this creation,
Broke the bow in many pieces,
Threw them back within the furnace,
Kept the workmen at the bellows,
Tried to forge the magic Sampo.
On the second day, the blacksmith
Downward bent and well examined,
On the bottom of the furnace;
From the fire, a skiff of metals,
Came a boat of purple color,
All the ribs were colored golden,
And the oars were forged from copper;
Thus the skiff was full of beauty,
But alas! a thing of evil;
Forth it rushes into trouble,
Hastens into every quarrel,
Hastes without a provocation
Into every evil combat.
Ilmarinen, metal artist,
Is not pleased with this creation,
Breaks the skiff in many fragments,
Throws them back within the furnace,
Keeps the workmen at the bellows,
Thus to forge the magic Sampo.
On the third day, Ilmarinen,
First of all the metal-workers,
Downward bent and well examined,
On the bottom of the furnace;
There be saw a heifer rising,
Golden were the horns of Kimmo,
On her head the Bear of heaven,
On her brow a disc of sunshine,
Beautiful the cow of magic;
But alas! she is ill-tempered,
Rushes headlong through the forest,
Rushes through the swamps and meadows,
Wasting all her milk in running.
Ilmarinen, the magician.
Is not pleased with this creation,
Cuts the magic cow in pieces,
Throws them in the fiery furnace,
Sets the workmen at the bellows,
Thus to forge the magic Sampo.
On the fourth day, Ilmarinen
Downward bent and well examined,
To the bottom of the furnace;
There beheld a plow in beauty
Rising from the fire of metals,
Golden was the point and plowshare,
And the beam was forged from copper,
And the handles, molten silver,
Beautiful the plow and wondrous;
But alas! it is ill-mannered,
Plows up fields of corn and barley,
Furrows through the richest meadows.
Ilmarinen, metal artist,
Is not pleased with this creation,
Quickly breaks the plow in pieces,
Throws them back within the furnace,
Lets the winds attend the bellows,
Lets the storm-winds fire the metals.

The Kalevala
Fiercely vie the winds of heaven,
East-wind rushing, West-wind roaring,
South-wind crying, North-wind howling,
Blow one day and then a second,
Blow the third from morn till even,
When the fire leaps through the windows,
Through the door the sparks fly upward,
Clouds of smoke arise to heaven;
With the clouds the black smoke mingles,
As the storm-winds ply the bellows.
On the third night Ilmarinen,
Bending low to view his metals,
On the bottom of the furnace,
Sees the magic Sampo rising,
Sees the lid in many colors.
Quick the artist of Wainola
Forges with the tongs and anvil,
Knocking with a heavy hammer,
Forges skilfully the Sampo;
On one side the flour is grinding,
On another salt is making,
On a third is money forging,
And the lid is many-colored.
Well the Sampo grinds when finished,
To and fro the lid in rocking,
Grinds one measure at the day-break,
Grinds a measure fit for eating,
Grinds a second for the market,
Grinds a third one for the store-house.
Joyfully the dame of Northland,
Louhi, hostess of Pohyola,
Takes away the magic Sampo,
To the hills of Sariola,
To the copper-bearing mountains,
Puts nine locks upon the wonder,
Makes three strong roots creep around it;
In the earth they grow nine fathoms,
One large root beneath the mountain,
One beneath the sandy sea-bed,
One beneath the mountain-dwelling.
Modestly pleads Ilmarinen
For the maiden's willing answer,
These the words of the magician:
"Wilt thou come with me, fair maiden,
Be my wife and queen forever?
I have forged for thee the Sampo,
Forged the lid in many colors."
Northland's fair and lovely daughter
Answers thus the metal-worker:
"Who will in the coming spring-time,
Who will in the second summer,
Guide the cuckoo's song and echo?
Who will listen to his calling,
Who will sing with him in autumn,
Should I go to distant regions,
Should this cheery maiden vanish
From the fields of Sariola,
From Pohyola's fens and forests,
Where the cuckoo sings and echoes?
Should I leave my father's dwelling,
Should my mother's berry vanish,

Lönnrot

Should these mountains lose their cherry,
Then the cuckoo too would vanish,
All the birds would leave the forest,
Leave the summit of the mountain,
Leave my native fields and woodlands,
Never shall I, in my life-time,
Say farewell to maiden freedom,
Nor to summer cares and labors,
Lest the harvest be ungarnered,
Lest the berries be ungathered,
Lest the song-birds leave the forest,
Lest the mermaids leave the waters,
Lest I sing with them no longer."
Ilmarinen, the magician,
The eternal metal-forger,
Cap awry and head dejected,
Disappointed, heavy-hearted,
Empty-handed, well considers,
How to reach his distant country,
Reach his much-loved home and kinded,
Gain the meadows of Wainola,
From the never-pleasant Northland,
From the darksome Sariola.
Louhi thus addressed the suitor:
"O thou blacksmith, Ilmarinen,
Why art thou so heavy-hearted,
Why thy visage so dejected?
Hast thou in thy mind to journey
From the vales and hills of Pohya,
To the meadows of Wainola,
To thy home in Kalevala?
This is Ilmarinen's answer:
"Thitherward my mind is tending,
To my home-land let me journey,
With my kindred let me linger,
Be at rest in mine own country."
Straightway Louhi, dame of Northland,
Gave the hero every comfort,
Gave him food and rarest viands,
Placed him in a boat of copper,
In a copper-banded vessel,
Called the winds to his assistance,
Made the North-wind guide him homeward.
Thus the skilful Ilmarinen
Travels toward his native country,
On the blue back of the waters,
Travels one day, then a second,
Till the third day evening brings him
To Wainola's peaceful meadows,
To his home in Kalevala.
Straightway ancient Wainamoinen
Thus addresses Ilmarinen:
"O my brother, metal-artist,
Thou eternal wonder-worker,
Didst thou forge the magic Sampo,
Forge the lid in many colors?"
Spake the brother, Ilmarinen,
These the words the master uttered:
"Yea, I forged the magic Sampo,
Forged the lid in many colors;
To and fro the lid in rocking

The Kalevala
Grinds one measure at the day-dawn,
Grinds a measure fit for eating,
Grinds a second for the market,
Grinds a third one for the store-house.
Louhi has the wondrous Sampo,
I have not the Bride of Beauty."

RUNE XI
LEMMINKAINEN'S LAMENT

This the time to sing of Ahti,
Son of Lempo, Kaukomieli,
Also known as Lemminkainen.
Ahti was the king of islands,
Grew amid the island-dwellings,
At the site of his dear mother,
On the borders of the ocean,
On the points of promontories.
Ahti fed upon the salmon,
Fed upon the ocean whiting,
Thus became a mighty hero,
In his veins the blood of ages,
Read erect and form commanding,
Growth of mind and body perfect
But alas! he had his failings,
Bad indeed his heart and morals,
Roaming in unworthy places,
Staying days and nights in sequences
At the homes of merry maidens,
At the dances of the virgins,
With the maids of braided tresses.
Up in Sahri lived a maiden,
Lived the fair and winsome Kulli,
Lovely as a summer-flower,
From a kingly house descended,
Grew to perfect form and beauty,
Living in her father's cottage,
Home of many ancient heroes,
Beautiful was she and queenly,
Praised throughout the whole of Ehstland;
From afar men came to woo her,
To the birthplace of the virgin,
To the household of her mother.
For his son the Day-star wooes her,
But she will not go to Sun-land,
Will not shine beside the Day-star,
In his haste to bring the summer.
For her son, the bright Moon wooes her,
But she will not go to Moon-land,
By the bright Moon will not glimmer,
Will not run through boundless ether.
For his son the Night-star wooes her,
But she will not go to Star-land,
Will not twinkle in the starlight,
Through the dreary nights in winter.
Lovers come from distant Ehstlaud,
Others come from far-off Ingern,
But they cannot win the maiden,
This the answer that she gives them
"Vainly are your praises lavished
Vainly is your silver offered,
Wealth and praise are no temptation;
Never shall I go to Ehstland,

The Kalevala
Never shall I go a-rowing
On the waters of the Ingern,
Shall not cross the Sahri-waters,
Never eat the fish of Ehstland,
Never taste the Ehstland viands.
Ingerland shall never see me,
Will not row upon her rivers,
Will not step within her borders;
Hunger there, and fell starvation,
Wood is absent, fuel wanting,
Neither water, wheat, nor barley,
Even rye is not abundant."
Lemminkainen of the islands,
Warlike hero, Kaukomieli,
Undertakes to win the maiden,
Woo and win the Sahri-flower,
Win a bride so highly honored,
Win the maid with golden tresses,
Win the Sahri maid of beauty;
But his mother gives him warning:
"Nay," replies his gray-haired mother,
"Do not woo, my son beloved,
Maiden of a higher station;
She will never make thee happy
With her lineage of Sahri."
Spake the hero, Lemminkainen,
These the words of Kaukomieli:
"Should I come from lowly station,
Though my tribe is not the highest,
I shall woo to please my fancy,
Woo the maiden fair and lovely,
Choose a wife for worth and beauty."
This the anxious mother's answer:
"Lemminkainen, son beloved,
Listen to advice maternal:
Do not go to distant Sahri,
To her tribe of many branches;
All the maidens there will taunt thee,
All the women will deride thee."
Lemminkainen, little hearing,
Answers thus his mother's pleading:
"I will still the sneers of women,
Silence all the taunts of maidens,
I will crush their haughty bosoms,
Smite the hands and cheeks of infants;
Surely this will check their insults,
Fitting ending to derision!"
This the answer of the mother:
"Woe is me, my son beloved!
Woe is me, my life hard-fated!
Shouldst thou taunt the Sahri daughters,
Or insult the maids of virtue,
Shouldst thou laugh them to derision,
There will rise a great contention,
Fierce the battle that will follow.
All the hosts of Sahri-suitors,
Armed in thousands will attack thee,
And will slay thee for thy folly."
Nothing listing, Lemminkainen,
Heeding not his mother's warning,
Led his war-horse from the stables,

Lönnrot

Quickly hitched the fiery charger,
Fleetly drove upon his journey,
To the distant Sahri-village,
There to woo the Sahri-flower,
There to win the Bride of Beauty.
All the aged Sahri-women,
All the young and lovely maidens
Laughed to scorn the coming stranger
Driving careless through the alleys,
Wildly driving through the court-yard,
Now upsetting in the gate-way,
Breaking shaft, and hame, and runner.
Then the fearless Lemminkainen,
Mouth awry and visage wrinkled,
Shook his sable locks and answered:
"Never in my recollection
Have I heard or seen such treatment,
Never have I been derided,
Never suffered sneers of women,
Never suffered scorn of virgins,
Not in my immortal life-time.
Is there any place befitting
On the Sahri-plains and pastures,
Where to join in songs and dances?
Is there here a hall for pleasure,
Where the Sahri-maidens linger,
Merry maids with braided tresses?"
Thereupon the Sahri-maidens
Answered from their promontory.,
"Room enough is there in Sahri,
Room upon the Sahri-pastures,
Room for pleasure-halls and dances;
Sing and dance upon our meadows,
Be a shepherd on the mountains,
Shepherd-boys have room for dancing;
Indolent the Sahri-children,
But the colts are fat and frisky."
Little caring, Lemminkainen
Entered service there as shepherd,
In the daytime on the pastures,
In the evening, making merry
At the games of lively maidens,
At the dances with the virgins,
With the maids with braided tresses.
Thus it was that Lemminkainen,
Thus the shepherd, Kaukomieli,
Quickly hushed the women's laughter,
Quickly quenched the taunts of maidens,
Quickly silenced their derision.
All the dames and Sahri-daughters
Soon were feasting Lemminkainen,
At his side they danced and lingered.
Only was there one among them,
One among the Sahri-virgins,
Harbored neither love nor wooers,
Favored neither gods nor heroes,
This the lovely maid Kyllikki,
This the Sahri's fairest flower.
Lemminkainen, full of pleasure,
Handsome hero, Kaukomieli,
Rowed a hundred boats in pieces,

The Kalevala
Pulled a thousand oars to fragments,
While he wooed the Maid of Beauty,
Tried to win the fair Kyllikki.
Finally the lovely maiden,
Fairest daughter of the Northland,
Thus addresses Lemminkainen:
"Why dost linger here, thou weak one,
Why dost murmur on these borders,
Why come wooing at my fireside,
Wooing me in belt of copper?
Have no time to waste upon thee,
Rather give this stone its polish,
Rather would I turn the pestle
In the heavy sandstone mortar;
Rather sit beside my mother
In the dwellings of my father.
Never shall I heed thy wooing,
Neither wights nor whisks I care for,
Sooner have a slender husband
Since I have a slender body;
Wish to have him fine of figure,
Since perchance I am well-shapen;
Wish to have him tall and stately,
Since my form perchance is queenly;
Never waste thy time in wooing
Saliri's maid and favored flower."
Time had gone but little distance,
Scarcely had a month passed over,
When upon a merry evening,
Where the maidens meet for dancing,
In the glen beyond the meadow,
On a level patch of verdure,
Came too soon the maid Kyllikki,
Sahri's pride, the Maid of Beauty;
Quickly followed Lemminkainen,
With his stallion proudly prancing,
Fleetest racer of the Northland,
Fleetly drives beyond the meadow,
Where the maidens meet for dancing,
Snatches quick the maid Kyllikki,
On the settle seats the maiden,
Quickly draws the leathern cover,
And adjusts the brichen cross-bar,
Whips his courser to a gallop.
With a rush, and roar, and rattle,
Speeds he homeward like the storm-wind,
Speaks these words to those that listen:
"Never, never, anxious maidens,
Must ye give the information,
That I carried off Kyllikki
To my distant home and kindred.
If ye do not heed this order,
Ye shall badly fare as maidens;
I shall sing to war your suitors,
Sing them under spear and broadsword,
That for months, and years, and ages,
Never ye will see their faces,
Never hear their merry voices,
Never will they tread these uplands,
Never will they join these dances,
Never will they drive these highways."

Lönnrot

Sad the wailing of Kyllikki,
Sad the weeping flower of Sahri!
Listen to her tearful pleading:
"Give, O give me back my freedom,
Free me from the throes of thralldom,
Let this maiden wander homeward,
By some foot-path let me wander
To my father who is grieving,
To my mother who is weeping;
Let me go or I will curse thee!
If thou wilt not give me freedom,
Wilt not let me wander homeward,
Where my loved ones wait my coming,
I have seven stalwart brothers,
Seven sons of father's brother,
Seven sons of mother's sister,
Who pursue the tracks of red-deer,
Hunt the hare upon the heather;
They will follow thee and slay thee,
Thus I'll gain my wished-for freedom."
Lemminkainen, little heeding,
Would not grant the maiden's wishes,
Would not heed her plea for mercy.
Spake again the waiting virgin,
Pride and beauty of the Northland:
"Joyful was I with my kindred,
Joyful born and softly nurtured
Merrily I spent my childhood,
Happy I, in virgin-freedom,
In the dwelling of my father,
By the bedside of my mother,
With my lineage in Sahri;
But alas! all joy has vanished,
All my happiness departed,
All my maiden beauty waneth
Since I met thine evil spirit,
Shameless hero of dishonor,
Cruel fighter of the islands,
Merciless in civil combat."
Spake the hero, Lemminkainen,
These the words of Kaukomieli:
"Dearest maiden, fair Kyllikki,
My sweet strawberry of Pohya,
Still thine anguish, cease thy weeping,
Be thou free from care and sorrow,
Never shall I do thee evil,
Never will my hands maltreat thee,
Never will mine arms abuse thee,
Never will my tongue revile thee,
Never will my heart deceive thee.
"Tell me why thou hast this anguish,
Why thou hast this bitter sorrow,
Why this sighing and lamenting,
Tell me why this wail of sadness?
Banish all thy cares and sorrows,
Dry thy tears and still thine anguish,
I have cattle, food, and shelter,
I have home, and friends, and kindred,
Kine upon the plains and uplands,
In the marshes berries plenty,
Strawberries upon the mountains

The Kalevala
I have kine that need no milking,
Handsome kine that need no feeding,
Beautiful if not well-tended;
Need not tie them up at evening,
Need not free them in the morning,
Need not hunt them, need not feed them,
Need not give them salt nor water.
"Thinkest thou my race is lowly,
Dost thou think me born ignoble,
Does my lineage agrieve thee?
Was not born in lofty station,
From a tribe of noble heroes,
From a worthy race descended;
But I have a sword of fervor,
And a spear yet filled with courage,
Surely these are well descended,
These were born from hero-races,
Sharpened by the mighty Hisi,
By the gods were forged and burnished;
Therefore will I give thee greatness,
Greatness of my race and nation,
With my broadsword filled with fervor,
With my spear still filled with courage."
Anxiously the sighing maiden
Thus addresses Lemminkainen:
"O thou Ahti, son of Lempo,
Wilt thou take this trusting virgin,
As thy faithful life-companion,
Take me under thy protection,
Be to me a faithful husband,
Swear to me an oath of honor,
That thou wilt not go to battle,
When for gold thou hast a longing,
When thou wishest gold and silver?"
This is Lemminkainen's answer:
I will swear an oath of honor,
That I'll never go to battle,
When for gold I feel a longing,
When I wish for gold and silver.
Swear thou also on thine honor,
Thou wilt go not to the village,
When desire for dance impels thee,
Wilt not visit village-dances."
Thus the two made oath together,
Registered their vows in heaven,
Vowed before omniscient Ukko,
Ne'er to go to war vowed Ahti,
Never to the dance, Kyllikki.
Lemminkainen, full of joyance,
Snapped his whip above his courser,
Whipped his racer to a gallop,
And these words the hero uttered:
"Fare ye well, ye Sahri-meadows,
Roots of firs, and stumps of birch-trees.
That I wandered through in summer,
That I travelled o'er in winter,
Where ofttimes in rainy seasons,
At the evening hour I lingered,
When I sought to win the virgin,
Sought to win the Maid of Beauty,
Fairest of the Sahri-flowers.

Lönnrot

Fare ye well, ye Sahri-woodlands,
Seas and oceans, lakes and rivers,
Vales and mountains, isles and inlets,
Once the home of fair Kyllikki!"
Quick the racer galloped homeward,
Galloped on along the highway,
Toward the meadows of Wainola,
To the plains of Kalevala.
As they neared the Ahti-dwellings,
Thus Kyllikki spake in sorrow:
"Cold and drear is thy cottage,
Seeming like a place deserted;
Who may own this dismal cabin,
Who the one so little honored?"
Spake the hero, Lemminkainen,
These the words that Ahti uttered:
"Do not grieve about my cottage,
Have no care about my chambers;
I shall build thee other dwellings,
I shall fashion them much better,
Beams, and posts, and sills, and rafters,
Fashioned from the sacred birch-wood."
Now they reach the home of Ahti,
Lemminkainen's home and birthplace,
Enter they his mother's cottage;
There they meet his aged mother,
These the words the mother uses:
"Long indeed hast thou been absent,
Long in foreign lands hast wandered,
Long in Sahri thou hast lingered!"
This is Lemminkainen's answer:
"All the host of Sahri-women,
All the chaste and lovely maidens,
All the maids with braided tresses,
Well have paid for their derision,
For their scorn and for their laughter,
That they basely heaped upon me.
I have brought the best among them
In my sledge to this thy cottage;
Well I wrapped her in my fur-robes,
Kept her warm enwrapped in bear-skin,
Brought her to my mother's dwelling,
As my faithful life-companion;
Thus I paid the scornful maidens,
Paid them well for their derision.
"Cherished mother of my being,
I have found the long-sought jewel,
I have won the Maid of Beauty,
Spread our couch with finest linen,
For our heads the softest pillows,
On our table rarest viands,
So that I may dwell in pleasure
With my spouse, the bride of honor,
With the pride of distant Sahri."
This the answer of the mother:
"Be thou praised, O gracious Ukko,
Loudly praised, O thou Creator,
Since thou givest me a daughter,
Ahti's bride, my second daughter,
Who can stir the fire at evening,
Who can weave me finest fabrics,

The Kalevala
Who can twirl the useful spindle,
Who can rinse my silken ribbons,
Who can full the richest garments.
"Son beloved, praise thy Maker,
For the winning of this virgin,
Pride and joy of distant Sahri
Kind indeed is thy Creator,
Wise the ever-knowing Ukko!
Pure the snow upon the mountains,
Purer still thy Bride of Beauty;
White the foam upon the ocean,
Whiter still her virgin-spirit;
Graceful on the lakes, the white-swan,
Still more graceful, thy companion:
Beautiful the stars in heaven,
Still more beautiful, Kyllikki.
Larger make our humble cottage,
Wider build the doors and windows,
Fashion thou the ceilings higher,
Decorate the walls in beauty,
Now that thou a bride hast taken
From a tribe of higher station,
Purest maiden of creation,
From the meadow-lands of Sahri,
From the upper shores of Northland."

RUNE XII
KYLLIKKI'S BROKEN VOW

Lemminkainen, artful husband,
Reckless hero, Kaukomieli,
Constantly beside his young wife.,
Passed his life in sweet contentment,
And the years rolled swiftly onward;
Ahti thought not of the battles,
Nor Kyllikki of the dances.
Once upon a time it happened
That the hero, Lemminkainen,
Went upon the lake a-fishing,
Was not home at early evening,
As the cruel night descended;
To the village went Kyllikki,
To the dance of merry maidens.
Who will tell the evil story,
Who will bear the information
To the husband, Lemminkainen?
Ahti's sister tells the story,
And the sister's name, Ainikki.
Soon she spreads the cruel tidings,
Straightway gives the information,
Of Kyllikki's perjured honor,
These words Ainikki utters:
"Ahti, my beloved brother,
To the village went Kyllikki,
To the hall of many strangers,
To the plays and village dances,
With the young men and the maidens,
With the maids of braided tresses,
To the halls of joy and pleasure."
Lemminkainen, much dejected,
Broken-hearted, flushed with anger,
Spake these words in measured accents:
"Mother dear, my gray-haired mother,
Wilt thou straightway wash my linen
In the blood of poison-serpents,
In the black blood of the adder?
I must hasten to the combat,
To the camp-fires of the Northland,
To the battle-fields of Lapland;
To the village went Kyllikki,
To the play of merry maidens,
To the games and village dances,
With the maids of braided tresses."
Straightway speaks the wife, Kyllikki:
"My beloved husband, Ahti,
Do not go to war, I pray thee.
In the evening I lay sleeping,
Slumbering I saw in dream-land
Fire upshooting from the chimney,
Flames arising, mounting skyward,
From the windows of this dwelling,
From the summits of these rafters,

The Kalevala

Piercing through our upper chambers,
Roaring like the fall of waters,
Leaping from the floor and ceiling,
Darting from the halls and doorways."
But the doubting Lemminkainen
Makes this answer to Kyllikki:
"I discredit dreams or women,
Have no faith in vows of maidens!
Faithful mother of my being,
Hither bring my mail of copper;
Strong desire is stirring in me
For the cup of deadly combat,
For the mead of martial conquest."
This the pleading mother's answer:
"Lemminkainen, son beloved,
Do not go to war I pray thee;
We have foaming beer abundant,
In our vessels beer of barley,
Held in casks by oaken spigots;
Drink this beer of peace and pleasure,
Let us drink of it together."
Spake the hero, Lemminkainen:
"I shall taste no more the viands,
In the home of false Kyllikki;
Rather would I drink the water
From the painted tips of birch-oars;
Sweeter far to me the water,
Than the beverage of dishonor,
At my mother's home and fireside!
"Hither bring my martial doublet,
Bring me now the sword of battle,
Bring my father's sword of honor;
I must go to upper Northland,
To the battle-fields of Lapland,
There to win me gold and silver."
This the anxious mother's answer:
"My beloved Kaukomieli,
We have gold in great abundance,
Gold and silver in the store-room;
Recently upon the uplands,
In the early hours of morning,
Toiled the workmen in the corn-fields,
Plowed the meadows filled with serpents,
When the plowshare raised the cover
From a chest of gold and silver,
Countless was the gold uncovered,
Hid beneath the grassy meadow;
This the treasure I have brought thee,
Take the countless gold in welcome."
Spake the hero, Lemminkainen:
"Do not wish thy household silver,
From the wars I'll earn my silver;
Gold and silver from the combat
Are to me of greater value
Than the wealth thou hast discovered.
Bring me now my heavy armor,
Bring me too my spear and broadsword;
To the Northland I must hasten,
To the bloody wars of Lapland,
Thither does my pride impel me,
Thitherward my heart is turning.

Lönnrot

"I have heard a tale of Lapland,
Some believe the wondrous story,
That a maid in Pimentola
Lives that does not care for suitors,
Does not care for bearded heroes."
This the aged mother's answer:
"Warlike Athi, son beloved,
In thy home thou hast Kyllikki,
Fairest wife of all the islands;
Strange to see two wives abiding
In the home of but one husband."
Spake the hero, Lemminkainen:
"To the village runs Kyllikki;
Let her run to village dances,
Let her sleep in other dwellings,
With the village youth find pleasure,
With the maids of braided tresses."
Seeks the mother to detain him,
Thus the anxious mother answers:
"Do not go, my son beloved,
Ignorant of Pohya-witchcraft,
To the distant homes of Northland
Till thou hast the art of magic,
Till thou hast some little wisdom
Do not go to fields of battle,
To the fires of Northland's children,
To the slaughter-fields of Lapland,
Till of magic thou art master.
There the Lapland maids will charm thee,
Turyalanders will bewitch thee,
Sing thy visage into charcoal,
Head and shoulders to the furnace,
Into ashes sing thy fore-arm,
Into fire direct thy footsteps."
Spake the warlike Lemminkainen:
Wizards often have bewitched me,
And the fascinating serpents;
Lapland wizards, three in number,
On an eve in time of summer,
Sitting on a rock at twilight,
Not a garment to protect them,
Once bewitched me with their magic;
This much they have taken from me,
This the sum of all my losses:
What the hatchet gains from flint-stone,
What the auger bores from granite,
What the heel chips from the iceberg,
And what death purloins from tomb-stones.
"Horribly the wizards threatened,
Tried to sink me with their magic,
In the water of the marshes,
In the mud and treacherous quicksand,
To my chin in mire and water;
But I too was born a hero,
Born a hero and magician,
Was not troubled by their magic.
"Straightway I began my singing,
Sang the archers with their arrows,
Sang the spearmen with their weapons,
Sang the swordsmen with their poniards,
Sang the singers with their singing,

The Kalevala

The enchanters with their magic,
To the rapids of the rivers,
To the highest fall of waters,
To the all-devouring whirlpool,
To the deepest depths of ocean,
Where the wizards still are sleeping,
Sleeping till the grass shoots upward
Through the beards and wrinkled faces,
Through the locks of the enchanters,
As they sleep beneath the billows."
Still entreats the anxious mother,
Still beseeches Lemminkainen,
Trying to restrain the hero,
While Kyllikki begs forgiveness;
This the language of the mother:
"Do not go, my son beloved,
To the villages of Northland,
Nor to Lapland's frigid borders;
Dire misfortune will befall thee,
Star of evil settle o'er thee,
Lemminkainen's end, destruction.
"Couldst thou speak in tongues a hundred,
I could not believe thee able,
Through the magic of thy singing,
To enchant the sons of Lapland
To the bottom of the ocean,
Dost not know the Tury-language,
Canst but speak the tongue of Suomi,
Canst not win by witless magic."
Lemminkainen, reckless hero,
Also known as Kaukomieli,
Stood beside his mother, combing
Out his sable locks and musing,
Brushing down his beard, debating,
Steadfast still in his decision,
Quickly hurls his brush in anger,
Hurls it to the wall opposing,
Gives his mother final answer,
These the words that Ahti uses:
"Dire misfortune will befall me,
Some sad fate will overtake me,
Evil come to Lemminkainen,
When the blood flows from that hair-brush,
When blood oozes from those bristles."
Thus the warlike Lemminkainen
Goes to never-pleasant Lapland,
Heeding not his mother's warning,
Heeding not her prohibition.
Thus the hero, Kaukomieli,
Quick equips himself for warfare,
On his head a copper helmet,
On his shoulders caps of copper,
On his body iron armor,
Steel, the belt around his body;
As he girds himself for battle,
Ahti thus soliloquizing:
"Strong the hero in his armor,
Strong indeed in copper helmet,
Powerful in mail of iron,
Stronger far than any hero
On the dismal shores of Lapland,

Need not fear their wise enchanters,
Need not fear their strongest foemen,
Need not fear a war with wizards."
Grasped he then the sword of battle,
Firmly grasped the heavy broadsword
That Tuoni had been grinding,
That the gods had brightly burnished,
Thrust it in the leathern scabbard,
Tied the scabbard to his armor.
How do heroes guard from danger,
Where protect themselves from evil?
Heroes guard their homes and firesides,
Guard their doors, and roofs, and windows,
Guard the posts that bold the torch-lights,
Guard the highways to the court-yard,
Guard the ends of all the gate-ways.
Heroes guard themselves from women,
Carefully from merry maidens;
If in this their strength be wanting,
Easy fall the heroes, victims
To the snares of the enchanters.
Furthermore are heroes watchful
Of the tribes of warlike giants,
Where the highway doubly branches,
On the borders of the blue-rock,
On the marshes filled with evil,
Near the mighty fall of waters,
Near the circling of the whirlpool,
Near the fiery springs and rapids.
Spake the stout-heart, Lemminkainen:
"Rise ye heroes of the broadsword,
Ye, the earth's eternal heroes,
From the deeps, ye sickle-bearers,
From the brooks, ye crossbow-shooters,
Come, thou forest, with thine archers,
Come, ye thickets, with your armies,
Mountain spirits, with your powers,
Come, fell Hisi, with thy horrors,
Water-mother, with thy dangers,
Come, Wellamo, with thy mermaids,
Come, ye maidens from the valleys,
Come, ye nymphs from winding rivers,
Be protection to this hero,
Be his day-and-night companions,
Body-guard to Lemminkainen,
Thus to blunt the spears of wizards,
Thus to dull their pointed arrows,
That the spears of the enchanters,
That the arrows of the archers,
That the weapons of the foemen,
May not harm this bearded hero.
"Should this force be insufficient,
I can call on other powers,
I can call the gods above me,
Call the great god of the heavens,
Him who gives the clouds their courses,
Him who rules through boundless ether,
Who directs the march of storm-winds.
"Ukko, thou O God above me,
Thou the father of creation,
Thou that speakest through the thunder,

The Kalevala
Thou whose weapon is the lightning,
Thou whose voice is borne by ether,
Grant me now thy mighty fire-sword,
Give me here thy burning arrows,
Lightning arrows for my quiver,
Thus protect me from all danger,
Guard me from the wiles of witches,
Guide my feet from every evil,
Help me conquer the enchanters,
Help me drive them from the Northland;
Those that stand in front of battle,
Those that fill the ranks behind me,
Those around me, those above me,
Those beneath me, help me banish,.
With their knives, and swords, and cross-bows,
With their spears of keenest temper,
With their tongues of evil magic;
Help me drive these Lapland wizards
To the deepest depths of ocean,
There to wrestle with Wellamo."
Then the reckless Lemminkainen
Whistled loudly for his stallion,
Called the racer from the hurdles,
Called his brown steed from the pasture,
Threw the harness on the courser,
Hitched the fleet-foot to the snow-sledge,
Leaped upon the highest cross-bench,
Cracked his whip above the racer,
And the steed flies onward swiftly,
Bounds the sleigh upon its journey,
And the golden plain re-echoes;
Travels one day, then a second,
Travels all the next day northward,
Till the third day evening brings him
To a sorry Northland village,
On the dismal shores of Lapland.
Here the hero, Lemminkainen,
Drove along the lowest highway,
Through the streets along the border,
To a court-yard in the hamlet,
Asked one standing in the doorway:
"Is there one within this dwelling,
That can loose my stallion's breastplate,
That can lift his heavy collar,
That these shafts can rightly lower?"
On the floor a babe was playing,
And the young child gave this answer:
"There is no one in this dwelling
That can loose thy stallion's breastplate,
That can lift his heavy collar,
That the shafts can rightly lower."
Lemminkainen, not discouraged,
Whips his racer to a gallop,
Rushes forward through the village,
On the middle of the highways,
To the court-yard in the centre,
Asks one standing in the threshold,
Leaning on the penthouse door-posts:
"Is there any one here dwelling
That can slip my stallion's bridle,
That can loose his leathern breast-straps,

That can tend my royal racer?"
From the fire-place spake a wizard,
From her bench the witch made answer:
"Thou canst find one in this dwelling,
That can slip thy courser's bridle,
That can loose his heavy breastplate,
That can tend thy royal racer.
There are here a thousand heroes
That can make thee hasten homeward,
That can give thee fleet-foot stallions,
That can chase thee to thy country,
Reckless rascal and magician,
To thy home and fellow minstrels,
To the uplands of thy father,
To the cabins of thy mother,
To the work-bench of thy brother,
To the dairy or thy sister,
Ere the evening star has risen,
Ere the sun retires to slumber."
Lemminkainen, little fearing,
Gives this answer to the wizard:
"I should slay thee for thy pertness,
That thy clatter might be silenced."
Then he whipped his fiery charger,
And the steed flew onward swiftly,
On the upper of the highways,
To the court-yard on the summit.
When the reckless Lemminkainen
Had approached the upper court-yard,
Uttered he the words that follow:
"O thou Hisi, stuff this watch-dog,
Lempo, stuff his throat and nostrils,
Close the mouth of this wild barker,
Bridle well the vicious canine,
That the watcher may be silent
While the hero passes by him."
Then he stepped within the court-room,
With his whip he struck the flooring,
From the floor arose a vapor,
In the fog appeared a pigmy,
Who unhitched the royal racer,
From his back removed the harness,
Gave the weary steed attention.
Then the hero, Lemminkainen,
Carefully advanced and listened.
No one saw the strange magician,
No one heard his cautious footsteps;
Heard he songs within the dwelling,
Through the moss-stuffed chinks heard voices.
Through the walls he beard them singing,
Through the doors the peals of laughter.
Then he spied within the court-rooms,
Lurking slyly in the hall-ways,
Found the court-rooms filled with singers,
By the walls were players seated,
Near the doors the wise men hovered,
Skilful ones upon the benches,
Near the fires the wicked wizards;
All were singing songs of Lapland,
Singing songs of evil Hisi.
Now the minstrel, Lemminkainen,

The Kalevala
Changes both his form and stature,
Passes through the inner door-ways,
Enters he the spacious court-hall,
And these words the hero utters:
"Fine the singing quickly ending,
Good the song that quickly ceases;
Better far to keep thy wisdom
Than to sing it on the house-tops."
Comes the hostess of Pohyola,
Fleetly rushing through the door-way,
To the centre of the court-room,
And addresses thus the stranger:
Formerly a dog lay watching,
Was a cur of iron-color,
Fond of flesh, a bone-devourer,
Loved to lick the blood of strangers.
Who then art thou of the heroes,
Who of all the host of heroes,
That thou art within my court-rooms,
That thou comest to my dwelling,
Was not seen without my portals,
Was not scented by my watch-dogs?
Spake the reckless Lemminkainen:
"Do not think that I come hither
Having neither wit nor wisdom,
Having neither art nor power,
Wanting in ancestral knowledge,
Lacking prudence of the fathers,
That thy watch-dogs may devour me.
"My devoted mother washed me,
When a frail and tender baby,
Three times in the nights of summer,
Nine times in the nights of autumn,
That upon my journeys northward
I might sing the ancient wisdom,
Thus protect myself from danger;
When at home I sing as wisely
As the minstrels of thy hamlet."
Then the singer, Lemminkainen,
Ancient hero, Kaukomieli,
Quick began his incantations,
Straightway sang the songs of witchcraft,
From his fur-robe darts the lightning,
Flames outshooting from his eye-balls,
From the magic of his singing
From his wonderful enchantment.
Sang the very best of singers
To the very worst of minstrels,
Filled their mouths with dust and ashes,
Piled the rocks upon their shoulders,
Stilled the best of Lapland witches,
Stilled the sorcerers and wizards.
Then he banished all their heroes,
Banished all their proudest minstrels,
This one hither, that one thither,
To the lowlands poor in verdure,
To the unproductive uplands,
To the oceans wanting whiting,
To the waterfalls of Rutya,
To the whirlpool hot and flaming,
To the waters decked with sea-foam,

Lönnrot

Into fires and boiling waters,
Into everlasting torment.
Then the hero, Lemminkainen,
Sang the foemen with their broadswords?
Sang the heroes with their weapons,
Sang the eldest, sang the youngest,
Sang the middle-aged, enchanted;
Only one he left his senses,
He a poor, defenseless shepherd,
Old and sightless, halt and wretched,
And the old man's name was Nasshut.
Spake the miserable shepherd:
"Thou hast old and young enchanted,
Thou hast banished all our heroes,
Why hast spared this wretched shepherd?"
This is Lemminkainen's answer:
"Therefore have I not bewitched thee:
Thou art old, and blind, and wretched
Feeble-minded thou, and harmless,
Loathsome now without my magic.
Thou didst, in thy better life-time,
When a shepherd filled with malice,
Ruin all thy mother's berries,
Make thy sister, too unworthy,
Ruin all thy brother's cattle,
Drive to death thy father's stallions,
Through the marshes, o'er the meadows,
Through the lowlands, o'er the mountains,
Heeding not thy mother's counsel."
Thereupon the wretched Nasshut,
Angry grew and swore for vengeance,
Straightway limping through the door-way,
Hobbled on beyond the court-yard,
O'er the meadow-lands and pastures,
To the river of the death-land,
To the holy stream and whirlpool,
To the kingdom of Tuoni,
To the islands of Manala;
Waited there for Kaukomieli,
Listened long for Lemminkainen,
Thinking he must pass this river
On his journey to his country,
On. the highway to the islands,
From the upper shores of Pohya,
From the dreary Sariola.

RUNE XIII
LEMMINKAINEN'S SECOND WOOING

Spake the ancient Lemminkainen
To the hostess of Pohyola:
"Give to me thy lovely daughter,
Bring me now thy winsome maiden,
Bring the best of Lapland virgins,
Fairest virgin of the Northland."
Louhi, hostess of Pohyola,
Answered thus the wild magician:
"I shall never give my daughter,
Never give my fairest maiden,
Not the best one, nor the worst one,
Not the largest, nor the smallest;
Thou hast now one wife-companion,
Thou has taken hence one hostess,
Carried off the fair Kyllikki."
This is Lemminkainen's answer:
To my home I took Kyllikki,
To my cottage on the island,
To my entry-gates and kindred;
Now I wish a better hostess,
Straightway bring thy fairest daughter,
Worthiest of all thy virgins,
Fairest maid with sable tresses."
Spake the hostess of Pohyola:
"Never will I give my daughter
To a hero false and worthless,
To a minstrel vain and evil;
Therefore, pray thou for my maiden,
Therefore, woo the sweet-faced flower,
When thou bringest me the wild-moose
From the Hisi fields and forests."
Then the artful Lemminkainen
Deftly whittled out his javelins,
Quickly made his leathern bow-string,
And prepared his bow and arrows,
And soliloquized as follows:
"Now my javelins are made ready,
All my arrows too are ready,
And my oaken cross-bow bended,
But my snow-shoes are not builded,
Who will make me worthy snow-shoes?"
Lemminkainen, grave and thoughtful,
Long reflected, well considered,
Where the snow-shoes could be fashioned,
Who the artist that could make them;
Hastened to the Kauppi-smithy,
To the smithy of Lylikki,
Thus addressed the snow-shoe artist:
"O thou skilful Woyalander,
Kauppi, ablest smith of Lapland,
Make me quick two worthy snow-shoes,
Smooth them well and make them hardy,
That in Tapio the wild-moose,

Lönnrot

Roaming through the Hisi-forests,
I may catch and bring to Louhi,
As a dowry for her daughter."
Then Lylikki thus made answer,
Kauppi gave this prompt decision:
"Lemminkainen, reckless minstrel,
Thou wilt hunt in vain the wild-moose,
Thou wilt catch but pain and torture,
In the Hisi fens and forests."
Little heeding, Lemminkainen
Spake these measures to Lylikki
"Make for me the worthy snow-shoes,
Quickly work and make them ready;
Go I will and catch the blue-moose
Where in Tapio it browses,
In the Hisi woods and snow-fields."
Then Lylikki, snow-shoe-maker,
Ancient Kauppi, master artist,
Whittled in the fall his show-shoes,
Smoothed them in the winter evenings,
One day working on the runners,
All the next day making stick-rings,
Till at last the shoes were finished,
And the workmanship was perfect.
Then he fastened well the shoe-straps,
Smooth as adder's skin the woodwork,
Soft as fox-fur were the stick-rings;
Oiled he well his wondrous snow-shoes
With the tallow of the reindeer;
When he thus soliloquizes,
These the accents of Lylikki:
"Is there any youth in Lapland,
Any in this generation,
That can travel in these snow-shoes,
That can move the lower sections?"
Spake the reckless Lemminkainen,
Full of hope, and life, and vigor:
Surely there is one in Lapland.
In this rising generation,
That can travel in these snow-shoes,
That the right and left can manage."
To his back he tied the quiver,
Placed the bow upon his shoulder,
With both hands he grasped his snow-cane,
Speaking meanwhile words as follow:
"There is nothing in the woodlands,
Nothing in the world of Ukko,
Nothing underneath the heavens,
In the uplands, in the lowlands,
Nothing in the snow-fields running,
Not a fleet deer of the forest,
That could not be overtaken
With the snow-shoes of Lylikki,
With the strides of Lemminkainen."
Wicked Hisi heard these measures,
Juntas listened to their echoes;
Straightway Hisi called the wild-moose,
Juutas fashioned soon a reindeer,
And the head was made of punk-wood,
Horns of naked willow branches,
Feet were furnished by the rushes,

The Kalevala
And the legs, by reeds aquatic,
Veins were made of withered grasses,
Eyes, from daisies of the meadows,
Ears were formed of water-flowers,
And the skin of tawny fir-bark,
Out of sappy wood, the muscles,
Fair and fleet, the magic reindeer.
Juutas thus instructs the wild-moose,
These the words of wicked Hisi:
Flee away, thou moose of Juutas,
Flee away, thou Hisi-reindeer,
Like the winds, thou rapid courser,
To the snow-homes of the ranger,
To the ridges of the mountains,
To the snow-capped hills of Lapland,
That thy hunter may be worn out,
Thy pursuer be tormented,
Lemminkainen be exhausted."
Thereupon the Hisi-reindeer,
Juutas-moose with branching antlers,
Fleetly ran through fen and forest,
Over Lapland's hills and valleys,
Through the open fields and court-yards,
Through the penthouse doors and gate-ways,
Turning over tubs of water,
Threw the kettles from the fire-pole,
And upset the dishes cooking.
Then arose a fearful uproar,
In the court-yards of Pohyola,
Lapland-dogs began their barking,
Lapland-children cried in terror,
Lapland-women roared with laughter,
And the Lapland-heroes shouted.
Fleetly followed Lemminkainen,
Followed fast, and followed faster,
Hastened on behind the wild-moose,
Over swamps and through the woodlands,
Over snow-fields vast and pathless,
Over high uprising mountains,
Fire out-shooting from his runners,
Smoke arising from his snow-cane:
Could not hear the wild-moose bounding,
Could not sight the flying fleet-foot;
Glided on through field and forest,
Glided over lakes and rivers,
Over lands beyond the smooth-sea,
Through the desert plains of Hisi,
Glided o'er the plains of Kalma,
Through the kingdom of Tuoni,
To the end of Kalma's empire,
Where the jaws of Death stand open,
Where the head of Kalma lowers,
Ready to devour the stranger,
To devour wild Lemminkainen;
But Tuoni cannot reach him,
Kalma cannot overtake him.
Distant woods are yet untraveled,
Far away a woodland corner
Stands unsearched by Kaukomieli,
In the North's extensive, borders,
In the realm of dreary Lapland.

Lönnrot

Now the hero, on his snow-shoes,
Hastens to the distant woodlands,
There to hunt the moose of Piru.
As he nears the woodland corner,
There he bears a frightful uproar,
From the Northland's distant borders,
From the dreary fields of Lapland,
Hears the dogs as they are barking,
Hears the children loudly screaming,
Hears the laughter or the women,
Hears the shouting of the heroes.
Thereupon wild Lemminkainen
Hastens forward on his snow-shoes,
To the place where dogs are barking,
To the distant woods of Lapland.
When the reckless Kaukomieli
Had approached this Hisi corner,
Straightway he began to question:
"Why this laughter or the women,
Why the screaming of the children,
Why the shouting of the heroes,
Why this barking of the watch-dogs?
This reply was promptly given:
"This the reason for this uproar,
Women laughing, children screaming,
Heroes shouting, watch-dogs barking
Hisi's moose came running hither,
Hither came the Piru-Reindeer,
Hither came with hoofs of silver,
Through the open fields and court-yards,
Through the penthouse doors and gate-ways,
Turning over tubs or water,
Threw the kettles from the fire-pole,
And upset the dishes cooking."
Then the hero, Lemminkainen,
Straightway summoned all his courage,
Pushed ahead his mighty snow-shoes,
Swift as adders in the stubble,
Levelled bushes in the marshes,
Like the swift and fiery serpents,
Spake these words of magic import,
Keeping balance with his snow-staff:
Come thou might of Lapland heroes,
Bring to me the moose of Juutas;
Come thou strength of Lapland-women,
And prepare the boiling caldron;
Come, thou might of Lapland children,
Bring together fire and fuel;
Come, thou strength of Lapland-kettles,
Help to boil the Hisi wild-moose."
Then with mighty force and courage,
Lemminkainen hastened onward,
Striking backward, shooting forward;
With a long sweep of his snow-shoe,
Disappeared from view the hero;
With the second, shooting further,
Was the hunter out of hearing,
With the third the hero glided
On the shoulders of the wild-moose;
Took a pole of stoutest oak-wood,
Took some bark-strings from the willow,

The Kalevala
Wherewithal to bind the moose-deer,
Bind him to his oaken hurdle.
To the moose he spake as follows:
"Here remain, thou moose of Juutas
Skip about, my bounding courser,
In my hurdle jump and frolic,
Captive from the fields of Piru,
From the Hisi glens and mountains."
Then he stroked the captured wild-moose,
Patted him upon his forehead,
Spake again in measured accents:
"I would like awhile to linger,
I would love to rest a moment
In the cottage of my maiden,
With my virgin, young and lovely."
Then the Hisi-moose grew angry,
Stamped his feet and shook his antlers,
Spake these words to Lemminkainen:
"Surely Lempo soon will got thee,
Shouldst thou sit beside the maiden,
Shouldst thou linger by the virgin."
Now the wild-moose stamps and rushes,
Tears in two the bands of willow,
Breaks the oak-wood pole in pieces,
And upturns the hunter's hurdle,
Quickly leaping from his captor,
Bounds away with strength of freedom,
Over hills and over lowlands,
Over swamps and over snow-fields,
Over mountains clothed in heather,
That the eye may not behold him,
Nor the hero's ear detect him.
Thereupon the mighty hunter
Angry grows, and much disheartened,
Starts again the moose to capture,
Gliding off behind the courser.
With his might he plunges forward;
At the instep breaks his snow-shoe,
Breaks the runners into fragments,
On the mountings breaks his javelins,
In the centre breaks his snow-staff,
And the moose bounds on before him,
Through the Hisi-woods and snow-fields,
Out of reach of Lemminkainen.
Then the reckless Kaukomieli
Looked with bended head, ill-humored,
One by one upon the fragments,
Speaking words of ancient wisdom:
"Northland hunters, never, never,
Go defiant to thy forests,
In the Hisi vales and mountains,
There to hunt the moose of Juutas,
Like this senseless, reckless hero;
I have wrecked my magic snow-shoes,
Ruined too my useful snow-staff,
And my javelins I have broken,
While the wild-moose runs in safety
Through the Hisi fields and forests."

Lönnrot

RUNE XIV
DEATH OF LEMMINKAINEN

Lemminkainen, much disheartened,
Deeply thought and long considered,
What to do, what course to follow,
Whether best to leave the wild-moose
In the fastnesses of Hisi,
And return to Kalevala,
Or a third time hunt the ranger,
Hoping thus to bring him captive,
Thus return at last a victor
To the forest home of Louhi,
To the joy of all her daughters,
To the wood-nymph's happy fireside.
Taking courage Lemminkainen
Spake these words in supplication:
"Ukko, thou O God above me,
Thou Creator of the heavens,
Put my snow-shoes well in order,
And endow them both with swiftness,
That I rapidly may journey
Over marshes, over snow-fields,
Over lowlands, over highlands,
Through the realms of wicked Hisi,
Through the distant plains of Lapland,
Through the paths of Lempo's wild-moose,
To the forest hills of Juutas.
To the snow-fields shall I journey,
Leave the heroes to the woodlands,
On the way to Tapiola,
Into Tapio's wild dwellings.
"Greeting bring I to the mountains,
Greeting to the vales and uplands,
Greet ye, heights with forests covered,
Greet ye, ever-verdant fir-trees,
Greet ye, groves of whitened aspen,
Greetings bring to those that greet you,
Fields, and streams, and woods of Lapland.
Bring me favor, mountain-woodlands,
Lapland-deserts, show me kindness,
Mighty Tapio, be gracious,
Let me wander through thy forests,
Let me glide along thy rivers,
Let this hunter search thy snow-fields,
Where the wild-moose herds in numbers
Where the bounding reindeer lingers.
"O Nyrikki, mountain hero,
Son of Tapio of forests,
Hero with the scarlet head-gear,
Notches make along the pathway,
Landmarks upward to the mountains,
That this hunter may not wander,
May not fall, and falling perish
In the snow-fields of thy kingdom,
Hunting for the moose of Hisi,

The Kalevala
Dowry for the pride of Northland.
"Mistress of the woods, Mielikki,
Forest-mother, formed in beauty,
Let thy gold flow out abundant,
Let thy silver onward wander,
For the hero that is seeking
For the wild-moose of thy kingdom;
Bring me here thy keys of silver,
From the golden girdle round thee;
Open Tapio's rich chambers,
And unlock the forest fortress,
While I here await the booty,
While I hunt the moose of Lempo.
"Should this service be too menial
Give the order to thy servants,
Send at once thy servant-maidens,
And command it to thy people.
Thou wilt never seem a hostess,
If thou hast not in thy service,
Maidens ready by the hundreds,
Thousands that await thy bidding,
Who thy herds may watch and nurture,
Tend the game of thy dominions.
"Tall and slender forest-virgin,
Tapio's beloved daughter,
Blow thou now thy honey flute-notes,
Play upon thy forest-whistle,
For the hearing of thy mistress,
For thy charming woodland-mistress,
Make her hear thy sweet-toned playing,
That she may arise from slumber.
Should thy mistress not awaken
At the calling of thy flute-notes,
Play again, and play unceasing,
Make the golden tongue re-echo."
Wild and daring Lemminkainen
Steadfast prays upon his journey,
Calling on the gods for succor,
Hastens off through fields and moorlands,
Passes on through cruel brush-wood,
To the colliery of Hisi,
To the burning fields of Lempo;
Glided one day, then a second,
Glided all the next day onward,
Till he came to Big-stone mountain,
Climbed upon its rocky summit,
Turned his glances to the north-west,
Toward the Northland moors and marshes;
There appeared the Tapio-mansion.
All the doors were golden-colored,
Shining in the gleam of sunlight
Through the thickets on the mountains,
Through the distant fields of Northland.
Lemminkainen, much encouraged,
Hastens onward from his station
Through the lowlands, o'er the uplands,
Over snow-fields vast and vacant,
Under snow-robed firs and aspens,
Hastens forward, happy-hearted,
Quickly reaches Tapio's court-yards,
Halts without at Tapio's windows,

Slyly looks into her mansion,
Spies within some kindly women,
Forest-dames outstretched before him,
All are clad in scanty raiment,
Dressed in soiled and ragged linens.
Spake the stranger Lemminkainen:
"Wherefore sit ye, forest-mothers,
In your old and simple garments,
In your soiled and ragged linen?
Ye, forsooth! are too untidy,
Too unsightly your appearance
In your tattered gowns appareled.
When I lived within the forest,
There were then three mountain castles,
One of horn and one of ivory,
And the third of wood constructed;
In their walls were golden windows,
Six the windows in each castle,
Through these windows I discovered
All the host of Tapio's mansion,
Saw its fair and stately hostess;
Saw great Tapio's lovely daughter,
Saw Tellervo in her beauty,
With her train of charming maidens;
All were dressed in golden raiment,
Rustled all in gold and silver.
Then the forest's queenly hostess,
Still the hostess of these woodlands,
On her arms wore golden bracelets,
Golden rings upon her fingers,
In her hair were sparkling, jewels,
On her bead were golden fillets,
In her ears were golden ear-rings,
On her neck a pearly necklace,
And her braidlets, silver-tinselled.
"Lovely hostess of the forest,
Metsola's enchanting mistress,
Fling aside thine ugly straw-shoes,
Cast away the shoes of birch-bark,
Doff thy soiled and ragged linen,
Doff thy gown of shabby fabric,
Don the bright and festive raiment,
Don the gown of merry-making,
While I stay within thy borders,
While I seek my forest-booty,
Hunt the moose of evil Hisi.
Here my visit will be irksome,
Here thy guest will be ill-humored,
Waiting in thy fields and woodlands,
Hunting here the moose of Lempo,
Finding not the Hisi-ranger,
Shouldst thou give me no enjoyment,
Should I find no joy, nor respite.
Long the eve that gives no pleasure,
Long the day that brings no guerdon!
"Sable-bearded god of forests,
In thy hat and coat of ermine,
Robe thy trees in finest fibers,
Deck thy groves in richest fabrics,
Give the fir-trees shining silver,
Deck with gold the slender balsams,

The Kalevala
Give the spruces copper belting,
And the pine-trees silver girdles,
Give the birches golden flowers,
Deck their stems with silver fret-work,
This their garb in former ages,
When the days and nights were brighter,
When the fir-trees shone like sunlight,
And the birches like the moonbeams;
Honey breathed throughout the forest,
Settled in the glens and highlands
Spices in the meadow-borders,
Oil out-pouring from the lowlands.
"Forest daughter, lovely virgin,
Golden maiden, fair Tulikki,
Second of the Tapio-daughters,
Drive the game within these borders,
To these far-extending snow-fields.
Should the reindeer be too sluggish,
Should the moose-deer move too slowly
Cut a birch-rod from the thicket,
Whip them hither in their beauty,
Drive the wild-moose to my hurdle,
Hither drive the long-sought booty
To the hunter who is watching,
Waiting in the Hisi-forests.
"When the game has started hither,
Keep them in the proper highway,
Hold thy magic hands before them,
Guard them well on either road-side,
That the elk may not escape thee,
May not dart adown some by-path.
Should, perchance, the moose-deer wander
Through some by-way of the forest,
Take him by the ears and antlers,
Hither lead the pride of Lempo.
"If the path be filled with brush-wood
Cast the brush-wood to the road-side;
If the branches cross his pathway,
Break the branches into fragments;
Should a fence of fir or alder
Cross the way that leads him hither.
Make an opening within it,
Open nine obstructing fences;
If the way be crossed by streamlets,
If the path be stopped by rivers,
Make a bridge of silken fabric,
Weaving webs of scarlet color,
Drive the deer-herd gently over,
Lead them gently o'er the waters,
O'er the rivers of thy forests,
O'er the streams of thy dominions.
"Thou, the host of Tapio's mansion,
Gracious host of Tapiola,
Sable-bearded god of woodlands,
Golden lord of Northland forests,
Thou, O Tapio's worthy hostess,
Queen of snowy woods, Mimerkki,
Ancient dame in sky-blue vesture,
Fenland-queen in scarlet ribbons,
Come I to exchange my silver,
To exchange my gold and silver;

Lönnrot

Gold I have, as old as moonlight,
Silver of the age of sunshine,
In the first of years was gathered,
In the heat and pain of battle;
It will rust within my pouches,
Soon will wear away and perish,
If it be not used in trading."
Long the hunter, Lemminkainen,
Glided through the fen and forest,
Sang his songs throughout the woodlands,
Through three mountain glens be sang them,
Sang the forest hostess friendly,
Sang he, also, Tapio friendly,
Friendly, all the forest virgins,
All of Metsola's fair daughters.
Now they start the herds of Lempo,
Start the wild-moose from his shelter,
In the realms of evil Hisi,
Tapio's highest mountain-region;
Now they drive the ranger homeward,
To the open courts of Piru,
To the hero that is waiting,
Hunting for the moose of Juutas.
When the herd had reached the castle,
Lemminkainen threw his lasso
O'er the antlers of the blue-moose,
Settled on the neck and shoulders
Of the mighty moose of Hisi.
Then the hunter, Kaukomieli,
Stroked his captive's neck in safety,
For the moose was well-imprisoned.
Thereupon gay Lemminkainen
Filled with joyance spake as follows:
"Pride of forests, queen of woodlands,
Metsola's enchanted hostess,
Lovely forest dame, Mielikki,
Mother-donor of the mountains,
Take the gold that I have promised,
Come and take away the silver;
Spread thy kerchief well before me,
Spread out here thy silken neck-wrap,
Underneath the golden treasure,
Underneath the shining silver,
that to earth it may not settle,
Scattered on the snows of winter."
Then the hero went a victor
To the dwellings of Pohyola,
And addressed these words to Louhi:
"I have caught the moose of Hisi,
In the Metsola-dominions,
Give, O hostess, give thy daughter,
Give to me thy fairest virgin,
Bride of mine to be hereafter."
Louhi, hostess of the Northland,
Gave this answer to the suitor:
"I will give to thee my daughter,
For thy wife my fairest maiden,
When for me thou'lt put a bridle
On the flaming horse of Hisi,
Rapid messenger of Lempo,
On the Hisi-plains and pastures."

The Kalevala

Nothing daunted, Lemminkainen
Hastened forward to accomplish
Louhi's second test of heroes,
On the cultivated lowlands,
On the sacred fields and forests.
Everywhere he sought the racer,
Sought the fire-expiring stallion,
Fire out-shooting from his nostrils.
Lemminkainen, fearless hunter,
Bearing in his belt his bridle,
On his shoulders, reins and halter,
Sought one day, and then a second,
Finally, upon the third day,
Went he to the Hisi-mountain,
Climbed, and struggled to the summit;
To the east he turned his glances,
Cast his eyes upon the sunrise,
There beheld the flaming courser,
On the heath among the far-trees.
Lempo's fire-expiring stallion
Fire and mingled smoke, out-shooting
From his mouth, and eyes, and nostrils.
Spake the daring Lemminkainen,
This the hero's supplication:
"Ukko, thou O God above me,
Thou that rulest all the storm-clouds,
Open thou the vault of heaven,
Open windows through the ether,
Let the icy rain come falling,
Lot the heavy hailstones shower
On the flaming horse of Hisi,
On the fire-expiring stallion."
Ukko, the benign Creator,
Heard the prayer of Lemminkainen,
Broke apart the dome of heaven,
Rent the heights of heaven asunder,
Sent the iron-hail in showers,
Smaller than the heads of horses,
Larger than the heads of heroes,
On the flaming steed of Lempo,
On the fire-expiring stallion,
On the terror of the Northland.
Lemminkainen, drawing nearer,
Looked with care upon the courser,
Then he spake the words that follow:
"Wonder-steed of mighty Hisi,
Flaming horse of Lempo's mountain,
Bring thy mouth of gold, assenting,
Gently place thy head of silver
In this bright and golden halter,
In this silver-mounted bridle.
I shall never harshly treat thee,
Never make thee fly too fleetly,
On the way to Sariola,
On the tracks of long duration,
To the hostess of Pohyola,
To her magic courts and stables,
Will not lash thee on thy journey;
I shall lead thee gently forward,
Drive thee with the reins of kindness,
Cover thee with silken blankets."

Then the fire-haired steed of Juutas,
Flaming horse of mighty Hisi,
Put his bead of shining silver,
In the bright and golden bead-stall,
In the silver-mounted bridle.
Thus the hero, Lemminkainen,
Easy bridles Lempo's stallion,
Flaming horse of evil Piru;
Lays the bits within his fire-mouth,
On his silver head, the halter,
Mounts the fire-expiring courser,
Brandishes his whip of willow,
Hastens forward on his journey,
Bounding o'er the hills and mountains,
Dashing through the valleys northward,
O'er the snow-capped hills of Lapland,
To the courts of Sariola.
Then the hero, quick dismounting,
Stepped within the court of Louhi,
Thus addressed the Northland hostess:
"I have bridled Lempo's fire-horse,
I have caught the Hisi-racer,
Caught the fire-expiring stallion,
In the Piru plains and pastures,
Ridden him within thy borders;
I have caught the moose of Lempo,
I have done what thou demandest;
Give, I pray thee, now thy daughter,
Give to me thy fairest maiden,
Bride of mine to be forever."
Louhi, hostess of Pohyola,
Made this answer to the suitor:
"I will only give my daughter,
Give to thee my fairest virgin,
Bride of thine to be forever,
When for me the swan thou killest
In the river of Tuoni,
Swimming in the black death-river,
In the sacred stream and whirlpool;
Thou canst try one cross-bow only,
But one arrow from thy quiver."
Then the reckless Lemminkainen,
Handsome hero, Kaukomieli,
Braved the third test of the hero,
Started out to hunt the wild-swan,
Hunt the long-necked, graceful swimmer,
In Tuoni's coal-black river,
In Manala's lower regions.
Quick the daring hunter journeyed,
Hastened off with fearless footsteps,
To the river of Tuoni,
To the sacred stream and whirlpool,
With his bow upon his shoulder,
With his quiver and one arrow.
Nasshut, blind and crippled shepherd,
Wretched shepherd of Pohyola,
Stood beside the death-land river,
Near the sacred stream and whirlpool,
Guarding Tuonela's waters,
Waiting there for Lemminkainen,
Listening there for Kaukomieli,

The Kalevala

Waiting long the hero's coming.
Finally he hears the footsteps
Of the hero on his journey,
Hears the tread of Lemminkainen,
As he journeys nearer, nearer,
To the river of Tuoni,
To the cataract of death-land,
To the sacred stream and whirlpool.
Quick the wretched shepherd, Nasshut,
From the death-stream sends a serpent,
Like an arrow from a cross-bow,
To the heart of Lemminkainen,
Through the vitals of the hero.
Lemminkainen, little conscious,
Hardly knew that be was injured,
Spake these measures as he perished.
"Ah! unworthy is my conduct,
Ah! unwisely have I acted,
That I did not heed my mother,
Did not take her goodly counsel,
Did not learn her words of magic.
Oh I for three words with my mother,
How to live, and bow to suffer,
In this time of dire misfortune,
How to bear the stings of serpents,
Tortures of the reed of waters,
From the stream of Tuonela!
"Ancient mother who hast borne me,
Who hast trained me from my childhood,
Learn, I pray thee, where I linger,
Where alas! thy son is lying,
Where thy reckless hero suffers.
Come, I pray thee, faithful mother,
Come thou quickly, thou art needed,
Come deliver me from torture,
From the death-jaws of Tuoni,
From the sacred stream and whirlpool."
Northland's old and wretched shepherd,
Nasshut, the despised protector
Of the flocks of Sariola,
Throws the dying Lemminkainen,
Throws the hero of the islands,
Into Tuonela's river,
To the blackest stream of death-land,
To the worst of fatal whirlpools.
Lemminkainen, wild and daring,
Helpless falls upon the waters,
Floating down the coal-black current,
Through the cataract and rapids
To the tombs of Tuonela.
There the blood-stained son of death-land,
There Tuoni's son and hero,
Cuts in pieces Lemminkainen,
Chops him with his mighty hatchet,
Till the sharpened axe strikes flint-sparks
From the rocks within his chamber,
Chops the hero into fragments,
Into five unequal portions,
Throws each portion to Tuoni,
In Manala's lowest kingdom,
Speaks these words when he has ended:

Lönnrot

"Swim thou there, wild Lemminkainen,
Flow thou onward in this river,
Hunt forever in these waters,
With thy cross-bow and thine arrow,
Shoot the swan within this empire,
Shoot our water-birds in welcome!"
Thus the hero, Lemminkainen,
Thus the handsome Kaukomieli,
The untiring suitor, dieth
In the river of Tuoni,
In the death-realm of Manala.

RUNE XV
LEMMINKAINEN'S RESTORATION

Lemminkainen's aged mother
Anxious roams about the islands,
Anxious wonders in her chambers,
What the fate of Lemminkainen,
Why her son so long has tarried;
Thinks that something ill has happened
To her hero in Pohyola.
Sad, indeed, the mother's anguish,
As in vain she waits his coming,
As in vain she asks the question,
Where her daring son is roaming,
Whether to the fir-tree mountain,
Whether to the distant heath-land,
Or upon the broad-sea's ridges,
On the floods and rolling waters,
To the war's contending armies,
To the heat and din of battle,
Steeped in blood of valiant heroes,
Evidence of fatal warfare.
Daily does the wife Kyllikki
Look about her vacant chamber,
In the home of Lemminkainen,
At the court of Kaukomieli;
Looks at evening, looks at morning,
Looks, perchance, upon his hair-brush,
Sees alas! the blood-drops oozing,
Oozing from the golden bristles,
And the blood-drops, scarlet-colored.
Then the beauteous wife, Kyllikki,
Spake these words in deeps of anguish:
"Dead or wounded is my husband,
Or at best is filled with trouble,
Lost perhaps in Northland forests,
In some glen unknown to heroes,
Since alas! the blood is flowing
From the brush of Lemminkainen,
Red drops oozing from the bristles."
Thereupon the anxious mother
Looks upon the bleeding hair-brush
And begins this wail of anguish:
"Woe is me, my life hard-fated,
Woe is me, all joy departed!
For alas! my son and hero,
Valiant hero of the islands,
Son of trouble and misfortune!
Some sad fate has overtaken
My ill-fated Lemminkainen!
Blood is flowing from his hair-brush,
Oozing from its golden bristles,
And the drops are scarlet-colored."
Quick her garment's hem she clutches,
On her arm she throws her long-robes,
Fleetly flies upon her journey;

Lönnrot

With her might she hastens northward,
Mountains tremble from her footsteps,
Valleys rise and heights are lowered,
Highlands soon become as lowlands,
All the hills and valleys levelled.
Soon she gains the Northland village,
Quickly asks about her hero,
These the words the mother utters:
"O thou hostess of Pohyola,
Where hast thou my Lemminkainen?
Tell me of my son and hero!"
Louhi, hostess of the Northland,
Gives this answer to the mother:
"Nothing know I of thy hero,
Of the hero of the islands;
Where thy son may be I know not,
Cannot lend the information;
Once I gave thy son a courser,
Hitched the racer to his snow-sledge,
This the last of Lemminkainen;
May perchance be drowned in Wuhne,
Frozen In the icy ocean,
Fallen prey to wolves in hunger,
In a bear's den may have perished."
Lemminkainen's mother answers:
"Thou art only speaking falsehoods,
Northland wolves cannot devour us,
Nor the bears kill Kaukomieli;
He can slay the wolves of Pohya
With the fingers of his left hand;
Bears of Northland he would silence
With the magic of his singing.
"Hostess of Pohyola, tell me
Whither thou hast sent my hero;
I shall burst thy many garners,
Shall destroy the magic Sampo,
If thou dost not tell me truly
Where to find my Lemminkainen."
Spake the hostess of Pohyola:
"I have well thy hero treated,
Well my court has entertained him,
Gave him of my rarest viands,
Fed him at my well-filled tables,
Placed him in a boat of copper,
Thus to float adown the current,
This the last of Lemminkainen;
Cannot tell where he has wandered.
Whether in the foam of waters,
Whether in the boiling torrent,
Whether in the drowning whirlpool."
Lemminkainen's mother answers:
Thou again art speaking falsely;
Tell me now the truth I pray thee,
Make an end of thy deception,
Where is now my Lemminkainen,
Whither hast thou sent my hero,
Young and daring son of Kalew?
If a third time thou deceivest,
I will send thee plagues, unnumbered,
I will send thee fell destruction,
Certain death will overtake thee."

The Kalevala

Spake the hostess of Pohyola:
"This the third time that I answer,
This the truth that I shall tell thee:
I have sent the Kalew-hero
To the Hisi-fields and forests,
There to hunt the moose of Lempo;
Sent him then to catch the fire-horse,
Catch the fire-expiring stallion,
On the distant plains of Juutas,
In the realm of cruel Hisi.
Then I sent him to the Death-stream,
In the kingdom of Tuoni,
With his bow and but one arrow,
There to shoot the swan as dowry
For my best and fairest daughter;
Have not heard about thy hero
Since he left for Tuonela;
May in misery have fallen,
May have perished in Manala;
Has not come to ask my daughter,
Has not come to woo the maiden,
Since he left to hunt the death-swan."
Now the mother seeks her lost one,
For her son she weeps and trembles,
Like the wolf she bounds through fenlands,
Like the bear, through forest thickets,
Like the wild-boar, through the marshes,
Like the hare, along the sea-coast,
To the sea-point, like the hedgehog
Like the wild-duck swims the waters,
Casts the rubbish from her pathway,
Tramples down opposing brush-wood,
Stops at nothing in her journey
Seeks a long time for her hero,
Seeks, and seeks, and does not find him.
Now she asks the trees the question,
And the forest gives this answer:
"We have care enough already,
Cannot think about thy matters;
Cruel fates have we to battle,
Pitiful our own misfortunes!
We are felled and chopped in pieces,
Cut in blocks for hero-fancy,
We are burned to death as fuel,
No one cares how much we suffer."
Now again the mother wanders,
Seeks again her long-lost hero,
Seeks, and seeks, and does not find him.
Paths arise and come to meet her,
And she questions thus the pathways:
"Paths of hope that God has fashioned,
Have ye seen my Lemminkainen,
Has my son and golden hero
Travelled through thy many kingdoms?"
Sad, the many pathways answer:
"We ourselves have cares sufficient,
Cannot watch thy son and hero,
Wretched are the lives of pathways,
Deep indeed our own misfortunes;
We are trodden by, the red-deer,
By the wolves, and bears, and roebucks,

Driven o'er by heavy cart-wheels,
By the feet of dogs are trodden,
Trodden under foot of heroes,
Foot-paths for contending armies."
Seeks again the frantic mother,
Seeks her long-lost son and hero,
Seeks, and seeks, and does not find him;
Finds the Moon within her orbit,
Asks the Moon in pleading measures:
"Golden Moon, whom God has stationed
In the heavens, the Sun's companion,
Hast thou seen my Kaukomieli,
Hast thou seen my silver apple,
Anywhere in thy dominions? "
Thus the golden Moon makes answer:
"I have trouble all-sufficient,
Cannot watch thy daring hero;
Long the journey I must travel,
Sad the fate to me befallen,
Pitiful mine own misfortunes,
All alone the nights to wander,
Shine alone without a respite,
In the winter ever watching,
In the summer sink and perish."
Still the mother seeks, and wanders,
Seeks, and does not find her hero,
Sees the Sun in the horizon,
And the mother thus entreats him:
Silver Sun, whom God has fashioned,
Thou that giveth warmth and comfort,
Hast thou lately seen my hero,
Hast thou seen my Lemminkainen,
Wandering in thy dominions?"
Thus the Sun in kindness answers:
"Surely has thy hero perished,
To ingratitude a victim;
Lemminkainen died and vanished
In Tuoni's fatal river,
In the waters of Manala,
In the sacred stream and whirlpool,
In the cataract and rapids,
Sank within the drowning current
To the realm of Tuonela,
To Manala's lower regions."
Lemminkainen's mother weeping,
Wailing in the deeps of anguish,
Mourns the fate of Kaukomieli,
Hastens to the Northland smithy,
To the forge of Ilmarinen,
These the words the mother utters:
"Ilmarinen, metal-artist,
Thou that long ago wert forging,
Forging earth a concave cover,
Yesterday wert forging wonders,
Forge thou now, immortal blacksmith,
Forge a rake with shaft of copper,
Forge the teeth of strongest metal,
Teeth in length a hundred fathoms,
And five hundred long the handle."
Ilmarinen does as bidden,
Makes the rake in full perfection.

The Kalevala

Lemminkainen's anxious mother
Takes the magic rake and hastens
To the river of Tuoni,
Praying to the Sun as follows:
"Thou, O Sun, by God created,
Thou that shinest on thy Maker,
Shine for me in heat of magic,
Give me warmth, and strength, and courage,
Shine a third time full of power,
Lull to sleep the wicked people,
Still the people of Manala,
Quiet all Tuoni's empire."
Thereupon the sun of Ukko,
Dearest child of the Creator,
Flying through the groves of Northland,
Sitting on a curving birch-tree,
Shines a little while in ardor,
Shines again in greater fervor,
Shines a third time full of power,
Lulls to sleep the wicked people
In the Manala home and kingdom,
Still the heroes with their broadswords,
Makes the lancers halt and totter,
Stills the stoutest of the spearmen,
Quiets Tuoni's ghastly empire.
Now the Sun retires in magic,
Hovers here and there a moment
Over Tuoni's hapless sleepers,
Hastens upward to his station,
To his Jumala home and kingdom.
Lemminkainen's faithful mother
Takes the rake of magic metals,
Rakes the Tuoni river bottoms,
Rakes the cataract and whirlpool,
Rakes the swift and boiling current
Of the sacred stream of death-land,
In the Manala home and kingdom.
Searching for her long-lost hero,
Rakes a long time, finding nothing;
Now she wades the river deeper,
To her belt in mud and water,
Deeper, deeper, rakes the death-stream,
Rakes the river's deepest caverns,
Raking up and down the current,
Till at last she finds his tunic,
Heavy-hearted, finds his jacket;
Rakes again and rakes unceasing,
Finds the hero's shoes and stockings,
Sorely troubled, finds these relics;
Now she wades the river deeper,
Rakes the Manala shoals and shallows,
Rakes the deeps at every angle;
As she draws the rake the third time
From the Tuoni shores and waters,
In the rake she finds the body
Of her long-lost Lemminkainen,
In the metal teeth entangled,
In the rake with copper handle.
Thus the reckless Lemminkainen,
Thus the son of Kalevala,
Was recovered from the bottom

Of the Manala lake and river.
There were wanting many fragments,
Half the head, a hand, a fore-arm,
Many other smaller portions,
Life, above all else, was missing.
Then the mother, well reflecting,
Spake these words in bitter weeping:
"From these fragments, with my magic,
I will bring to life my hero."
Hearing this, the raven answered,
Spake these measures to the mother:
"There is not in these a hero,
Thou canst not revive these fragments;
Eels have fed upon his body,
On his eyes have fed the whiting;
Cast the dead upon the waters,
On the streams of Tuonela,
Let him there become a walrus,
Or a seal, or whale, or porpoise."
Lemminkainen's mother does not
Cast the dead upon the waters,
On the streams of Tuonela,
She again with hope and courage,
Rakes the river lengthwise, crosswise,
Through the Manala pools and caverns,
Rakes up half the head, a fore-arm,
Finds a hand and half the back-bone,
Many other smaller portions;
Shapes her son from all the fragments,
Shapes anew her Lemminkainen,
Flesh to flesh with skill she places,
Gives the bones their proper stations,
Binds one member to the other,
Joins the ends of severed vessels,
Counts the threads of all the venules,
Knits the parts in apposition;
Then this prayer the mother offers:
"Suonetar, thou slender virgin,
Goddess of the veins of heroes,
Skilful spinner of the vessels,
With thy slender, silver spindle,
With thy spinning-wheel of copper,
Set in frame of molten silver,
Come thou hither, thou art needed;
Bring the instruments for mending,
Firmly knit the veins together,
At the end join well the venules,
In the wounds that still are open,
In the members that are injured.
"Should this aid be inefficient;
There is living in the ether,
In a boat enriched with silver,
In a copper boat, a maiden,
That can bring to thee assistance.
Come, O maiden, from the ether,
Virgin from the belt of heaven,
Row throughout these veins, O maiden,
Row through all these lifeless members,
Through the channels of the long-bones,
Row through every form of tissue.
Set the vessels in their places,

The Kalevala
Lay the heart in right position,
Make the pulses beat together,
Join the smallest of the veinlets,
And unite with skill the sinews.
Take thou now a slender needle,
Silken thread within its eyelet,
Ply the silver needle gently,
Sew with care the wounds together.
"Should this aid be inefficient,
Thou, O God, that knowest all things,
Come and give us thine assistance,
Harness thou thy fleetest racer
Call to aid thy strongest courser,
In thy scarlet sledge come swiftly,
Drive through all the bones and channels,
Drive throughout these lifeless tissues,
Drive thy courser through each vessel,
Bind the flesh and bones securely,
In the joints put finest silver,
Purest gold in all the fissures.
"Where the skin is broken open,
Where the veins are torn asunder,
Mend these injuries with magic;
Where the blood has left the body,
There make new blood flow abundant;
Where the bones are rudely broken,
Set the parts in full perfection;
Where the flesh is bruised and loosened,
Touch the wounds with magic balsam,
Do not leave a part imperfect;
Bone, and vein, and nerve, and sinew,
Heart, and brain, and gland, and vessel,
Heal as Thou alone canst heal them."
These the means the mother uses,
Thus she joins the lifeless members,
Thus she heals the death-like tissues,
Thus restores her son and hero
To his former life and likeness;
All his veins are knit together,
All their ends are firmly fastened,
All the parts in apposition,
Life returns, but speech is wanting,
Deaf and dumb, and blind, and senseless.
Now the mother speaks as follows:
"Where may I procure the balsam,
Where the drops of magic honey,
To anoint my son and hero,
Thus to heal my Lemminkainen,
That again his month may open,
May again begin his singing,
Speak again in words of wonder,
Sing again his incantations?
"Tiny bee, thou honey-birdling,
Lord of all the forest flowers,
Fly away and gather honey,
Bring to me the forest-sweetness,
Found in Metsola's rich gardens,
And in Tapio's fragrant meadows,
From the petals of the flowers,
From the blooming herbs and grasses,
Thus to heal my hero's anguish,

Lönnrot

Thus to heal his wounds of evil."
Thereupon the honey-birdling
Flies away on wings of swiftness,
Into Metsola's rich gardens,
Into Tapio's flowery meadows,
Gathers sweetness from the meadows,
With the tongue distills the honey
From the cups of seven flowers,
From the bloom of countless grasses;
Quick from Metsola returning,
Flying, humming darting onward,
With his winglets honey-laden,
With the store of sweetest odors,
To the mother brings the balsam.
Lemminkainen's anxious mother
Takes the balm of magic virtues,
And anoints the injured hero,
Heals his wounds and stills his anguish;
But the balm is inefficient,
For her son is deaf and speechless.
Then again out-speaks the mother:
Lemminkainen's Restoration.
"Little bee, my honey-birdling,
Fly away in one direction,
Fly across the seven oceans,
In the eighth, a magic island,
Where the honey is enchanted,
To the distant Turi-castles,
To the chambers of Palwoinen;
There the honey is effective,
There, the wonder-working balsam,
This may heal the wounded hero;
Bring me of this magic ointment,
That I may anoint his eyelids,
May restore his injured senses."
Thereupon the honey-birdling
Flew away o'er seven oceans,
To the old enchanted island;
Flies one day, and then a second,
On the verdure does not settle,
Does not rest upon the flowers;
Flies a third day, fleetly onward,
Till a third day evening brings him
To the island in the ocean,
To the meadows rich in honey,
To the cataract and fire-flow,
To the sacred stream and whirlpool.
There the honey was preparing,
There the magic balm distilling
In the tiny earthen vessels,
In the burnished copper kettles,
Smaller than a maiden's thimble,
Smaller than the tips of fingers.
Faithfully the busy insect
Gathers the enchanted honey
From the magic Turi-cuplets
In the chambers of Palwoinen.
Time had gone but little distance,
Ere the bee came loudly humming
Flying fleetly, honey-laden;
In his arms were seven vessels,

The Kalevala

Seven, the vessels on each shoulder;
All were filled with honey-balsam,
With the balm of magic virtues.
Lemminkainen's tireless mother
Quick anoints her speechless hero,
With the magic Turi-balsam,
With the balm of seven virtues;
Nine the times that she anoints him
With the honey of Palwoinen,
With the wonder-working balsam;
But the balm is inefficient,
For the hero still is speechless.
Then again out-speaks the mother:
"Honey-bee, thou ether birdling,
Fly a third time on thy journey,
Fly away to high Jumala,
Fly thou to the seventh heaven,
Honey there thou'lt find abundant,
Balsam of the highest virtue,
Only used by the Creator,
Only made from the breath of Ukko.
God anoints his faithful children,
With the honey of his wisdom,
When they feel the pangs of sorrow,
When they meet the powers of evil.
Dip thy winglets in this honey,
Steep thy plumage in His sweetness,
Hither bring the all-sufficient
Balsam of the great Creator;
This will still my hero's anguish,
This will heal his wounded tissues,
This restore his long-lost vision,
Make the Northland hills re-echo
With the magic of his singing,
With his wonderful enchantment."
Thus the honey-bee made answer:
"I can never fly to heaven,
To the seventh of the heavens,
To the distant home of Ukko,
With these wings of little virtue."
Lemminkainen's mother answered:
"Thou canst surely fly to heaven,
To the seventh of the heavens,
O'er the Moon, beneath the sunshine,
Through the dim and distant starlight.
On the first day, flying upward,
Thou wilt near the Moon in heaven,
Fan the brow of Kootamoinen;
On the second thou canst rest thee
On the shoulders of Otava;
On the third day, flying higher,
Rest upon the seven starlets,
On the heads of Hetewanè;
Short the journey that is left thee,
Inconsiderable the distance
To the home of mighty Ukko,
To the dwellings of the blessed."
Thereupon the bee arising,
From the earth flies swiftly upward,
Hastens on with graceful motion,
By his tiny wings borne heavenward,

Lönnrot

In the paths of golden moonbeams,
Touches on the Moon's bright borders,
Fans the brow of Kootamoinen,
Rests upon Otava's shoulders,
Hastens to the seven starlets.,
To the heads of Hetewanè,
Flies to the Creator's castle,
To the home of generous Ukko,
Finds the remedy preparing,
Finds the balm of life distilling,
In the silver-tinted caldrons,
In the purest golden kettles;
On one side, heart-easing honey,
On a second, balm of joyance,
On the third, life-giving balsam.
Here the magic bee, selecting,
Culls the sweet, life-giving balsam,
Gathers too, heart-easing honey,
Heavy-laden hastens homeward.
Time had traveled little distance,
Ere the busy bee came humming
To the anxious mother waiting,
In his arms a hundred cuplets,
And a thousand other vessels,
Filled with honey, filled with balsam,
Filled with the balm of the Creator.
Lemminkainen's mother quickly
Takes them on her, tongue and tests them,
Finds a balsam all-sufficient.
Then the mother spake as follows:
"I have found the long-sought balsam,
Found the remedy of Ukko,
Where-with God anoints his people,
Gives them life, and faith, and wisdom,
Heals their wounds and stills their anguish,
Makes them strong against temptation,
Guards them from the evil-doers."
Now the mother well anointing,
Heals her son, the magic singer,
Eyes, and ears, and tongue, and temples,
Breaks, and cuts, and seams, anointing,
Touching well the life-blood centres,
Speaks these words of magic import
To the sleeping Lemminkainen:
"Wake, arise from out thy slumber,
From the worst of low conditions,
From thy state of dire misfortune!"
Slowly wakes the son and hero,
Rises from the depths of slumber,
Speaks again in magic accents,
These the first words of the singer:
"Long, indeed, have I been sleeping,
Long unconscious of existence,
But my sleep was full of sweetness,
Sweet the sleep in Tuonela,
Knowing neither joy nor sorrow!"
This the answer of his mother:
"Longer still thou wouldst have slumbered,
Were it not for me, thy mother;
Tell me now, my son beloved,
Tell me that I well may hear thee,

The Kalevala
Who enticed thee to Manala,
To the river of Tuoni,
To the fatal stream and whirlpool?"
Then the hero, Lemminkainen,
Gave this answer to his mother:
"Nasshut, the decrepit shepherd
Of the flocks of Sariola,
Blind, and halt, and poor, and wretched,
And to whom I did a favor;
From the slumber-land of envy
Nasshut sent me to Manala,
To the river of Tuoni;
Sent a serpent from the waters,
Sent an adder from the death-stream,
Through the heart of Lemminkainen;
Did not recognize the serpent,
Could not speak the serpent-language,
Did not know the sting of adders."
Spake again the ancient mother:
"O thou son of little insight,
Senseless hero, fool-magician,
Thou didst boast betimes thy magic
To enchant the wise enchanters,
On the dismal shores of Lapland,
Thou didst think to banish heroes,
From the borders of Pohyola;
Didst not know the sting of serpents,
Didst not know the reed of waters,
Nor the magic word-protector!
Learn the origin of serpents,
Whence the poison of the adder.
"In the floods was born the serpent,
From the marrow of the gray-duck,
From the brain of ocean-swallows;
Suoyatar had made saliva,
Cast it on the waves of ocean,
Currents drove it outward, onward,
Softly shone the sun upon it,
By the winds 'twas gently cradled,
Gently nursed by winds and waters,
By the waves was driven shoreward,
Landed by the surging billows.
Thus the serpent, thing of evil,
Filling all the world with trouble,
Was created in the waters
Born from Suoyatar, its maker."
Then the mother of the hero
Rocked her son to rest and comfort,
Rocked him to his former being,
To his former life and spirit,
Into greater magic powers;
Wiser, handsomer than ever
Grew the hero of the islands;
But his heart was full of trouble,
And his mother, ever watchful,
Asked the cause of his dejection.
This is Lemminkainen's answer:
"This the cause of all my sorrow;
Far away my heart is roaming,
All my thoughts forever wander
To the Northland's blooming virgins,

Lönnrot

To the maids of braided tresses.
Northland's ugly hostess, Louhi,
Will not give to me her daughter,
Fairest maiden of Pohyola,
Till I kill the swan of Mana,
With my bow and but one arrow,
In the river of Tuoni.
Lemminkainen's mother answers,
In the sacred stream and whirlpool.
"Let the swan swim on in safety,
Give the water-bird his freedom,
In the river of Manala,
In the whirlpool of Tuoni;
Leave the maiden in the Northland.,
With her charms and fading beauty;
With thy fond and faithful mother,
Go at once to Kalevala,
To thy native fields and fallows.
Praise thy fortune, all sufficient,
Praise, above all else, thy Maker.
Ukko gave thee aid when needed,
Thou wert saved by thy Creator,
From thy long and hopeless slumber,
In the waters of Tuoni,
In the chambers of Manala.
I unaided could not save thee,
Could not give the least assistance;
God alone, omniscient Ukko,
First and last of the creators,
Can revive the dead and dying,
Can protect his worthy people
From the waters of Manala, .
From the fatal stream and whirlpool,
In the kingdom of Tuoni."
Lemminkainen, filled with wisdom,
With his fond and faithful mother,
Hastened straightway on his journey
To his distant home and kindred,
To the Wainola fields and meadows,
To the plains of Kalevala.

* * * * *

Here I leave my Kaukomieli,
Leave my hero Lemminkainen,
Long I leave him from my singing,
Turn my song to other heroes,
Send it forth on other pathways,
Sing some other golden legend.

RUNE XVI
WAINAMOINEN'S BOAT-BUILDING

Wainamoinen, ancient minstrel,
The eternal wisdom-singer,
For his boat was working lumber,
Working long upon his vessel,
On a fog-point jutting seaward,
On an island, forest-covered;
But the lumber failed the master,
Beams were wanting for his vessel,
Beams and scantling, ribs and flooring.
Who will find for him the lumber,
Who procure the timber needed
For the boat of Wainamoinen,
For the bottom of his vessel?
Pellerwoinen of the prairies,
Sampsa, slender-grown and ancient,
He will seek the needful timber,
He procure the beams of oak-wood
For the boat of Wainamoinen,
For the bottom of his vessel.
Soon he starts upon his journey
To the eastern fields and forests,
Hunts throughout the Northland mountain
To a second mountain wanders,
To a third he hastens, searching,
Golden axe upon his shoulder,
In his hand a copper hatchet.
Comes an aspen-tree to meet him
Of the height of seven fathoms.
Sampsa takes his axe of copper,
Starts to fell the stately aspen,
But the aspen quickly halting,
Speaks these words to Pellerwoinen:
"Tell me, hero, what thou wishest,
What the service thou art needing?"
Sampsa Pellerwoinen answers:
"This indeed, the needed service
That I ask of thee, O aspen:
Need thy lumber for a vessel,
For the boat of Wainamoinen,
Wisest of the wisdom-singers."
Quick and wisely speaks the aspen,
Thus its hundred branches answer:
"All the boats that have been fashioned
From my wood have proved but failures;
Such a vessel floats a distance,
Then it sinks upon the bottom
Of the waters it should travel.
All my trunk is filled with hollows,
Three times in the summer seasons
Worms devour my stem and branches,
Feed upon my heart and tissues."
Pellerwoinen leaves the aspen,
Hunts again through all the forest,

Lönnrot

Wanders through the woods of Northland,
Where a pine-tree comes to meet him,
Of the height of fourteen fathoms.
With his axe he chops the pine-tree,
Strikes it with his axe of copper,
As he asks the pine this question:
"Will thy trunk give worthy timber
For the boat of Wainamoinen,
Wisest of the wisdom-singers?"
Loudly does the pine-tree answer:
"All the ships that have been fashioned
From my body are unworthy;
I am full of imperfections,
Cannot give thee needed timber
Wherewithal to build thy vessel;
Ravens live within ray branches,
Build their nests and hatch their younglings
Three times in my trunk in summer."
Sampsa leaves the lofty pine-tree,
Wanders onward, onward, onward,
To the woods of gladsome summer,
Where an oak-tree comes to meet him,
In circumference, three fathoms,
And the oak he thus addresses:
"Ancient oak-tree, will thy body
Furnish wood to build a vessel,
Build a boat for Wainamoinen,
Master-boat for the magician,
Wisest of the wisdom-singers?"
Thus the oak replies to Sampsa:
"I for thee will gladly furnish
Wood to build the hero's vessel;
I am tall, and sound, and hardy,
Have no flaws within my body;
Three times in the months of summer,
In the warmest of the seasons,
Does the sun dwell in my tree-top,
On my trunk the moonlight glimmers,
In my branches sings the cuckoo,
In my top her nestlings slumber."
Now the ancient Pellerwoinen
Takes the hatchet from his shoulder,
Takes his axe with copper handle,
Chops the body of the oak-tree;
Well he knows the art of chopping.
Soon he fells the tree majestic,
Fells the mighty forest-monarch,
With his magic axe and power.
From the stems he lops the branches,
Splits the trunk in many pieces,
Fashions lumber for the bottom,
Countless boards, and ribs, and braces,
For the singer's magic vessel,
For the boat of the magician.
Wainamoinen, old and skilful,
The eternal wonder-worker,
Builds his vessel with enchantment,
Builds his boat by art of magic,
From the timber of the oak-tree,
From its posts, and planks, and flooring.
Sings a song, and joins the frame-work;

The Kalevala

Sings a second, sets the siding;
Sings a third time, sets the row-locks;
Fashions oars, and ribs, and rudder,
Joins the sides and ribs together.
When the ribs were firmly fastened,
When the sides were tightly jointed,
Then alas! three words were wanting,
Lost the words of master-magic,
How to fasten in the ledges,
How the stern should be completed,
How complete the boat's forecastle.
Then the ancient Wainamoinen,
Wise and wonderful enchanter,
Heavy-hearted spake as follows:
"Woe is me, my life hard-fated!
Never will this magic vessel
Pass in safety o'er the water,
Never ride the rough sea-billows."
Then he thought and long considered,
Where to find these words of magic,
Find the lost-words of the Master:
"From the brains of countless swallows,
From the heads of swans in dying,
From the plumage of the gray-duck?"
For these words the hero searches,
Kills of swans a goodly number,
Kills a flock of fattened gray-duck,
Kills of swallows countless numbers,
Cannot find the words of magic,
Not the lost-words of the Master.
Wainamoinen, wisdom-singer,
Still reflected and debated:
"I perchance may find the lost-words
On the tongue of summer-reindeer,
In the mouth of the white squirrel."
Now again he hunts the lost-words,
Hastes to find the magic sayings,
Kills a countless host of reindeer,
Kills a rafterful of squirrels,
Finds of words a goodly number,
But they are of little value,
Cannot find the magic lost-word.
Long he thought and well considered:
"I can find of words a hundred
In the dwellings of Tuoni,
In the Manala fields and castles."
Wainamoinen quickly journeys
To the kingdom of Tuoni,
There to find the ancient wisdom,
There to learn the secret doctrine;
Hastens on through fen and forest,
Over meads and over marshes,
Through the ever-rising woodlands,
Journeys one week through the brambles,
And a second through the hazels,
Through the junipers the third week,
When appear Tuoni's islands,
And the Manala fields and castles.
Wainamoinen, brave and ancient,
Calls aloud in tones of thunder,
To the Tuonela deeps and dungeons,

Lönnrot

And to Manala's magic castle:
"Bring a boat, Tuoni's daughter,
Bring a ferry-boat, O maiden,
That may bear me o'er this channel,
O'er this black and fatal river."
Quick the daughter of Tuoni,
Magic maid of little stature,
Tiny virgin of Manala,
Tiny washer of the linen,
Tiny cleaner of the dresses,
At the river of Tuoni,
In Manala's ancient castles,
Speaks these words to Wainamoinen,
Gives this answer to his calling:
"Straightway will I bring the row-boat,
When the reasons thou hast given
Why thou comest to Manala
In a hale and active body."
Wainamoinen, old and artful.,
Gives this answer to the maiden:
"I was brought here by Tuoni,
Mana raised me from the coffin."
Speaks the maiden of Manala:
"This a tale of wretched liars;
Had Tuoni brought thee hither,
Mana raised thee from the coffin,
Then Tuoni would be with thee,
Manalainen too would lead thee,
With Tuoni's hat upon thee,
On thy hands, the gloves of Mana;
Tell the truth now, Wainamoinen,
What has brought thee to Manala?"
Wainamoinen, artful hero,
Gives this answer, still finessing:
"Iron brought me to Manala,
To the kingdom of Tuoni."
Speaks the virgin of the death-land,
Mana's wise and tiny daughter:
"Well I know that this is falsehood,
Had the iron brought thee hither,
Brought thee to Tuoni's kingdom,
Blood would trickle from thy vesture,
And the blood-drops, scarlet-colored.
Speak the truth now, Wainamoinen,
This the third time that I ask thee."
Wainamoinen, little heeding,
Still finesses to the daughter:
"Water brought me to Manala,
To the kingdom of Tuoui."
This the tiny maiden's answer:
"Well I know thou speakest falsely;
If the waters of Manala,
If the cataract and whirlpool,
Or the waves had brought thee hither,
From thy robes the drops would trickle,
Water drip from all thy raiment.
Tell the truth and I will serve thee,
What has brought thee to Manala?"
Then the wilful Wainamoinen
Told this falsehood to the maiden:
"Fire has brought me to Manala,

The Kalevala

To the kingdom of Tuoni."
Spake again Tuoni's daughter:
"Well I know the voice of falsehood.
If the fire had brought thee hither,
Brought thee to Tuoni's empire,
Singed would be thy locks and eyebrows,
And thy beard be crisped and tangled.
O, thou foolish Wainamoinen,
If I row thee o'er the ferry,
Thou must speak the truth in answer,
This the last time I will ask thee;
Make an end of thy deception.
What has brought thee to Manala,
Still unharmed by pain or sickness,
Still untouched by Death's dark angel
Spake the ancient Wainamoinen:
"At the first I spake, not truly,
Now I give thee rightful answer:
I a boat with ancient wisdom,
Fashioned with my powers of magic,
Sang one day and then a second,
Sang the third day until evening,
When I broke the magic main-spring,
Broke my magic sledge in pieces,
Of my song the fleetest runners;
Then I come to Mana's kingdom,
Came to borrow here a hatchet,
Thus to mend my sledge of magic,
Thus to join the parts together.
Send the boat now quickly over,
Send me, quick, Tuoni's row-boat,
Help me cross this fatal river,
Cross the channel of Manala."
Spake the daughter of Tuoni,
Mana's maiden thus replying:
"Thou art sure a stupid fellow,
Foresight wanting, judgment lacking,
Having neither wit nor wisdom,
Coming here without a reason,
Coming to Tuoni's empire;
Better far if thou shouldst journey
To thy distant home and kindred;
Man they that visit Mana,
Few return from Maria's kingdom."
Spake the good old Wainamoinen:
"Women old retreat from danger,
Not a man of any courage,
Not the weakest of the heroes.
Bring thy boat, Tuoni's daughter,
Tiny maiden of Manala,
Come and row me o'er the ferry."
Mana's daughter does as bidden,
Brings her boat to Wainamoinen,
Quickly rows him through the channel,
O'er the black and fatal river,
To the kingdom of Manala,
Speaks these words to the magician:
"Woe to thee! O Wainamoinen!
Wonderful indeed, thy magic,
Since thou comest to Manala,
Comest neither dead nor dying."

Lönnrot

Tuonetar, the death-land hostess,
Ancient hostess of Tuoni,
Brings him pitchers filled with strong-beer,
Fills her massive golden goblets,
Speaks these measures to the stranger:
"Drink, thou ancient Wainamoinen,
Drink the beer of king Tuoni!"
Wainamoinen, wise and cautious,
Carefully inspects the liquor,
Looks a long time in the pitchers,
Sees the spawning of the black-frogs,
Sees the young of poison-serpents,
Lizards, worms, and writhing adders,
Thus addresses Tuonetar:
"Have not come with this intention,
Have not come to drink thy poisons,
Drink the beer of Tuonela;
Those that drink Tuoni's liquors,
Those that sip the cups of Mana,
Court the Devil and destruction,
End their lives in want and ruin."
Tuonetar makes this answer:
"Ancient minstrel, Wainamoinen,
Tell me what has brought thee hither,
Brought thee to the, realm of Mana,
To the courts of Tuonela,
Ere Tuoni sent his angels
To thy home in Kalevala,
There to cut thy magic life-thread."
Spake the singer, Wainamoinen:
"I was building me a vessel,
At my craft was working, singing,
Needed three words of the Master,
How to fasten in the ledges,
How the stern should be completed,
How complete the boat's forecastle.
This the reason of my coming
To the empire of Tuoni,
To the castles of Manala:
Came to learn these magic sayings,
Learn the lost-words of the Master."
Spake the hostess, Tuonetar:
"Mana never gives these sayings,
Canst not learn them from Tuoni,
Not the lost-words of the Master;
Thou shalt never leave this kingdom,
Never in thy magic life-time,
Never go to Kalevala,
To Wainola's peaceful meadows.
To thy distant home and country."
Quick the hostess, Tuonetar,
Waves her magic wand of slumber
O'er the head of Wainamoinen,
Puts to rest the wisdom-hero,
Lays him on the couch of Mana,
In the robes of living heroes,
Deep the sleep that settles o'er him.
In Manala lived a woman,
In the kingdom of Tuoni,
Evil witch and toothless wizard,
Spinner of the threads of iron,

The Kalevala
Moulder of the bands of copper,
Weaver of a hundred fish-nets,
Of a thousand nets of copper,
Spinning in the days of summer,
Weaving in the winter evenings,
Seated on a rock in water.
In the kingdom of Tuoni
Lived a man, a wicked wizard,
Three the fingers of the hero,
Spinner he of iron meshes,
Maker too of nets of copper,
Countless were his nets of metal,
Moulded on a rock in water,
Through the many days of summer.
Mana's son with crooked fingers,
Iron-pointed, copper fingers,
Pulls of nets, at least a thousand,
Through the river of Tuoni,
Sets them lengthwise, sets them crosswise,
In the fatal, darksome river,
That the sleeping Wainamomen,
Friend and brother of the waters,
May not leave the isle of Mana,
Never in the course of ages,
Never leave the death-land castles,
Never while the moonlight glimmers
On the empire of Tuoni.
Wainamoinen, wise and wary,
Rising from his couch of slumber,
Speaks these words as he is waking:
"Is there not some mischief brewing,
Am I not at last in danger,
In the chambers of Tuoni,
In the Manala home and household?"
Quick he changes his complexion,
Changes too his form and feature,
Slips into another body;
Like a serpent in a circle,
Rolls black-dyed upon the waters;
Like a snake among the willows,
Crawls he like a worm of magic,
Like an adder through the grasses,
Through the coal-black stream of death-land,
Through a thousand nets of copper
Interlaced with threads of iron,
From the kingdom of Tuoni,
From the castles of Manala.
Mana's son, the wicked wizard,
With his iron-pointed fingers,
In the early morning hastens
To his thousand nets of copper,
Set within the Tuoni river,
Finds therein a countless number
Of the death-stream fish and serpents;
Does not find old Wainamoinen,
Wainamoinen, wise and wary,
Friend and fellow of the waters.
When the wonder-working hero
Had escaped from Tuonela,
 Spake he thus in supplication:
"Gratitude to thee, O Ukko,

Lönnrot

Do I bring for thy protection!
Never suffer other heroes,
 Of thy heroes not the wisest,
To transgress the laws of nature;
Never let another singer,
While he lives within the body,
Cross the river of Tuoni,
As thou lovest thy creations.
Many heroes cross the channel,
Cross the fatal stream of Mana,
Few return to tell the story,
Few return from Tuonela,
From Manala's courts and castles."
Wainamoinen calls his people,
On the plains of Kalevala,
Speaks these words of ancient wisdom,
To the young men, to the maidens,
To the rising generation:
"Every child of Northland, listen:
If thou wishest joy eternal,
Never disobey thy parents,
Never evil treat the guiltless,
Never wrong the feeble-minded,
Never harm thy weakest fellow,
Never stain thy lips with falsehood,
Never cheat thy trusting neighbor,
Never injure thy companion,
Lest thou surely payest penance
In the kingdom of Tuoni,
In the prison of Manala;
There, the home of all the wicked,
There the couch of the unworthy,
There the chambers of the guilty.
Underneath Manala's fire-rock
Are their ever-flaming couches,
For their pillows hissing serpents,
Vipers green their writhing covers,
For their drink the blood of adders,
For their food the pangs of hunger,
Pain and agony their solace;
If thou wishest joy eternal,
Shun the kingdom of Tuoui!"

RUNE XVII
WAINAMOINEN FINDS THE LOST-WORD

Wainamoinen, old and truthful,
Did not learn the words of magic
In Tuoni's gloomy regions,
In the kingdom of Manala.
Thereupon he long debated,
Well considered, long reflected,
Where to find the magic sayings;
When a shepherd came to meet him,
Speaking thus to Wainamoinen:
"Thou canst find of words a hundred,
Find a thousand wisdom-sayings,
In the mouth of wise Wipunen,
In the body of the hero;
To the spot I know the foot-path,
To his tomb the magic highway,
Trodden by a host of heroes;
Long the distance thou must travel,
On the sharpened points of needles;
Then a long way thou must journey
On the edges of the broadswords;
Thirdly thou must travel farther
On the edges of the hatchets."
Wainamoinen, old and trustful,
Well considered all these journeys,
Travelled to the forge and smithy,
Thus addressed the metal-worker:
"Ilmarinen, worthy blacksmith,
Make a shoe for me of iron,
Forge me gloves of burnished copper,
Mold a staff of strongest metal,
Lay the steel upon the inside,
Forge within the might of magic;
I am going on a journey
To procure the magic sayings,
Find the lost-words of the Master,
From the mouth of the magician,
From the tongue of wise Wipunen."
Spake the artist, Ilmarinen:
"Long ago died wise Wipunen,
Disappeared these many ages,
Lays no more his snares of copper,
Sets no longer traps of iron,
Cannot learn from him the wisdom,
Cannot find in him the lost-words."
Wainamoinen, old and hopeful,
Little heeding, not discouraged,
In his metal shoes and armor,
Hastens forward on his journey,
Runs the first day fleetly onward,
On the sharpened points of needles;
'Wearily he strides the second,
On the edges of the broadswords
Swings himself the third day forward,

Lönnrot

On the edges of the hatchets.
Wise Wipunen, wisdom-singer,
Ancient bard, and great magician,
With his magic songs lay yonder,
Stretched beside him, lay his sayings,
On his shoulder grew the aspen,
On each temple grew the birch-tree,
On his mighty chin the alder,
From his beard grew willow-bushes,
From his mouth the dark green fir-tree,
And the oak-tree from his forehead.
Wainamoinen, coming closer,
Draws his sword, lays bare his hatchet
From his magic leathern scabbard,
Fells the aspen from his shoulder,
Fells the birch-tree from his temples,
From his chin he fells the alder,
From his beard, the branching willows,
From his mouth the dark-green fir-tree,
Fells the oak-tree from his forehead.
Now he thrusts his staff of iron
Through the mouth of wise Wipunen,
Pries his mighty jaws asunder,
Speaks these words of master-magic:
"Rise, thou master of magicians,
From the sleep of Tuonela,
From thine everlasting slumber!"
Wise Wipunen, ancient singer,
Quickly wakens from his sleeping,
Keenly feels the pangs of torture,
From the cruel staff of iron;
Bites with mighty force the metal,
Bites in twain the softer iron,
Cannot bite the steel asunder,
Opens wide his mouth in anguish.
Wainamoinen of Wainola,
In his iron-shoes and armor,
Careless walking, headlong stumbles
In the spacious mouth and fauces
Of the magic bard, Wipunen.
Wise Wipunen, full of song-charms,
Opens wide his mouth and swallows
Wainamoinen and his magic,
Shoes, and staff, and iron armor.
Then outspeaks the wise Wipunen:
"Many things before I've eaten,
Dined on goat, and sheep, and reindeer,
Bear, and ox, and wolf, and wild-boar,
Never in my recollection,
Have I tasted sweeter morsels!"
Spake the ancient Wainamoinen:
"Now I see the evil symbols,
See misfortune hanging o'er me,
In the darksome Hisi-hurdles,
In the catacombs of Kalma."
Wainamoinen long considered
How to live and how to prosper,
How to conquer this condition.
In his belt he wore a poniard,
With a handle hewn from birch-wood,
From the handle builds a vessel,

The Kalevala
Builds a boat through magic science;
In this vessel rows he swiftly
Through the entrails of the hero,
Rows through every gland and vessel
Of the wisest of magicians.
Old Wipunen, master-singer,
Barely feels the hero's presence,
Gives no heed to Wainamoinen.
Then the artist of Wainola
Straightway sets himself to forging,
Sets at work to hammer metals;
Makes a smithy from his armor,
Of his sleeves he makes the bellows,
Makes the air-valve from his fur-coat,
From his stockings, makes the muzzle,
Uses knees instead of anvil,
Makes a hammer of his fore-arm;
Like the storm-wind roars the bellows,
Like the thunder rings the anvil;
Forges one day, then a second,
Forges till the third day closes,
In the body of Wipunen,
In the sorcerer's abdomen.
Old Wipunen, full of magic,
Speaks these words in wonder, guessing:
"Who art thou of ancient heroes,
Who of all the host of heroes?
Many heroes I have eaten,
And of men a countless number,
Have not eaten such as thou art;
Smoke arises from my nostrils,
From my mouth the fire is streaming,
In my throat are iron-clinkers.
"Go, thou monster, hence to wander,
Flee this place, thou plague of Northland,
Ere I go to seek thy mother,
Tell the ancient dame thy mischief;
She shall bear thine evil conduct,
Great the burden she shall carry;
Great a mother's pain and anguish,
When her child runs wild and lawless;
Cannot comprehend the meaning,
Nor this mystery unravel,
Why thou camest here, O monster,
Camest here to give me torture.
Art thou Hisi sent from heaven,
Some calamity from Ukko?
Art, perchance, some new creation,
Ordered here to do me evil?
If thou art some evil genius,
Some calamity from Ukko,
Sent to me by my Creator,
Then am I resigned to suffer
God does not forsake the worthy,
Does not ruin those that trust him,
Never are the good forsaken.
If by man thou wert created,
If some hero sent thee hither,
I shall learn thy race of evil,
Shall destroy thy wicked tribe-folk.
"Thence arose the violation,

Thence arose the first destruction,
Thence came all the evil-doings:
From the neighborhood of wizards,
From the homes of the magicians,
From the eaves of vicious spirits,
From the haunts of fortune-tellers,
From the cabins of the witches,
From the castles of Tuoni,
From the bottom of Manala,
From the ground with envy swollen,
From Ingratitude's dominions,
From the rocky shoals and quicksands,
From the marshes filled with danger,
From the cataract's commotion,
From the bear-caves in the mountains,
From the wolves within the thickets,
From the roarings of the pine-tree,
From the burrows of the fox-dog,
From the woodlands of the reindeer,
From the eaves and Hisi-hurdles,
From the battles of the giants,
From uncultivated pastures,
From the billows of the oceans,
From the streams of boiling waters,
From the waterfalls of Rutya,
From the limits of the storm-clouds,
From the pathways of the thunders,
From the flashings of the lightnings,
From the distant plains of Pohya,
From the fatal stream and whirlpool,
From the birthplace of Tuoni.
"Art thou coming from these places?
Hast thou, evil, hastened hither,
To the heart of sinless hero,
To devour my guiltless body,
To destroy this wisdom-singer?
Get thee hence, thou dog of Lempo,
Leave, thou monster from Manala,
Flee from mine immortal body,
Leave my liver, thing of evil,
In my body cease thy forging,
Cease this torture of my vitals,
Let me rest in peace and slumber.
"Should I want in means efficient,
Should I lack the magic power
To outroot thine evil genius,
I shall call a better hero,
Call upon a higher power,
To remove this dire misfortune,
To annihilate this monster.
I shall call the will of woman,
From the fields, the old-time heroes?
Mounted heroes from the sand-hills,
Thus to rescue me from danger,
From these pains and ceaseless tortures.
"If this force prove inefficient,
Should not drive thee from my body,
Come, thou forest, with thy heroes,
Come, ye junipers and pine-trees,
With your messengers of power,
Come, ye mountains, with your wood-nymphs,

The Kalevala

Come, ye lakes, with all your mermaids,
Come, ye hundred ocean-spearmen,
Come, torment this son of Hisi,
Come and kill this evil monster.
"If this call is inefficient,
Does not drive thee from my vitals,
Rise, thou ancient water-mother,
With thy blue-cap from the ocean,
From the seas, the lakes, the rivers,
Bring protection to thy hero,
Comfort bring and full assistance,
That I guiltless may not suffer,
May not perish prematurely.
"Shouldst thou brave this invocation,
Kapè, daughter of Creation,
Come, thou beauteous, golden maiden,
Oldest of the race of women,
Come and witness my misfortunes,
Come and turn away this evil,
Come, remove this biting torment,
Take away this plague of Piru.
"If this call be disregarded,
If thou wilt not leave me guiltless,
Ukko, on the arch of heaven,
In the thunder-cloud dominions,
Come thou quickly, thou art needed,
Come, protect thy tortured hero,
Drive away this magic demon,
Banish ever his enchantment,
With his sword and flaming furnace,
With his fire-enkindling bellows.
"Go, thou demon, hence to wander,
Flee, thou plague of Northland heroes;
Never come again for shelter,
Nevermore build thou thy dwelling
In the body of Wipunen;
Take at once thy habitation
To the regions of thy kindred,
To thy distant fields and firesides;
When thy journey thou hast ended,
Gained the borders of thy country,
Gained the meads of thy Creator,
Give a signal of thy coming,
Rumble like the peals of thunder,
Glisten like the gleam of lightning,
Knock upon the outer portals,
Enter through the open windows,
Glide about the many chambers,
Seize the host and seize the hostess,
Knock their evil heads together,
Wring their necks and hurl their bodies
To the black-dogs of the forest.
"Should this prove of little value,
Hover like the bird of battle,
O'er the dwellings of the master,
Scare the horses from the mangers,
From the troughs affright the cattle,
Twist their tails, and horns, and forelocks,
Hurl their carcasses to Lempo.
"If some scourge the winds have sent me,
Sent me on the air of spring-tide,

Brought me by the frosts of winter,
Quickly journey whence thou camest,
On the air-path of the heavens,
Perching not upon some aspen,
Resting not upon the birch-tree;
Fly away to copper mountains,
That the copper-winds may nurse thee,
Waves of ether, thy protection.
"Didst those come from high Jumala,
From the hems of ragged snow-clouds,
Quick ascend beyond the cloud-space,
Quickly journey whence thou camest,
To the snow-clouds, crystal-sprinkled,
To the twinkling stars of heaven
There thy fire may burn forever,
There may flash thy forked lightnings,
In the Sun's undying furnace.
"Wert thou sent here by the spring-floods,
Driven here by river-torrents?
Quickly journey whence thou camest,
Quickly hasten to the waters,
To the borders of the rivers,
To the ancient water-mountain,
That the floods again may rock thee,
And thy water-mother nurse thee.
"Didst thou come from Kalma's kingdom,
From the castles of the death-land?
Haste thou back to thine own country,
To the Kalma-halls and castles,
To the fields with envy swollen,
Where contending armies perish.
"Art thou from the Hisi-woodlands,
From ravines in Lempo's forest,
From the thickets of the pine-wood,
From the dwellings of the fir-glen?
Quick retrace thine evil footsteps
To the dwellings of thy master,
To the thickets of thy kindred;
There thou mayest dwell at pleasure,
Till thy house decays about thee,
Till thy walls shall mould and crumble.
Evil genius, thee I banish,
Got thee hence, thou horrid monster,
To the caverns of the white-bear,
To the deep abysm of serpents,
To the vales, and swamps, and fenlands,
To the ever-silent waters,
To the hot-springs of the mountains,
To the dead-seas of the Northland,
To the lifeless lakes and rivers,
To the sacred stream and whirlpool.
"Shouldst thou find no place of resting,
I will banish thee still farther,
To the Northland's distant borders,
To the broad expanse of Lapland,
To the ever-lifeless deserts,
To the unproductive prairies,
Sunless, moonless, starless, lifeless,
In the dark abyss of Northland;
This for thee, a place befitting,
Pitch thy tents and feast forever

The Kalevala
On the dead plains of Pohyola.
"Shouldst thou find no means of living,
I will banish thee still farther,
To the cataract of Rutya,
To the fire-emitting whirlpool,
Where the firs are ever falling,
To the windfalls of the forest;
Swim hereafter in the waters
Of the fire-emitting whirlpool,
Whirl thou ever in the current
Of the cataract's commotion,
In its foam and boiling waters.
Should this place be unbefitting,
I will drive thee farther onward,
To Tuoni's coal-black river,
To the endless stream of Mana,
Where thou shalt forever linger;
Thou canst never leave Manala,
Should I not thy head deliver,
Should I never pay thy ransom;
Thou canst never safely journey
Through nine brother-rams abutting,
Through nine brother-bulls opposing,
Through nine brother-stallions thwarting,
Thou canst not re-cross Death-river
Thickly set with iron netting,
Interlaced with threads of copper.
"Shouldst thou ask for steeds for saddle,
Shouldst thou need a fleet-foot courser,
I will give thee worthy racers,
I will give thee saddle-horses;
Evil Hisi has a charger,
Crimson mane, and tail, and foretop,
Fire emitting from his nostrils,
As he prances through his pastures;
Hoofs are made of strongest iron,
Legs are made of steel and copper,
Quickly scales the highest mountains,
Darts like lightning through the valleys,
When a skilful master rides him.
"Should this steed be insufficient,
I will give thee Lempo's snow-shoes,
Give thee Hisi's shoes of elm-wood,
Give to thee the staff of Piru,
That with these thou mayest journey
Into Hisi's courts and castles,
To the woods and fields of Juutas;
If the rocks should rise before thee,
Dash the flinty rocks in pieces,
Hurl the fragments to the heavens;
If the branches cross thy pathway,
Make them turn aside in greeting;
If some mighty hero hail thee,
Hurl him headlong to the woodlands.
"Hasten hence, thou thing of evil,
Heinous monster, leave my body,
Ere the breaking of the morning
Ere the Sun awakes from slumber,
Ere the sinning of the cuckoo;
Haste away, thou plague of Northland,
Haste along the track of' moonbeams,

Wander hence, forever wander,
To the darksome fields or Pohya.
"If at once thou dost not leave me,
I will send the eagle's talons,
Send to thee the beaks of vultures,
To devour thine evil body,
Hurl thy skeleton to Hisi.
Much more quickly cruel Lempo
Left my vitals when commanded,
When I called the aid of Ukko,
Called the help of my Creator.
Flee, thou motherless offendant,
Flee, thou fiend of Sariola,
Flee, thou hound without a master,
Ere the morning sun arises,
Ere the Moon withdraws to slumber!"
Wainamoinen, ancient hero,
Speaks at last to old Wipunen:
"Satisfied am I to linger
In these old and spacious caverns,
Pleasant here my home and dwelling;
For my meat I have thy tissues,
Have thy heart, and spleen, and liver,
For my drink the blood of ages,
Goodly home for Wainamoinen.
"I shall set my forge and bellows
Deeper, deeper in thy vitals;
I shall swing my heavy hammer,
Swing it with a greater power
On thy heart, and lungs, and liver;
I shall never, never leave thee
Till I learn thine incantations,
Learn thy many wisdom-sayings,
Learn the lost-words of the Master;
Never must these words be bidden,
Earth must never lose this wisdom,
Though the wisdom-singers perish."
Old Wipunen, wise magician,
Ancient prophet, filled with power,
Opens fall his store of knowledge,
Lifts the covers from his cases,
Filled with old-time incantations,
Filled with songs of times primeval,
Filled with ancient wit and wisdom;
Sings the very oldest folk-songs,
Sings the origin of witchcraft,
Sings of Earth and its beginning
Sings the first of all creations,
Sings the source of good and evil
Sung alas! by youth no longer,
Only sung in part by heroes
In these days of sin and sorrow.
Evil days our land befallen.
Sings the orders of enchantment.
How, upon the will of Ukko,
By command of the Creator,
How the air was first divided,
How the water came from ether,
How the earth arose from water,
How from earth came vegetation,
Fish, and fowl, and man, and hero.

The Kalevala
Sings again the wise Wipunen,
How the Moon was first created,
How the Sun was set in heaven,
Whence the colors of the rainbow,
Whence the ether's crystal pillars,
How the skies with stars were sprinkled.
Then again sings wise Wipunen,
Sings in miracles of concord,
Sings in magic tones of wisdom,
Never was there heard such singing;
Songs he sings in countless numbers,
Swift his notes as tongues of serpents,
All the distant hills re-echo;
Sings one day, and then a second,
Sings a third from dawn till evening,
Sings from evening till the morning;
Listen all the stars of heaven,
And the Moon stands still and listens
Fall the waves upon the deep-sea,
In the bay the tides cease rising,
Stop the rivers in their courses,
Stops the waterfall of Rutya,
Even Jordan ceases flowing,
And the Wuoksen stops and listens.
When the ancient Wainamoinen
Well had learned the magic sayings,
Learned the ancient songs and legends,
Learned the words of ancient wisdom,
Learned the lost-words of the Master,
Well had learned the secret doctrine,
He prepared to leave the body
Of the wisdom-bard, Wipunen,
Leave the bosom of the master,
Leave the wonderful enchanter.
Spake the hero, Wainamoinen:
"O, thou Antero Wipunen,
Open wide thy mouth and fauces,
I have found the magic lost-words,
I will leave thee now forever,
Leave thee and thy wondrous singing,
Will return to Kalevala,
To Wainola's fields and firesides."
Thus Wipunen spake in answer:
"Many are the things I've eaten,
Eaten bear, and elk, and reindeer,
Eaten ox, and wolf, and wild-boar,
Eaten man, and eaten hero,
Never, never have I eaten
Such a thing as Wainamoinen;
Thou hast found what thou desirest,
Found the three words of the Master;
Go in peace, and ne'er returning,
Take my blessing on thy going."
Thereupon the bard Wipunen
Opens wide his mouth, and wider;
And the good, old Wainamoinen
Straightway leaves the wise enchanter,
Leaves Wipunen's great abdomen;
From the mouth he glides and journeys
O'er the hills and vales of Northland,
Swift as red-deer or the forest,

Lönnrot

Swift as yellow-breasted marten,
To the firesides of Wainola,
To the plains of Kalevala.
Straightway hastes he to the smithy
Of his brother, Ilmarinen,
Thus the iron-artist greets him:
Hast thou found the long-lost wisdom,
Hast thou heard the secret doctrine,
Hast thou learned the master magic,
How to fasten in the ledges,
How the stern should be completed,
How complete the ship's forecastle?
Wainamoinen thus made answer:
"I have learned of words a hundred,
Learned a thousand incantations,
Hidden deep for many ages,
Learned the words of ancient wisdom,
Found the keys of secret doctrine,
Found the lost-words of the Master."
Wainamoinen, magic-builder,
Straightway journeys to his vessel,
To the spot of magic labor,
Quickly fastens in the ledges,
Firmly binds the stern together
And completes the boat's forecastle.
Thus the ancient Wainamoinen
Built the boat with magic only,
And with magic launched his vessel,
Using not the hand to touch it,
Using not the foot to move it,
Using not the knee to turn it,
Using nothing to propel it.
Thus the third task was completed,
For the hostess of Pohyola,
Dowry for the Maid of Beauty
Sitting on the arch of heaven,
On the bow of many colors.

RUNE XVIII

THE RIVAL SUITORS

Wainamoinen, old and truthful,
Long considered, long debated,
How to woo and win the daughter
Of the hostess of Pohyola,
How to lead the Bride of Beauty,
Fairy maiden of the rainbow,
To the meadows of Wainola,
From the dismal Sariola.
Now he decks his magic vessel,
Paints the boat in blue and scarlet,
Trims in gold the ship's forecastle,
Decks the prow in molten silver;
Sings his magic ship down gliding,
On the cylinders of fir-tree:
Now erects the masts of pine-wood,
On each mast the sails of linen,
Sails of blue, and white, and scarlet,
Woven into finest fabric.
Wainamoinen, the magician,
Steps aboard his wondrous vessel,
Steers the bark across the waters,
On the blue back of the broad-sea,
Speaks these words in sailing northward,
Sailing to the dark Pohyola:
"Come aboard my ship, O Ukko,
Come with me, thou God of mercy,
To protect thine ancient hero,
To support thy trusting servant,
On the breasts of raging billows,
On the far out-stretching waters.
"Rock, O winds, this wondrous vessel,
Causing not a single ripple;
Rolling waves, bear ye me northward,
That the oar may not be needed
In my journey to Pohyola,
O'er this mighty waste of waters."
Ilmarinen's beauteous sister,
Fair and goodly maid, Annikki,
Of the Night and Dawn, the daughter,
Who awakes each morning early,
Rises long before the daylight,
Stood one morning on the sea-shore,
Washing in the foam her dresses,
Rinsing out her silken ribbons,
On the bridge of scarlet color,
On the border of the highway,
On a headland jutting seaward,
On the forest-covered island.
Here Annikki, looking round her,
Looking through the fog and ether,
Looking through the clouds of heaven,
Gazing far out on the blue-sea,
Sees the morning sun arising,

Lönnrot

Glimmering along the billows,
Looks with eyes of distant vision
Toward the sunrise on the waters,
Toward the winding streams of Suomi,
Where the Wina-waves were flowing.
There she sees, on the horizon,
Something darkle in the sunlight,
Something blue upon the billows,
Speaks these words in wonder guessing:
What is this upon the surges,
What this blue upon the waters,
What this darkling in the sunlight?
'Tis perhaps a flock of wild-geese,
Or perchance the blue-duck flying;
Then upon thy wings arising,
Fly away to highest heaven.
"Art thou then a shoal of sea-trout,
Or perchance a school of salmon?
Dive then to the deep sea-bottom,
In the waters swim and frolic.
"Art thou then a cliff of granite,
Or perchance a mighty oak-tree,
Floating on the rough sea-billows?
May the floods then wash and beat thee
Break thee to a thousand fragments."
Wainamoinen, sailing northward,
Steers his wondrous ship of magic
Toward the headland jutting seaward,
Toward the island forest-covered.
Now Annikki, goodly maiden,
Sees it is the magic vessel
Of a wonderful enchanter,
Of a mighty bard and hero,
And she asks this simple question:
"Art thou then my father's vessel,
Or my brother's ship of magic?
Haste away then to thy harbor,
To thy refuge in Wainola.
Hast thou come a goodly distance?
Sail then farther on thy journey,
Point thy prow to other waters."
It was not her father's vessel,
Not a sail-boat from the distance,
'Twas the ship of Wainamoinen,
Bark of the eternal singer;
Sails within a hailing distance,
Swims still nearer o'er the waters,
Brings one word and takes another,
Brings a third of magic import.
Speaks the goodly maid, Annikki,
Of the Night and Dawn, the daughter,
To the sailor of the vessel:
"Whither sailest, Wainamoinen,
Whither bound, thou friend of waters,
Pride and joy of Kalevala?"
From the vessel Wainamomen
Gives this answer to the maiden:
"I have come to catch some sea-trout,
Catch the young and toothsome whiting,
Hiding in tbese-reeds and rushes."
This the answer of Annikki:

The Kalevala

"Do not speak to me in falsehood,
Know I well the times of fishing;
Long ago my honored father
Was a fisherman in Northland,
Came to catch the trout and whiting,
Fished within these seas and rivers.
Very well do I remember
How the fisherman disposes,
How he rigs his fishing vessel,
Lines, and gaffs, and poles, and fish-nets;
Hast not come a-fishing hither.
Whither goest, Wainamoinen,
Whither sailest, friend of waters?
Spake the ancient Wainamoinen:
"I have come to catch some wild-geese,
Catch the hissing birds of Suomi,
In these far-extending borders,
In the Sachsensund dominions."
Good Annikki gives this answer:
"Know I well a truthful speaker,
Easily detect a falsehood;
Formerly my aged father
Often came a-hunting hither,
Came to hunt the hissing wild-geese,
Hunt the red-bill of these waters.
Very well do I remember
How the hunter rigs his vessel,
Bows, and arrows, knives, and quiver,
Dogs enchained within the vessel,
Pointers hunting on the sea-shore,
Setters seeking in the marshes,
Tell the truth now Wainamoinen,
Whither is thy vessel sailing?"
Spake the hero of the Northland:
"To the wars my ship is sailing,
To the bloody fields of battle,
Where the streams run scarlet-colored,
Where the paths are paved with bodies!"
These the words of fair Annikki:
"Know I well the paths to battle.
Formerly my aged father
Often sounded war's alarum,
Often led the hosts to conquest;
In each ship a hundred rowers,
And in arms a thousand heroes,
Oil the prow a thousand cross-bows,
Swords, and spears, and battle-axes;
Know I well the ship of battle.
Speak Do longer fruitless falsehoods,
Whither sailest, Wainamoinen,
Whither steerest, friend of waters?
These the words of Wainamoinen:
"Come, O maiden, to my vessel,
In my magic ship be seated,
Then I'll give thee truthful answer."
Thus Annikki, silver-tinselled,
Answers ancient Wainamoinen:
"With the winds I'll fill thy vessel,
To thy bark I'll send the storm-winds
And capsize thy ship of magic,
Break in pieces its forecastle,

Lönnrot

If the truth thou dost not tell me,
If thou dost not cease thy falsehoods,
If thou dost not tell me truly
Whither sails thy magic vessel."
These the words of Wainamoinen:
"Now I make thee truthful answer,
Though at first I spake deception:
I am sailing to the Northland
To the dismal Sariola,
Where the ogres live and flourish,
Where they drown the worthy heroes,
There to woo the Maid of Beauty
Sitting on the bow of heaven,
Woo and win the fairy virgin,
Bring her to my home and kindred,
To the firesides of Walnola."
Then Aunikki, graceful maiden,
Of the Night and Dawn, the daughter,
As she heard the rightful answer,
Knew the truth was fully spoken,
Straightway left her coats unbeaten,
Left unwashed her linen garments,
Left unrinsed her silks and ribbons
On the highway by the sea-shore,
On the bridge of scarlet color
On her arm she threw her long-robes,
Hastened off with speed of roebuck
To the shops of Ilmarinen,
To the iron-forger's furnace,
To the blacksmith's home and smithy,
Here she found the hero-artist,
Forging out a bench of iron,
And adorning it with silver.
Soot lay thick upon his forehead,
Soot and coal upon his shoulders.
On the threshold speaks Annikki,
These the words his sister uses:
"Ilmarinen, dearest brother,
Thou eternal artist-forger,
Forge me now a loom of silver,
Golden rings to grace my fingers,
Forge me gold and silver ear-rings,
Six or seven golden girdles,
Golden crosslets for my bosom,
For my head forge golden trinkets,
And I'll tell a tale surprising,
Tell a story that concerns thee
Truthfully I'll tell the story."
Then the blacksmith Ilmarinen
Spake and these the words he uttered:
"If thou'lt tell the tale sincerely,
I will forge the loom of silver,
Golden rings to grace thy fingers,
Forge thee gold and silver ear-rings,
Six or seven golden girdles,
Golden crosslets for thy bosom,
For thy head forge golden trinkets;
But if thou shouldst tell me falsely,
I shall break thy beauteous jewels,
Break thine ornaments in pieces,
Hurl them to the fire and furnace,

The Kalevala

Never forge thee other trinkets."
This the answer of Annikki:
"Ancient blacksmith, Ilmarinen,
Dost thou ever think to marry
Her already thine affianced,
Beauteous Maiden of the Rainbow,
Fairest virgin of the Northland,
Chosen bride of Sariola?
Shouldst thou wish the Maid of Beauty,
Thou must forge, and forge unceasing,
Hammering the days and nights through;
Forge the summer hoofs for horses,
Forge them iron hoofs for winter,
In the long nights forge the snow-sledge,
Gaily trim it in the daytime,
Haste thou then upon thy journey
To thy wooing in the Northland,
To the dismal Sariola;
Thither journeys one more clever,
Sails another now before thee,
There to woo thy bride affianced,
Thence to lead thy chosen virgin,
Woo and win the Maid of Beauty;
Three long years thou hast been wooing.
Wainamoinen now is sailing
On the blue back of the waters,
Sitting at his helm of copper;
On the prow are golden carvings,
Beautiful his boat of magic,
Sailing fleetly o'er the billows,
To the never-pleasant Northland,
To the dismal Sariola."
Ilmarinen stood in wonder,
Stood a statue at the story;
Silent grief had settled o'er him,
Settled o'er the iron-artist;
From one hand the tongs descended,
From the other fell the hammer,
As the blacksmith made this answer:
"Good Annikki, worthy sister,
I shall forge the loom of silver,
Golden rings to grace thy fingers,
Forge thee gold and silver ear-rings,
Six or seven golden girdles,
Golden crosslets for thy bosom;
Go and heat for me the bath-room,
Fill with heat the honey-chambers,
Lay the faggots on the fire-place,
Lay the smaller woods around them,
Pour some water through the ashes,
Make a soap of magic virtue,
Thus to cleanse my blackened visage,
Thus to cleanse the blacksmith's body,
Thus remove the soot and ashes."
Then Annikki, kindly sister,
Quickly warmed her brother's bath-room,
Warmed it with the knots of fir-trees,
That the thunder-winds had broken;
Gathered pebbles from the fire-stream,
Threw them in the heating waters;
Broke the tassels from the birch-trees,

Lönnrot

Steeped the foliage in honey,
Made a lye from milk and ashes,
Made of these a strong decoction,
Mixed it with the fat and marrow
Of the reindeer of the mountains,
Made a soap of magic virtue,
Thus to cleanse the iron-artist,
Thus to beautify the suitor,
Thus to make the hero worthy.
Ilmarinen, ancient blacksmith,
The eternal metal-worker,
Forged the wishes of his sister,
Ornaments for fair Annikki,
Rings, and bracelets, pins and ear-drops,
Forged for her six golden girdles,
Forged a weaving loom of silver,
While the maid prepared the bath-room,
Set his toilet-room in order.
To the maid he gave the trinkets,
Gave the loom of molten silver,
And the sister thus made answer:
"I have heated well thy bath-room,
Have thy toilet-things in order,
Everything as thou desirest;
Go prepare thyself for wooing,
Lave thy bead to flaxen whiteness,
Make thy cheeks look fresh and ruddy,
Lave thyself in Love's aroma,
That thy wooing prove successful."
Ilmarinen, magic artist,
Quick repairing to his bath-room,
Bathed his head to flaxen whiteness,
Made his cheeks look fresh and ruddy,
Laved his eyes until they sparkled
Like the moonlight on the waters;
Wondrous were his form and features,
And his cheeks like ruddy berries.
These the words of Ilmarinen:
"Fair Annikki, lovely sister,
Bring me now my silken raiment,
Bring my best and richest vesture,
Bring me now my softest linen,
That my wooing prove successful."
Straightway did the helpful sister
Bring the finest of his raiment,
Bring the softest of his linen,
Raiment fashioned by his mother;
Brought to him his silken stockings,
Brought him shoes of marten-leather,
Brought a vest of sky-blue color,
Brought him scarlet-colored trousers,
Brought a coat with scarlet trimming,
Brought a red shawl trimmed in ermine
Fourfold wrapped about his body;
Brought a fur-coat made of seal-skin,
Fastened with a thousand bottons,
And adorned with countless jewels;
Brought for him his magic girdle,
Fastened well with golden buckles,
That his artist-mother fashioned;
Brought him gloves with golden wristlets,

The Kalevala
That the Laplanders had woven
For a head of many ringlets;
Brought the finest cap in Northland,
That his ancient father purchased
When he first began his wooing.
Ilmarinen, blacksmith-artist,
Clad himself to look his finest,
When he thus addressed a servant:
"Hitch for me a fleet-foot racer,
Hitch him to my willing snow-sledge,
For I start upon a journey
To the distant shores of Pohya,
To the dismal Sariola."
Spake the servant thus in answer:
"Thou hast seven fleet-foot racers,
Munching grain within their mangers,
Which of these shall I make ready?"
Spake the blacksmith, Ilmarinen:
"Take the fleetest of my coursers,
Put the gray steed in the harness,
Hitch him to my sledge of magic;
Place six cuckoos on the break-board,
Seven bluebirds on the cross-bars,
Thus to charm the Northland maidens,
Thus to make them look and listen,
As the cuckoos call and echo.
Bring me too my largest bear-skin,
Fold it warm about the cross-bench;
Bring me then my marten fur-robes,
As a cover and protection."
Straightway then the trusty servant
Of the blacksmith, Ilmarinen,
Put the gray steed in the harness,
Hitched the racer to the snow-sledge,
Placed six cuckoos on the break-board,
Seven bluebirds on the cross-bars,
On the front to sing and twitter;
Then he brought the largest bear-skin,
Folded it upon the cross-bench;
Brought the finest robes of marten,
Warm protection for the master.
Ilmarinen, forger-artist,
The eternal metal-worker,
Earnestly entreated Ukko:
"Send thy snow-flakes, Ukko, father,
Let them gently fall from heaven,
Let them cover all the heather,
Let them hide the berry-bushes,
That my sledge may glide in freedom
O'er the hills to Sariola!"
Ukko sent the snow from heaven,
Gently dropped the crystal snow-flakes,
Lending thus his kind assistance
To the hero, Ilmarinen,
On his journey to the Northland.
Reins in hand, the ancient artist
Seats him in his metal snow-sledge,
And beseeches thus his Master:
"Good luck to my reins and traces,
Good luck to my shafts and runners!
God protect my magic snow-sledge,

Lönnrot

Be my safeguard on my journey
To the dismal Sariola!"
Now the ancient Ilmarinen
Draws the reins upon the racer,
Snaps his whip above the courser,
To the gray steed gives this order,
And the charger plunges northward:
"Haste away, my flaxen stallion,
Haste thee onward, noble white-face,
To the never-pleasant Pohya,
To the dreary Sariola!"
Fast and faster flies the fleet-foot,
On the curving snow-capped sea-coast,
On the borders of the lowlands,
O'er the alder-hills and mountains.
Merrily the steed flies onward,
Bluebirds singing, cuckoos calling,
On the sea-shore looking northward,
Through the sand and falling snow-flakes
Blinding winds, and snow, and sea-foam,
Cloud the hero, Ilmarinen,
As he glides upon his journey,
Looking seaward for the vessel
Of the ancient Wainamoinen;
Travels one day, then a second,
Travels all the next day northward,
Till the third day Ilmarinen
Overtakes old Wainamoinen,
Rails him in his magic vessel,
And addresses thus the minstrel:
"O thou ancient Wainamoinen,
Let us woo in peace the maiden,
Fairest daughter or the Northland,
Sitting on the bow of heaven,
Let each labor long to win her,
Let her wed the one she chooses,
Him selecting, let her follow."
Wainamoinen thus makes answer:
"I agree to thy proposal,
Let us woo in peace the maiden,
Not by force, nor faithless measures,
Shall we woo the Maid of Beauty,
Let her follow him she chooses;
Let the unsuccessful suitor
Harbor neither wrath nor envy
For the hero that she follows."
Thus agreeing, on they journey,
Each according to his pleasure;
Fleetly does the steed fly onward,
Quickly flies the magic vessel,
Sailing on the broad-sea northward;
Ilmarinen's fleet-foot racer
Makes the hills of Northland tremble,
As he gallops on his journey
To the dismal Sariola.
Wainamoinen calls the South-winds,
And they fly to his assistance;
Swiftly sails his ship of beauty,
Swiftly plows the rough sea-billows
In her pathway to Pohyola.
Time had gone but little distance,

The Kalevala

Scarce a moment had passed over,
Ere the dogs began their barking,
In the mansions of the Northland,
In the courts of Sariola,
Watch-dogs of the court of Louhi;
Never had they growled so fiercely,
Never had they barked so loudly,
Never with their tails had beaten
Northland into such an uproar.
Spake the master of Pohyola:
"Go and learn, my worthy daughter,
Why the watch-dogs have been barking,
Why the black-dog signals danger."
Quickly does the daughter answer:
"I am occupied, dear father,
I have work of more importance,
I must tend my flock of lambkins,
I must turn the nether millstone,
Grind to flour the grains of barley,
Run the grindings through the sifter,
Only have I time for grinding."
Lowly growls the faithful watch-dog,
Seldom does he growl so strangely.
Spake the master of Pohyola:
"Go and learn, my trusted consort,
Why the Northland dogs are barking,
Why the black-dog signals danger."
Thus his aged wife makes answer;
"Have no time, nor inclination,
I must feed my hungry household,
Must prepare a worthy dinner,
I must bake the toothsome biscuit,
Knead the dough till it is ready,
Only have I strength for kneading."
Spake the master of Pohyola:
"Dames are always in a hurry,
Maidens too are ever busy,
Whether warming at the oven,
Or asleep upon their couches;
Go my son, and learn the danger,
Why the black-dog growls displeasure,"
Quickly does the son give answer:
"Have no time, nor inclination,
Am in haste to grind my hatchet;
I must chop this log to cordwood,
For the fire must cut the faggots,
I must split the wood in fragments,
Large the pile and small the fire-wood,
Only have I strength for chopping."
Still the watch-dog growls in anger,
Growl the whelps within the mansion,
Growl the dogs chained in the kennel,
Growls the black-dog on the hill-top,
Setting Northland in an uproar.
Spake the master of Pohyola:
"Never, never does my black-dog
Growl like this without a reason;
Never does he bark for nothing,
Does not growl at angry billows,
Nor the sighing of the pine-trees."
Then the master of Pohyola

Went himself to learn the reason
For the barking of the watch-dogs;
Strode he through the spacious court-yard,
Through the open fields beyond it,
To the summit of the uplands.
Looking toward his black-dog barking,
He beholds the muzzle pointed
To a distant, stormy hill-top,
To a mound with alders covered;
There he learned the rightful reason,
Why his dogs had barked so loudly,
Why had growled the wool-tail bearer,
Why his whelps had signalled danger.
At full sail, he saw a vessel,
And the ship was scarlet-colored,
Entering the bay of Lempo;
Saw a sledge of magic colors,
Gliding up the curving sea-shore,
O'er the snow-fields of Pohyola.
Then the master of the Northland
Hastened straightway to his dwelling,
Hastened forward to his court-room,
These the accents of the master:
"Often strangers journey hither,
On the blue back of the ocean,
Sailing in a scarlet vessel,
Rocking in the bay of Lempo;
Often strangers come in sledges
To the honey-lands of Louhi."
Spake the hostess of Pohyola:
How shall we obtain a token
Why these strangers journey hither?
My beloved, faithful daughter,
Lay a branch upon the fire-place,
Let it burn with fire of magic
If it trickle drops of scarlet,
War and bloodshed do they bring us;
If it trickle drops of water,
Peace and plenty bring the strangers."
Northland's fair and slender maiden,
Beautiful and modest daughter,
Lays a sorb-branch on the fire-place,
Lights it with the fire of magic;
Does not trickle drops of scarlet,
Trickles neither blood, nor water,
From the wand come drops of honey.
From the corner spake Suowakko,
This the language of the wizard:
"If the wand is dripping honey,
Then the strangers that are coming
Are but worthy friends and suitors."
Then the hostess of the Northland,
With the daughter of the hostess,
Straightway left their work, and hastened
From their dwelling to the court-yard;
Looked about in all directions,
Turned their eyes upon the waters,
Saw a magic-colored vessel
Rocking slowly in the harbor,
Having sailed the bay of Lempo,
Triple sails, and masts, and rigging,

The Kalevala

Sable was the nether portion,
And the upper, scarlet-colored,
At the helm an ancient hero
Leaning on his oars of copper;
Saw a fleet-foot racer running,
Saw a red sledge lightly follow,
Saw the magic sledge emblazoned,
Guided toward the courts of Louhi;
Saw and heard six golden cuckoos
Sitting on the break-board, calling,
Seven bluebirds richly colored
Singing from the yoke and cross-bar;
In the sledge a magic hero,
Young, and strong, and proud, and handsome,
Holding reins upon the courser.
Spake the hostess of Pohyola:
"Dearest daughter, winsome maiden,
Dost thou wish a noble suitor?
Should these heroes come to woo thee,
Wouldst thou leave thy home and country,
Be the bride of him that pleases,
Be his faithful life-companion?
"He that comes upon the waters,
Sailing in a magic vessel,
Having sailed the bay of Lempo,
Is the good, old Wainamoinen;
In his ship are countless treasures,
Richest presents from Wainola.
"He that rides here in his snow-sledge
In his sledge of magic beauty,
With the cuckoos and the bluebirds,
Is the blacksmith, Ilmarinen,
Cometh hither empty-handed,
Only brings some wisdom-sayings.
When they come within the dwelling,
Bring a bowl of honeyed viands,
Bring a pitcher with two handles,
Give to him that thou wouldst follow
Give it to old Wainamoinen,
Him that brings thee countless treasures,
Costly presents in his vessel,
Priceless gems from Kalevala."
Spake the Northland's lovely daughter,
This the language of the maiden
"Good, indeed, advice maternal,
But I will not wed for riches,
Wed no man for countless treasures;
For his worth I'll choose a husband,
For his youth and fine appearance,
For his noble form and features;
In the olden times the maidens
Were not sold by anxious mothers
To the suitors that they loved not.
I shall choose without his treasures
Ilmarinen for his wisdom,
For his worth and good behavior,
Him that forged the wondrous Sampo,
Hammered thee the lid in colors."
Spake the hostess of Pohyola:
"Senseless daughter, child of folly,
Thus to choose the ancient blacksmith,

From whose brow drips perspiration,
Evermore to rinse his linen,
Lave his hands, and eyes, and forehead,
Keep his ancient house in order;
Little use his wit and wisdom
When compared with gold and silver."
This the answer of the daughter:
"I will never, never, never,
Wed the ancient Wainamoinen
With his gold and priceless jewels;
Never will I be a helpmate
To a hero in his dotage,
Little thanks my compensation."
Wainamoinen, safely landing
In advance of Ilmarinen,
Pulls his gaily-covered vessel
From the waves upon the sea-beach,
On the cylinders of birch-wood,
On the rollers copper-banded,
Straightway hastens to the guest-room
Of the hostess of Pohyola,
Of the master of the Northland,
Speaks these words upon the threshold
To the famous Maid of Beauty:
"Come with me, thou lovely virgin,
Be my bride and life-companion,
Share with me my joys and sorrows,
Be my honored wife hereafter!"
This the answer of the maiden:
"Hast thou built for me the vessel,
Built for me the ship of magic
From the fragments of the distaff,
From the splinters of the spindle?"
Wainamoinen thus replying:
"I have built the promised vessel,
Built the wondrous ship for sailing,
Firmly joined the parts by magic;
It will weather roughest billows,
Will outlive the winds and waters,
Swiftly glide upon the blue-back
Of the deep and boundless ocean
It will ride the waves in beauty,
Like an airy bubble rising,
Like a cork on lake and river,
Through the angry seas of Northland,
Through Pohyola's peaceful waters."
Northland's fair and slender daughter
Gives this answer to her suitor:
"Will not wed a sea-born hero,
Do not care to rock the billows,
Cannot live with such a husband
Storms would bring us pain and trouble,
Winds would rack our hearts and temples;
Therefore thee I cannot follow,
Cannot keep thy home in order,
Cannot be thy life-companion,
Cannot wed old Wainamoinen."

RUNE XIX
ILMARINEN'S WOOING

Ilmarinen, hero-blacksmith,
The eternal metal-worker,
Hastens forward to the court-room
Of the hostess of Pohyola,
Of the master of the Northland,
Hastens through the open portals
Into Louhi's home and presence.
Servants come with silver pitchers,
Filled with Northland's richest brewing;
Honey-drink is brought and offered
To the blacksmith of Wainola,
Ilmarinen thus replying:
"I shall not in all my life-time
Taste the drink that thou hast brought me,
Till I see the Maid of Beauty,
Fairy Maiden of the Rainbow;
I will drink with her in gladness,
For whose hand I journey hither."
Spake the hostess of Pohyola:
"Trouble does the one selected
Give to him that wooes and watches;
Not yet are her feet in sandals,
Thine affianced is not ready.
Only canst thou woo my daughter,
Only canst thou win the maiden,
When thou hast by aid of magic
Plowed the serpent-field of Hisi,
Plowed the field of hissing vipers,
Touching neither beam nor handles.
Once this field was plowed by Piru,
Lempo furrowed it with horses,
With a plowshare made of copper,
With a beam of flaming iron;
Never since has any hero
Brought this field to cultivation."
Ilmarinen of Wainola
Straightway hastens to the chamber
Of the Maiden of the Rainbow,
Speaks these words in hesitation:
"Thou of Night and Dawn the daughter,
Tell me, dost thou not remember
When for thee I forged the Sampo,
Hammered thee the lid in colors?
Thou didst swear by oath the strougest,
By the forge and by the anvil,
By the tongs and by the hammer,
In the ears of the Almighty,
And before omniscient Ukko,
Thou wouldst follow me hereafter,
Be my bride, my life-companion,
Be my honored wife forever.
Now thy mother is exacting,
Will not give to me her daughter,

Till by means of magic only,
I have plowed the field of serpents,
Plowed the hissing soil of Hisi."
The affianced Bride of Beauty
Gives this answer to the suitor:
"O, thou blacksmith, Ilmarinen,
The eternal wonder-forger,
Forge thyself a golden plowshare,
Forge the beam of shining silver,
And of copper forge the handles;
Then with ease, by aid of magic,
Thou canst plow the field of serpents,
Plow the hissing soil of Hisi."
Ilmarinen, welcome suitor,
Straightway builds a forge and smithy,
Places gold within the furnace,
In the forge he lays the silver,
Forges then a golden plowshare,
Forges, too, a beam of silver,
Forges handles out of copper,
Forges boots and gloves of iron,
Forges him a mail of metal,
For his limbs a safe protection,
Safe protection for his body.
Then a horse of fire selecting,
Harnesses the flaming stallion,
Goes to plow the field of serpents,
Plow the viper-lands of Hisi.
In the field were countless vipers,
Serpents there of every species,
Crawling, writhing, hissing, stinging,
Harmless all against the hero,
Thus he stills the snakes of Lempo:
"Vipers, ye by God created,
Neither best nor worst of creatures,
Ye whose wisdom comes from Ukko,
And whose venom comes from Hisi,
Ukko is your greater Master,
By His will your heads are lifted;
Get ye hence before my plowing,
Writ-he ye through the grass and stubble,
Crawl ye to the nearest thicket,
Keep your heads beneath the heather,
Hunt our holes to Mana's kingdom
If your poison-heads be lifted,
Then will mighty Ukko smite them
'With his iron-pointed arrows,
With the lightning of his anger."
Thus the blacksmith, Ilmarinen,
Safely plows the field of serpents,
Lifts the vipers in his plowing,
Buries them beneath the furrow,
Harmless all against his magic.
When the task had been completed,
Ilmarinen, quick returning,
Thus addressed Pohyola's hostess:
"I have plowed the field of Hisi,
Plowed the field of hissing serpents,
Stilled and banished all the vipers;
Give me, ancient dame, thy daughter,
Fairest maiden of the Northland.

The Kalevala
Spake the hostess of Pohyola:
"Shall not grant to thee my daughter,
Shall not give my lovely virgin,
Till Tuoni's bear is muzzled,
Till Manala's wolf is conquered,
In the forests of the Death-land,
In the boundaries of Mana.
Hundreds have been sent to hunt him,
So one yet has been successful,
All have perished in Manala."
Thereupon young Ilmarinen
To the maiden's chamber hastens,
Thus addresses his affianced:
"Still another test demanded,
I must go to Tuonela,
Bridle there the bear of Mana,
Bring him from the Death-land forests,
From Tuoni's grove and empire!
This advice the maiden gives him:
"O thou artist, Ilmarinen,
The eternal metal-worker,
Forge of steel a magic bridle,
On a rock beneath the water,
In the foaming triple currents;
Make the straps of steel and copper,
Bridle then the bear of Mana,
Lead him from Tuoni's forests."
Then the blacksmith, Ilmarinen,
Forged of steel a magic bridle,
On a rock beneath the water,
In the foam of triple currents;
Made the straps of steel and copper,
Straightway went the bear to muzzle,
In the forests of the Death-land,
Spake these words in supplication:
"Terhenetar, ether-maiden,
Daughter of the fog and snow-flake,
Sift the fog and let it settle
O'er the bills and lowland thickets,
Where the wild-bear feeds and lingers,
That he may not see my coming,
May not hear my stealthy footsteps!"
Terhenetar hears his praying,
Makes the fog and snow-flake settle
On the coverts of the wild-beasts;
Thus the bear he safely bridles,
Fetters him in chains of magic,
In the forests of Tuoni,
In the blue groves of Manala.
When this task had been completed,
Ilmarinen, quick returning,
Thus addressed the ancient Louhi:
"Give me, worthy dame, thy daughter,
Give me now my bride affianced,
I have brought the bear of Mana
From Tuoni's fields and forests."
Spake the hostess of Pohyola
To the blacksmith, Ilmarinen:
"I will only give my daughter,
Give to thee the Maid of Beauty,
When the monster-pike thou catchest

In the river of Tuoni,
In Manala's fatal waters,
Using neither hooks, nor fish-nets,
Neither boat, nor fishing-tackle;
Hundreds have been sent to catch him,
No one yet has been successful,
All have perished in Manala."
Much disheartened, Ilmarinen
Hastened to the maiden's chamber,
Thus addressed the rainbow-maiden:
"Now a third test is demanded,
Much more difficult than ever;
I must catch the pike of Mana,
In the river of Tuoni,
And without my fishing-tackle,
Hard the third test of the hero!
This advice the maiden gives him:
"O thou hero, Ilmarinen,
Never, never be discouraged:
In thy furnace, forge an eagle,
From the fire of ancient magic;
He will catch the pike of Mana,
Catch the monster-fish in safety,
From the death-stream of Tuoni,
From Manala's fatal waters."
Then the suitor, Ilmarinen,
The eternal artist-forgeman,
In the furnace forged an eagle
From the fire of ancient wisdom;
For this giant bird of magic
Forged he talons out of iron,
And his beak of steel and copper;
Seats himself upon the eagle,
On his back between the wing-bones,
Thus addresses he his creature,
Gives the bird of fire, this order:
"Mighty eagle, bird of beauty,
Fly thou whither I direct thee,
To Tuoni's coal-black river,
To the blue deeps of the Death-stream,
Seize the mighty fish of Mana,
Catch for me this water-monster."
Swiftly flies the magic eagle,
Giant-bird of worth and wonder,
To the river of Tuoni,
There to catch the pike of Mana;
One wing brushes on the waters,
While the other sweeps the heavens;
In the ocean dips his talons,
Whets his beak on mountain-ledges.
Safely landing, Ilmarinen,
The immortal artist-forger,
Hunts the monster of the Death-stream,
While the eagle hunts and fishes
In the waters of Manala.
From the river rose a monster,
Grasped the blacksmith, Ilmarinen,
Tried to drag him to his sea-cave;
Quick the eagle pounced upon him,
With his metal-beak he seized him,
Wrenched his head, and rent his body,

The Kalevala
Hurled him back upon the bottom
Of the deep and fatal river,
Freed his master, Ilmarinen.
Then arose the pike of Mana,
Came the water-dog in silence,
Of the pikes was not the largest,
Nor belonged he to the smallest;
Tongue the length of double hatchets,
eeth as long as fen-rake handles,
Mouth as broad as triple streamlets,
Back as wide as seven sea-boats,
Tried to snap the magic blacksmith,
Tried to swallow Ilmarinen.
Swiftly swoops the mighty eagle,
Of the birds was not the largest,
Nor belonged he to the smallest;
Mouth as wide as seven streamlets,
Tongue as long as seven javelins,
Like five crooked scythes his talons;
Swoops upon the pike of Mana.
Quick the giant fish endangered,
Darts and flounders in the river,
Dragging down the mighty eagle,
Lashing up the very bottom
To the surface of the river;
When the mighty bird uprising
Leaves the wounded pike in water,
Soars aloft on worsted pinions
To his home in upper ether;
Soars awhile, and sails, and circles,
Circles o'er the reddened waters,
Swoops again on lightning-pinions,
Strikes with mighty force his talons
Into the shoulder of his victim;
Strikes the second of his talons
On the flinty mountain-ledges,
On the rocks with iron hardened;
From the cliffs rebound his talons,
Slip the flinty rocks o'erhanging,
And the monster-pike resisting
Dives again beneath the surface
To the bottom of the river,
From the talons of the eagle;
Deep, the wounds upon the body
Of the monster of Tuoni.
Still a third time soars the eagle,
Soars, and sails, and quickly circles,
Swoops again upon the monster,
Fire out-shooting from his pinoins,
Both his eyeballs flashing lightning;
With his beak of steel and copper
Grasps again the pike of Mana
Firmly planted are his talons
In the rocks and in his victim,
Drags the monster from the river,
Lifts the pike above the waters,
From Tuoni's coal-black river,
From the blue-back of Manala.
Thus the third time does the eagle
Bring success from former failures;
Thus at last the eagle catches

Lönnrot

Mana's pike, the worst of fishes,
Swiftest swimmer of the waters,
From the river of Tuoni;
None could see Manala's river,
For the myriad of fish-scales;
Hardly could one see through ether,
For the feathers of the eagle,
Relicts of the mighty contest.
Then the bird of copper talons
Took the pike, with scales of silver,
To the pine-tree's topmost branches,
To the fir-tree plumed with needles,
Tore the monster-fish in pieces,
Ate the body of his victim,
Left the head for Ilmarinen.
Spake the blacksmith to the eagle:
"O thou bird of evil nature,
What thy thought and what thy motive?
Thou hast eaten what I needed,
Evidence of my successes;
Thoughtless eagle, witless instinct,
Thus to mar the spoils of conquest!"
But the bird of metal talons
Hastened onward, soaring upward,
Rising higher into ether,
Rising, flying, soaring, sailing,
To the borders of the long-clouds,
Made the vault of ether tremble,
Split apart the dome of heaven,
Broke the colored bow of Ukko,
Tore the Moon-horns from their sockets,
Disappeared beyond the Sun-land,
To the home of the triumphant.
Then the blacksmith, Ilmarinen,
Took the pike-head to the hostess
Of the ever-dismal Northland,
Thus addressed the ancient Louhi:
"Let this head forever serve thee
As a guest-bench for thy dwelling,
Evidence of hero-triumphs;
I have caught the pike of Mana,
I have done as thou demandest,
Three my victories in Death-land,
Three the tests of magic heroes;
Wilt thou give me now thy daughter,
Give to me the Maid of Beauty?"
Spake the hostess of Pohyola:
"Badly is the test accomplished,
Thou has torn the pike in pieces,
From his neck the head is severed,
Of his body thou hast eaten,
Brought to me this worthless relic!
These the words of Ilmarinen:
"When the victory is greatest,
Do we suffer greatest losses!
From the river of Tuoni,
From the kingdom of Manala,
I have brought to thee this trophy,
Thus the third task is completed.
Tell me is the maiden ready,
Wilt thou give the bride affianced?

The Kalevala

Spake the hostess of Pohyola:
"I will give to thee my daughter,
Will prepare my snow-white virgin,
For the suitor, Ilmarinen;
Thou hast won the Maid of Beauty,
Bride is she of thine hereafter,
Fit companion of thy fireside,
Help and joy of all thy lifetime."
On the floor a child was sitting,
And the babe this tale related.
"There appeared within this dwelling,
Came a bird within the castle,
From the East came flying hither,
From the East, a monstrous eagle,
One wing touched the vault of heaven,
While the other swept the ocean;
With his tail upon the waters,
Reached his beak beyond the cloudlets,
Looked about, and eager watching,
Flew around, and sailing, soaring,
Flew away to hero-castle,
Knocked three times with beak of copper
On the castle-roof of iron;
But the eagle could not enter.
"Then the eagle, looking round him,
Flew again, and sailed, and circled,
Flew then to the mothers' castle,
Loudly rapped with heavy knocking
On the mothers' roof of copper;
But the eagle could not enter.
"Then the eagle, looking round him,
Flew a third time, sailing, soaring,
Flew then to the virgins' castle,
Knocked again with beak of copper,
On the virgins' roof of linen,
Easy for him there to enter;
Flew upon the castle-chimney,
Quick descending to the chamber,
Pulled the clapboards from the studding,
Tore the linen from the rafters,
Perched upon the chamber-window,
Near the walls of many colors,
On the cross-bars gaily-feathered,
Looked upon the curly-beaded,
Looked upon their golden ringlets,
Looked upon the snow-white virgins,
On the purest of the maidens,
On the fairest of the daughters,
On the maid with pearly necklace,
On the maiden wreathed in flowers;
Perched awhile, and looked, admiring,
Swooped upon the Maid of Beauty,
On the purest of the virgins,
On the whitest, on the fairest,
On the stateliest and grandest,
Swooped upon the rainbow-daughter
Of the dismal Sariola;
Grasped her in his mighty talons,
Bore away the Maid of Beauty,
Maid of fairest form and feature,
Maid adorned with pearly necklace,

Lönnrot

Decked in feathers iridescent,
Fragrant flowers upon her bosom,
Scarlet band around her forehead,
Golden rings upon her fingers,
Fairest maiden of the Northland."
Spake the hostess of Pohyola,
When the babe his tale had ended:
"Tell me bow, my child beloved,
Thou hast learned about the maiden,
Hast obtained the information,
How her flaxen ringlets nestled,
How the maiden's silver glistened,
How the virgin's gold was lauded.
Shone the silver Sun upon thee,
Did the moonbeams bring this knowledge?"
From the floor the child made answer:
"Thus I gained the information,
Moles of good-luck led me hither,
To the home, of the distinguished,
To the guest-room of the maiden,
Good-name bore her worthy father,
He that sailed the magic vessel;
Better-name enjoyed the mother,
She that baked the bread of barley,
She that kneaded wheaten biscuits,
Fed her many guests in Northland.
"Thus the information reached me,
Thus the distant stranger heard it,
Heard the virgin had arisen:
Once I walked within the court-yard,
Stepping near the virgin's chamber,
At an early hour of morning,
Ere the Sun had broken slumber
Whirling rose the soot in cloudlets,
Blackened wreaths of smoke came rising
From the chamber of the maiden,
From thy daughter's lofty chimney;
There the maid was busy grinding,
Moved the handles of the millstone
Making voices like the cuckoo,
Like the ducks the side-holes sounded,
And the sifter like the goldfinch,
Like the sea-pearls sang the grindstones.
"Then a second time I wandered
To the border of the meadow
In the forest was the maiden
Rocking on a fragrant hillock,
Dyeing red in iron vessels,
And in copper kettles, yellow.
"Then a third time did I wander
To the lovely maiden's window;
There I saw thy daughter weaving,
Heard the flying of her shuttle,
Heard the beating of her loom-lathe,
Heard the rattling of her treddles,
Heard the whirring of her yarn-reel."
Spake the hostess of Pohyola:
"Now alas! beloved daughter,
I have often taught this lesson:
'Do not sing among the pine-trees,
Do not call adown the valleys,

The Kalevala
Do not hang thy head in walking,
Do not bare thine arms, nor shoulders,
Keep the secrets of thy bosom,
Hide thy beauty and thy power.'
"This I told thee in the autumn,
Taught thee in the summer season,
Sang thee in the budding spring-time,
Sang thee when the snows were falling:
'Let us build a place for hiding,
Let us build the smallest windows,
Where may weave my fairest daughter,
Where my maid may ply her shuttle,
Where my joy may work unnoticed
By the heroes of the Northland,
By the suitors of Wainola.'"
From the floor the child made answer,
Fourteen days the young child numbered;
"Easy 'tis to hide a war-horse
In the Northland fields and stables;
Hard indeed to hide a maiden,
Having lovely form and features!
Build of stone a distant castle
In the middle of the ocean,
Keep within thy lovely maiden,
Train thou there thy winsome daughter,
Not long hidden canst thou keep her.
Maidens will not grow and flourish,
Kept apart from men and heroes,
Will not live without their suitors,
Will not thrive without their wooers;
Thou canst never hide a maiden,
Neither on the land nor water."
Now the ancient Wainamoinen,
Head down-bent and heavy-hearted,
Wanders to his native country,
To Wainola's peaceful meadows,
To the plains of Kalevala,
Chanting as he journeys homeward:
"I have passed the age for wooing,
Woe is me, rejected suitor,
Woe is me, a witless minstrel,
That I did not woo and marry,
When my face was young and winsome,
When my hand was warm and welcome!
Youth dethrones my age and station,
Wealth is nothing, wisdom worthless,
When a hero goes a-wooing
With a poor but younger brother.
Fatal error that a hero
Does not wed in early manhood,
In his youth does not be master
Of a worthy wife and household."
Thus the ancient Wainamoinen
Sends the edict to his people:
"Old men must not go a-wooing,
Must not swim the sea of anger,
Must not row upon a wager,
Must not run a race for glory,
With the younger sons of Northland."

RUNE XX
THE BREWING OF BEER

Now we sing the wondrous legends,
Songs of wedding-feasts and dances,
Sing the melodies of wedlock,
Sing the songs of old tradition;
Sing of Ilmarinen's marriage
To the Maiden of the Rainbow,
Fairest daughter of the Northland,
Sing the drinking-songs of Pohya.
Long prepared they for the wedding
In Pohyola's halls and chambers,
In the courts of Sariola;
Many things that Louhi ordered,
Great indeed the preparations
For the marriage of the daughter,
For the feasting of the heroes,
For the drinking of the strangers,
For the feeding of the poor-folk,
For the people's entertainment.
Grew an ox in far Karjala,
Not the largest, nor the smallest,
Was the ox that grew in Suomi;
But his size was all-sufficient,
For his tail was sweeping Jamen,
And his head was over Kemi,
Horns in length a hundred fathoms,
Longer than the horns his mouth was;
Seven days it took a weasel
To encircle neck and shoulders;
One whole day a swallow journeyed
From one horn-tip to the other,
Did not stop between for resting.
Thirty days the squirrel travelled
From the tail to reach the shoulders,
But he could not gain the horn-tip
Till the Moon had long passed over.
This young ox of huge dimensions,
This great calf of distant Suomi,
Was conducted from Karjala
To the meadows of Pohyola;
At each horn a hundred heroes,
At his head and neck a thousand.
When the mighty ox was lassoed,
Led away to Northland pastures,
Peacefully the monster journeyed
By the bays of Sariola,
Ate the pasture on the borders;
To the clouds arose his shoulders,
And his horns to highest heaven.
Not in all of Sariola
Could a butcher be discovered
That could kill the ox for Louhi,
None of all the sons of Northland,
In her hosts of giant people,
In her rising generation,
In the hosts of those grown older.

The Kalevala
Came a hero from a distance,
Wirokannas from Karelen,
And these words the gray-beard uttered:
"Wait, O wait, thou ox of Suomi,
Till I bring my ancient war-club;
Then I'll smite thee on thy forehead,
Break thy skull, thou willing victim!
Nevermore wilt thou in summer
Browse the woods of Sariola,
Bare our pastures, fields, and forests;
Thou, O ox, wilt feed no longer
Through the length and breadth of Northland,
On the borders of this ocean!"
When the ancient Wirokannas
Started out the ox to slaughter,
When Palwoinen swung his war-club,
Quick the victim turned his forehead,
Flashed his flaming eyes upon him;
To the fir-tree leaped the hero,
In the thicket hid Palwoinen,
Hid the gray-haired Wirokannas.
Everywhere they seek a butcher,
One to kill the ox of Suomi,
In the country of Karelen,
And among the Suomi-giants,
In the quiet fields of Ehstland,
On the battle-fields of Sweden,
Mid the mountaineers of Lapland,
In the magic fens of Turya;
Seek him in Tuoni's empire,
In the death-courts of Manala.
Long the search, and unsuccessful,
On the blue back of the ocean,
On the far-outstretching pastures.
There arose from out the sea-waves,
Rose a hero from the waters,
On the white-capped, roaring breakers,
From the water's broad expanses;
Nor belonged he to the largest,
Nor belonged he to the smallest;
Made his bed within a sea-shell,
Stood erect beneath a flour-sieve,
Hero old, with hands of iron,
And his face was copper-colored;
Quick the hero full unfolded,
Like the full corn from the kernel.
On his head a hat of flint-stone,
On his feet were sandstone-sandals,
In his hand a golden cleaver,
And the blade was copper-handled.
Thus at last they found a butcher,
Found the magic ox a slayer.
Nothing has been found so mighty
That it has not found a master.
As the sea-god saw his booty,
Quickly rushed he on his victim,
Hurled him to his knees before him,
Quickly felled the calf of Suomi,
Felled the young ox of Karelen.
Bountifully meat was furnished;
Filled at least a thousand hogsheads

Lönnrot

Of his blood were seven boatfuls,
And a thousand weight of suet,
For the banquet of Pohyola,
For the marriage-feast of Northland.
In Pohyola was a guest-room,
Ample was the hall of Louhi,
Was in length a hundred furlongs,
And in breadth was nearly fifty;
When upon the roof a rooster
Crowed at break of early morning,
No one on the earth could hear him;
When the dog barked at one entrance,
None could hear him at the other.
Louhi, hostess of Pohyola,
Hastens to the hall and court-room,
In the centre speaks as follows:
"Whence indeed will come the liquor,
Who will brew me beer from barley,
Who will make the mead abundant,
For the people of the Northland,
Coming to my daughter's marriage,
To her drinking-feast and nuptials?
Cannot comprehend the malting,
Never have I learned the secret,
Nor the origin of brewing."
Spake an old man from his corner:
"Beer arises from the barley,
Comes from barley, hops, and water,
And the fire gives no assistance.
Hop-vine was the son of Remu,
Small the seed in earth was planted,
Cultivated in the loose soil,
Scattered like the evil serpents
On the brink of Kalew-waters,
On the Osmo-fields and borders.
There the young plant grew and flourished,
There arose the climbing hop-vine,
Clinging to the rocks and alders.
"Man of good-luck sowed the barley
On the Osmo hills and lowlands,
And the barley grew and flourished,
Grew and spread in rich abundance,
Fed upon the air and water,
On the Osmo plains and highlands,
On the fields of Kalew-heroes.
"Time had travelled little distance,
Ere the hops in trees were humming,
Barley in the fields was singing,
And from Kalew's well the water,
This the language of the trio:
'Let us join our triple forces,
Join to each the other's powers;
Sad alone to live and struggle,
Little use in working singly,
Better we should toil together.'
"Osmotar, the beer-preparer,
Brewer of the drink refreshing,
Takes the golden grains of barley,
Taking six of barley-kernels,
Taking seven tips of hop-fruit,
Filling seven cups with water,

The Kalevala
On the fire she sets the caldron,
Boils the barley, hops, and water,
Lets them steep, and seethe, and bubble
Brewing thus the beer delicious,
In the hottest days of summer,
On the foggy promontory,
On the island forest-covered;
Poured it into birch-wood barrels,
Into hogsheads made of oak-wood.
"Thus did Osmotar of Kalew
Brew together hops and barley,
Could not generate the ferment.
Thinking long and long debating,
Thus she spake in troubled accents:
'What will bring the effervescence,
Who will add the needed factor,
That the beer may foam and sparkle,
May ferment and be delightful?'
Kalevatar, magic maiden,
Grace and beauty in her fingers,
Swiftly moving, lightly stepping,
In her trimly-buckled sandals,
Steps upon the birch-wood bottom,
Turns one way, and then another,
In the centre of the caldron;
Finds within a splinter lying
From the bottom lifts the fragment,
Turns it in her fingers, musing:
'What may come of this I know not,
In the hands of magic maidens,
In the virgin hands of Kapo,
Snowy virgin of the Northland!'
"Kalevatar took the splinter
To the magic virgin, Kapo,
Who by unknown force and insight,
Rubbed her hands and knees together,
And produced a snow-white squirrel;
Thus instructed she her creature,
Gave the squirrel these directions:
'Snow-white squirrel, mountain-jewel,
Flower of the field and forest,
Haste thee whither I would send thee,
Into Metsola's wide limits,
Into Tapio's seat of wisdom;
Hasten through the heavy tree-tops,
Wisely through the thickest branches,
That the eagle may not seize thee,
Thus escape the bird of heaven.
Bring me ripe cones from the fir-tree,
From the pine-tree bring me seedlings,
Bring them to the hands of Kapo,
For the beer of Osmo's daughter.'
Quickly hastened forth the squirrel,
Quickly sped the nimble broad-tail,
Swiftly hopping on its journey
From one thicket to another,
From the birch-tree to the aspen,
From the pine-tree to the willow,
From the sorb-tree to the alder,
Jumping here and there with method,
Crossed the eagle-woods in safety,

Lönnrot

Into Metsola's wide limits,
Into Tapio's seat of wisdom;
There perceived three magic pine-trees,
There perceived three smaller fir-trees,
Quickly climbed the dark-green branches,
Was not captured by the eagle,
Was not mangled in his talons;
Broke the young cones from the fir-tree,
Cut the shoots of pine-tree branches,
Hid the cones within his pouches,
Wrapped them in his fur-grown mittens
Brought them to the hands of Kapo,
To the magic virgin's fingers.
Kapo took the cones selected,
Laid them in the beer for ferment,
But it brought no effervescence,
And the beer was cold and lifeless.
"Osmotar, the beer-preparer,
Kapo, brewer of the liquor,
Deeply thought and long considered:
'What will bring the effervescence,
Who will lend me aid efficient,
That the beer may foam and sparkle,
May ferment and be refreshing?'
"Kalevatar, sparkling maiden,
Grace and beauty in her fingers,
Softly moving, lightly stepping,
In her trimly-buckled sandals,
Steps again upon the bottom,
Turns one way and then another,
In the centre of the caldron,
Sees a chip upon the bottom,
Takes it from its place of resting,
Looks upon the chip and muses
'What may come of this I know not,
In the hands of mystic maidens,
In the hands of magic Kapo,
In the virgin's snow-white fingers.'
"Kalevatar took the birch-chip
To the magic maiden, Kapo,
Gave it to the white-faced maiden.
Kapo, by the aid of magic,
Rubbed her hands and knees together,
And produced a magic marten,
And the marten, golden-breasted;
Thus instructed she her creature,
Gave the marten these directions.
'Thou, my golden-breasted marten,
Thou my son of golden color,
Haste thou whither I may send thee,
To the bear-dens of the mountain,
To the grottoes of the growler,
Gather yeast upon thy fingers,
Gather foam from lips of anger,
From the lips of bears in battle,
Bring it to the hands of Kapo,
To the hands of Osmo's daughter.'
"Then the marten golden-breasted,
Full consenting, hastened onward,
Quickly bounding on his journey,
Lightly leaping through the distance

The Kalevala

Leaping o'er the widest rivers,
Leaping over rocky fissures,
To the bear-dens of the mountain,
To the grottoes of the growler,
Where the wild-bears fight each other,
Where they pass a dread existence,
Iron rocks, their softest pillows,
In the fastnesses of mountains;
From their lips the foam was dripping,
From their tongues the froth of anger;
This the marten deftly gathered,
Brought it to the maiden, Kapo,
Laid it in her dainty fingers.
"Osmotar, the beer-preparer,
Brewer of the beer of barley,
Used the beer-foam as a ferment;
But it brought no effervescence,
Did not make the liquor sparkle.
"Osmotar, the beer-preparer,
Thought again, and long debated:
'Who or what will bring the ferment,
Th at my beer may not be lifeless?'
"Kalevatar, magic maiden,
Grace and beauty in her fingers,
Softly moving, lightly stepping,
In her trimly-buckled sandals,
Steps again upon the bottom,
Turns one way and then another,
In the centre of the caldron,
Sees a pod upon the bottom,
Lifts it in her snow-white fingers,
urns it o'er and o'er, and muses:
'What may come of this I know not,
In the hands of magic maidens,
In the hands of mystic Kapo,
In the snowy virgin's fingers?'
"Kalevatar, sparkling maiden,
Gave the pod to magic Kapo;
Kapo, by the aid of magic,
Rubbed the pod upon her knee-cap,
And a honey-bee came flying
From the pod within her fingers,
Kapo thus addressed her birdling:
'Little bee with honeyed winglets,
King of all the fragrant flowers,
Fly thou whither I direct thee,
To the islands in the ocean,
To the water-cliffs and grottoes,
Where asleep a maid has fallen,
Girdled with a belt of copper
By her side are honey-grasses,
By her lips are fragrant flowers,
Herbs and flowers honey-laden;
Gather there the sweetened juices,
Gather honey on thy winglets,
From the calyces of flowers,
From the tips of seven petals,
Bring it to the hands of Kapo,
To the hands of Osmo's daughter.'
"Then the bee, the swift-winged birdling,
Flew away with lightning-swiftness

Lönnrot

On his journey to the islands,
O'er the high waves of the ocean;
Journeyed one day, then a second,
Journeyed all the next day onward,
Till the third day evening brought him
To the islands in the ocean,
To the water-cliffs and grottoes;
Found the maiden sweetly sleeping,
In her silver-tinselled raiment,
Girdled with a belt of copper,
In a nameless meadow, sleeping,
In the honey-fields of magic;
By her side were honeyed grasses,
By her lips were fragrant flowers,
Silver stalks with golden petals;
Dipped its winglets in the honey,
Dipped its fingers in the juices
Of the sweetest of the flowers,
Brought the honey back to Kapo,
To the mystic maiden's fingers.
"Osmotar, the beer-preparer,
Placed the honey in the liquor;
Kapo mixed the beer and honey,
And the wedding-beer fermented;
Rose the live beer upward, upward,
From the bottom of the vessels,
Upward in the tubs of birch-wood,
Foaming higher, higher, higher,
Till it touched the oaken handles,
Overflowing all the caldrons;
To the ground it foamed and sparkled,
Sank away in sand and gravel.
"Time had gone but little distance,
Scarce a moment had passed over,
Ere the heroes came in numbers
To the foaming beer of Northland,
Rushed to drink the sparkling liquor.
Ere all others Lemminkainen
Drank, and grew intoxicated
On the beer of Osmo's daughter,
On the honey-drink of Kalew.
"Osmotar, the beer-preparer,
Kapo, brewer of the barley,
Spake these words in saddened accents:
'Woe is me, my life hard-fated,
Badly have I brewed the liquor,
Have not brewed the beer in wisdom,
Will not live within its vessels,
Overflows and fills Pohyola!'
"From a tree-top sings the redbreast,
From the aspen calls the robin:
'Do not grieve, thy beer is worthy,
Put it into oaken vessels,
Into strong and willing barrels
Firmly bound with hoops of copper.'
"Thus was brewed the beer or Northland,
At the hands of Osmo's daughter;
This the origin of brewing
Beer from Kalew-hops and barley;
Great indeed the reputation
Of the ancient beer of Kalew,

The Kalevala
Said to make the feeble hardy,
Famed to dry the tears of women,
Famed to cheer the broken-hearted,
Make the aged young and supple,
Make the timid brave and mighty,
Make the brave men ever braver,
Fill the heart with joy and gladness,
Fill the mind with wisdom-sayings,
Fill the tongue with ancient legends,
Only makes the fool more foolish."
When the hostess of Pohyola
Heard how beer was first fermented,
Heard the origin of brewing,
Straightway did she fill with water
Many oaken tubs and barrels;
Filled but half the largest vessels,
Mixed the barley with the water,
Added also hops abundant;
Well she mixed the triple forces
In her tubs of oak and birch-wood,
Heated stones for months succeeding,
Thus to boil the magic mixture,
Steeped it through the days of summer,
Burned the wood of many forests,
Emptied all the, springs of Pohya;
Daily did the, forests lesson,
And the wells gave up their waters,
Thus to aid the hostess, Louhi,
In the brewing of the liquors,
From the water, hops, and barley,
And from honey of the islands,
For the wedding-feast of Northland,
For Pohyola's great carousal
And rejoicings at the marriage
Of the Malden of the Rainbow
To the blacksmith, Ilmarinen,
Metal-worker of Wainola.
Smoke is seen upon the island,
Fire, upon the promontory,
Black smoke rising to the heavens
From the fire upon the island;
Fills with clouds the half of Pohya,
Fills Karelen's many hamlets;
All the people look and wonder,
This the chorus of the women:
"Whence are rising all these smoke-clouds,
Why this dreadful fire in Northland?
Is not like the smoke of camp-fires,
Is too large for fires of shepherds!"
Lemminkainen's ancient mother
Journeyed in the early morning
For some water to the fountain,
Saw the smoke arise to heaven,
In the region of Pohyola,
These the words the mother uttered:
"'Tis the smoke of battle-heroes,
From the beat of warring armies!"
Even Ahti, island-hero,
Ancient wizard, Lemminkainen,
Also known as Kaukomieli,
Looked upon the scene in wonder,

Lönnrot

Thought awhile and spake as follows:
"I would like to see this nearer,
Learn the cause of all this trouble,
Whence this smoke and great confusion,
Whether smoke from heat of battle,
Or the bonfires of the shepherds."
Kaukomieli gazed and pondered,
Studied long the rising smoke-clouds;
Came not from the heat of battle,
Came not from the shepherd bonfires;
Heard they were the fires of Louhi
Brewing beer in Sariola,
On Pohyola's promontory;
Long and oft looked Lemminkainen,
Strained in eagerness his vision,
Stared, and peered, and thought, and wondered,
Looked abashed and envy-swollen,
"O beloved, second mother,
Northland's well-intentioned hostess,
Brew thy beer of honey-flavor,
Make thy liquors foam and sparkle,
For thy many friends invited,
Brew it well for Lemminkainen,
For his marriage in Pohyola
With the Maiden of the Rainbow."
Finally the beer was ready,
Beverage of noble heroes,
Stored away in casks and barrels,
There to rest awhile in silence,
In the cellars of the Northland,
In the copper-banded vessels,
In the magic oaken hogsheads,
Plugs and faucets made of copper.
Then the hostess of Pohyola
kilfully prepared the dishes,
Laid them all with careful fingers
In the boiling-pans and kettles,
Ordered countless loaves of barley,
Ordered many liquid dishes,
All the delicacies of Northland,
For the feasting of her people,
For their richest entertainment,
For the nuptial songs and dances,
At the marriage of her daughter
With the blacksmith, Ilmarinen.
When the loaves were baked and ready.
When the dishes all were seasoned,
Time had gone but little distance,
Scarce a moment had passed over,
Ere the beer, in casks imprisoned,
Loudly rapped, and sang, and murmured:
"Come, ye heroes, come and take me,
Come and let me cheer your spirits,
Make you sing the songs of wisdom,
That with honor ye may praise me,
Sing the songs of beer immortal!"
Straightway Louhi sought a minstrel,
Magic bard and artist-singer,
That the beer might well be lauded,
Might be praised in song and honor.
First as bard they brought a salmon,

The Kalevala

Also brought a pike from ocean,
But the salmon had no talent,
And the pike had little wisdom;
Teeth of pike and gills of salmon
Were not made for singing legends.
Then again they sought a singer,
Magic minstrel, beer-enchanter,
Thus to praise the drink of heroes,
Sing the songs of joy and gladness;
And a boy was brought for singing;
But the boy had little knowledge,
Could not praise the beer in honor;
Children's tongues are filled with questions,
Children cannot speak in wisdom,
Cannot sing the ancient legends.
Stronger grew the beer imprisoned
In the copper-banded vessels,
Locked behind the copper faucets,
Boiled, and foamed, and sang, and murmured:
"If ye do not bring a singer,
That will sing my worth immortal,
That will sing my praise deserving,
I will burst these bands of copper,
Burst the heads of all these barrels;
Will not serve the best of heroes
Till he sings my many virtues."
Louhi, hostess of Pohyola,
Called a trusted maiden-servant,
Sent her to invite the people
To the marriage of her daughter,
These the words that Louhi uttered:
"O my trusted, truthful maiden,
Servant-maid to me belonging,
Call together all my people,
Call the heroes to my banquet,
Ask the rich, and ask the needy,
Ask the blind and deaf, and crippled,
Ask the young, and ask the aged;
Go thou to the hills, and hedges,
To the highways, and the by-ways,
Urge them to my daughter's wedding;
Bring the blind, and sorely troubled,
In my boats upon the waters,
In my sledges bring the halting,
With the old, and sick, and needy;
Ask the whole of Sariola,
Ask the people of Karelen,
Ask the ancient Wainamoinen,
Famous bard and wisdom-singer;
But I give command explicit
Not to ask wild Lemminkainen,
Not the island-dweller, Ahti!"
This the question of the servant:
"Why not ask wild Lemminkainen,
Ancient islander and minstrel?"
Louhi gave this simple answer:
"Good the reasons that I give thee
Why the wizard, Lemminkainen,
Must not have an invitation
To my daughter's feast and marriage
Ahti courts the heat of battle,

Lönnrot

Lemminkainen fosters trouble,
Skilful fighter of the virtues;
Evil thinking, acting evil,
He would bring but pain and sorrow,
He would jest and jeer at maidens
In their trimly buckled raiment,
Cannot ask the evil-minded!"
Thus again the servant questions:
"Tell me how to know this Ahti,
Also known as Lemminkainen,
That I may not ask him hither;
Do not know the isle of Ahti,
Nor the home of Kaukomieli
Spake the hostess of Pohyola:
"Easy 'tis to know the wizard,
Easy find the Ahti-dwelling:
Ahti lives on yonder island,
On that point dwells Lemminkainen,
In his mansion near the water,
Far at sea his home and dwelling."
Thereupon the trusted maiden
Spread the wedding-invitations
To the people of Pohyola,
To the tribes of Kalevala;
Asked the friendless, asked the homeless
Asked the laborers and shepherds,
Asked the fishermen and hunters,
Asked the deaf, the dumb, the crippled,
Asked the young, and asked the aged,
Asked the rich, and asked the needy;
Did not give an invitation
To the reckless Lemminkainen,
Island-dweller of the ocean.

RUNE XXI
ILMARINEN'S WEDDING-FEAST

Louhi, hostess of the Northland,
Ancient dame of Sariola,
While at work within her dwelling,
Heard the whips crack on the fenlands,
Heard the rattle of the sledges;
To the northward turned her glances,
Turned her vision to the sunlight,
And her thoughts ran on as follow:
"Who are these in bright apparel,
On the banks of Pohya-waters,
Are they friends or hostile armies?"
Then the hostess of the Northland
Looked again and well considered,
Drew much nearer to examine,
Found they were not hostile armies,
Found that they were friends and suitors.
In the midst was Ilmarinen,
Son-in-law to ancient Louhi.
When the hostess of Pohyola
Saw the son-in-law approaching
She addressed the words that follow:
"I had thought the winds were raging,
That the piles of wood were falling,
Thought the pebbles in commotion,
Or perchance the ocean roaring;
Then I hastened nearer, nearer,
Drew still nearer and examined,
Found the winds were not in battle,
Found the piles of wood unshaken,
Found the ocean was not roaring,
Nor the pebbles in commotion,
Found my son-in-law was coming
With his heroes and attendants,
Heroes counted by the hundreds.
"Should you ask of me the question,
How I recognized the bridegroom
Mid the hosts of men and heroes,
I should answer, I should tell you:
'As the hazel-bush in copses,
As the oak-tree in the forest,
As the Moon among the planets;
Drives the groom a coal-black courser,
Running like the famished black-dog,
Flying like the hungry raven,
Graceful as the lark at morning,
Golden cuckoos, six in number,
Twitter on the birchen cross-bow;
There are seven bluebirds singing
On the racer's hame and collar."
Noises hear they in the court-yard,
On the highway hear the sledges,
To the court comes Ilmarinen,
With his body-guard of heroes;

Lönnrot

In the midst the chosen suitor,
Not too far in front of others,
Not too far behind his fellows.
Spake the hostess of Pohyola:
"Hie ye hither, men and heroes,
Haste, ye watchers, to the stables,
There unhitch the suitor's stallion,
Lower well the racer's breast-plate,
There undo the straps and buckles,
Loosen well the shafts and traces,
And conduct the suitor hither,
Give my son-in-law good welcome!"
Ilmarinen turned his racer
Into Louhi's yard and stables,
And descended from his snow-sledge.
Spake the hostess of Pohyola:
"Come, thou servant of my bidding,
Best of all my trusted servants,
Take at once the bridegroom's courser
From the shafts adorned with silver,
From the curving arch of willow,
Lift the harness trimmed in copper,
Tie the white-face to the manger,
Treat the suitor's steed with kindness,
Lead him carefully to shelter
By his soft and shining bridle,
By his halter tipped with silver;
Let him roll among the sand-hills,
On the bottoms soft and even,
On the borders of the snow-banks,
In the fields of milky color.
"Lead the hero's steed to water,
Lead him to the Pohya-fountains,
Where the living streams are flowing,
Sweet as milk of human kindness,
From the roots of silvery birches,
Underneath the shade of aspens.
"Feed the courser of the suitor,
On the sweetest corn and barley,
On the summer-wheat and clover,
In the caldron steeped in sweetness;
Feed him at the golden manger,
In the boxes lined with copper,
At my manger richly furnished,
In the warmest of the stables;
Tie him with a silk-like halter,
To the golden rings and staples,
To the hooks of purest silver,
Set in beams of birch and oak-wood;
Feed him on the hay the sweetest,
Feed him on the corn nutritious,
Give the best my barns can furnish.
"Curry well the suitor's courser
With the curry-comb of fish-bone,
Brush his hair with silken brushes,
Put his mane and tail in order,
Cover well with flannel blankets,
Blankets wrought in gold and silver,
Buckles forged from shining copper.
"Come, ye small lads of the village,
Lead the suitor to my chambers,

The Kalevala
With your auburn locks uncovered,
From your hands remove your mittens,
See if ye can lead the hero
Through the door without his stooping,
Lifting not the upper cross-bar,
Lowering not the oaken threshold,
Moving not the birchen casings,
Great the hero who must enter.
"Ilmarinen is too stately,
Cannot enter through the portals,
Not the son-in-law and bridegroom,
Till the portals have been heightened;
Taller by a head the suitor
Than the door-ways of the mansion."
Quick the servants of Pohyola
Tore away the upper cross-bar,
That his cap might not be lifted;
Made the oaken threshold lower
That the hero might not stumble;
Made the birch-wood portals wider,
Opened full the door of welcome,
Easy entrance for the suitor.
Speaks the hostess of the Northland
As the bridegroom freely passes
Through the doorway of her dwelling:
"Thanks are due to thee, O Ukko,
That my son-in-law has entered!
Let me now my halls examine;
Make the bridal chambers ready,
Finest linen on my tables,
Softest furs upon my benches,
Birchen flooring scrubbed to whiteness,
All my rooms in perfect order."
Then the hostess of Pohyola
Visited her spacious dwelling,
Did not recognize her chambers;
Every room had been remodeled,
Changed by force of mighty magic;
All the halls were newly burnished,
Hedge-hog bones were used for ceilings,
Bones of reindeer for foundations,
Bones of wolverine for door-sills,
For the cross-bars bones of roebuck,
Apple-wood were all the rafters,
Alder-wood, the window-casings,
Scales of trout adorned the windows,
And the fires were set in flowers.
All the seats were made of silver,
All the floors of copper-tiling,
Gold-adorned were all the tables,
On the floor were silken mattings,
Every fire-place set in copper,
Every hearth-stone cut from marble,
On each shelf were colored sea-shells,
Kalew's tree was their protection.
To the court-room came the hero,
Chosen suitor from Wainola,
These the words of Ilmarinen:
"Send, O Ukko, health and pleasure
To this ancient home and dwelling,
To this mansion richly fashioned!"

Spake the hostess of Pohyola:
"Let thy coming be auspicious
To these halls of thee unworthy,
To the home of thine affianced,
To this dwelling lowly fashioned,
Mid the lindens and the aspens.
"Come, ye maidens that should serve me,
Come, ye fellows from the village,
Bring me fire upon the birch-bark,
Light the fagots of the fir-tree,
That I may behold the bridegroom,
Chosen suitor of my daughter,
Fairy Maiden of the Rainbow,
See the color of his eyeballs,
Whether they are blue or sable,
See if they are warm and faithful."
Quick the young lads from the village
Brought the fire upon the birch-bark,
Brought it on the tips of pine-wood;
And the fire and smoke commingled
Roll and roar about the hero,
Blackening the suitor's visage,
And the hostess speaks as follows;
"Bring the fire upon a taper,
On the waxen tapers bring it!"
Then the maidens did as bidden,
Quickly brought the lighted tapers,
Made the suitor's eyeballs glisten,
Made his cheeks look fresh and ruddy;
Made his eyes of sable color
Sparkle like the foam of waters,
Like the reed-grass on the margin,
Colored as the ocean jewels,
Iridescent as the rainbow.
"Come, ye fellows of the hamlet,
Lead my son-in-law and hero
To the highest seat at table,
To the seat of greatest honor,
With his back upon the blue-wall,
Looking on my bounteous tables,
Facing all the guests of Northland."
Then the hostess of Pohyola
Served her guests in great abundance,
Richest drinks and rarest viands,
First of all she, served the bridegroom
On his platters, honeyed biscuit,
And the sweetest river salmon,
Seasoned butter, roasted bacon,
All the dainties of Pohyola.
Then the helpers served the others,
Filled the plates of all invited
With the varied food of Northland.
Spake the hostess of Pohyola:
"Come, ye maidens from the village,
Hither bring the beer in pitchers,
In the urns with double handles,
To the many guests in-gathered,
Ere all others, serve the bridegroom."
Thereupon the merry maidens
Brought the beer in silver pitchers
From the copper-banded vessels,

The Kalevala

For the wedding-guests assembled;
And the beer, fermenting, sparkled
On the beard of Ilmarinen,
On the beards of many heroes.
When the guests had all partaken
Of the wondrous beer of barley,
Spake the beer in merry accents
Through the tongues of the magicians,
Through the tongue of many a hero,
Through the tongue of Wainamoinen,
Famed to be the sweetest singer
Of the Northland bards and minstrels,
These the words of the enchanter:
"O thou beer of honeyed flavor,
Let us not imbibe in silence,
Let some hero sing thy praises,
Sing thy worth in golden measures;
Let the hostess start the singing,
Let the bridegroom sound thy virtues!
Have our songs thus quickly vanished,
Have our joyful tongues grown silent?
Evil then has been the brewing,
Then the beer must be unworthy,
That it does not cheer the singer,
Does not move the merry minstrel,
That the golden guests are joyless,
And the cuckoo is not singing.
Never will these benches echo
Till the bench-guests chant thy virtues;
Nor the floor resound thy praises
Till the floor-guests sing in concord;
Nor the windows join the chorus
Till the window-guests have spoken;
All the tables will keep silence
Till the heroes toast thy virtues;
Little singing from the chimney
Till the chimney-guests have chanted."
On the floor a child was sitting,
Thus the little boy made answer:
"I am small and young in singing,
Have perchance but little wisdom;
Be that as it may, my seniors,
Since the elder minstrels sing not,
Nor the heroes chant their legends,
Nor the hostess lead the singing,
I will sing my simple stories,
Sing my little store of knowledge,
To the pleasure of the evening,
To the joy of the invited."
Near the fire reclined an old man,
And the gray-beard thus made answer:
"Not the time for children's singing,
Children's wisdom is too ready,
Children's songs are filled with trifles,
Filled with shrewd and vain deceptions,
Maiden-songs are full of follies;
Leave the songs and incantations
To the ancient wizard-singers;
Leave the tales of times primeval
To the minstrel of Wainola,
To the hero of the Northland,

Lönnrot

To the, ancient Wainamoinen."
Thereupon Osmoinen answered:
"Are there not some sweeter singers
In this honored congregation,
That will clasp their hands together,
Sing the ancient songs unbroken,
Thus begin the incantations,
Make these ancient halls re-echo
For the pleasure of the evening,
For the joy of the in-gathered?"
From the hearth-stone spake, the gray-beard
"Not a singer of Pohyola,
Not a minstrel, nor magician,
That was better skilled in chanting
Legends of the days departed,
Than was I when I was singing,
In my years of vain ambition;
Then I chanted tales of heroes,
On the blue back of the waters,
Sang the ballads of my people,
In the vales and on the mountains,
Through the verdant fields and forests;
Sweet my voice and skilled my singing,
All my songs were highly lauded,
Rippled like the quiet rivers,
Easy-flowing like the waters,
Easy-gliding as the snow-shoes,
Like the ship upon the ocean.
"Woe is me, my days are ended,
Would not recognize my singing,
All its sweetness gone to others,
Flows no more like rippling waters,
Makes no more the hills re-echo!
Now my songs are full of discord,
Like the rake upon the stubble,
Like the sledge upon the gravel,
Like the boat upon the sea-shore!"
Then the ancient Wainamoinen
Spake these words in magic measures:
"Since no other bard appeareth
That will clasp my hand in singing,
I will sing some simple legends,
Sing my, garnered store of wisdom,
Make these magic halls re-echo
With my tales of ancient story,
Since a bard I was created,
Born an orator and singer;
Do not ask the ways of others,
Follow not the paths of strangers."
Wainamoinen, famous minstrel,
Song's eternal, wise supporter,
Then began the songs of pleasure,
Made the halls resound with joyance,
Filled the rooms with wondrous singing;
Sang the ancient bard-magician
All the oldest wisdom-sayings,
Did not fail in voice nor legends,
All the wisest thoughts remembered.
Thus the ancient Wainamoinen
Sang the joy of all assembled,
To the pleasure of the evening,

The Kalevala
To the merriment of maidens,
To the happiness of heroes;
All the guests were stilled in wonder
At the magic of his singing,
At the songs of the magician.
Spake again wise Wainamoinen,
When his wonder-tales had ended:
"I have little worth or power,
Am a bard of little value,
Little consequence my singing,
Mine abilities as nothing,
If but Ukko, my Creator,
Should intone his wisdom-sayings,
Sing the source of good and evil,
Sing the origin of matter,
Sing the legends of omniscience,
Sing his songs in full perfection.
God could sing the floods to honey,
Sing the sands to ruddy berries,
Sing the pebbles into barley,
Sing to beer the running waters,
Sing to salt the rocks of ocean,
Into corn-fields sing the forests,
Into gold the forest-fruitage,
Sing to bread the hills and mountains,
Sing to eggs the rounded sandstones;
He could touch the springs of magic,
He could turn the keys of nature,
And produce within thy pastures,
Hurdles filled with sheep and reindeer,
Stables filled with fleet-foot stallions,
Kine in every field and fallow;
Sing a fur-robe for the bridegroom,
For the bride a coat of ermine,
For the hostess, shoes of silver,
For the hero, mail of copper.
"Grant O Ukko, my Creator,
God of love, and truth, and justice,
Grant thy blessing on our feasting,
Bless this company assembled,
For the good of Sariola,
For the happiness of Northland!
May this bread and beer bring joyance,
May they come in rich abundance,
May they carry full contentment
To the people of Pohyola,
To the cabin and the mansion;
May the hours we spend in singing,
In the morning, in the evening,
Fill our hearts with joy and gladness!
Hear us in our supplications,
Grant to us thy needed blessings,
Send enjoyment, health, and comfort,
To the people here assembled,
To the host and to the hostess,
To the bride and to the bridegroom,
To the sons upon the waters,
To the daughters at their weavings,
To the hunters on the mountains,
To the shepherds in the fenlands,
That our lives may end in honor,

Lönnrot

That we may recall with pleasure
Ilmarinen's magic marriage
To the Maiden of the Rainbow,
Snow-white virgin of the Northland."

The Kalevala

RUNE XXII
THE BRIDE S FAREWELL

When the marriage was completed,
When the many guests had feasted,
At the wedding of the Northland,
At the Dismal-land carousal,
Spake the hostess of Pohyola
To the blacksmith, Ilmarinen:
"Wherefore, bridegroom, dost thou linger,
Why art waiting, Northland hero?
Sittest for the father's pleasure,
For affection of the mother,
For the splendor of the maidens,
For the beauty of the daughter?
Noble son-in-law and brother,
Wait thou longer, having waited
Long already for the virgin,
Thine affianced is not ready,
Not prepared, thy life-companion,
Only are her tresses braided.
"Chosen bridegroom, pride of Pohya,
Wait thou longer, having waited
Long already for the virgin,
Thy beloved is preparing,
Only is one hand made ready.
"Famous artist, Ilmarinen,
Wait still longer, having waited
Long already for the virgin,
Thy beloved is not ready,
Only is one foot in fur-shoes,"
Spake again the ancient Louhi:
"Chosen suitor of my daughter,
Thou hast thrice in kindness waited,
Wait no longer for the virgin,
Thy beloved now is ready,
Well prepared thy life-companion,
Fairy Maiden of the Rainbow.
"Beauteous daughter, join thy suitor,
Follow him, thy chosen husband,
Very near is the uniting,
Near indeed thy separation.
At thy hand the honored bridegroom,
Near the door he waits to lead thee,
Guide thee to his home and kindred;
At the gate his steed is waiting,
Restless champs his silver bridle,
And the sledge awaits thy presence.
"Thou wert anxious for a suitor,
Ready to accept his offer,
Wert in haste to take his jewels,
Place his rings upon thy fingers;
Now, fair daughter, keep thy promise;
To his sledge, with happy footsteps,
Hie in haste to join the bridegroom,
Gaily journey to the village

Lönnrot

With thy chosen life-companion,
With thy suitor, Ilmarinen.
Little hast thou looked about thee,
Hast not raised thine eyes above thee,
Beauteous maiden of the Northland,
Hast thou made a rueful bargain,
Full of wailing thine engagement,
And thy marriage full of sorrow,
That thy father's ancient cottage
Thou art leaving now forever,
Leaving also friends and kindred,
For the, blacksmith, Ilmarinen?
"O how beautiful thy childhood,
In thy father's dwelling-places,
Nurtured like a tender flower,
Like the strawberry in spring-time
Soft thy couch and sweet thy slumber,
Warm thy fires and rich thy table;
From the fields came corn in plenty,
From the highlands, milk and berries,
Wheat and barley in abundance,
Fish, and fowl, and hare, and bacon,
From thy father's fields and forests.
"Never wert thou, child, in sorrow,
Never hadst thou grief nor trouble,
All thy cares were left to fir-trees,
All thy worry to the copses,
All thy weeping to the willows,
All thy sighing to the lindens,
All thy thinking to the aspens
And the birches on the mountains,
Light and airy as the leaflet,
As a butterfly in summer,
Ruddy as a mountain-berry,
Beautiful as vernal flowers.
"Now thou leavest home and kindred,
Wanderest to other firesides,
Goest to another mother,
Other sisters, other brothers,
Goest to a second father,
To the servant-folk of strangers,
From thy native hills and lowlands.
There and here the homes will differ,
Happier thy mother's hearth-stone;
Other horns will there be sounded,
Other portals there swing open,
Other hinges there be creaking;
There the doors thou canst not enter
Like the daughters of Wainola,
Canst not tend the fires and ovens
As will please the minds of strangers.
"Didst thou think, my fairest maiden,
Thou couldst wed and on the morrow
Couldst return, if thou shouldst wish it,
To thy father's court and dwelling?
Not for one, nor two, nor three days,
Wilt thou leave thy mother's chambers,
Leave thy sisters and thy brothers,
Leave thy father's hills and lowlands.
Long the time the wife must wander,
Many months and years must wander,

The Kalevala
Work, and struggle, all her life long,
Even though the mother liveth.
Great, indeed, must be the changes
When thou comest back to Pohya,
Changed, thy friends and nearest kindred,
Changed, thy father's ancient dwellings,
Changed, the valleys and the mountains,
Other birds will sing thy praises!"
When the mother thus had spoken,
Then the daughter spake, departing:
"In my early days of childhood
Often I intoned these measures:
'Art a virgin, yet no virgin,
Guided by an aged mother,
In a brother's fields and forests,
In the mansion of a father!
Only wilt become a virgin,
Only when thou hast a suitor,
Only when thou wedst a hero,
One foot on the father's threshold,
And the other for the snow-sledge
That will speed thee and thy husband
To his native vales and highlands!'
"I have wished thus many summers,
Sang it often in my childhood,
Hoped for this as for the flowers,
Welcome as the birds of spring-time.
Thus fulfilled are all my wishes,
Very near is my departure,
One foot on my father's threshold,
And the, other for the journey
With my husband to his people;
Cannot understand the reason
That has changed my former feelings,
Cannot leave thee now with gladness,
Cannot go with great rejoicing
From my dear, old home and kindred,
Where as maiden I have lingered,
From the courts where I was nurtured,
From my father's band and guidance,
From my faithful mother's counsel.
Now I go, a maid of sorrow,
Heavy-hearted to the bridegroom,
Like the bride of Night in winter,
Like the ice upon the rivers.
"Such is not the mind of others,
Other brides of Northland heroes;
Others do not leave unhappy,
Have no tears, nor cares, nor sorrows,
I alas! must weep and murmur,
Carry to my grave great sadness,
Heart as dark as Death's black river.
"Such the feelings of the happy,
Such the minds of merry maidens:
Like the early dawn of spring-time,
Like the rising Sun in summer
No such radiance awaits me,
With my young heart filled with terror;
Happiness is not my portion,
Like the flat-shore of the ocean,
Like the dark rift of the storm-cloud,

Lönnrot

Like the cheerless nights of winter!
Dreary is the day in autumn,
Dreary too the autumn evening,
Still more dreary is my future!"
An industrious old maiden,
Ever guarding home and kindred,
Spake these words of doubtful comfort:
"Dost thou, beauteous bride, remember,
Canst thou not recall my counsels?
These the words that I have taught thee:
'Look not joyfully for suitors,
Never heed the tongues of wooers,
Look not in the eyes of charmers,
At their feet let fall thy vision.
He that hath a mouth for sweetness,
He that hath an eye for beauty,
Offers little that will comfort;
Lempo sits upon his forehead,
In his mouth dwells dire Tuoni.'
"Thus, fair bride, did I advise thee,
Thus advised my sister's daughter:
Should there come the best of suitors,
Noblest wooers, proudest lovers,
Give to all these wisdom-sayings,
Let thine answer be as follows:
'Never will I think it wisdom,
Never will it be my pleasure,
To become a second daughter,
Linger with my husband's mother;
Never shall I leave my father,
Never wander forth to bondage,
At the bidding of a bridegroom:
Never shall I be a servant,
Wife and slave to any hero,
Never will I be submissive
To the orders of a husband.'
"Fairest bride, thou didst not heed me,
Gav'st no thought to my advices,
Didst not listen to my counsel;
Wittingly thy feet have wandered
Into boiling tar and water,
Hastened to thy suitor's snow-sledge,
To the bear-dens of thy husband,
On his sledge to be ill-treated,
Carried to his native country,
To the bondage of his people,
There, a subject to his mother.
Thou hast left thy mother's dwelling,
To the schooling of the master;
Hard indeed the master's teachings,
Little else than constant torture;
Ready for thee are his bridles,
Ready for thy bands the shackles,
Were not forged for any other;
Soon, indeed, thou'lt feel the hardness,
Feel the weight of thy misfortune,
Feel thy second father's censure,
And his wife's inhuman treatment,
Hear the cold words or thy brother,
Quail before thy haughty sister.
"Listen, bride, to what I tell thee:

The Kalevala

In thy home thou wert a jewel,
Wert thy father's pride and pleasure,
'Moonlight,' did thy father call thee,
And thy mother called thee 'Sunshine,'
'Sea-foam' did thy brother call thee,
And thy sister called thee 'Flower.'
When thou leavest home and kindred
Goest to a second mother,
Often she will give thee censure,
Never treat thee as her daughter,
Rarely will she give thee counsel,
Never will she sound thy praises.
'Brush-wood,' will the father call thee,
'Sledge of Rags,' thy husband's mother,
'Flight of Stairs,' thy stranger brother,
'Scare-crow,' will the sister call thee,
Sister of thy blacksmith-husband;
Then wilt think of my good counsels,
Then wilt wish in tears and murmurs,
That as steam thou hadst ascended,
That as smoke thy soul had risen,
That as sparks thy life had vanished.
As a bird thou canst not wander
From thy nest to circle homeward,
Canst not fall and die like leaflets,
As the sparks thou canst not perish,
Like the smoke thou canst not vanish.
"Youthful bride, and darling sister,
Thou hast bartered all thy friendships,
Hast exchanged thy loving father,
Thou hast left thy faithful mother
For the mother of thy husband;
Hast exchanged thy loving brother,
Hast renounced thy gentle sister,
For the kindred of thy suitor;
Hast exchanged thy snow-white covers
For the rocky couch of sorrow;
Hast exchanged these crystal waters
For the waters of Wainola;
Hast renounced these sandy sea-shores
For the muddy banks of Kalew;
Northland glens thou hast forsaken
For thy husband's barren meadows;
Thou hast left thy berry-mountains
For the stubble-fields and deserts.
"Thou, O maiden, hast been thinking
Thou wouldst happy be in wedlock;
Neither work, nor care, nor sorrow,
From this night would be thy portion,
With thy husband for protection.
Not to sleep art thou conducted,
Not to happiness, nor joyance,
Wakefulness, thy night-companion,
And thy day-attendant, trouble;
Often thou wilt drink of sorrow,
Often long for vanished pleasures.
"When at home thou hadst no head-gear,
Thou hadst also little sadness;
When thy couch was not of linen,
No unhappiness came nigh thee;
Head-gear brings but pain and sorrow,

Linen breeds bad dispositions,
Linen brings but deeps of anguish,
And the flax untimely mourning.
"Happy in her home, the maiden,
Happy at her father's fireside,
Like the master in his mansion,
Happy with her bows and arrows.
'Tis not thus with married women;
Brides of heroes may be likened
To the prisoners of Moskva,
Held in bondage by their masters.
"As a wife, must weep and labor,
Carry trouble on both shoulders;
When the next hour passes over,
Thou must tend the fire and oven,
Must prepare thy husband's dinner,
Must direct thy master's servants.
When thine evening meal is ready,
Thou must search for bidden wisdom
In the brain of perch and salmon,
In the mouths of ocean whiting,
Gather wisdom from the cuckoo,
Canst not learn it from thy mother,
Mother dear of seven daughters;
Cannot find among her treasures
Where were born the human instincts,
Where were born the minds of heroes,
Whence arose the maiden's beauty,
Whence the beauty of her tresses,
Why all life revives in spring-time.
"Weep, O weep, my pretty young bride.
When thou weepest, weep sincerely,
Weep great rivers from thine eyelids,
Floods of tears in field and fallow,
Lakelets in thy father's dwelling;
Weep thy rooms to overflowing,
Shed thy tears in great abundance,
Lest thou weepest on returning
To thy native hills and valleys,
When thou visitest thy father
In the smoke of waning glory,
On his arm a withered tassel.
"Weep, O weep, my lovely maiden,
When thou weepest, weep in earnest,
Weep great rivers from thine eyelids;
If thou dost not weep sincerely,
Thou wilt weep on thy returning
To thy Northland home and kindred,
When thou visitest thy mother
Old and breathless near the hurdles,
In her arms a barley-bundle.
"Weep, O weep, sweet bride of beauty,
When thou weepest, weep profusely;
If thou dost not weep in earnest,
Thou wilt weep on thy returning
To thy native vales and highlands,
When thou visitest thy brother
Lying wounded by the way-side,
In his hand but empty honors.
"Weep, O weep, my sister's daughter,
Weep great rivers from thine eyelids;

The Kalevala

If thou dost not weep sufficient,
Thou wilt weep on thy returning
To the scenes of happy childhood,
When thou visitest thy sister
Lying, prostrate in the meadow,
In her hand a birch-wood mallet."
When the ancient maid had ended,
Then the young bride sighed in anguish,
Straightway fell to bitter weeping,
  Spake these words in deeps of sorrow:
"O, ye sisters, my beloved,
Ye companions of my childhood,
Playmates of my early summers,
Listen to your sister's counsel:
Cannot comprehend the reason,
Why my mind is so dejected,
Why this weariness and sadness,
This untold and unseen torture,
Cannot understand the meaning
Of this mighty weight of sorrow!
Differently I had thought it,
I had hoped for greater pleasures,
I had hoped to sing as cuckoos,
On the hill-tops call and echo,
When I had attained this station,
Reached at last the goal expectant;
But I am not like the cuckoo,
Singing, merry on the hill-tops;
I am like the songless blue-duck,
As she swims upon the waters,
Swims upon the cold, cold ocean,
Icicles upon her pinions.
"Ancient father, gray-haired mother,
Whither do ye wish to lead me,
Whither take this bride, thy daughter,
That this sorrow may pass over,
Where this heavy heart may lighten,
Where this grief may turn to gladness?
Better it had been, O mother,
Hadst thou nursed a block of birch-wood,
Hadst thou clothed the colored sandstone,
Rather than this hapless maiden,
For the fulness of these sorrows,
For this keen and killing trouble.
Many sympathizers tell me:
'Foolish bride, thou art ungrateful,
Do not grieve, thou child of sorrow,
Thou hast little cause for weeping.'
"O, deceive me not, my people,
Do not argue with me falsely,
For alas! I have more troubles
Than the waterfalls have pebbles,
Than the Ingerland has willows,
Than the Suomi-hills have berries;
Never could the Pohya plow-horse
Pull this mighty weight of sorrow,
Shaking not his birchen cross-bar,
Breaking not his heavy collar;
Never could the Northland reindeer
Heavy shod and stoutly harnessed,
Draw this load of care and trouble."

Lönnrot

By the stove a babe was playing,
And the young child spake as follows:
"Why, O fair bride, art thou weeping,
Why these tears of pain and sadness?
Leave thy troubles to the elk-herds,
And thy grief to sable fillies,
Let the steeds of iron bridles
Bear the burden of thine anguish,
Horses have much larger foreheads,
Larger shoulders, stronger sinews,
And their necks are made for labor,
Stronger are their bones and muscles,
Let them bear thy heavy burdens.
There is little good in weeping,
Useless are thy tears of sorrow;
Art not led to swamps and lowlands,
Nor to banks of little rivers;
Thou art led to fields of flowers,
Led to fruitful trees and forests,
Led away from beer of Pohya
To the sweeter mead of Kalew.
At thy shoulder waits thy husband,
On thy right side, Ilmarinen,
Constant friend and life-protector,
He will guard thee from all evil;
Husband ready, steed in waiting,
Gold-and-silver-mounted harness,
Hazel-birds that sing and flutter
On the courser's yoke and cross-bar;
Thrushes also sing and twitter
Merrily on hame and collar,
Seven bluebirds, seven cuckoos,
Sing thy wedding-march in concord.
"Be no longer full of sorrow,
Dry thy tears, thou bride of beauty,
Thou hast found a noble husband,
Better wilt thou fare than ever,
By the side of Ilmarinen,
Artist husband, metal-master,
Bread-provider of thy table,
On the arm of the fish-catcher,
On the breast of the elk-hunter,
By the side of the bear-killer.
Thou hast won the best of suitors,
Hast obtained a mighty hero;
Never idle is his cross-bow,
On the nails his quivers hang not,
Neither are his dogs in kennel,
Active agents is his bunting.
Thrice within the budding spring-time
In the early hours of morning
He arises from his fare-couch,
From his slumber in the brush-wood,
Thrice within the sowing season,
On his eyes the deer has fallen,
And the branches brushed his vesture,
And his locks been combed by fir-boughs.
Hasten homeward with thy husband,
Where thy hero's friends await thee,
Where his forests sing thy welcome.
"Ilmarinen there possesses

The Kalevala
All the birds that fly in mid-air,
All the beasts that haunt the woodlands,
All that feed upon the mountains,
All that graze on hill and valley,
Sheep and cattle by the thousands;
Sweet the grass upon his meadows,
Sweet the barley in his uplands,
In the lowlands corn abundant,
Wheat upon the elm-wood fallows,
Near the streamlets rye is waving,
Waving grain on many acres,
On his mountains gold and silver,
Rich his mines of shining copper,
Highlands filled with magic metals,
Chests of jewels in his store-house,
All the wealth of Kalevala."

RUNE XXIII
OSMOTAR THE BRIDE-ADVISER

Now the bride must be instructed,
Who will teach the Maid of Beauty,
Who instruct the Rainbow-daughter?
Osmotar, the wisdom-maiden,
Kalew's fair and lovely virgin,
Osmotar will give instructions
To the bride of Ilmarinen,
To the orphaned bride of Pohya,
Teach her how to live in pleasure,
How to live and reign in glory,
Win her second mother's praises,
Joyful in her husband's dwelling.
Osmotar in modest accents
Thus the anxious bride addresses;
"Maid of Beauty, lovely sister,
Tender plant of Louhi's gardens,
Hear thou what thy sister teaches,
Listen to her sage instructions:
Go thou hence, my much beloved,
Wander far away, my flower,
Travel on enwrapped in colors,
Glide away in silks and ribbons,
From this house renowned and ancient,
From thy father's halls and court-yards
Haste thee to thy husband's village,
Hasten to his mother's household;
Strange, the rooms in other dwellings,
Strange, the modes in other hamlets.
"Full of thought must be thy going,
And thy work be well considered,
Quite unlike thy home in Northland,
On the meadows of thy father,
On the high-lands of thy brother,
Singing through thy mother's fenlands,
Culling daisies with thy sister.
"When thou goest from thy father
Thou canst take whatever pleases,
Only three things leave behind thee:
Leave thy day-dreams to thy sister,
Leave thou kindness for thy mother,
To thy brother leave thy labors,
Take all else that thou desirest.
Throw away thine incantations,
Cast thy sighing to the pine-trees,
And thy maidenhood to zephyrs,
Thy rejoicings to the couches,
Cast thy trinkets to the children,
And thy leisure to the gray-beards,
Cast all pleasures to thy playmates,
Let them take them to the woodlands,
Bury them beneath the mountain.
"Thou must hence acquire new habits,
Must forget thy former customs,

The Kalevala

Mother-love must be forsaken,
Thou must love thy husband's mother,
Lower must thy head be bended,
Kind words only must thou utter.
"Thou must hence acquire new habits,
Must forget thy former customs,
Father-love must be forsaken,
Thou must love thy husband's father,
Lower must thy head be bended,
Kind words only must thou utter.
"Thou must hence acquire new habits,
Must forget thy former customs,
Brother-love must be forsaken,
Thou must love thy husband's brother,
Lower must thy head be bended,
Kind words only must thou utter.
"Thou must hence acquire new habits
Must forget thy former customs,
Sister-love must be forsaken,
Thou must love thy husband's sister,
Lower must thy head be bended,
Kind words only must thou utter.
"Never in the course of ages,
Never while the moonlight glimmers,
Wickedly approach thy household,
Nor unworthily, thy servants,
Nor thy courts with indiscretion;
Let thy dwellings sing good manners,
And thy walls re-echo virtue.
After mind the hero searches.
And the best of men seek honor,
Seek for honesty and wisdom;
If thy home should be immoral,
If thine inmates fail in virtue,
Then thy gray-beards would be black-dogs
In sheep's clothing at thy firesides;
All thy women would be witches,
Wicked witches in thy chambers,
And thy brothers be as serpents
Crawling through thy husband's mansion;
All thy sisters would be famous
For their evil thoughts and conduct.
"Equal honors must be given
To thy husband's friends and kindred;
Lower must thy head be bended,
Than within thy mother's dwelling,
Than within thy father's guest-room,
When thou didst thy kindred honor.
Ever strive to give good counsel,
Wear a countenance of sunshine,
Bear a head upon thy shoulders
Filled with wise and ancient sayings;
Open bright thine eyes at morning
To behold the silver sunrise,
Sharpen well thine ears at evening,
Thus to hear the rooster crowing;
When he makes his second calling,
Straightway thou must rise from slumber,
Let the aged sleep in quiet;
Should the rooster fail to call thee,
Let the moonbeams touch thine eyelids,

Lönnrot

Let the Great Bear be thy keeper
Often go thou and consult them,
Call upon the Moon for counsel,
Ask the Bear for ancient wisdom,
From the stars divine thy future;
When the Great Bear faces southward,
When his tail is pointing northward,
This is time to break with slumber,
Seek for fire within the ashes,
Place a spark upon the tinder,
Blow the fire through all the fuel.
If no spark is in the ashes,
Then go wake thy hero-husband,
Speak these words to him on waking:
'Give me fire, O my beloved,
Give a single spark, my husband,
Strike a little fire from flintstone,
Let it fall upon my tinder.'
"From the spark, O Bride of Beauty,
Light thy fires, and heat thine ovens,
In the holder, place the torch-light,
Find thy pathway to the stables,
There to fill the empty mangers;
If thy husband's cows be lowing,
If thy brother's steeds be neighing,
Then the cows await thy coming,
And the steeds for thee are calling,
Hasten, stooping through the hurdles,
Hasten through the yards and stables,
Feed thy husband's cows with pleasure,
Feed with care the gentle lambkins,
Give the cows the best of clover,
Hay, and barley, to the horses,
Feed the calves of lowing mothers,
Feed the fowl that fly to meet thee.
"Never rest upon the haymow,
Never sleep within the hurdles,
When the kine are fed and tended,
When the flocks have all been watered;
Hasten thence, my pretty matron,
Like the snow-flakes to thy dwelling,
There a crying babe awaits thee,
Weeping in his couch neglected,
Cannot speak and tell his troubles,
Speechless babe, and weeping infant,
Cannot say that he is hungry,
Whether pain or cold distresses,
Greets with joy his mother's footsteps.
Afterward repair in silence
To thy husband's rooms and presence,
Early visit thou his chambers,
In thy hand a golden pitcher,
On thine arm a broom of birch-wood,
In thy teeth a lighted taper,
And thyself the fourth in order.
Sweep thou then thy hero's dwelling,
Dust his benches and his tables,
Wash the flooring well with water.
"If the baby of thy sister
Play alone within his corner,
Show the little child attention,

Bathe his eyes and smoothe his ringlets,
Give the infant needed comforts;
Shouldst thou have no bread of barley,
In his hand adjust some trinket.
"Lastly, when the week has ended,
Give thy house a thorough cleansing,
Benches, tables, walls, and ceilings;
What of dust is on the windows,
Sweep away with broom of birch-twigs,
All thy rooms must first be sprinkled,
at the dust may not be scattered,
May not fill the halls and chambers.
Sweep the dust from every crevice,
Leave thou not a single atom;
Also sweep the chimney-corners,
Do not then forget the rafters,
Lest thy home should seem untidy,
Lest thy dwelling seem neglected.
"Hear, O maiden, what I tell thee,
Learn the tenor of my teaching:
Never dress in scanty raiment,
Let thy robes be plain and comely,
Ever wear the whitest linen,
On thy feet wear tidy fur-shoes,
For the glory of thy husband,
For the honor of thy hero.
Tend thou well the sacred sorb-tree,
Guard the mountain-ashes planted
In the court-yard, widely branching;
Beautiful the mountain-ashes,
Beautiful their leaves and flowers,
Still more beautiful the berries.
Thus the exiled one demonstrates
That she lives to please her husband,
Tries to make her hero happy.
"Like the mouse, have ears for hearing,
Like the hare, have feet for running,
Bend thy neck and turn thy visage
Like the juniper and aspen,
Thus to watch with care thy goings,
Thus to guard thy feet from stumbling,
That thou mayest walk in safety.
"When thy brother comes from plowing,
And thy father from his garners,
And thy husband from the woodlands,
From his chopping, thy beloved,
Give to each a water-basin,
Give to each a linen-towel,
Speak to each some pleasant greeting.
"When thy second mother hastens
To thy husband's home and kindred,
In her hand a corn-meal measure,
Haste thou to the court to meet her,
Happy-hearted, bow before her,
Take the measure from her fingers,
Happy, bear it to thy husband.
"If thou shouldst not see distinctly
What demands thy next attention,
Ask at once thy hero's mother:
'Second mother, my beloved,
Name the task to be accomplished

Lönnrot

By thy willing second daughter,
Tell me how to best perform it.'
"This should be the mother's answer:
'This the manner of thy workings,
Thus thy daily work accomplish:
Stamp with diligence and courage,
Grind with will and great endurance,
Set the millstones well in order,
Fill the barley-pans with water,
Knead with strength the dough for baking,
Place the fagots on the fire-place,
That thy ovens may be heated,
Bake in love the honey-biscuit,
Bake the larger loaves of barley,
Rinse to cleanliness thy platters,
Polish well thy drinking-vessels.
"If thou hearest from the mother,
From the mother of thy husband,
That the cask for meal is empty,
Take the barley from the garners,
Hasten to the rooms for grinding.
When thou grindest in the chambers,
Do not sing in glee and joyance,
Turn the grinding-stones in silence,
To the mill give up thy singing,
Let the side-holes furnish music;
Do not sigh as if unhappy,
Do not groan as if in trouble,
Lest the father think thee weary,
Lest thy husband's mother fancy
That thy groans mean discontentment,
That thy sighing means displeasure.
Quickly sift the flour thou grindest,
Take it to the casks in buckets,
Bake thy hero's bread with pleasure,
Knead the dough with care and patience,
That thy biscuits may be worthy,
That the dough be light and airy.
"Shouldst thou see a bucket empty,
Take the bucket on thy shoulder,
On thine arm a silver-dipper,
Hasten off to fill with water
From the crystal river flowing;
Gracefully thy bucket carry,
Bear it firmly by the handles,
Hasten houseward like the zephyrs,
Hasten like the air of autumn;
Do not tarry near the streamlet,
At the waters do not linger,
That the father may not fancy,
Nor the ancient dame imagine,
That thou hast beheld thine image,
Hast admired thy form and features,
Hast admired thy grace and beauty
In the mirror of the fountain,
In the crystal streamlet's eddies.
"Shouldst thou journey to the woodlands,
There to gather aspen-fagots,
Do not go with noise and bustle,
Gather all thy sticks in silence,
Gather quietly the birch-wood,

The Kalevala
That the father may not fancy,
And the mother not imagine,
That thy calling came from anger,
And thy noise from discontentment.
"If thou goest to the store-house
To obtain the flour of barley,
Do not tarry on thy journey,
On the threshold do not linger,
That the father may not fancy,
And the mother not imagine,
That the meal thou hast divided
With the women of the village.
"If thou goest to the river,
There to wash thy birchen platters,
There to cleanse thy pans and buckets,
Lest thy work be done in neatness,
Rinse the sides, and rinse the handles,
Rinse thy pitchers to perfection,
Spoons, and forks, and knives, and goblets,
Rinse with care thy cooking-vessels,
Closely watch the food-utensils,
That the dogs may not deface them,
That the kittens may not mar them,
That the eagles may not steal them,
That the children may not break them;
Many children in the village,
Many little heads and fingers,
That will need thy careful watching,
Lest they steal the things of value.
"When thou goest to thy bathing,
Have the brushes ready lying
In the bath-room clean and smokeless;
Do not, linger in the water,
At thy bathing do not tarry,
That the father may not fancy,
And the mother not imagine,
Thou art sleeping on the benches,
Rolling in the laps of comfort.
"From thy bath, when thou returnest,
To his bathing tempt the father,
Speak to him the words that follow:
'Father of my hero-husband,
Clean are all the bath-room benches,
Everything in perfect order;
Go and bathe for thine enjoyment,
Pour the water all-sufficient,
I will lend thee needed service.'
"When the time has come for spinning,
When the hours arrive for weaving,
Do not ask the help of others,
Look not in the stream for knowledge,
For advice ask not the servants,
Nor the spindle from the sisters,
Nor the weaving-comb from strangers.
Thou thyself must do the spinning,
With thine own hand ply the shuttle,
Loosely wind the skeins of wool-yarn,
Tightly wind the balls of flax-thread,
Wind them deftly in the shuttle
Fit the warp upon the rollers,
Beat the woof and warp together,

Lönnrot

Swiftly ply the weaver's shuttle,
Weave good cloth for all thy vestments,
Weave of woolen, webs for dresses
From the finest wool of lambkins,
One thread only in thy weaving.
"Hear thou what I now advise thee:
Brew thy beer from early barley,
From the barley's new-grown kernels,
Brew it with the magic virtues,
Malt it with the sweets of honey,
Do not stir it with the birch-rod,
Stir it with thy skilful fingers;
When thou goest to the garners,
Do not let the seed bring evil,
Keep the dogs outside the brew-house,
Have no fear of wolves in hunger,
Nor the wild-beasts of the mountains,
When thou goest to thy brewing,
Shouldst thou wander forth at midnight.
"Should some stranger come to see thee,
Do not worry for his comfort;
Ever does the worthy household
Have provisions for the stranger,
Bits of meat, and bread, and biscuit,
Ample for the dinner-table;
Seat the stranger in thy dwelling,
Speak with him in friendly accents,
Entertain the guest with kindness,
While his dinner is preparing.
When the stranger leaves thy threshold,
When his farewell has been spoken,
Lead him only to the portals,
Do not step without the doorway,
That thy husband may not fancy,
And the mother not imagine,
Thou hast interest in strangers.
"Shouldst thou ever make a journey
To the centre of the village,
There to gain some needed object,
While thou speakest in the hamlet,
Let thy words be full of wisdom,
That thou shamest not thy kindred,
Nor disgrace thy husband's household.
"Village-maidens oft will ask thee,
Mothers of the hamlet question:
'Does thy husband's mother greet thee
As in childhood thou wert greeted,
In thy happy home in Pohya?'
Do not answer in negation,
Say that she has always given
Thee the best of her provisions,
Given thee the kindest greetings,
Though it be but once a season.
"Listen well to what I tell thee:
As thou goest from thy father
To thy husband's distant dwelling,
Thou must not forget thy mother,
Her that gave thee life and beauty,
Her that nurtured thee in childhood,
Many sleepless nights she nursed thee;
Often were her wants neglected,

The Kalevala

Numberless the times she rocked thee;
Tender, true, and ever faithful,
Is the mother to her daughter.
She that can forget her mother,
Can neglect the one that nursed her,
Should not visit Mana's castle,
In the kingdom of Tuoni;
In Manala she would suffer,
Suffer frightful retribution,
Should her mother be forgotten;
Should her dear one be neglected,
Mana's daughters will torment her,
And Tuoni's sons revile her,
They will ask her much as follows:
'How couldst thou forget thy mother,
How neglect the one that nursed thee?
Great the pain thy mother suffered,
Great the trouble that thou gavest
When thy loving mother brought thee
Into life for good or evil,
When she gave thee earth-existence,
When she nursed thee but an infant,
When she fed thee in thy childhood,
When she taught thee what thou knowest,
Mana's punishments upon thee,
Since thy mother is forgotten!'"
On the floor a witch was sitting,
Near the fire a beggar-woman,
One that knew the ways of people,
These the words the woman uttered:
"Thus the crow calls in the winter:
'Would that I could be a singer,
And my voice be full of sweetness,
But, alas! my songs are worthless,
Cannot charm the weakest creature;
I must live without the singing
Leave the songs to the musicians,
Those that live in golden houses,
In the homes of the beloved;
Homeless therefore I must wander,
Like a beggar in the corn-fields,
And with none to do me honor.'
"Hear now, sister, what I tell thee,
Enter thou thy husband's dwelling,
Follow not his mind, nor fancies,
As my husband's mind I followed;
As a flower was I when budding,
Sprouting like a rose in spring-time,
Growing like a slender maiden,
Like the honey-gem of glory,
Like the playmates of my childhood,
Like the goslings of my father,
Like the blue-ducks of my mother,
Like my brother's water-younglings,
Like the bullfinch of my sister;
Grew I like the heather-flower,
Like the berry of the meadow,
Played upon the sandy sea-shore,
Rocked upon the fragrant upland,
Sang all day adown the valley,
Thrilled with song the hill and mountain,

Filled with mirth the glen and forest,
Lived and frolicked in the woodlands.
"Into traps are foxes driven
By the cruel pangs of hunger,
Into traps, the cunning ermine;
Thus are maidens wooed and wedded,
In their hunger for a husband.
Thus created is the virgin,
Thus intended is the daughter,
Subject to her hero-husband,
Subject also to his mother.
"Then to other fields I hastened,
Like a berry from the border,
Like a cranberry for roasting,
Like a strawberry for dinner;
All the elm-trees seemed to wound me,
All the aspens tried to cut me,
All the willows tried to seize me,
All the forest tried to slay me.
Thus I journeyed to my husband,
Thus I travelled to his dwelling,
Was conducted to his mother.
Then there were, as was reported,
Six compartments built of pine-wood,
Twelve the number of the chambers,
And the mansion filled with garrets,
Studding all the forest border,
Every by-way filled with flowers
Streamlets bordered fields of barley,
Filled with wheat and corn, the islands,
Grain in plenty in the garners,
Rye unthrashed in great abundance,
Countless sums of gold and silver,
Other treasures without number.
When my journey I had ended,
When my hand at last was given,
Six supports were in his cabin,
Seven poles as rails for fencing.
Filled with anger were the bushes,
All the glens disfavor showing,
All the walks were lined with trouble,
Evil-tempered were the forests,
Hundred words of evil import,
Hundred others of unkindness.
Did not let this bring me sorrow,
Long I sought to merit praises,
Long I hoped to find some favor,
Strove most earnestly for kindness;
When they led me to the cottage,
There I tried some chips to gather,
Knocked my head against the portals
Of my husband's lowly dwelling.
"At the door were eyes of strangers,
Sable eyes at the partition,
Green with envy in his cabin,
Evil heroes in the back-ground,
From each mouth the fire was streaming,
From each tongue the sparks out-flying,
Flying from my second father,
From his eyeballs of unkindness.
Did not let this bring me trouble,

The Kalevala
Tried to live in peace and pleasure,
In the homestead of my husband
In humility I suffered,
Skipped about with feet of rabbit,
Flew along with steps of ermine,
Late I laid my head to slumber,
Early rose as if a servant,
Could not win a touch of kindness,
Could not merit love nor honor,
Though I had dislodged the mountains,
Though the rocks had I torn open.
"Then I turned the heavy millstone,
Ground the flour with care and trouble,
Ground the barley-grains in patience,
That the mother might be nourished,
That her fury-throat might swallow
What might please her taste and fancy,.
From her gold-enamelled platters,
From the corner of her table.
"As for me, the hapless daughter,
All my flour was from the siftings
On the table near the oven,
Ate I from the birchen ladle;
Oftentimes I brought the mosses
Gathered in the lowland meadows,
Baked them into loaves for eating;
Brought the water from the river,
Thirsty, sipped it from the dipper,
Ate of fish the worst in Northland,
Only smelts, and worthless swimmers,
Rocking in my boat of birch-bark
Never ate I fish or biscuit
From my second mother's fingers.
"Blades I gathered in the summers,
Twisted barley-stalks in winter,
Like the laborers of heroes,
Like the servants sold in bondage.
In the thresh-house of my husband,
Evermore to me was given
Flail the heaviest and longest,
And to me the longest lever,
On the shore the strongest beater,
And the largest rake in haying;
No one thought my burden heavy,
No one thought that I could suffer,
Though the best of heroes faltered,
And the strongest women weakened.
"Thus did I, a youthful housewife,
At the right time, all my duties,
Drenched myself in perspiration,
Hoped for better times to follow;
But I only rose to labor,
Knowing neither rest nor pleasure.
I was blamed by all the household,
With ungrateful tongues derided,
Now about my awkward manners,
Now about my reputation,
Censuring my name and station.
Words unkind were heaped upon me,
Fell like hail on me unhappy,
Like the frightful flash of lightning,

Lönnrot

Like the heavy hail of spring-time.
I did not despair entirely,
Would have lived to labor longer
Underneath the tongue of malice,
But the old-one spoiled Lay temper,
Roused my deepest ire and hatred
Then my husband grew a wild-bear,
Grew a savage wolf of Hisi.
"Only then I turned to weeping,
And reflected in my chamber,
Thought of all my former pleasures
Of the happy days of childhood,
Of my father's joyful firesides,
Of my mother's peaceful cottage,
Then began I thus to murmur:
'Well thou knowest, ancient mother,
How to make thy sweet bud blossom,
How to train thy tender shootlet;
Did not know where to ingraft it,
Placed, alas! the little scion
In the very worst of places,
On an unproductive hillock,
In the hardest limb of cherry,
Where it could not grow and flourish,
There to waste its life, in weeping,
Hapless in her lasting sorrow.
Worthier had been my conduct
In the regions that are better,
In the court-yards that are wider,
In compartments that are larger,
Living with a loving husband,
Living with a stronger hero.
Shoe of birch-bark was my suitor,
Shoe of Laplanders, my husband;
Had the body of a raven,
Voice and visage like the jackdaw,
Mouth and claws were from the black-wolf,
The remainder from the wild-bear.
Had I known that mine affianced
Was a fount of pain and evil,
To the hill-side I had wandered,
Been a pine-tree on the highway,
Been a linden on the border,
Like the black-earth made my visage,
Grown a beard of ugly bristles,
Head of loam and eyes of lightning,
For my ears the knots of birches,
For my limbs the trunks of aspens.'
"This the manner of my singing
In the hearing of my husband,
Thus I sang my cares and murmurs
Thus my hero near the portals
Heard the wail of my displeasure,
Then he hastened to my chamber;
Straightway knew I by his footsteps,
Well concluded be was angry,
'Knew it by his steps implanted;
All the winds were still in slumber,
Yet his sable locks stood endwise,
Fluttered round his bead in fury,
While his horrid mouth stood open;

The Kalevala
To and fro his eyes were rolling,
In one hand a branch of willow,
In the other, club of alder;
Struck at me with might of malice,
Aimed the cudgel at my forehead.
"When the evening had descended,
When my husband thought of slumber
Took he in his hand a whip-stalk,
With a whip-lash made of deer-skin,
Was not made for any other,
Only made for me unhappy.
"When at last I begged for mercy,
When I sought a place for resting,
By his side I courted slumber,
Merciless, my husband seized me,
Struck me with his arm of envy,
Beat me with the whip of torture,
Deer-skin-lash and stalk of birch-wood.
From his couch I leaped impulsive,
In the coldest night of winter,
But the husband fleetly followed,
Caught me at the outer portals,
Grasped me by my streaming tresses,
Tore my ringlets from my forehead,
Cast in curls upon the night-winds
To the freezing winds of winter.
What the aid that I could ask for,
Who could free me from my torment?
Made I shoes of magic metals,
Made the straps of steel and copper,
Waited long without the dwelling,
Long I listened at the portals,
Hoping he would end his ravings,
Hoping he would sink to slumber,
But he did not seek for resting,
Did not wish to still his fury.
Finally the cold benumbed me;
As an outcast from his cabin,
I was forced to walk and wander,
When I, freezing, well reflected,
This the substance of my thinking:
'I will not endure this torture,
Will not bear this thing forever,
Will not bear this cruel treatment,
Such contempt I will not suffer
In the wicked tribe of Hisi,
In this nest of evil Piru.'
"Then I said, 'Farewell forever!'
To my husband's home and kindred,
To my much-loved home and husband;
Started forth upon a journey
To my father's distant hamlet,
Over swamps and over snow-fields,
Wandered over towering mountains,
Over hills and through the valleys,
To my brother's welcome meadows,
To my sister's home and birthplace.
"There were rustling withered pine-trees.
Finely-feathered firs were fading,
Countless ravens there were cawing,
All the jackdaws harshly singing,

Lönnrot

This the chorus of the ravens:
'Thou hast here a home no longer,
This is not the happy homestead
Of thy merry days of childhood.'
"Heeding not this woodland chorus,
Straight I journeyed to the dwelling
Of my childhood's friend and brother,
Where the portals spake in concord,
And the hills and valleys answered,
This their saddened song and echo:
'Wherefore dost thou journey hither,
Comest thou for joy or sorrow,
To thy father's old dominions?
Here unhappiness awaits thee,
Long departed is thy father,
Dead and gone to visit Ukko,
Dead and gone thy faithful mother,
And thy brother is a stranger,
While his wife is chill and heartless!'
"Heeding not these many warnings,
Straightway to my brother's cottage
Were my weary feet directed,
Laid my hand upon the door-latch
Of my brother's dismal cottage,
But the latch was cold and lifeless.
When I wandered to the chamber,
When I waited at the doorway,
There I saw the heartless hostess,
But she did not give me greeting,
Did not give her hand in welcome;
Proud, alas! was I unhappy,
Did not make the first advances,
Did not offer her my friendship,
And my hand I did not proffer;
Laid my hand upon the oven,
All its former warmth departed!
On the coal I laid my fingers,
All the latent heat had left it.
On the rest-bench lay my brother,
Lay outstretched before the fire-place,
Heaps of soot upon his shoulders,
Heaps of ashes on his forehead.
Thus the brother asked the stranger,
Questioned thus his guest politely:
'Tell me what thy name and station,
Whence thou comest o'er the waters!'
This the answer that I gave him:
Hast thou then forgot thy sister,
Does my brother not remember,
Not recall his mother's daughter
We are children of one mother,
Of one bird were we the fledgelings,
In one nest were hatched and nurtured.'
"Then the brother fell to weeping,
From his eyes great tear-drops flowing,
To his wife the brother whispered,
Whispered thus unto the housewife.
'Bring thou beer to give my sister,
Quench her thirst and cheer her spirits.'
"Full of envy, brought the sister
Only water filled with evil,

The Kalevala

Water for the infant's eyelids,
Soap and water from the bath-room.
"To his wife the brother whispered,
Whispered thus unto the housewife:
'Bring thou salmon for my sister,
For my sister so long absent,
Thus to still her pangs of hunger.'
"Thereupon the wife obeying,
Brought, in envy, only cabbage
That the children had been eating,
And the house-dogs had been licking,
Leavings of the black-dog's breakfast.
"Then I left my brother's dwelling,
Hastened to the ancient homestead,
To my mother's home deserted;
Onward, onward did I wander,
Hastened onward by the cold-sea,
Dragged my body on in anguish,
To the cottage-doors of strangers,
To the unfamiliar portals,
For the care of the neglected,
For the needy of the village,
For the children poor and orphaned.
"There are many wicked people,
Many slanderers of women,
Many women evil-minded,
That malign their sex through envy.
Many they with lips of evil,
That belie the best of maidens,
Prove the innocent are guilty
Of the worst of misdemeanors,
Speak aloud in tones unceasing,
Speak, alas! with wicked motives,
Spread the follies of their neighbors
Through the tongues of self-pollution.
Very few, indeed, the people
That will feed the poor and hungry,
That will bid the stranger welcome;
Very few to treat her kindly,
Innocent, and lone, and needy,
Few to offer her a shelter
From the chilling storms of winter,
When her skirts with ice are stiffened,
Coats of ice her only raiment!
"Never in my days of childhood,
Never in my maiden life-time,
Never would believe the story
Though a hundred tongues had told
Though a thousand voices sang it,
That such evil things could happen,
That such misery could follow,
Such misfortune could befall one
Who has tried to do her duty,
Who has tried to live uprightly,
Tried to make her people happy."
Thus the young bride was instructed,
Beauteous Maiden of the Rainbow,
Thus by Osmotar, the teacher.

RUNE XXIV
THE BRIDE'S FAREWELL.

Osmotar, the bride-instructor,
Gives the wedding-guests this counsel,
Speaks these measures to the bridegroom:
"Ilmarinen, artist-brother,
Best of all my hero-brothers,
Of my mother's sons the dearest,
Gentlest, truest, bravest, grandest,
Listen well to what I tell thee
Of the Maiden of the Rainbow,
Of thy beauteous life-companion
Bridegroom, praise thy fate hereafter,
Praise forever thy good fortune;
If thou praisest, praise sincerely,
Good the maiden thou hast wedded,
Good the bride that Ukko gives thee,
Graciously has God bestowed her.
Sound her praises to thy father,
Praise her virtues to thy mother,
Let thy heart rejoice in secret,
That thou hast the Bride of Beauty,
Lovely Maiden of the Rainbow!
"Brilliant near thee stands the maiden,
At thy shoulder thy companion,
Happy under thy protection,
Beautiful as golden moonlight,
Beautiful upon thy bosom,
Strong to do thy kindly bidding,
Labor with thee as thou wishest,
Rake the hay upon thy meadows,
Keep thy home in full perfection,
Spin for thee the finest linen,
Weave for thee the richest fabrics,
Make for thee the softest raiment,
Make thy weaver's loom as merry
As the cuckoo of the forest;
Make the shuttle glide in beauty
Like the ermine of the woodlands;
Make the spindle twirl as deftly
As the squirrel spins the acorn;
Village-maidens will not slumber
While thy young bride's loom is humming,
While she plies the graceful shuttle.
"Bridegroom of the Bride of Beauty,
Noblest of the Northland heroes,
Forge thyself a scythe for mowing,
Furnish it with oaken handle,
Carve it in thine ancient smithy,
Hammer it upon thine anvil,
Have it ready for the summer,
For the merry days of sunshine;
Take thy bride then to the lowlands,
Mow the grass upon thy meadows,
Rake the hay when it is ready,

The Kalevala
Make the reeds and grasses rustle,
Toss the fragrant heads of clover,
Make thy hay in Kalevala
When the silver sun is shining.
"When the time has come for weaving,
To the loom attract the weaver,
Give to her the spools and shuttles,
Let the willing loom be worthy,
Beautiful the frame and settle;
Give to her what may be needed,
That the weaver's song may echo,
That the lathe may swing and rattle,
Ma y be heard within the village,
That the aged may remark it,
And the village-maidens question:
'Who is she that now is weaving,
What new power now plies the shuttle?'
"Make this answer to the question:
'It is my beloved weaving,
My young bride that plies the shuttle.'
"Shall the weaver's weft be loosened,
Shall the young bride's loom be tightened?
Do not let the weft be loosened,
Nor the weaver's loom be tightened;
Such the weaving of the daughters
Of the Moon beyond the cloudlets;
Such the spinning of the maidens
Of the Sun in high Jumala,
Of the daughters of the Great Bear,
Of the daughters of the Evening.
Bridegroom, thou beloved hero,
Brave descendant of thy fathers,
When thou goest on a journey,
When thou drivest on the highway,
Driving with the Rainbow-daughter,
Fairest bride of Sariola,
Do not lead her as a titmouse,
As a cuckoo of the forest,
Into unfrequented places,
Into copses of the borders,
Into brier-fields and brambles,
Into unproductive marshes;
Let her wander not, nor stumble
On opposing rocks and rubbish.
Never in her father's dwelling,
Never in her mother's court-yard,
Has she fallen into ditches,
Stumbled hard against the fences,
Run through brier-fields, nor brambles,
Fallen over rocks, nor rubbish.
"Magic bridegroom of Wainola,
Wise descendant of the heroes,
Never let thy young wife suffer,
Never let her be neglected,
Never let her sit in darkness,
Never leave her unattended.
Never in her father's mansion,
In the chambers of her mother,
Has she sat alone in darkness,
Has she suffered for attention;
Sat she by the crystal window,

Lönnrot

Sat and rocked, in peace and plenty,
Evenings for her father's pleasure,
Mornings for her mother's sunshine.
Never mayest thou, O bridegroom,
Lead the Maiden of the Rainbow
To the mortar filled with sea-grass,
There to grind the bark for cooking,
There to bake her bread from stubble,
There to knead her dough from tan-bark
Never in her father's dwelling,
Never in her mother's mansion,
Was she taken to the mortar,
There to bake her bread from sea-grass.
Thou shouldst lead the Bride of Beauty
To the garner's rich abundance,
There to draw the till of barley,
Grind the flour and knead for baking,
There to brew the beer for drinking,
Wheaten flour for honey-biscuits.
"Hero-bridegroom of Wainola,
Never cause thy Bride of Beauty
To regret her day of marriage;
Never make her shed a tear-drop,
Never fill her cup with sorrow.
Should there ever come an evening
When thy wife shall feel unhappy,
Put the harness on thy racer,
Hitch the fleet-foot to the snow-sled;
Take her to her father's dwelling,
To the household of her mother;
Never in thy hero-lifetime,
Never while the moonbeams glimmer,
Give thy fair spouse evil treatment,
Never treat her as thy servant;
Do not bar her from the cellar,
Do not lock thy best provisions
Never in her father's mansion,
Never by her faithful mother
Was she treated as a hireling.
Honored bridegroom of the Northland,
Proud descendant of the fathers,
If thou treatest well thy young wife,
Worthily wilt thou be treated;
When thou goest to her homestead,
When thou visitest her father,
Thou shalt meet a cordial welcome.
"Censure not the Bride of Beauty,
Never grieve thy Rainbow-maiden,
Never say in tones reproachful,
She was born in lowly station,
That her father was unworthy;
Honored are thy bride's relations,
From an old-time tribe, her kindred;
When of corn they sowed a measure,
Each one's portion was a kernel;
When they sowed a cask of flax-seed,
Each received a thread of linen.
Never, never, magic husband,
Treat thy beauty-bride unkindly,
Teach her not with lash of servants,
Strike her not with thongs of leather;

The Kalevala
Never has she wept in anguish
From the birch-whip of her mother.
Stand before her like a rampart,
Be to her a strong protection,
Do not let thy mother chide her,
Let thy father not upbraid her,
Never let thy guests offend her;
Should thy servants bring annoyance,
They may need the master's censure;
Do not harm the Bride of Beauty,
Never injure her thou lovest;
Three long years hast thou been wooing,
Hoping every mouth to win her.
"Counsel with the bride of heaven,
To thy young wife give instruction,
Kindly teach thy bride in secret,
In the long and dreary evenings,
When thou sittest at the fireside;
Teach one year, in words of kindness,
Teach with eyes of love a second,
In the third year teach with firmness.
If she should not heed thy teaching,
Should not hear thy kindly counsel
After three long years of effort,
Cut a reed upon the lowlands,
Cut a nettle from the border,
Teach thy wife with harder measures.
In the fourth year, if she heed not,
Threaten her with sterner treatment,
With the stalks of rougher edges,
Use not yet the thongs of leather,
Do not touch her with the birch-whip.
If she does not heed this warning,
Should she pay thee no attention,
Cut a rod upon the mountains,
Or a willow in the valleys,
Hide it underneath thy mantle,
That the stranger may not see it,
Show it to thy wife in secret,
Shame her thus to do her duty,
Strike not yet, though disobeying.
Should she disregard this warning,
Still refuse to heed thy wishes,
Then instruct her with the willow,
Use the birch-rod from the mountains
In the closet of thy dwelling,
In the attic of thy mansion;
Strike, her not upon the common,
Do not conquer her in public,
Lest the villagers should see thee,
Lest the neighbors hear her weeping,
And the forests learn thy troubles.
Touch thy wife upon the shoulders,
Let her stiffened back be softened.
Do not touch her on the forehead,
Nor upon the ears, nor visage;
If a ridge be on her forehead,
Or a blue mark on her eyelids,
Then her mother would perceive it,
And her father would take notice,
All the village-workmen see it,

Lönnrot

And the village-women ask her
'Hast thou been in heat of battle,
Hast thou struggled in a conflict,
Or perchance the wolves have torn thee,
Or the forest-bears embraced thee,
Or the black-wolf be thy husband,
And the bear be thy protector?'"
By the fire-place lay a gray-beard,
On the hearth-stone lay a beggar,
And the old man spake as follows:
"Never, never, hero-husband,
Follow thou thy young wife's wishes,
Follow not her inclinations,
As, alas! I did, regretful;
Bought my bride the bread of barley,
Veal, and beer, and best of butter,
Fish and fowl of all descriptions,
Beer I bought, home-brewed and sparkling,
Wheat from all the distant nations,
All the dainties of the Northland;
All of this was unavailing,
Gave my wife no satisfaction,
Often came she to my chamber,
Tore my sable locks in frenzy,
With a visage fierce and frightful,
With her eyeballs flashing anger,
Scolding on and scolding ever,
Ever speaking words of evil,
Using epithets the vilest,
Thought me but a block for chopping.
Then I sought for other measures,
Used on her my last resources,
Cut a birch-whip in the forest,
And she spake in tones endearing;
Cut a juniper or willow,
And she called me 'hero-darling';
When with lash my wife I threatened,
Hung she on my neck with kisses."
Thus the bridegroom was instructed,
Thus the last advices given.
Then the Maiden of the Rainbow,
Beauteous bride of Ilmarinen,
Sighing heavily and moaning,
Fell to weeping, heavy-hearted,
Spake these words from depths of sorrow:
"Near, indeed, the separation,
Near, alas! the time for parting,
Near the time for my departure;
O the anguish of the parting,
O the pain of separation,
From these walls renowned and ancient,
From this village of the Northland,
From these scenes of peace and plenty,
Where my faithful mother taught me,
Where my father gave instruction
To me in my happy childhood,
When my years were few and tender!
As a child I did not fancy,
Never thought of separation
From the confines of this cottage,
From these dear old hills and mountains,

The Kalevala
But, alas! I now must journey,
Since I now cannot escape it;
Empty is the bowl of parting,
All the farewell-beer is taken,
And my husband's sledge is waiting,
With the break-board looking southward,
Looking from my father's dwelling.
"How shall I give compensation,
How repay, on my departure,
All the kindness of my mother,
All the counsel of my father,
All the friendship of my brother,
All my sister's warm affection?
Gratitude to thee, dear father,
For my former-life and blessings,
For the comforts of thy table,
For the pleasures of my childhood!
Gratitude to thee, dear mother,
For thy tender care and guidance,
For my birth and for my culture,
Nurtured by thy purest life-blood!
Gratitude to thee, dear brother,
Gratitude to thee, sweet sister,
To the servants of my childhood,
To my many friends and playmates!
"Never, never, aged father,
Never, thou, beloved mother,
Never, ye, my kindred spirits,
Never harbor care, nor sorrow,
Never fall to bitter weeping,
Since thy child has gone to others,
To the distant home of strangers,
To the meadows of Wainola,
From her father's fields and firesides.
Shines the Sun of the Creator,
Shines the golden Moon of Ukko,
Glitter all the stars of heaven,
In the firmament of ether,
Full as bright on other homesteads;
Not upon my father's uplands,
Not upon my home in childhood,
Shines the Star of Joyance only.
"Now the time has come for parting
From my father's golden firesides,
From my brother's welcome hearth-stone,
From the chambers of my sister,
From my mother's happy dwelling;
Now I leave the swamps and lowlands,
Leave the grassy vales and mountains,
Leave the crystal lakes and rivers,
Leave the shores and sandy shallows,
Leave the white-capped surging billows,
Where the maidens swim and linger,
Where the mermaids sing and frolic;
Leave the swamps to those that wander,
Leave the corn-fields to the plowman,
Leave the forests to the weary,
Leave the heather to the rover,
Leave the copses to the stranger,
Leave the alleys to the beggar,
Leave the court-yards to the rambler,

Lönnrot

Leave the portals to the servant,
Leave the matting to the sweeper,
Leave the highways to the roebuck,
Leave the woodland-glens to lynxes,
Leave the lowlands to the wild-geese,
And the birch-tree to the cuckoo.
Now I leave these friends of childhood,
Journey southward with my husband,
To the arms of Night and Winter,
O'er the ice-grown seas of Northland.
"Should I once again, returning,
Pay a visit to my tribe-folk,
Mother would not hear me calling,
Father would not see me weeping,
Calling at my mother's grave-stone,
'Weeping o'er my buried father,
On their graves the fragrant flowers,
Junipers and mournful willows,
Verdure from my mother's tresses,
From the gray-beard of my father.
"Should I visit Sariola,
Visit once again these borders,
No one here would bid me welcome.
Nothing in these hills would greet me,
Save perchance a few things only,
By the fence a clump of osiers,
And a land-mark at the corner,
Which in early youth I planted,
When a child of little stature.
"Mother's kine perhaps will know me,
Which so often I have watered,
Which I oft have fed and tended,
Lowing now at my departure,
In the pasture cold and cheerless;
Sure my mother's kine will welcome
Northland's daughter home returning.
Father's steeds may not forget me,
Steeds that I have often ridden,
When a maiden free and happy,
Neighing now for me departing,
In the pasture of my brother,
In the stable of my father;
Sure my father's steeds will know me,
Bid Pohyola's daughter welcome.
Brother's faithful dogs may know me,
That I oft have fed and petted,
Dogs that I have taught to frolic,
That now mourn for me departing,
In their kennels in the court-yard,
In their kennels cold and cheerless;
Sure my brother's dogs will welcome
Pohya's daughter home returning.
But the people will not know me,
When I come these scenes to visit,
Though the fords remain as ever,
Though unchanged remain the rivers,
Though untouched the flaxen fish-nets
On the shores await my coming.
"Fare thou well, my dear old homestead,
Fare ye well, my native bowers;
It would give me joy unceasing

The Kalevala
Could I linger here forever.
Now farewell, ye halls and portals,
Leading to my father's mansion;
It would give me joy unceasing
Could I linger here forever.
Fare ye well, familiar gardens
Filled with trees and fragrant flowers;
It would give me joy unceasing,
Could I linger here forever.
Send to all my farewell greetings,
To the fields, and groves, and berries;
Greet the meadows with their daisies,
Greet the borders with their fences,
Greet the lakelets with their islands,
Greet the streams with trout disporting,
Greet the hills with stately pine-trees,
And the valleys with their birches.
Fare ye well, ye streams and lakelets,
Fertile fields, and shores of ocean,
All ye aspens on the mountains,
All ye lindens of the valleys,
All ye beautiful stone-lindens,
All ye shade-trees by the cottage,
All ye junipers and willows,
All ye shrubs with berries laden,
Waving grass and fields of barley,
Arms of elms, and oaks, and alders,
Fare ye well, dear scenes of childhood,
Happiness of days departed!"
Ending thus, Pohyola's daughter
Left her native fields and fallows,
Left the darksome Sariola,
With her husband, Ilmarinen,
Famous son of Kalevala.
But the youth remained for singing,
This the chorus of the children:
"Hither came a bird of evil'
Flew in fleetness from the forest,
Came to steal away our virgin,
Came to win the Maid of Beauty;
Took away our fairest flower,
Took our mermaid from the waters,
Won her with his youth and beauty,
With his keys of ancient wisdom.
Who will lead us to the sea-beach,
Who conduct us to the rivers?
Now the buckets will be idle,
On the hooks will rest the fish-poles,
Now unswept will lie the matting,
And unswept the halls of birch-wood,
Copper goblets be unburnished,
Dark the handles of the pitchers,
Fare thou well, dear Rainbow Maiden."
Ilmarinen, happy bridegroom,
Hastened homeward with the daughter
Of the hostess of Pohyola,
With the beauty of the Northland
Fleetly flew the hero's snow-sledge,
Loudly creaked, and roared, and rattled
Down the banks of Northland waters,
By the side of Honey-inlet,

Lönnrot

On the back of Sandy Mountain.
Stones went rolling from the highway,
Like the winds the sledge flew onward,
On the yoke rang hoops of iron,
Loud the spotted wood resounded,
Loudly creaked the bands of willow,
All the birchen cross-bars trembled,
And the copper-bells rang music,
In the racing of the fleet-foot,
In the courser's gallop homeward;
Journeyed one day, then a second,
Journeyed still the third day onward,
In one hand the reins of magic,
While the other grasped the maiden,
One foot resting on the cross-bar,
And the other in the fur-robes.
Merrily the steed flew homeward,
Quickly did the highways shorten,
Till at last upon the third day,
As the sun was fast declining,
There appeared the blacksmith's furnace,
Nearer, Ilmarinen's dwelling,
Smoke arising high in ether,
Clouds of smoke to lofty heaven,
From the village of Wainola,
From the suitor's forge and smithy,
From the chimneys of the hero,
From the home of the successful.

BOOK II

RUNE XXV

WAINAMOINEN'S WEDDING-SONGS.

At the home of Ilmarinen
Long had they been watching, waiting,
For the coming of the blacksmith,
With his bride from Sariola.
Weary were the eyes of watchers,
Waiting from the father's portals,
Looking from the mother's windows;
Weary were the young knees standing
At the gates of the magician;
Weary grew the feet of children,
Tramping to the walls and watching;
Worn and torn, the shoes of heroes,
Running on the shore to meet him.
Now at last upon a morning
Of a lovely day in winter,
Heard they from the woods the rumble
Of a snow-sledge swiftly bounding.
Lakko, hostess of Wainola,
She the lovely Kalew-daughter,
Spake these words in great excitement:
"'Tis the sledge of the magician,
Comes at last the metal-worker
From the dismal Sariola,
By his side the Bride of Beauty!
Welcome, welcome, to this hamlet,
Welcome to thy mother's hearth-stone,
To the dwelling of thy father,
By thine ancestors erected!"
Straightway came great Ilmarinen
To his cottage drove the blacksmith,
To the fireside of his father,
To his mother's ancient dwelling.
Hazel-birds were sweetly singing
On the newly-bended collar;
Sweetly called the sacred cuckoos
From the summit of the break-board;
Merry, jumped the graceful squirrel
On the oaken shafts and cross-bar.
Lakko, Kalew's fairest hostess,
Beauteous daughter of Wainola,
Spake these words of hearty welcome:
"For the new moon hopes the village,
For the sun, the happy maidens,
For the boat, the swelling water;
I have not the moon expected,
For the sun have not been waiting,
I have waited for my hero,
Waited for the Bride of Beauty;
Watched at morning, watched at evening,
Did not know but some misfortune,

Lönnrot

Some sad fate had overtaken
Bride and bridegroom on their journey;
Thought the maiden growing weary,
Weary of my son's attentions,
Since he faithfully had promised
To return to Kalevala,
Ere his foot-prints had departed
From the snow-fields of his father.
Every morn I looked and listened,
Constantly I thought and wondered
When his sledge would rumble homeward,
When it would return triumphant
To his home, renowned and ancient.
Had a blind and beggared straw-horse
Hobbled to these shores awaiting,
With a sledge of but two pieces,
Well the steed would have been lauded,
Had it brought my son beloved,
Had it brought the Bride of Beauty.
Thus I waited long, impatient,
Looking out from morn till even,
Watching with my head extended,
With my tresses streaming southward,
With my eyelids widely opened,
Waiting for my son's returning
To this modest home of heroes,
To this narrow place of resting.
Finally am I rewarded,
For the sledge has come triumphant,
Bringing home my son and hero,
By his side the Rainbow maiden,
Red her cheeks, her visage winsome,
Pride and joy of Sariola.
"Wizard-bridegroom of Wainola,
Take thy-courser to the stable,
Lead him to the well-filled manger,
To the best of grain and clover;
Give to us thy friendly greetings,
Greetings send to all thy people.
When thy greetings thou hast ended,
Then relate what has befallen
To our hero in his absence.
Hast thou gone without adventure
To the dark fields of Pohyola,
Searching for the Maid of Beauty?
Didst thou scale the hostile ramparts,
Didst thou take the virgin's mansion,
Passing o'er her mother's threshold,
Visiting the halls of Louhi?
"But I know without the asking,
See the answer to my question:
Comest from the North a victor,
On thy journey well contented;
Thou hast brought the Northland daughter,
Thou hast razed the hostile portals,
Thou hast stormed the forts of Louhi,
Stormed the mighty walls opposing,
On thy journey to Pohyola,
To the village of the father.
In thy care the bride is sitting,
In thine arms, the Rainbow-maiden,

The Kalevala
At thy side, the pride of Northland,
Mated to the highly-gifted.
Who has told the cruel story,
Who the worst of news has scattered,
That thy suit was unsuccessful,
That in vain thy steed had journeyed?
Not in vain has been thy wooing,
Not in vain thy steed has travelled
To the dismal homes of Lapland;
He has journeyed heavy laden,
Shaken mane, and tail, and forelock,
Dripping foam from lips and nostrils,
Through the bringing of the maiden,
With the burden of the husband.
"Come, thou beauty, from the snow-sledge,
Come, descend thou from the cross-bench,
Do not linger for assistance,
Do not tarry to be carried;
If too young the one that lifts thee,
If too proud the one in waiting,
Rise thou, graceful, like a young bird,
Hither glide along the pathway,
On the tan-bark scarlet- colored,
That the herds of kine have evened,
That the gentle lambs have trodden,
Smoothened by the tails of horses.
Haste thou here with gentle footsteps,
Through the pathway smooth and tidy,
On the tiles of even surface,
On thy second father's court-yard,
To thy second mother's dwelling,
To thy brother's place of resting,
To thy sister's silent chambers.
Place thy foot within these portals,
Step across this waiting threshold,
Enter thou these halls of joyance,
Underneath these painted rafters,
Underneath this roof of ages.
During all the winter evenings,
Through the summer gone forever,
Sang the tiling made of ivory,
Wishing thou wouldst walk upon it;
Often sang the golden ceiling,
Hoping thou wouldst walk beneath it,
And the windows often whistled,
Asking thee to sit beside them;
Even on this merry morning,
Even on the recent evening,
Sat the aged at their windows,
On the sea-shore ran the children,
Near the walls the maidens waited,
Ran the boys upon the highway,
There to watch the young bride's coming,
Coming with her hero-husband.
"Hail, ye courtiers of Wainola,
With the heroes of the fathers,
Hail to thee, Wainola's hamlet,
Hail, ye halls with heroes peopled,
Hail, ye rooms with all your inmates,
Hail to thee, sweet golden moonlight,
Hail to thee, benignant Ukko,

Lönnrot

Hail companions of the bridegroom!
Never has there been in Northland
Such a wedding-train of honor,
Never such a bride of beauty.
"Bridegroom, thou beloved hero,
Now untie the scarlet ribbons,
And remove the silken muffler,
Let us see the honey-maiden,
See the Daughter of the Rainbow.
Seven years hast thou been wooing,
Hast thou brought the maid affianced,
Wainamoinen's Wedding-Songs.
Hast thou sought a sweeter cuckoo,
Sought one fairer than the moonlight,
Sought a mermaid from the ocean?
But I know without the asking,
See the answer to my question:
Thou hast brought the sweet-voiced cuckoo,
Thou hast found the swan of beauty
Plucked the sweetest flower of Northland,
Culled the fairest of the jewels,
Gathered Pohya's sweetest berry!"
Sat a babe upon the matting,
And the young child spake as follows:
"Brother, what is this thou bringest,
Aspen-log or trunk of willow,
Slender as the mountain-linden?
Bridegroom, well dost thou remember,
Thou hast hoped it all thy life-time,
Hoped to bring the Maid of Beauty,
Thou a thousand times hast said it,
Better far than any other,
Not one like the croaking raven,
Nor the magpie from the border,
Nor the scarecrow from the corn-fields,
Nor the vulture from the desert.
What has this one done of credit,
In the summer that has ended?
Where the gloves that she has knitted,
Where the mittens she has woven?
Thou hast brought her empty-handed,
Not a gift she brings thy father;
In thy chests the nice are nesting,
Long-tails feeding on thy vestments,
And thy bride, cannot repair them."
Lakko hostess of Wainola,
She the faithful Kalew-daughter,
Hears the young child's speech in wonder,
Speaks these words of disapproval:
Silly prattler, cease thy talking,
Thou Last spoken in dishonor;
Let all others be astonished,
Reap thy malice on thy kindred,
must not harm the Bride of Beauty,
Rainbow-daughter of the Northland.
False indeed is this thy Prattle,
All thy words are full or evil,
Fallen from thy tongue of mischief
From the lips of one unworthy.
Excellent the hero's young bride,
Best of all in Sariola,

The Kalevala

Like the strawberry in summer,
Like the daisy from the meadow,
Like the cuckoo from the forest,
Like the bluebird from the aspen,
Like the redbreast from the heather,
Like the martin from the linden;
Never couldst thou find in Ehstland
Such a virgin as this daughter,
Such a graceful beauteous maiden,
With such dignity of Carriage,
With such arms of pearly whiteness,
With a neck so fair and lovely.
Neither is she empty-handed,
She has brought us furs abundant,
Brought us many silken garments,
Richest weavings of Pohyola.
Many beauteous things the maiden,
With the spindle has accomplished,
Spun and woven with her fingers
Dresses of the finest texture
She in winter has upfolded,
Bleached them in the days of spring-time,
Dried them at the hour of noon-day,
For our couches finest linen,
For our heads the softest pillows,
For our comfort woollen blankets,
For our necks the silken ribbons."
To the bride speaks gracious Lakko:
"Goodly wife, thou Maid of Beauty,
Highly wert thou praised as daughter,
In thy father's distant country;
Here thou shalt be praised forever
By the kindred of thy husband;
Thou shalt never suffer sorrow,
Never give thy heart to grieving;
In the swamps thou wert not nurtured,
Wert not fed beside the brooklets;
Thou wert born 'neath stars auspicious,
Nurtured from the richest garners,
Thou wert taken to the brewing
Of the sweetest beer in Northland.
"Beauteous bride from Sariola,
Shouldst thou see me bringing hither
Casks of corn, or wheat, or barley;
Bringing rye in great abundance,
They belong to this thy household;
Good the plowing of thy husband,
Good his sowing and his reaping.
"Bride of Beauty from the Northland,
Thou wilt learn this home to manage,
Learn to labor with thy kindred;
Good the home for thee to dwell in,
Good enough for bride and daughter.
At thy hand will rest the milk-pail,
And the churn awaits thine order;
It is well here for the maiden,
Happy will the young bride labor,
Easy are the resting-benches;
Here the host is like thy father,
Like thy mother is the hostess,
All the sons are like thy brothers,

Lönnrot

Like thy sisters are the daughters.
"Shouldst thou ever have a longing
For the whiting of the ocean,
For thy, father's Northland salmon,
For thy brother's hazel-chickens,
Ask them only of thy husband,
Let thy hero-husband bring them.
There is not in all of Northland,
Not a creature of the forest,
Not a bird beneath the ether,
Not a fish within the waters,
Not the largest, nor the smallests
That thy husband cannot capture.
It is well here for the maiden,
Here the bride may live in freedom,
Need not turn the heavy millstone,
Need not move the iron pestle;
Here the wheat is ground by water,
For the rye, the swifter current,
While the billows wash the vessels
And the surging waters rinse them.
Thou hast here a lovely village,
Finest spot in all of Northland,
In the lowlands sweet the verdure,
in the uplands, fields of beauty,
With the lake-shore near the hamlet,
Near thy home the running water,
Where the goslings swim and frolic,
Water-birds disport in numbers."
Thereupon the bride and bridegroom
Were refreshed with richest viands,
Given food and drink abundant,
Fed on choicest bits of reindeer,
On the sweetest loaves of barley,
On the best of wheaten biscuits,
On the richest beer of Northland.
Many things were on the table,
Many dainties of Wainola,
In the bowls of scarlet color,
In the platters deftly painted,
Many cakes with honey sweetened,
To each guest was butter given,
Many bits of trout and whiting,
Larger salmon carved in slices,
With the knives of molten silver,
Rimmed with gold the silver handles,
Beer of barley ceaseless flowing,
Honey-drink that was not purchased,
In the cellar flows profusely,
Beer for all, the tongues to quicken,
Mead and beer the minds to freshen.
Who is there to lead the singing,
Lead the songs of Kalevala?
Wainamoinen, old and truthful,
The eternal, wise enchanter,
Quick begins his incantations,
Straightway sings the songs that follow.
"Golden brethren, dearest kindred,
Ye, my loved ones, wise and worthy
Ye companions, highly-gifted,
Listen to my simple sayings:

The Kalevala
Rarely stand the geese together,
Sisters do not mate each other,
Not together stand the brothers,
Nor the children of one mother,
In the countries of the Northland.
"Shall we now begin the singing,
Sing the songs of old tradition?
Singers can but sing their wisdom,
And the cuckoo call the spring-time,
And the goddess of the heavens
Only dyes the earth in beauty;
So the goddesses of weaving
Can but weave from dawn till twilight,
Ever sing the youth of Lapland
In their straw-shoes full of gladness,
When the coarse-meat of the roebuck,
Or of blue-moose they have eaten.
Wherefore should I not be singing,
And the children not be chanting
Of the biscuits of Wainola,
Of the bread of Kalew-waters?
Even Sing the lads of Lapland
In their straw-shoes filled with joyance,
Drinking but a cup of water,
Eating but the bitter tan-bark.
Wherefore should I not be singing,
And the children not be chanting
Of the beer of Kalevala,
Brewed from barley in perfection,
Dressed in quaint and homely costume,
As they sit beside their hearth-stones.
Wherefore should I not be singing,
And the children too be chanting
Underneath these painted rafters,
In these halls renowned and ancient?
This the place for men to linger,
This the court-room for the maidens,
Near the foaming beer of barley,
Honey-brewed in great abundance,
Very near, the salmon-waters,
Near, the nets for trout and whiting,
Here where food is never wanting,
Where the beer is ever brewing.
Here Wainola's sons assemble,
Here Wainola's daughters gather,
Here they never eat in trouble,
Here they live without regretting,
In the life-time of the landlord,
While the hostess lives and prospers.
"Who shall first be sung and lauded?
Shall it be the bride or bridegroom?
Let us praise the bridegroom's father,
Let the hero-host be chanted,
Him whose home is in the forest,
Him who built upon the mountains,
Him who brought the trunks of lindens,
With their tops and slender branches,
Brought them to the best of places,
Joined them skilfully together,
For the mansion of the nation,
For this famous hero-dwelling,

Lönnrot

Walls procured upon the lowlands,
Rafters from the pine and fir-tree,
From the woodlands beams of oak-wood,
From the berry-plains the studding,
Bark was furnished by the aspen,
And the mosses from the fenlands.
Trimly builded is this mansion,
In a haven warmly sheltered;
Here a hundred men have labored,
On the roof have stood a thousand,
As this spacious house was building,
As this roof was tightly jointed.
Here the ancient mansion-builder,
When these rafters were erected,
Lost in storms his locks of sable,
Scattered by the winds of heaven.
Often has the hero-landlord
On the rocks his gloves forgotten,
Left his hat upon the willows,
Lost his mittens in the marshes;
Oftentimes the mansion-builder,
In the early hours of morning,
Ere his workmen had awakened,
Unperceived by all the village,
Has arisen from his slumber,
Left his cabin the snow-fields,
Combed his locks among the branches,
Bathed his eyes in dews of morning.
"Thus obtained the pleasant landlord
Friends to fill his spacious dwelling,
Fill his benches with magicians,
Fill his windows with enchanters,
Fill his halls with wizard-singers,
Fill his floors with ancient speakers,
Fill his ancient court with strangers,
Fill his hurdles with the needy;
Thus the Kalew-host is lauded.
"Now I praise the genial hostess,
Who prepares the toothsome dinner,
Fills with plenty all her tables,
Bakes the honeyed loaves of barley,
Kneads the dough with magic fingers,
With her arms of strength and beauty,
Bakes her bread in copper ovens,
Feeds her guests and bids them welcome,
Feeds them on the toothsome bacon,
On the trout, and pike, and whiting,
On the rarest fish in ocean,
On the dainties of Wainola.
"Often has the faithful hostess
Risen from her couch in silence,
Ere the crowing of the watcher,
To prepare the wedding-banquet,
Make her tables look attractive.
Brew the honey-beer of wedlock.
Excellently has the housewife,
Has the hostess filled with wisdom,
Brewed the beer from hops and barley,
From the corn of Kalevala,
From the wheat-malt honey-seasoned,
Stirred the beer with graceful fingers,

The Kalevala

At the oven in the penthouse,
In the chamber swept and polished.
Neither did the prudent hostess,
Beautiful, and full of wisdom,
Let the barley sprout too freely,
Lest the beer should taste of black-earth,
Be too bitter in the brewing,
Often went she to the garners,
Went alone at hour of midnight,
Was not frightened by the black-wolf,
Did not fear the beasts of woodlands.
"Now the hostess I have lauded,
Let me praise the favored suitor,
Now the honored hero-bridegroom,
Best of all the village-masters.
Clothed in purple is the hero,
Raiment brought from distant nations,
Tightly fitting to his body;
Snugly sets his coat of ermine,
To the floor it hangs in beauty,
Trailing from his neck and shoulders,
Little of his vest appearing,
Peeping through his outer raiment,
Woven by the Moon's fair daughters,
And his vestment silver-tinselled.
Dressed in neatness is the suitor,
Round his waist a belt of copper,
Hammered by the Sun's sweet maidens,
Ere the early fires were lighted,
Ere the fire had been discovered.
Dressed in richness is the bridegroom,
On his feet are silken stockings,
Silken ribbons on his ankles,
Gold and silver interwoven.
Dressed in beauty is the bridegroom,
On his feet are shoes of deer-skin,
Like the swans upon the water,
Like the blue-duck on the sea-waves,
Like the thrush among the willows,
Like the water-birds of Northland.
Well adorned the hero-suitor,
With his locks of golden color,
With his gold-beard finely braided,
Hero-hat upon his forehead,
Piercing through the forest branches,
Reaching to the clouds of heaven,
Bought with countless gold and silver,
Priceless is the suitor's head-gear.
"Now the bridegroom has been lauded,
I will praise the young bride's playmate,
Day-companion in her childhood,
In the maiden's magic mansion.
Whence was brought the merry maiden,
From the village of Tanikka?
Thence was never brought the playmate,
Playmate of the bride in childhood.
Has she come from distant nations,
From the waters of the Dwina,
O'er the ocean far-outstretching?
Not from Dwina came the maiden,
Did not sail across the waters;

Lönnrot

Grew as berry in the mountains,
As a strawberry of sweetness,
On the fields the child of beauty,
In the glens the golden flower.
Thence has come the young bride's playmate,
Thence arose her fair companion.
Tiny are her feet and fingers,
Small her lips of scarlet color,
Like the maiden's loom of Suomi;
Eyes that shine in kindly beauty
Like the twinkling stars of heaven;
Beam the playmate's throbbing temples
Like the moonlight on the waters.
Trinkets has the bride's companion,
On her neck a golden necklace,
In her tresses, silken ribbons,
On her arms are golden bracelets,
Golden rings upon her fingers,
Pearls are set in golden ear-rings,
Loops of gold upon her temples,
And with pearls her brow is studded.
Northland thought the Moon was shining
When her jeweled ear-ringsglistened;
Thought the Sun had left his station
When her girdle shone in beauty;
Thought a ship was homeward sailing
When her colored head-gear fluttered.
Thus is praised the bride's companion,
Playmate of the Rainbow-maiden.
"Now I praise the friends assembled,
All appear in graceful manners;
If the old are wise and silent,
All the youth are free and merry,
All the guests are fair and worthy.
Never was there in Wainola,
Never will there be in Northland,
Such a company assembled;
All the children speak in joyance,
All the aged move sedately;
Dressed in white are all the maidens,
Like the hoar-frost of the morning,
Like the welcome dawn of spring-time,
Like the rising of the daylight.
Silver then was more abundant,
Gold among the guests in plenty,
On the hills were money, pockets,
Money-bags along the valleys,
For the friends that were invited,
For the guests in joy assembled.
All the friends have now been lauded,
Each has gained his meed of honor."
Wainamoinen, old and truthful,
Song-deliverer of Northland,
Swung himself upon the fur-bench
Or his magic sledge of copper,
Straightway hastened to his hamlet,
Singing as he journeyed onward,
Singing charms and incantations,
Singing one day, then a second,
All the third day chanting legends.
On the rocks the runners rattled,

The Kalevala

Hung the sledge upon a birch-stump,
Broke it into many pieces,
With the magic of his singing;
Double were the runners bended,
All the parts were torn asunder,
And his magic sledge was ruined.
Then the good, old Wainamoinen
Spake these words in meditation:
"Is there one among this number,
In this rising generation,
Or perchance among the aged,
In the passing generation,
That will go to Mana's kingdom,
To the empire of Tuoni,
There to get the magic auger
From the master of Manala,
That I may repair my snow-sledge,
Or a second sledge may fashion?"
What the younger people answered
Was the answer of the aged:
"Not among the youth of Northland,
Nor among the aged heroes,
Is there one of ample courage,
That has bravery sufficient,
To attempt the reckless journey
To the kingdom of Tuoni,
To Manala's fields and castles,
Thence to bring Tuoni's auger,
Wherewithal to mend thy snow-sledge,
Build anew thy sledge of magic."
Thereupon old Wainamoinen,
The eternal wisdom-singer,
Went again to Mana's empire,
To the kingdom of Tuoni,
Crossed the sable stream of Deathland,
To the castles of Manala,
Found the auger of Tuoni,
Brought the instrument in safety.
Straightway sings old Wainamoinen,
Sings to life a purple forest,
In the forest, slender birches,
And beside them, mighty oak-trees,
Shapes them into shafts and runners,
Moulds them by his will and power,
Makes anew his sledge of magic.
On his steed he lays the harness,
Binds him to his sledge securely,
Seats himself upon the cross-bench,
And the racer gallops homeward,
To the manger filled and waiting,
To the stable of his master;
Brings the ancient Wainamoinen,
Famous bard and wise enchanter,
To the threshold of his dwelling,
To his home in Kalevala.

RUNE XXVI
ORIGIN OF THE SERPENT.

Ahti, living on the island,
Near the Kauko-point and harbor,
Plowed his fields for rye and barley,
Furrowed his extensive pastures,
Heard with quickened ears an uproar,
Heard the village in commotion,
Heard a noise along the sea-shore,
Heard the foot-steps on the ice-plain,
Heard the rattle of the sledges;
Quick his mind divined the reason,
Knew it was Pohyola's wedding,
Wedding of the Rainbow-virgin.
Quick he stopped in disappointment,
Shook his sable locks in envy,
Turned his hero-head in anger,
While the scarlet blood ceased flowing
Through his pallid face and temples;
Ceased his plowing and his sowing,
On the field he left the furrows,
On his steed he lightly mounted,
Straightway galloped fleetly homeward
To his well-beloved mother,
To his mother old and golden,
Gave his mother these directions,
These the words of Lemminkainen:
"My beloved, faithful mother,
Quickly bring me beer and viands,
Bring me food for I am hungry,
Food and drink for me abundant,
Have my bath-room quickly heated,
Quickly set the room in order,
That I may refresh my body,
Dress myself in hero-raiment."
Lemminkainen's aged mother
Brings her hero food in plenty,
Beer and viands for the hungry,
For her thirsting son and hero;
Quick she heats the ancient bath-room,
Quickly sets his bath in order.
Then the reckless Lemminkainen
Ate his meat with beer inspiring,
Hastened to his bath awaiting;
Only was the bullfinch bathing,
With the many-colored bunting;
Quick the hero laved his temples,
Laved himself to flaxen whiteness,
Quick returning to his mother,
Spake in haste the words that follow:
"My beloved, helpful mother,
Go at once to yonder mountain,
To the store-house on the hill-top,
Bring my vest of finest texture,
Bring my hero-coat of purple,

The Kalevala

Bring my suit of magic colors,
Thus to make me look attractive,
Thus to robe myself in beauty."
First the ancient mother asked him,
Asked her son this simple question:
"Whither dost thou go, my hero?
Dost thou go to hunt the roebuck,
Chase the lynx upon the mountains,
Shoot the squirrel in the woodlands?"
Spake the reckless Lemminkainen,
Also known as Kaukomieli:
"Worthy mother of my being,
Go I not to hunt the roebuck,
Chase the lynx upon the mountains,
Shoot the squirrel on the tree-tops;
I am going to Pohyola,
To the feasting of her people.
Bring at once my purple vestments,
Straightway bring my nuptial outfit,
Let me don it for the marriage
Of the maiden of the Northland."
But the ancient dame dissented,
And the wife forebade the husband;
Two of all the best of heroes,
Three of nature's fairest daughters,
Strongly urged wild Lemminkainen
Not to go to Sariola,
To Pohyola's great carousal,
To the marriage-feast of Northland,
"Since thou hast not been invited,
Since they do not wish thy presence."
Spake the reckless Lemminkainen.
These the words of Kaukomieli:
"Where the wicked are invited,
There the good are always welcome,
Herein lies my invitation;
I am constantly reminded
By this sword of sharpened edges,
By this magic blade and scabbard,
That Pohyola needs my presence."
Lemminkainen's aged mother
Sought again to stay her hero:
"Do not go, my son beloved,
To the feasting in Pohyola;
Full of horrors are the highways,
On the road are many wonders,
Three times Death appears to frighten,
Thrice destruction hovers over!"
Spake the reckless Lemminkainen,
These the words of Kaukomieli:
"Death is seen by aged people,
Everywhere they see perdition,
Death can never frighten heroes,
Heroes do not fear the spectre;
Be that as it may, dear mother,
Tell that I may understand thee,
Name the first of all destructions,
Name the first and last destroyers!"
Lemminkainen's mother answered:
"I will tell thee, son and hero,
Not because I wish to speak it,

Lönnrot

But because the truth is worthy;
I will name the chief destruction,
Name the first of the destroyers.
When thou hast a distance journeyed,
Only one day hast thou travelled,
Comes a stream along the highway,
Stream of fire of wondrous beauty,
In the stream a mighty fire-spout,
In the spout a rock uprising,
On the rock a fiery hillock,
On the top a flaming eagle,
And his crooked beak he sharpens,
Sharpens too his bloody talons,
For the coming of the stranger,
For the people that approach him."
Spake the reckless Lemminkainen,
Handsome hero, Kaukomieli:
"Women die beneath the eagle,
Such is not the death of heroes;
Know I well a magic lotion,
That will heal the wounds of eagles;
Make myself a steed of alders,
That will walk as my companion,
That will stride ahead majestic;
As a duck I'll drive behind him,
Drive him o'er the fatal waters,
Underneath the flaming eagle,
With his bloody beak and talons.
Worthy mother of my being,
Name the second of destroyers."
Lemminkainen's mother answered:
"This the second of destroyers:
When thou hast a distance wandered,
Only two clays hast thou travelled,
Comes a pit of fire to meet thee,
In the centre of the highway,
Eastward far the pit extending,
Stretches endless to the westward,
Filled with burning coals and pebbles,
Glowing with the heat of ages;
Hundreds has this monster swallowed,
In his jaws have thousands perished,
Hundreds with their trusty broadswords,
Thousands on their fiery chargers."
Spake the reckless Lemminkainen,
Handsome hero, Kaukomieli:
"Never will the hero perish
In the jaws of such a monster;
Know I well the means of safety,
Know a remedy efficient:
I will make of snow a master,
On the snow-clad fields, a hero,
Drive the snow-man on before me,
Drive him through the flaming vortex,
Drive him through the fiery furnace,
With my magic broom of copper;
I will follow in his shadow,
Follow close the magic image,
Thus escape the frightful monster,
With my golden locks uninjured,
With my flowing beard untangled.

The Kalevala

Ancient mother of my being,
Name the last of the destructions,
Name the third of the destroyers."
Lemminkainen's mother answered:
"This the third of fatal dangers:
Hast thou gone a greater distance,
Hast thou travelled one day longer,
To the portals of Pohyola,
To the narrowest of gate-ways,
There a wolf will rise to meet thee,
There the black-bear sneak upon thee-,
In Pohyola's darksome portals,
Hundreds in their jaws have perished,
Have devoured a thousand heroes;
Wherefore will they not destroy thee,
Since thy form is unprotected?"
Spake the reckless Lemminkainen,
Handsome hero, Kaukomieli:
"Let them eat the gentle lambkins,
Feed upon their tender tissues,
They cannot devour this hero;
I am girded with my buckler,
Girded with my belt of copper,
Armlets wear I of the master,
From the wolf and bear protected,
Will not hasten to Untamo.
I can meet the wolf of Lempo,
For the bear I have a balsam,
For his mouth I conjure bridles,
For the wolf, forge chains of iron;
I will smite them as the willow,
Chop them into little fragments,
Thus I'll gain the open court-yard,
Thus triumphant end my journey."
Lemminkainen's mother answered:
"Then thy journey is not ended,
Greater dangers still await thee,
Great the wonders yet before thee,
Horrors three within thy pathway;
Three great dangers of the hero
Still await thy reckless footsteps,
These the worst of all thy dangers:
When thou hast still farther wandered,
Thou wilt reach the Court of Pohya,
Where the walls are forged from iron,
And from steel the outer bulwark;
Rises from the earth to heaven,
Back again to earth returning;
Double spears are used for railings,
On each spear are serpents winding,
On each rail are stinging adders;
Lizards too adorn the bulwarks,
Play their long tails in the sunlight,
Hissing lizards, venomed serpents,
Jump and writhe upon the rampart,
Turn their horrid heads to meet thee;
On the greensward lie the monsters,
On the ground the things of evil,
With their pliant tongues of venom,
Hissing, striking, crawling, writhing;
One more horrid than the others,

Lies before the fatal gate-way,
Longer than the longest rafters,
Larger than the largest portals;
Hisses with the tongue of anger,
Lifts his head in awful menace,
Raises it to strike none other
Than the hero of the islands."
Spake the warlike Lemminkainen,
Handsome hero, Kaukomieli:
"By such things the children perish,
Such is not the death of heroes;
Know I well the fire to manage,
I can quench the flames of passion,
I can meet the prowling wild-beasts,
Can appease the wrath of serpents,
I can heal the sting of adders,
I have plowed the serpent-pastures,
Plowed the adder-fields of Northland;
While my hands were unprotected,
Held the serpents in my fingers,
Drove the adders to Manala,
On my hands the blood of serpents,
On my feet the fat of adders.
Never will thy hero stumble
On the serpents of the Northland;
With my heel I'll crush the monsters,
Stamp the horrid things to atoms;
I will banish them from Pohya,
Drive them to Manala's kingdom,
Step within Pohyola's mansion,
Walk the halls of Sariola!"
Lemminkainen's mother answered:
"Do not go, my son beloved,
To the firesides of Pohyola,
Through the Northland fields and fallows;
There are warriors with broadswords,
Heroes clad in mail of copper,
Are on beer intoxicated,
By the beer are much embittered;
They will charm thee, hapless creature,
On the tips of swords of magic;
Greater heroes have been conjured,
Stronger ones have been outwitted."
Spake the reckless Lemminkainen:
"Formerly thy son resided
In the hamlets of Pohyola;
Laplanders cannot enchant me,
Nor the Turyalanders harm me
I the Laplander will conjure,
Charm him with my magic powers,
Sing his shoulders wide asunder,
In his chin I'll sing a fissure,
Sing his collar-bone to pieces,
Sing his breast to thousand fragments."
Lemminkainen's mother answered:
"Foolish son, ungrateful wizard,
Boasting of thy former visit,
Boasting of thy fatal journey!
Once in Northland thou wert living,
In the homesteads of Pohyola;
There thou tried to swim the whirlpool,

The Kalevala

Tasted there the dog-tongue waters,
Floated down the fatal current,
Sank beneath its angry billows;
Thou hast seen Tuoni's river,
Thou hast measured Mana's waters,
There to-day thou wouldst be sleeping,
Had it not been for thy mother!
What I tell thee well remember,
Shouldst thou gain Pohyola's chambers,
Filled with stakes thou'lt find the court-yard,
These to hold the heads of heroes;
There thy head will rest forever,
Shouldst thou go to Sariola."
Spake the warlike Lemminkainen:
"Fools indeed may heed thy counsel,
Cowards too may give attention;
Those of seven conquest-summers
Cannot heed such weak advising.
Bring to me my battle-armor.
Bring my magic mail of copper,
Bring me too my father's broadsword,
Keep the old man's blade from rusting;
Long it has been cold and idle,
Long has lain in secret places,
Long and constantly been weeping,
Long been asking for a bearer."
Then he took his mail of copper,
Took his ancient battle-armor,
Took his father's sword of magic,
Tried its point against the oak-wood,
Tried its edge upon the sorb-tree;
In his hand the blade was bended,
Like the limber boughs of willow,
Like the juniper in summer.
Spake the hero, Lemminkainen:
"There is none in Pohya's hamlets,
In the courts of Sariola,
That with me can measure broadswords,
That can meet this blade ancestral."
From the nail he took a cross-bow,
Took the strongest from the rafters,
Spake these words in meditation:
"I shall recognize as worthy,
Recognize that one a hero
That can bend this mighty cross-bow,
That can break its magic sinews,
In the hamlets of Pohyola."
Lemminkainen, filled with courage,
Girds himself in suit of battle,
Dons his mighty mail of copper,
To his servant speaks as follows:
"Trusty slave, and whom I purchased,
Whom I bought with gold and silver,
Quick prepare my fiery charger,
Harness well my steed of battle;
I am going to the feasting,
To the banquet-fields of Lempo."
Quick obeys the faithful servant,
Hitches well the noble war-horse,
Quick prepares the fire-red stallion,
Speaks these words when all is I ready:

Lönnrot

"I have done what thou hast hidden,
Ready harnessed is the charger,
Waiting to obey his master."
Comes the hour of the departing
f the hero, Lemminkainen,
Right hand ready, left unwilling,
All his anxious fingers pain him,
Till at last in full obedience,
All his members give permission;
Starts the hero on his journey,
While the mother gives him counsel,
At the threshold of the dwelling,
At the highway of the court-yard:
Child of courage, my beloved,
Son of strength, my wisdom-hero,
If thou goest to the feasting,
Shouldst thou reach the great carousal,
Drink thou only a half a cupful,
Drink the goblet to the middle,
Always give the half remaining,
Give the worse half to another,
To another more unworthy;
In the lower half are serpents,
Worms, and frogs, and hissing lizards,
Feeding on the slimy bottom."
Furthermore she tells her hero,
Gives her son these sage directions,
On the border of the court-yard,
At the portals farthest distant:
"If thou goest to the banquet,
Shouldst thou reach the great carousal,
Occupy but half the settle,
Take but half a stride in walking,
Give the second half to others,
To another less deserving;
Only thus thou'lt be a hero,
Thus become a son immortal;
In the guest-rooms look courageous,
Bravely move about the chambers,
In the gatherings of heroes,
With the hosts of magic valor."
Thereupon wild Lemminkainen
Quickly leaped upon the cross-bench
Of his battle-sledge of wonder,
Raised his pearl-enamelled birch-rod,
Snapped his whip above his charger,
And the steed flew onward fleetly,
Galloped on his distant journey.
He had travelled little distance,
When a flight of hazel-chickens
Quick arose before his coming,
Flew before the foaming racer.
There were left some feathers lying,
Feathers of the hazel-chickens,
Lying in the hero's pathway.
These the reckless Lemminkainen
Gathered for their magic virtues,
Put them in his pouch of leather,
Did not know what things might happen
On his journey to Pohyola;
All things have some little value,

The Kalevala
In a strait all things are useful.
Then he drove a little distance,
Galloped farther on the highway,
When his courser neighed in danger,
And the fleet-foot ceased his running.
Then the stout-heart, Lemminkainen,
Handsome hero, Kaukomieli,
Rose upon his seat in wonder,
Craned his neck and looked about him
Found it as his mother told him,
Found a stream of fire opposing;
Ran the fire-stream like a river,
Ran across the hero's pathway.
In the river was a fire-fall,
In the cataract a fire-rock,
On the rock a fiery hillock,
On its summit perched an eagle,
From his throat the fire was streaming
To the crater far below him,
Fire out-shooting from his feathers,
Glowing with a fiery splendor;
Long he looked upon the hero,
Long he gazed on Lemminkainen,
Then the eagle thus addressed him:
Whither art thou driving, Ahti,
Whither going, Lemminkainen?"
Kaukomieli spake in answer:
"To the feastings of Pohyola,
To the drinking-halls of Louhi,
To the banquet of her people;
Move aside and let me journey,
Move a little from my pathway,
Let this wanderer pass by thee,
I am warlike Lemminkainen."
This the answer of the eagle,
Screaming from his throat of splendor:
"Though thou art wild Lemminkainen,
I shall let thee wander onward,
Through my fire-throat let thee journey,
Through these flames shall be thy passage
To the banquet-halls of Louhi,
To Pohyola's great carousal!"
Little heeding, Kaukomieli
Thinks himself in little trouble,
Thrusts his fingers in his pockets,
Searches in his pouch of leather,
Quickly takes the magic feathers,
Feathers from the hazel-chickens,
Rubs them into finest powder,
Rubs them with his magic fingers
Whence a flight of birds arises,
Hazel-chickens from the feathers,
Large the bevy of the young birds.
Quick the wizard, Lemminkainen,
Drives them to the eagle's fire-mouth,
Thus to satisfy his hunger,
Thus to quench the fire out-streaming.
Thus escapes the reckless hero,
Thus escapes the first of dangers,
Passes thus the first destroyer,
On his journey to Pohyola.

Lönnrot

With his whip he strikes his courser,
With his birch-whip, pearl-enamelled;
Straightway speeds the fiery charger,
Noiselessly upon his journey,
Gallops fast and gallops faster,
Till the flying steed in terror
Neighs again and ceases running.
Lemminkainen, quickly rising,
Cranes his neck and looks about him,
Sees his mother's words were truthful,
Sees her augury well-taken.
Lo! before him yawned a fire-gulf,
Stretching crosswise through his pathway;
Far to east the gulf extending,
To the west an endless distance,
Filled with stones and burning pebbles,
Running streams of burning matter.
Little heeding, Lemminkainen
Cries aloud in prayer to Ukko:
"Ukko, thou O God above me,
Dear Creator, omnipresent,
From the north-west send a storm-cloud,
From the east, dispatch a second,
From the south send forth a third one;
Let them gather from the south-west,
Sew their edges well together,
Fill thou well the interspaces,
Send a snow-fall high as heaven,
Let it fall from upper ether,
Fall upon the flaming fire-pit,
On the cataract and whirlpool!"
Mighty Ukko, the Creator,
Ukko, father omnipresent,
Dwelling in the courts of heaven,
Sent a storm-cloud from the north-west,
From the east he sent a second,
From the south despatched a third one,
Let them gather from the south-west,
Sewed their edges well together,
Filled their many interspaces,
Sent a snow-fall high as heaven,
From the giddy heights of ether,
Sent it seething to the fire-pit,
On the streams of burning matter;
From the snow-fall in the fire-pond,
Grows a lake with rolling billows.
Quick the hero, Lemminkainen,
Conjures there of ice a passage
From one border to the other,
Thus escapes his second danger,
Thus his second trouble passes.
Then the reckless Lemminkainen
Raised his pearl-enamelled birch-rod,
Snapped his whip above his racer,
And the steed flew onward swiftly,
Galloped on his distant journey
O'er the highway to Pohyola;
Galloped fast and galloped faster,
Galloped on a greater distance,
When the stallion loudly neighing,
Stopped and trembled on the highway,

The Kalevala
Then the lively Lemminkainen
Raised himself upon the cross-bench,
Looked to see what else had happened;
Lo ! a wolf stands at the portals,
in the passage-way a black-bear,
At the high-gate of Pohyola,
At the ending of the journey.
Thereupon young Lemminkainen,
Handsome hero, Kaukomieli,
Thrusts his fingers in his pockets,
Seeks his magic pouch of leather,
Pulls therefrom a lock of ewe-wool,
Rubs it firmly in his fingers,
In his hands it falls to powder;
Breathes the breath of life upon it,
When a flock of sheep arises,
Goats and sheep of sable color;
On the flock the black-wolf pounces,
And the wild-bear aids the slaughter,
While the reckless Lemminkainen
Rushes by them on his journey;
Gallops on a little distance,
To the court of Sariola,
Finds the fence of molten iron,
And of steel the rods and pickets,
In the earth a hundred fathoms,
To the azure sky, a thousand,
Double-pointed spears projecting;
On each spear were serpents twisted,
Adders coiled in countless numbers,
Lizards mingled with the serpents,
Tails entangled pointing earthward,
While their heads were skyward whirling,
Writhing, hissing mass of evil.
Then the stout-heart, Kaukomieli,
Deeply thought and long considered:
"It is as my mother told me,
This the wall that she predicted,
Stretching from the earth to heaven;
Downward deep are serpents creeping,
Deeper still the rails extending;
High as highest flight of eagles,
Higher still the wall shoots upward."
But the hero, Lemminkainen,
Little cares, nor feels disheartened,
Draws his broadsword from its scabbard,
Draws his mighty blade ancestral,
Hews the wall with might of magic,
Breaks the palisade in pieces,
Hews to atoms seven pickets,
Chops the serpent-wall to fragments;
Through the breach he quickly passes
To the portals of Pohyola.
In the way, a serpent lying,
Lying crosswise in the entry,
Longer than the longest rafters,
Larger than the posts of oak-wood;
Hundred-eyed, the heinous serpent,
And a thousand tongues, the monster,
Eyes as large as sifting vessels,
Tongues as long as shafts of javelins,

Teeth as large as hatchet-handles,
Back as broad as skiffs of ocean.
Lemminkainen does not venture
Straightway through this host opposing,
Through the hundred heads of adders,
Through the thousand tongues of serpents.
Spake the magic Lemminkainen:
"Venomed viper, thing of evil,
Ancient adder of Tuoni,
Thou that crawlest in the stubble,
Through the flower-roots of Lempo,
Who has sent thee from thy kingdom,
Sent thee from thine evil coverts,
Sent thee hither, crawling, writhing,
In the pathway I would travel?
Who bestowed thy mouth of venom,
Who insisted, who commanded,
Thou shouldst raise thy head toward heaven,
Who thy tail has given action?
Was this given by the father,
Did the mother give this power,
Or the eldest of the brothers,
Or the youngest of the sisters,
Or some other of thy kindred?
"Close thy mouth, thou thing of evil,
Hide thy pliant tongue of venom,
In a circle wrap thy body,
Coil thou like a shield in silence,
Give to me one-half the pathway,
Let this wanderer pass by thee,
Or remove thyself entirely;
Get thee hence to yonder heather,
Quick retreat to bog and stubble,
Hide thyself in reeds and rushes,
In the brambles of the lowlands.
Like a ball of flax enfolding,
Like a sphere of aspen-branches,
With thy head and tail together,
Roll thyself to yonder mountain;
In the heather is thy dwelling,
Underneath the sod thy caverns.
Shouldst thou raise thy head in anger,
Mighty Ukko will destroy it,
Pierce it with his steel-tipped arrows,
With his death-balls made of iron!"
Hardly had the hero ended,
When the monster, little heeding,
Hissing with his tongue in anger,
Plying like the forked lightning,
Pounces with his mouth of venom
At the head of Lemminkainen;
But the hero, quick recalling,
Speaks the master-words of knowledge,
Words that came from distant ages,
Words his ancestors had taught him,
Words his mother learned in childhood,
These the words of Lemminkainen:
"Since thou wilt not heed mine order,
Since thou wilt not leave the highway,
Puffed with pride of thine own greatness,
Thou shall burst in triple pieces.

The Kalevala
Leave thy station for the borders,
I will hunt thine ancient mother,
Sing thine origin of evil,
How arose thy head of horror;
Suoyatar, thine ancient mother,
Thing of evil, thy creator!"
"Suoyatar once let her spittle
Fall upon the waves of ocean;
This was rocked by winds and waters,
Shaken by the ocean-currents,
Six years rocked upon the billows,
Rocked in water seven summers,
On the blue-back of the ocean,
On the billows high as heaven;
Lengthwise did the billows draw it,
And the sunshine gave it softness,
To the shore the billows washed it,
On the coast the waters left it.
"Then appeared Creation's daughters,
Three the daughters thus appearing,
On the roaring shore of ocean,
There beheld the spittle lying,
And the daughters spake as follows:
'What would happen from this spittle,
Should the breath of the Creator
Fall upon the writhing matter,
Breathe the breath of life upon it,
Give the thing the sense of vision?
"The Creator heard these measures,
Spake himself the words that follow:
'Evil only comes from evil,
This is the expectoration
Of fell Suoyatar, its mother;
Therefore would the thing be evil,
Should I breathe a soul within it,
Should I give it sense of vision.'
"Hisi heard this conversation,
Ever ready with his mischief,
Made himself to be creator,
Breathed a soul into the spittle,
To fell Suoyatar's fierce anger.
Thus arose the poison-monster,
Thus was born the evil serpent,
This the origin of evil.
"Whence the life that gave her action'?
From the carbon-pile of Hisi.
Whence then was her heart created?
From the heart-throbs of her mother
Whence arose her brain of evil?
From the foam of rolling waters.
Whence was consciousness awakened?
From the waterfall's commotion.
Whence arose her head of venom?
From the seed-germs of the ivy.
Whence then came her eyes of fury?
From the flaxen seeds of Lempo.
Whence the evil ears for hearing?
From the foliage of Hisi.
Whence then was her mouth created?
This from Suoyatar's foam-currents
Whence arose thy tongue of anger r

Lönnrot

From the spear of Keitolainen.
Whence arose thy fangs of poison?
From the teeth of Mana's daughter.
Whence then was thy back created?
From the carbon-posts of Piru.
How then was thy tail created?
From the brain of the hobgoblin.
Whence arose thy writhing entrails?
From the death-belt of Tuoni.
"This thine origin, O Serpent,
This thy charm of evil import,
Vilest thing of God's creation,
Writhing, hissing thing of evil,
With the color of Tuoni,
With the shade of earth and heaven,
With the darkness of the storm-cloud.
Get thee hence, thou loathsome monster,
Clear the pathway of this hero.
I am mighty Lemminkainen,
On my journey to Pohyola,
To the feastings and carousals,
In the halls of darksome Northland."
Thereupon the snake uncoiling,
Hundred-eyed and heinous monster,
Crawled away to other portals,
That the hero, Kaukomieli,
Might proceed upon his errand,
To the dismal Sariola,
To the feastings and carousals
In the banquet-halls of Pohya.

RUNE XXVII
THE UNWELCOME GUEST.

I have brought young Kaukomieli,
Brought the Islander and hero,
Also known as Lemminkainen,
Through the jaws of death and ruin,
Through the darkling deeps of Kalma,
To the homesteads of Pohyola,
To the dismal courts of Louhi;
Now must I relate his doings,
Must relate to all my bearers,
How the merry Lemminkainen,
Handsome hero, Kaukomieli,
Wandered through Pohyola's chambers,
Through the halls of Sariola,
How the hero went unbidden
To the feasting and carousal,
Uninvited to the banquet.
Lemminkainen full of courage,
Full of life, and strength, and magic.
Stepped across the ancient threshold,
To the centre of the court-room,
And the floors of linwood trembled,
Walls and ceilings creaked and murmured.
Spake the reckless Lemminkainen,
These the words that Ahti uttered:
"Be ye greeted on my coming,
Ye that greet, be likewise greeted!
Listen, all ye hosts of Pohya;
Is there food about this homestead,
Barley for my hungry courser,
Beer to give a thirsty stranger?"
Sat the host of Sariola
At the east end of the table,
Gave this answer to the questions:
"Surely is there in this homestead,
For thy steed an open stable,
Never will this host refuse thee,
Shouldst thou act a part becoming,
Worthy, coming to these portals,
Waiting near the birchen rafters,
In the spaces by the kettles,
By the triple hooks of iron."
Then the reckless Lemminkainen
Shook his sable locks and answered:
"Lempo may perchance come hither,
Let him fill this lowly station,
Let him stand between the kettles,
That with soot he may be blackened.
Never has my ancient father,
Never has the dear old hero,
Stood upon a spot unworthy,
At the portals near the rafters;
For his steed the best of stables,
Food and shelter gladly furnished,

Lönnrot

And a room for his attendants,
Corners furnished for his mittens,
Hooks provided for his snow-shoes,
Halls in waiting for his helmet.
Wherefore then should I not find here
What my father found before me?"
To the centre walked the hero,
Walked around the dining table,
Sat upon a bench and waited,
On a bench of polished fir-wood,
And the kettle creaked beneath him.
Spake the reckless Lemminkainen:
"As a guest am I unwelcome,
Since the waiters bring no viands,
Bring no dishes to the stranger?"
Ilpotar, the Northland hostess,
Then addressed the words that follow:
"Lemminkainen, thou art evil,
Thou art here, but not invited,
Thou hast not the look of kindness,
Thou wilt give me throbbing temples,
Thou art bringing pain and sorrow.
All our beer is in the barley,
All the malt is in the kernel,
All our grain is still ungarnered,
And our dinner has been eaten;
Yesterday thou shouldst have been here,
Come again some future season."
Whereupon wild Lemminkainen
Pulled his mouth awry in anger,
Shook his coal-black locks and answered:
"All the tables here are empty,
And the feasting-time is over;
All the beer has left the goblets,
Empty too are all the pitchers,
Empty are the larger vessels.
O thou hostess of Pohyola,
Toothless dame of dismal Northland,
Badly managed is thy wedding,
And thy feast is ill-conducted,
Like the dogs hast thou invited;
Thou hast baked the honey-biscuit,
Wheaten loaves of greatest virtue,
Brewed thy beer from hops and barley,
Sent abroad thine invitations,
Six the hamlets thou hast honored,
Nine the villages invited
By thy merry wedding-callers.
Thou hast asked the poor and lowly,
Asked the hosts of common people,
Asked the blind, and deaf, and crippled,
Asked a multitude of beggars,
Toilers by the day, and hirelings;
Asked the men of evil habits,
Asked the maids with braided tresses,
I alone was not invited.
How could such a slight be given,
Since I sent thee kegs of barley?
Others sent thee grain in cupfuls,
Brought it sparingly in dippers,
While I sent thee fullest measure,

The Kalevala
Sent the half of all my garners,
Of the richest of my harvest,
Of the grain that I had gathered.
Even now young Lemminkainen,
Though a guest of name and station
Has no beer, no food, no welcome,
Naught for him art thou preparing,
Nothing cooking in thy kettles,
Nothing brewing in thy cellars
For the hero of the Islands,
At the closing of his journey."
Ilpotar, the ancient hostess,
Gave this order to her servants:
"Come, my pretty maiden-waiter,
Servant-girl to me belonging,
Lay some salmon to the broiling,
Bring some beer to give the stranger!"
Small of stature was the maiden,
Washer of the banquet-platters,
Rinser of the dinner-ladles,
Polisher of spoons of silver,
And she laid some food in kettles,
Only bones and beads of whiting,
Turnip-stalks and withered cabbage,
Crusts of bread and bits of biscuit.
Then she brought some beer in pitchers,
Brought of common drink the vilest,
That the stranger, Lemminkainen,
Might have drink, and meat in welcome,
Thus to still his thirst and hunger.
Then the maiden spake as follows:
"Thou art sure a mighty hero,
Here to drink the beer of Pohya,
Here to empty all our vessels!"
Then the minstrel, Lemminkainen,
Closely handled all the pitchers,
Looking to the very bottoms;
There beheld he writhing serpents,
In the centre adders swimming,
On the borders worms and lizards.
Then the hero, Lemminkainen,
Filled with anger, spake as follows:
Get ye hence, ye things of evil,
Get ye hence to Tuonela,
With the bearer of these pitchers,
With the maid that brought ye hither,
Ere the evening moon has risen,
Ere the day-star seeks the ocean!
O thou wretched beer of barley,
Thou hast met with great dishonor,
Into disrepute hast fallen,
But I'll drink thee, notwithstanding,
And the rubbish cast far from me."
Then the hero to his pockets
Thrust his first and unnamed finger,
Searching in his pouch of leather;
Quick withdraws a hook for fishing,
Drops it to the pitcher's bottom,
Through the worthless beer of barley;
On his fish-book hang the serpents,
Catches many hissing adders,

Lönnrot

Catches frogs in magic numbers,
Catches blackened worms in thousands,
Casts them to the floor before him,
Quickly draws his heavy broad sword,
And decapitates the serpents.
Now he drinks the beer remaining,
When the wizard speaks as follows:
"As a guest am I unwelcome,
Since no beer to me is given
That is worthy of a hero;
Neither has a ram been butchered,
Nor a fattened calf been slaughtered,
Worthy food for Lemminkainen."
Then the landlord of Pohyola
Answered thus the Island-minstrel:
"Wherefore hast thou journeyed hither,
Who has asked thee for thy presence?
Spake in answer Lemminkainen:
"Happy is the guest invited,
Happier when not expected;
Listen, son of Pohylander,
Host of Sariola, listen:
Give me beer for ready payment,
Give me worthy drink for money!"
Then the landlord of Pohyola,
In bad humor, full of anger,
Conjured in the earth a lakelet,
At the feet of Kaukomieli,
Thus addressed the Island-hero:
"Quench thy thirst from yonder lakelet,
There, the beer that thou deservest!"
Little heeding, Lemminkainen
To this insolence made answer:
"I am neither bear nor roebuck,
That should drink this filthy water,
Drink the water of this lakelet."
Ahti then began to conjure,
Conjured he a bull before him,
Bull with horns of gold and silver,
And the bull drank from the lakelet,
Drank he from the pool in pleasure.
Then the landlord of Pohyola
There a savage wolf created,
Set him on the floor before him
To destroy the bull of magic,
Lemminkainen, full of courage,
Conjured up a snow-white rabbit,
Set him on the floor before him
To attract the wolf's attention.
Then the landlord of Pohyola
Conjured there a dog of Lempo,
Set him on the floor before him
To destroy the magic rabbit.
Lemminkainen, full of mischief,
Conjured on the roof a squirrel,
That by jumping on the rafters
He might catch the dog's attention.
But the master of the Northland
Conjured there a golden marten,
And he drove the magic squirrel
From his seat upon the rafters.

The Kalevala
Lemminkainen, full of mischief,
Made a fox of scarlet color,
And it ate the golden marten.
Then the master of Pohyola
Conjured there a hen to flutter
Near the fox of scarlet color.
Lemminkainen, full of mischief,
Thereupon a hawk created,
That with beak and crooked talons
He might tear the hen to pieces.
Spake the landlord of Pohyola,
These the words the tall man uttered:
"Never will this feast be bettered
Till the guests are less in number;
I must do my work as landlord,
Get thee hence, thou evil stranger,
Cease thy conjurings of evil,
Leave this banquet of my people,
Haste away, thou wicked wizard,
To thine Island-home and people!
Spake the reckless Lemminkainen:
"Thus no hero will be driven,
Not a son of any courage
Will be frightened by thy presence,
Will be driven from thy banquet."
Then the landlord of Pohyola
Snatched his broadsword from the rafters,
Drew it rashly from the scabbard,
Thus addressing Lemminkainen:
"Ahti, Islander of evil,
Thou the handsome Kaukomieli,
Let us measure then our broadswords,
Let our skill be fully tested;
Surely is my broadsword better
Than the blade within thy scabbard."
Spake the hero, Lemminkainen.
"That my blade is good and trusty,
Has been proved on heads of heroes,
Has on many bones been tested;
Be that as it may, my fellow,
Since thine order is commanding,
Let our swords be fully tested,
Let us see whose blade is better.
Long ago my hero-father
Tested well this sword in battle,
Never failing in a conflict.
Should his son be found less worthy?"
Then he grasped his mighty broadsword,
Drew the fire-blade from the scabbard
Hanging from his belt of copper.
Standing on their hilts their broadswords,
Carefully their blades were measured,
Found the sword of Northland's master
Longer than the sword of Ahti
By the half-link of a finger.
Spake the reckless Lemminkainen.
"Since thou hast the longer broadsword,
Thou shalt make the first advances,
I am ready for thy weapon."
Thereupon Pohyola's landlord
With the wondrous strength of anger,

Lönnrot

Tried in vain to slay the hero,
Strike the crown of Lemminkainen;
Chipped the splinters from the rafters,
Cut the ceiling into fragments,
Could not touch the Island-hero.
Thereupon brave Kaukomieli,
Thus addressed Pohyola's master:
"Have the rafters thee offended?
What the crimes they have committed,
Since thou hewest them in pieces?
Listen now, thou host of Northland,
Reckless landlord of Pohyola,
Little room there is for swordsmen
In these chambers filled with women;
We shall stain these painted rafters,
Stain with blood these floors and ceilings;
Let us go without the mansion,
In the field is room for combat,
On the plain is space sufficient;
Blood looks fairer in the court-yard,
Better in the open spaces,
Let it dye the snow-fields scarlet."
To the yard the heroes hasten,
There they find a monstrous ox-skin,
Spread it on the field of battle;
On the ox-skin stand the swordsmen.
Spake the hero, Lemminkainen:
"Listen well, thou host of Northland,
Though thy broadsword is the longer,
Though thy blade is full of horror,
Thou shalt have the first advantage;
Use with skill thy boasted broadsword
Ere the final bout is given,
Ere thy head be chopped in pieces;
Strike with skill, or thou wilt perish,
Strike, and do thy best for Northland."
Thereupon Pohyola's landlord
Raised on high his blade of battle,
Struck a heavy blow in anger,
Struck a second, then a third time,
But he could not touch his rival,
Could Dot draw a single blood-drop
From the veins of Lemminkainen,
Skillful Islander and hero.
Spake the handsome Kaukomieli:
"Let me try my skill at fencing,
Let me swing my father's broadsword,
Let my honored blade be tested!"
But the landlord of Pohyola,
Does not heed the words of Ahti,
Strikes in fury, strikes unceasing,
Ever aiming, ever missing.
When the skillful Lemminkainen
Swings his mighty blade of magic,
Fire disports along his weapon,
Flashes from his sword of honor,
Glistens from the hero's broadsword,
Balls of fire disporting, dancing,
On the blade of mighty Ahti,
Overflow upon the shoulders
Of the landlord of Pohyola.

The Kalevala
Spake the hero, Lemminkainen:
"O thou son of Sariola,
See! indeed thy neck is glowing
Like the dawning of the morning,
Like the rising Sun in ocean!"
Quickly turned Pohyola's landlord,
Thoughtless host of darksome Northland,
To behold the fiery splendor
Playing on his neck and shoulders.
Quick as lightning, Lemminkainen,
With his father's blade of battle,
With a single blow of broadsword,
With united skill and power,
Lopped the head of Pohya's master;
As one cleaves the stalks of turnips,
As the ear falls from the corn-stalk,
As one strikes the fins from salmon,
Thus the head rolled from the shoulders
Of the landlord of Pohyola,
Like a ball it rolled and circled.
In the yard were pickets standing,
Hundreds were the sharpened pillars,
And a head on every picket,
Only one was left un-headed.
Quick the victor, Lemminkainen,
Took the head of Pohya's landlord,
Spiked it on the empty picket.
Then the Islander, rejoicing,
Handsome hero, Kaukomieli,
Quick returning to the chambers,
Crave this order to the hostess:
"Evil maiden, bring me water,
Wherewithal to cleanse my fingers
From the blood of Northland's master,
Wicked host of Sariola."
Ilpotar, the Northland hostess,
Fired with anger, threatened vengeance,
Conjured men with heavy broadswords,
Heroes clad in copper-armor,
Hundred warriors with their javelins,
And a thousand bearing cross-bows,
To destroy the Island-hero,
For the death of Lemminkainen.
Kaukomieli soon discovered
That the time had come for leaving,
That his presence was unwelcome
At the feasting of Pohyola,
At the banquet of her people.

RUNE XXVIII
THE MOTHER'S COUNSEL.

Ahti, hero of the Islands,
Wild magician, Lemminkainen,
Also known as Kaukomieli,
Hastened from the great carousal,
From the banquet-halls of Louhi,
From the ever-darksome Northland,
From the dismal Sariola.
Stormful strode he from the mansion,
Hastened like the smoke of battle,
From the court-yard of Pohyola,
Left his crimes and misdemeanors
In the halls of ancient Louhi.
Then he looked in all directions,
Seeking for his tethered courser,
Anxious looked in field and stable,
But he did not find his racer;
Found a black thing in the fallow,
Proved to be a clump of willows.
Who will well advise the hero,
Who will give him wise directions,
Guide the wizard out of trouble,
Give his hero-locks protection,
Keep his magic head from danger
From the warriors of Northland?
Noise is beard within the village,
And a din from other homesteads,
From the battle-hosts of Louhi,
Streaming from the doors and window,
Of the homesteads of Pohyola.
Thereupon young Lemminkainen,
Handsome Islander and hero,
Changing both his form and features,
Clad himself in other raiment,
Changing to another body,
Quick became a mighty eagle,
Soared aloft on wings of magic,
Tried to fly to highest heaven,
But the moonlight burned his temples,
And the sunshine singed his feathers.
Then entreating, Lemminkainen,
Island-hero, turned to Ukko,
This the prayer that Ahti uttered:
"Ukko, God of love and mercy,
Thou the Wisdom of the heavens,
Wise Director of the lightning,
Thou the Author of the thunder,
Thou the Guide of all the cloudlets,
Give to me thy cloak of vapor,
Throw a silver cloud around me,
That I may in its protection
Hasten to my native country,
To my mother's Island-dwelling,
Fly to her that waits my coming,

The Kalevala

With a mother's grave forebodings."
Farther, farther, Lemminkainen
Flew and soared on eagle-pinions,
Looked about him, backwards, forwards,
Spied a gray-hawk soaring near him,
In his eyes the fire of splendor,
Like the eyes of Pohyalanders,
Like the eyes of Pohya's spearmen,
And the gray-hawk thus addressed him:
"Ho! There! hero, Lemminkainen,
Art thou thinking of our combat
With the hero-heads of Northland?"
Thus the Islander made answer,
These the words of Kaukomieli:
"O thou gray-hawk, bird of beauty,
Fly direct to Sariola,
Fly as fast as wings can bear thee;
When thou hast arrived in safety,
On the plains of darksome Northland,
Tell the archers and the spearmen,
They will never catch the eagle,
In his journey from Pohyola,
To his Island-borne and fortress."
Then the Ahti-eagle hastened
Straightway to his mother's cottage,
In his face the look of trouble,
In his heart the pangs of sorrow.
Ahti's mother ran to meet him,
When she spied him in the pathway,
Walking toward her island-dwelling;
These the words the mother uttered:
"Of my sons thou art the bravest,
Art the strongest of my children;
Wherefore then comes thine annoyance,
On returning from Pohyola?
Wert thou worsted at the banquet,
At the feast and great carousal?
At thy cups, if thou wert injured,
Thou shalt here have better treatment
Thou shalt have the cup thy father
Brought me from the hero-castle."
Spake the reckless Lemminkainen:
"Worthy mother, thou that nursed me,
If I had been maimed at drinking,
I the landlord would have worsted,
Would have slain a thousand heroes,
Would have taught them useful lessons."
Lemminkainen's mother answered:
"Wherefore then art thou indignant,
Didst thou meet disgrace and insult,
Did they rob thee of thy courser?
Buy thou then a better courser
With the riches of thy mother,
With thy father's horded treasures."
Spake the hero, Lemminkainen:
"Faithful mother of my being,
If my steed had been insulted,
If for him my heart was injured,
I the landlord would have punished,
Would have punished all the horsemen,
All of Pohya's strongest riders."

Lönnrot

Lemminkainen's mother answered:
"Tell me then thy dire misfortune,
What has happened to my hero,
On his journey to Pohyola?
Have the Northland maidens scorned thee,
Have the women ridiculed thee?
If the maidens scorned thy presence.
If the women gave derision,
There are others thou canst laugh at,
Thou canst scorn a thousand women."
Said the reckless Lemminkainen:
"Honored mother, fond and faithful,
If the Northland dames had scorned me
Or the maidens laughed derision,
I the maidens would have punished,
Would have scorned a thousand women."
Lemminkainen's mother answered:
"Wherefore then are thou indignant,
Thus annoyed, and heavy-hearted,
On returning from Pohyola?
Was thy feasting out of season,
Was the banquet-beer unworthy,
Were thy dreams of evil import
When asleep in darksome Northland?"
This is Lemminkainen's answer:
"Aged women may remember
What they dream on beds of trouble;
I have seen some wondrous visions,
Since I left my Island-cottage.
My beloved, helpful mother,
Fill my bag with good provisions,
Flour and salt in great abundance,
Farther must thy hero wander,
He must leave his home behind him,
Leave his pleasant Island-dwelling,
Journey from this home of ages;
Men are sharpening their broadswords,
Sharpening their spears and lances,
For the death of Lemminkainen."
Then again the mother questioned,
Hurriedly she asked the reason:
"Why the men their swords were whetting,
Why their spears are being sharpened."
Spake the reckless Lemminkainen,
Handsome hero, Kaukomieli:
"Therefore do they whet their broadswords,
Therefore sharpen they their lances:
It is for thy son's destruction,
At his heart are aimed their lances.
In the court-yard of Pohyola,
There arose a great contention,
Fierce the battle waged against me;
But I slew the Northland hero,
Killed the host of Sariola;
Quick to arms rose Louhi's people,
All the spears and swords of Northland
Were directed at thy hero;
All of Pohya turned against me,
Turned against a single foeman."
This the answer of the mother:
"I had told thee this beforehand,

The Kalevala
I had warned thee of this danger,
And forbidden thee to journey
To the hostile fields of Northland.
Here my hero could have lingered,
Passed his life in full contentment,
Lived forever with his mother,
With his mother for protection,
In the court-yard with his kindred;
Here no war would have arisen,
No contention would have followed.
Whither wilt thou go, my hero,
Whither will my loved one hasten,
To escape thy fierce pursuers,
To escape from thy misdoings,
From thy sins to bide in safety,
From thy crimes and misdemeanors,
That thy head be not endangered,
That thy body be not mangled,
That thy locks be not outrooted?"
Spake the reckless Lemminkainen:
"Know I not a spot befitting,
Do not know a place of safety,
Where to hide from my pursuers,
That will give me sure protection
From the crimes by me committed.
Helpful mother of my being,
Where to flee wilt thou advise me?"
This the answer of the mother:
"I do not know where I can send thee;
Be a pine-tree on the mountain,
Or a juniper in lowlands?
Then misfortune may befall thee;
Often is the mountain pine-tree
Cut in splints for candle-lighters;
And the juniper is often
Peeled for fence-posts for the pastures.
Go a birch-tree to the valleys,
Or an elm-tree to the glenwood?
Even then may trouble find thee,
Misery may overtake thee;
Often is the lowland birch-tree
Cut to pieces in the ware-house;
Often is the elm-wood forest
Cleared away for other plantings.
Be a berry on the highlands,
Cranberry upon the heather,
Strawberry upon the mountains,
Blackberry along the fences?
Even there will trouble find thee,
There misfortune overtake thee,
For the berry-maids would pluck thee,
Silver-tinselled girls would get thee.
Be a pike then in the ocean,
Or a troutlet in the rivers?
Then would trouble overtake thee,
Would become thy life-companion;
Then the fisherman would catch thee,
Catch thee in his net of flax-thread,
Catch thee with his cruel fish-hook.
Be a wolf then in the forest,
Or a black-bear in the thickets?

Lönnrot

Even then would trouble find thee,
And disaster cross thy pathway;
Sable hunters of the Northland
Have their spears and cross-bows ready
To destroy the wolf and black-bear."
Spake the reckless Lemminkainen:
"Know I well the worst of places,
Know where Death will surely follow,
Where misfortune's eye would find me;
Since thou gavest me existence,
Gavest nourishment in childhood,
Whither shall I flee for safety,
Whither hide from death and danger?
In my view is fell destruction,
Dire misfortune hovers o'er me;
On the morrow come the spearmen,
Countless warriors from Pohya,
Ahti's head their satisfaction."
This the answer of the mother:
"I can name a goodly refuge,
Name a land of small dimensions,
Name a distant ocean-island,
Where my son may live in safety.
Thither archers never wander,
There thy head cannot be severed;
But an oath as strong as heaven,
Thou must swear before thy mother;
Thou wilt not for sixty summers
Join in war or deadly combat,
Even though thou wishest silver,
Wishest gold and silver treasures."
Spake the grateful Lemminkainen:
"I will swear an oath of honor,
That I'll not in sixty summers
Draw my sword in the arena,
Test the warrior in battle;
I have wounds upon my shoulders,
On my breast two scars of broadsword,
Of my former battles, relies,
Relies of my last encounters,
On the battle-fields of Northland,
In the wars with men and heroes."
Lemminkainen's mother answered:
"Go thou, take thy father's vessel,
Go and bide thyself in safety,
Travel far across nine oceans;
In the tenth, sail to the centre,
To the island, forest-covered,
To the cliffs above the waters,
Where thy father went before thee,
Where he hid from his pursuers,
In the times of summer conquests,
In the darksome days of battle;
Good the isle for thee to dwell in,
Goodly place to live and linger;
Hide one year, and then a second,
In the third return in safety
To thy mother's island dwelling,
To thy father's ancient mansion,
To my hero's place of resting."

RUNE XXIX
THE ISLE OF REFUGE.

Lemminkainen, full of joyance,
Handsome hero, Kaukomieli,
Took provisions in abundance,
Fish and butter, bread and bacon,
Hastened to the Isle of Refuge,
Sailed away across the oceans,
Spake these measures on departing:
"Fare thee well, mine Island-dwelling,
I must sail to other borders,
To an island more protective,
Till the second summer passes;
Let the serpents keep the island,
Lynxes rest within the glen-wood,
Let the blue-moose roam the mountains,
Let the wild-geese eat the barley.
Fare thee well, my helpful mother!
When the warriors of the Northland,
From the dismal Sariola,
Come with swords, and spears, and cross-bows,
Asking for my head in vengeance,
Say that I have long departed,
Left my mother's Island-dwelling,
When the barley had been garnered."
Then he launched his boat of copper,
Threw the vessel to the waters,
From the iron-banded rollers,
From the cylinders of oak-wood,
On the masts the sails he hoisted,
Spread the magic sails of linen,
In the stern the hero settled
And prepared to sail his vessel,
One hand resting on the rudder.
Then the sailor spake as follows,
These the words of Lemminkainen:
"Blow, ye winds, and drive me onward,
Blow ye steady, winds of heaven,
Toward the island in the ocean,
That my bark may fly in safety
To my father's place of refuge,
To the far and nameless island!"
Soon the winds arose as bidden,
Rocked the vessel o'er the billows,
O'er the blue-back of the waters,
O'er the vast expanse of ocean;
Blew two months and blew unceasing,
Blew a third month toward the island,
Toward his father's Isle of Refuge.
Sat some maidens on the seaside,
On the sandy beach of ocean,
Turned about in all directions,
Looking out upon the billows;
One was waiting for her brother,
And a second for her father,

Lönnrot

And a third one, anxious, waited
For the coming of her suitor;
There they spied young Lemminkainen,
There perceived the hero's vessel
Sailing o'er the bounding billows;
It was like a hanging cloudlet,
Hanging twixt the earth and heaven.
Thus the island-maidens wondered,
Thus they spake to one another:
"What this stranger on the ocean,
What is this upon the waters?
Art thou one of our sea-vessels?
Wert thou builded on this island?
Sail thou straightway to the harbor,
To the island-point of landing
That thy tribe may be discovered."
Onward did the waves propel it,
Rocked his vessel o'er the billows,
Drove it to the magic island,
Safely landed Lemminkainen
On the sandy shore and harbor.
Spake he thus when he had landed,
These the words that Ahti uttered:
"Is there room upon this island,
Is there space within this harbor,
Where my bark may lie at anchor,
Where the sun may dry my vessel?"
This the answer of the virgins,
Dwellers on the Isle of Refuge:
"There is room within this harbor,
On this island, space abundant,
Where thy bark may lie at anchor,
Where the sun may dry thy vessel;
Lying ready are the rollers,
Cylinders adorned with copper;
If thou hadst a hundred vessels,
Shouldst thou come with boats a thousand,
We would give them room in welcome."
Thereupon wild Lemminkainen
Rolled his vessel in the harbor,
On the cylinders of copper,
Spake these words when he had ended:
"Is there room upon this island,
Or a spot within these forests,
Where a hero may be hidden
From the coming din of battle,
From the play of spears and arrows?"
Thus replied the Island-maidens:
"There are places on this island,
On these plains a spot befitting
Where to hide thyself in safety,
Hero-son of little valor.
Here are many, many castles,
Many courts upon this island;
Though there come a thousand heroes,
Though a thousand spearmen follow,
Thou canst hide thyself in safety."
Spake the hero, Lemminkainen:
"Is there room upon this island,
Where the birch-tree grows abundant,
Where this son may fell the forest,

The Kalevala

And may cultivate the fallow?"
Answered thus the Island-maidens:
"There is not a spot befitting,
Not a place upon the island,
Where to rest thy wearied members,
Not the smallest patch of birch-wood,
Thou canst bring to cultivation.
All our fields have been divided,
All these woods have been apportioned,
Fields and forests have their owners."
Lemminkainen asked this question,
These the words of Kaukomieli:
"Is there room upon this island,
Worthy spot in field or forest,
Where to Sing my songs of magic,
Chant my gathered store of wisdom,
Sing mine ancient songs and legends?"
Answered thus the Island-maidens:
"There is room upon this island,
Worthy place in these dominions,
Thou canst sing thy garnered wisdom,
Thou canst chant thine ancient legends,
Legends of the times primeval,
In the forest, in the castle,
On the island-plains and pastures."
Then began the reckless minstrel
To intone his wizard-sayings;
Sang he alders to the waysides,
Sang the oaks upon the mountains,
On the oak-trees sang be branches,
On each branch he sang an acorn,
On the acorns, golden rollers,
On each roller, sang a cuckoo;
Then began the cuckoos, calling,
Gold from every throat came streaming,
Copper fell from every feather,
And each wing emitted silver,
Filled the isle with precious metals.
Sang again young Lemminkainen,
Conjured on, and sang, and chanted,
Sang to precious stones the sea-sands,
Sang the stones to pearls resplendent,
Robed the groves in iridescence,
Sang the island full of flowers,
Many-colored as the rainbow.
Sang again the magic minstrel,
In the court a well he conjured,
On the well a golden cover,
On the lid a silver dipper,
That the boys might drink the water,
That the maids might lave their eyelids.
On the plains he conjured lakelets,
Sang the duck upon the waters,
Golden-cheeked and silver-headed,
Sang the feet from shining copper;
And the Island-maidens wondered,
Stood entranced at Ahti's wisdom,
At the songs of Lemminkainen,
At the hero's magic power.
Spake the singer, Lemminkainen,
Handsome hero, Kaukomieli:

Lönnrot

"I would sing a wondrous legend,
Sing in miracles of sweetness,
If within some hall or chamber,
I were seated at the table.
If I sing not in the castle,
In some spot by walls surrounded
Then I sing my songs to zephyrs,
Fling them to the fields and forests."
Answered thus the Island-maidens:
"On this isle are castle-chambers,
Halls for use of magic singers,
Courts complete for chanting legends,
Where thy singing will be welcome,
Where thy songs will not be scattered
To the forests of the island,
Nor thy wisdom lost in ether."
Straightway Lemminkainen journeyed
With the maidens to the castle;
There he sang and conjured pitchers
On the borders of the tables,
Sang and conjured golden goblets
Foaming with the beer of barley;
Sang he many well-filled vessels,
Bowls of honey-drink abundant,
Sweetest butter, toothsome biscuit,
Bacon, fish, and veal, and venison,
All the dainties of the Northland,
Wherewithal to still his hunger.
But the proud-heart, Lemminkainen,
Was not ready for the banquet,
Did not yet begin his feasting,
Waited for a knife of silver,
For a knife of golden handle;
Quick he sang the precious metals,
Sang a blade from purest silver,
To the blade a golden handle,
Straightway then began his feasting,
Quenched his thirst and stilled his hunger,
Charmed the maidens on the island.
Then the minstrel, Lemminkainen,
Roamed throughout the island-hamlets,
To the joy of all the virgins,
All the maids of braided tresses;
Wheresoe'er he turned his footsteps,
There appeared a maid to greet him;
When his hand was kindly offered,
There his band was kindly taken;
When he wandered out at evening,
Even in the darksome places,
There the maidens bade him welcome;
There was not an island-village
Where there were not seven castles,
In each castle seven daughters,
And the daughters stood in waiting,
Gave the hero joyful greetings,
Only one of all the maidens
Whom he did not greet with pleasure.
Thus the merry Lemminkainen
Spent three summers in the ocean,
Spent a merry time in refuge,
In the hamlets on the island,

The Kalevala
To the pleasure of the maidens,
To the joy of all the daughters;
Only one was left neglected,
She a poor and graceless spinster,
On the isle's remotest border,
In the smallest of the hamlets.
'Then he thought about his journey
O'er the ocean to his mother,
To the cottage of his father.
There appeared the slighted spinster,
To the Northland son departing,
Spake these words to Lemminkainen:
"O, thou handsome Kaukomieli,
Wisdom-bard, and magic singer,
Since this maiden thou hast slighted,
May the winds destroy thy vessel,
Dash thy bark to countless fragments
On the ocean-rocks and ledges!"
Lemminkainen's thoughts were homeward,
Did not heed the maiden's murmurs,
Did not rise before the dawning
Of the morning on the island,
To the pleasure of the maiden
Of the much-neglected hamlet.
Finally at close of evening,
He resolved to leave the island,
He resolved to waken early,
Long before the dawn of morning;
Long before the time appointed,
He arose that he might wander
Through the hamlets of the island,
Bid adieu to all the maidens,
On the morn of his departure.
As he wandered hither, thither,
Walking through the village path-ways
To the last of all the hamlets;
Saw he none of all the castle-,
Where three dwellings were not standing;
Saw he none of all the dwellings
Where three heroes were not watching;
Saw he none of all the heroes,
Who was not engaged in grinding
Swords, and spears, and battle-axes,
For the death of Lemminkainen.
And these words the hero uttered:
"Now alas! the Sun arises
From his couch within the ocean,
On the frailest of the heroes,
On the saddest child of Northland;
On my neck the cloak of Lempo
Might protect me from all evil,
Though a hundred foes assail me,
Though a thousand archers follow."
Then he left the maids ungreeted,
Left his longing for the daughters
Of the nameless Isle of Refuge,
With his farewell-words unspoken,
Hastened toward the island-harbor,
Toward his magic bark at anchor;
But he found it burned to ashes,
Sweet revenge had fired his vessel,

Lighted by the slighted spinster.
Then he saw the dawn of evil,
Saw misfortune hanging over,
Saw destruction round about him.
Straightway he began rebuilding
Him a magic sailing-vessel,
New and wondrous, full of beauty;
But the hero needed timber,
Boards, and planks, and beams, and braces,
Found the smallest bit of lumber,
Found of boards but seven fragments,
Of a spool he found three pieces,
Found six pieces of the distaff;
With these fragments builds his vessel,
Builds a ship of magic virtue,
Builds the bark with secret knowledge,
Through the will of the magician;
Strikes one blow, and builds the first part,
Strikes a second, builds the centre,
Strikes a third with wondrous power,
And the vessel is completed.
Thereupon the ship he launches,
Sings the vessel to the ocean,
And these words the hero utters:
"Like a bubble swim these waters,
Like a flower ride the billows;
Loan me of thy magic feathers,
Three, O eagle, four, O raven,
For protection to my vessel,
Lest it flounder in the ocean!"
Now the sailor, Lemminkainen,
Seats himself upon the bottom
Of the vessel he has builded,
Hastens on his journey homeward,
Head depressed and evil-humored,
Cap awry upon his forehead,
Mind dejected, heavy-hearted,
That he could not dwell forever
In the castles of the daughters
Of the nameless Isle of Refuge.
Spake the minstrel, Lemminkainen,
Handsome hero, Kaukomieli:
"Leave I must this merry island,
Leave her many joys and pleasures,
Leave her maids with braided tresses,
Leave her dances and her daughters,
To the joys of other heroes;
But I take this comfort with me:
All the maidens on the island,
Save the spinster who was slighted,
Will bemoan my loss for ages,
Will regret my quick departure;
They will miss me at the dances,
In the halls of mirth and joyance,
In the homes of merry maidens,
On my father's Isle of Refuge."
Wept the maidens on the island,
Long lamenting, loudly calling
To the hero sailing homeward:
"Whither goest, Lemminkainen,
Why depart, thou best of heroes?

The Kalevala
Dost thou leave from inattention,
Is there here a dearth of maidens,
Have our greetings been unworthy?"
Sang the magic Lemminkainen
To the maids as he was sailing,
This in answer to their calling:
"Leaving not for want of pleasure,
Do not go from dearth of women
Beautiful the island-maidens,
Countless as the sands their virtues.
This the reason of my going,
I am longing for my home-land,
Longing for my mother's cabins,
For the strawberries of Northland,
For the raspberries of Kalew,
For the maidens of my childhood,
For the children of my mother."
Then the merry Lemminkainen
Bade farewell to all the island;
Winds arose and drove his vessel
On the blue-back of the ocean,
O'er the far-extending waters,
Toward the island of his mother.
On the shore were grouped the daughters
Of the magic Isle of Refuge,
On the rocks sat the forsaken,
Weeping stood the island-maidens,
Golden daughters, loud-lamenting.
Weep the maidens of the island
While the sail-yards greet their vision,
While the copper-beltings glisten;
Do not weep to lose the sail-yards,
Nor to lose the copper-beltings;
Weep they for the loss of Ahti,
For the fleeing Kaukomieli
Guiding the departing vessel.
Also weeps young Lemminkainen,
Sorely weeps, and loud-lamenting,
Weeps while he can see the island,
While the island hill-tops glisten;
Does not mourn the island-mountains,
Weeps he only for the maidens,
Left upon the Isle of Refuge.
Thereupon sailed Kaukomieli
On the blue-back of the ocean;
Sailed one day, and then a second,
But, alas! upon the third day,
There arose a mighty storm-wind,
And the sky was black with fury.
Blew the black winds from the north-west,
From the south-east came the whirlwind,
Tore away the ship's forecastle,
Tore away the vessel's rudder,
Dashed the wooden hull to pieces.
Thereupon wild Lemminkainen
Headlong fell upon the waters;
With his head he did the steering,
With his hands and feet, the rowing;
Swam whole days and nights unceasing,
Swam with hope and strength united,
Till at last appeared a cloudlet,

Lönnrot

Growing cloudlet to the westward,
Changing to a promontory,
Into land within the ocean.
Swiftly to the shore swam Ahti,
Hastened to a magic castle,
Found therein a hostess baking,
And her daughters kneading barley,
And these words the hero uttered:
"O, thou hostess, filled with kindness,
Couldst thou know my pangs of hunger,
Couldst thou guess my name and station,
Thou wouldst hasten to the storehouse,
Bring me beer and foaming liquor,
Bring the best of thy provisions,
Bring me fish, and veal, and bacon,
Butter, bread, and honeyed biscuits,
Set for me a wholesome dinner,
Wherewithal to still my hunger,
Quench the thirst of Lemminkainen.
Days and nights have I been swimming,
Buffeting the waves of ocean,
Seemed as if the wind protected,
And the billows gave me shelter,"
Then the hostess, filled with kindness,
Hastened to the mountain storehouse,
Cut some butter, veal, and bacon,
Bread, and fish, and honeyed biscuit,
Brought the best of her provisions,
Brought the mead and beer of barley,
Set for him a toothsome dinner,
Wherewithal to still his hunger,
Quench the thirst of Lemminkainen.
When the hero's feast had ended,
Straightway was a magic vessel
Given by the kindly hostess
To the weary Kaukomieli,
Bark of beauty, new and hardy,
Wherewithal to aid the stranger
In his journey to his home-land,
To the cottage of his mother.
Quickly sailed wild Lemminkainen
On the blue-back of the ocean;
Sailed he days and nights unceasing,
Till at last he reached the borders
Of his own loved home and country;
There beheld he scenes familiar,
Saw the islands, capes, and rivers,
Saw his former shipping-stations,
Saw he many ancient landmarks,
Saw the mountains with their fir-trees,
Saw the pine-trees on the hill-tops,
Saw the willows in the lowlands;
Did not see his father's cottage,
Nor the dwellings of his mother.
Where a mansion once had risen,
There the alder-trees were growing,
Shrubs were growing on the homestead,
Junipers within the court-yard.
Spake the reckless Lemminkainen:
"In this glen I played and wandered,
On these stones I rocked for ages,

The Kalevala

On this lawn I rolled and tumbled,
Frolicked on these woodland-borders,
When a child of little stature.
Where then is my mother's dwelling,
Where the castles of my father?
Fire, I fear, has found the hamlet,
And the winds dispersed the ashes."
Then he fell to bitter weeping,
Wept one day and then a second,
Wept the third day without ceasing;
Did not mourn the ancient homestead,
Nor the dwellings of his father;
Wept he for his darling mother,
Wept he for the dear departed,
For the loved ones of the island.
Then he saw the bird of heaven,
Saw an eagle flying near him,
And he asked the bird this question:
"Mighty eagle, bird majestic,
Grant to me the information,
Where my mother may have wandered,
Whither I may go and find her!"
But the eagle knew but little,
Only knew that Ahti's people
Long ago together perished;
And the raven also answered
That his people had been scattered
By the swords, and spears, and arrows,
Of his enemies from Pohya.
Spake the hero, Lemminkainen:
"Faithful mother, dear departed,
Thou who nursed me in my childhood,
Art thou dead and turned to ashes,
Didst thou perish for my follies,
O'er thy head are willows weeping,
Junipers above thy body,
Alders watching o'er thy slumbers?
This my punishment for evil,
This the recompense of folly!
Fool was I, a son unworthy,
That I measured swords in Northland
With the landlord of Pohyola,
To my tribe came fell destruction,
And the death of my dear mother,
Through my crimes and misdemeanors."
Then the ministrel [sic] looked about him,
Anxious, looked in all directions,
And beheld some gentle foot-prints,
Saw a pathway lightly trodden
Where the heather had been beaten.
Quick as thought the path he followed,
Through the meadows, through the brambles,
O'er the hills, and through the valleys,
To a forest, vast and cheerless;
Travelled far and travelled farther,
Still a greater distance travelled,
To a dense and hidden glenwood,
In the middle of the island;
Found therein a sheltered cabin,
Found a small and darksome dwelling
Built between the rocky ledges,

Lönnrot

In the midst of triple pine-trees;
And within he spied his mother,
Found his gray-haired mother weeping.
Lemminkainen loud rejoices,
Cries in tones of joyful greetings,
These the words that Ahti utters:
"Faithful mother, well-beloved,
Thou that gavest me existence,
Happy I, that thou art living,
That thou hast not yet departed
To the kingdom of Tuoni,
To the islands of the blessed,
I had thought that thou hadst perished,
Hadst been murdered by my foemen,
Hadst been slain with bows and arrows.
Heavy are mine eyes from weeping,
And my checks are white with sorrow,
Since I thought my mother slaughtered
For the sins I had committed!"
Lemminkainen's mother answered:
"Long, indeed, hast thou been absent,
Long, my son, hast thou been living
In thy father's Isle of Refuge,
Roaming on the secret island,
Living at the doors of strangers,
Living in a nameless country,
Refuge from the Northland foemen."
Spake the hero, Lemminkainen:
"Charming is that spot for living,
Beautiful the magic island,
Rainbow-colored was the forest,
Blue the glimmer of the meadows,
Silvered were, the pine-tree branches,
Golden were the heather-blossoms;
All the woodlands dripped with honey,
Eggs in every rock and crevice,
Honey flowed from birch and sorb-tree,
Milk in streams from fir and aspen,
Beer-foam dripping from the willows,
Charming there to live and linger,
All their edibles delicious.
This their only source of trouble:
Great the fear for all the maidens,
All the heroes filled with envy,
Feared the coming of the stranger;
Thought that all the island-maidens,
Thought that all the wives and daughters,
All the good, and all the evil,
Gave thy son too much attention;
Thought the stranger, Lemminkainen,
Saw the Island-maids too often;
Yet the virgins I avoided,
Shunned the good and shunned the evil,
Shunned the host of charming daughters,
As the black-wolf shuns the sheep-fold,
As the hawk neglects the chickens."

RUNE XXX
THE FROST-FIEND.

Lemminkainen, reckless minstrel,
Handsome hero, Kaukomieli,
Hastens as the dawn is breaking,
At the dawning of the morning,
To the resting-place of vessels,
To the harbor of the island,
Finds the vessels sorely weeping,
Hears the wailing of the rigging,
And the ships intone this chorus:
"Must we wretched lie forever
In the harbor of this island,
Here to dry and fall in pieces?
Ahti wars no more in Northland,
Wars no more for sixty summers,
Even should he thirst for silver,
Should he wish the gold of battle."
Lemminkainen struck his vessels
With his gloves adorned with copper,
And addressed the ships as follows:
"Mourn no more, my ships of fir-wood,
Strong and hardy is your rigging,
To the wars ye soon may hasten,
Hasten to the seas of battle;
Warriors may swarm your cabins
Ere to-morrow's morn has risen.!'"
Then the reckless Lemminkainen
Hastened to his aged mother,
Spake to her the words that follow:
"Weep no longer, faithful mother,
Do not sorrow for thy hero,
Should he leave for scenes of battle,
For the hostile fields of Pohya;
Sweet revenge has fired my spirit,
And my soul is well determined,
To avenge the shameful insult
That the warriors of Northland
Gave to thee, defenseless woman."
To restrain him seeks his mother,
Warns her son again of danger:
"Do not go, my son beloved,
To the wars in Sariola;
There the jaws of Death await thee,
Fell destruction lies before thee!"
Lemminkainen, little heeding,
Still determined, speaks as follows:
"Where may I secure a swordsman,
Worthy of my race of heroes,
To assist me in the combat?
Often I have heard of Tiera,
Heard of Kura of the islands,
This one I will take to help me,
Magic hero of the broadsword;
He will aid me in the combat,

Will protect me from destruction."
Then he wandered to the islands,
On the way to Tiera's hamlet,
These the words that Ahti utters
As he nears the ancient dwellings:
Dearest friend, my noble Tiera,
My beloved hero-brother,
Dost thou other times remember,
When we fought and bled together,
On the battle-fields of Northland?
There was not an island-village
Where there were not seven mansions,
In each mansion seven heroes,
And not one of all these foemen
Whom we did not slay with broadswords,
Victims of our skill and valor."
Near the window sat the father
Whittling out a javelin-handle;
Near the threshold sat the mother
Skimming cream and making butter;
Near the portal stood the brother
Working on a sledge of birch-wood
Near the bridge-pass were the sisters
Washing out their varied garments.
Spake the father from the window,
From the threshold spake the mother,
From the portals spake the brother,
And the sisters from the bridge-pass:
"Tiera has no time for combat,
And his broadsword cannot battle;
Tiera is but late a bridegroom,
Still unveiled his bride awaits him."
Near the hearth was Tiera lying,
Lying by the fire was Kura,
Hastily one foot was shoeing,
While the other lay in waiting.
From the hook he takes his girdle,
Buckles it around his body,
Takes a javelin from its resting,
Not the largest, nor the smallest,
Buckles on his mighty scabbard,
Dons his heavy mail of copper;
On each javelin pranced a charger,
Wolves were howling from his helmet,
On the rings the bears were growling.
Tiera poised his mighty javelin,
Launched the spear upon its errand;
Hurled the shaft across the pasture,
To the border of the forest,
O'er the clay-fields of Pohyola,
O'er the green and fragrant meadows,
Through the distant bills of Northland.
Then great Tiera touched his javelin
To the mighty spear of Ahti,
Pledged his aid to Lemminkainen,
As his combatant and comrade.
Thereupon wild Kaukomieli
Pushed his boat upon the waters;
Like the serpent through the heather,
Like the creeping of the adder,
Sails the boat away to Pohya,

The Kalevala
O'er the seas of Sariola.
Quick the wicked hostess, Louhi,
Sends the black-frost of the heavens
To the waters of Pohyola,
O'er the far-extending sea-plains,
Gave the black-frost these directions:
"Much-loved Frost, my son and hero,
Whom thy mother has instructed,
Hasten whither I may send thee,
Go wherever I command thee,
Freeze the vessel of this hero,
Lemminkainen's bark of magic,
On the broad back of the ocean,
On the far-extending waters;
Freeze the wizard in his vessel,
Freeze to ice the wicked Ahti,
That he never more may wander,
Never waken while thou livest,
Or at least till I shall free him,
Wake him from his icy slumber!"
Frost, the son of wicked parents,
Hero-son of evil manners,
Hastens off to freeze the ocean,
Goes to fasten down the flood-gates,
Goes to still the ocean-currents.
As he hastens on his journey,
Takes the leaves from all the forest,
Strips the meadows of their verdure,
Robs the flowers of their colors.
When his journey he had ended,
Gained the border of the ocean,
Gained the sea-shore curved and endless,
On the first night of his visit,
Freezes he the lakes and rivers,
Freezes too the shore of ocean,
Freezes not the ocean-billows,
Does not check the ocean-currents.
On the sea a finch is resting,
Bird of song upon the waters,
But his feet are not yet frozen,
Neither is his head endangered.
When the second night Frost lingered,
He began to grow important,
He became a fierce intruder,
Fearless grew in his invasions,
Freezes everything before him;
Sends the fiercest cold of Northland,
Turns to ice the boundless waters.
Ever thicker, thicker, thicker,
Grew the ice on sea and ocean,
Ever deeper, deeper, deeper,
Fell the snow on field and forest,
Froze the hero's ship of beauty,
Cold and lifeless bark of Ahti;
Sought to freeze wild Lemminkainen,
Freeze him lifeless as his vessel,
Asked the minstrel for his life-blood,
For his ears, and feet, and fingers.
Then the hero, Lemminkainen,
Angry grew and filled with magic,
Hurled the black-frost to the fire-god,

Threw him to the fiery furnace,
Held him in his forge of iron,
Then addressed the frost as follows:
"Frost, thou evil son of Northland,
Dire and only son of Winter,
Let my members not be stiffened,
Neither ears, nor feet, nor fingers,
Neither let my head be frozen.
Thou hast other things to feed on,
Many other beads to stiffen;
Leave in peace the flesh of heroes,
Let this minstrel pass in safety,
Freeze the swamps, and lakes, and rivers,
Fens and forests, bills and valleys;
Let the cold stones grow still colder,
Freeze the willows in the waters,
Let the aspens freeze and suffer,
Let the bark peel from the birch-trees,
Let the Pines burst on the mountains,
Let this hero pass in safety,
Do not let his locks be stiffened.
"If all these prove insufficient,
Feed on other worthy matters;
Let the hot stones freeze asunder,
Let the flaming rocks be frozen,
Freeze the fiery blocks of iron,
Freeze to ice the iron mountains;
Stiffen well the mighty Wuoksi,
Let Imatra freeze to silence;
Freeze the sacred stream and whirlpool,
Let their boiling billows stiffen,
Or thine origin I'll sing thee,
Tell thy lineage of evil.
Well I know thine evil nature,
Know thine origin and power,
Whence thou camest, where thou goest,
Know thine ancestry of evil.
Thou wert born upon the aspen,
Wert conceived upon the willows,
Near the borders of Pohyola,
In the courts of dismal Northland;
Sin-begotten was thy father,
And thy mother was Dishonor.
"While in infancy who fed thee
While thy mother could not nurse thee?
Surely thou wert fed by adders,
Nursed by foul and slimy serpents;
North-winds rocked thee into slumber,
Cradled thee in roughest weather,
In the worst of willow-marshes,
In the springs forever flowing,
Evil-born and evil-nurtured,
Grew to be an evil genius,
Evil was thy mind and spirit,
And the infant still was nameless,
Till the name of Frost was given
To the progeny of evil.
"Then the young lad lived in hedges,
Dwelt among the weeds and willows,
Lived in springs in days of summer,
On the borders of the marshes,

The Kalevala
Tore the lindens in the winter,
Stormed among the glens and forests,
Raged among the sacred birch-trees,
Rattled in the alder-branches,
Froze the trees, the shoots, the grasses,
Evened all the plains and prairies,
Ate the leaves within the woodlands,
Made the stalks drop down their blossoms,
Peeled the bark on weeds and willows.
"Thou hast grown to large proportions,
Hast become too tall and mighty;
Dost thou labor to benumb me,
Dost thou wish mine ears and fingers,
Of my feet wouldst thou deprive me?
Do not strive to freeze this hero,
In his anguish and misfortune;
In my stockings I shall kindle
Fire to drive thee from my presence,
In my shoes lay flaming faggots,
Coals of fire in every garment,
Heated sandstones in my rigging;
Thus will hold thee at a distance.
Then thine evil form I'll banish
To the farthest Northland borders;
When thy journey is completed,
When thy home is reached in safety,
Freeze the caldrons in the castle,
Freeze the coal upon the hearthstone,
In the dough, the hands of women,
On its mother's lap, the infant,
Freeze the colt beside its mother.
"If thou shouldst not heed this order,
I shall banish thee still farther,
To the carbon-piles of Hisi,
To the chimney-hearth of Lempo,
Hurl thee to his fiery furnace,
Lay thee on the iron anvil,
That thy body may be hammered
With the sledges of the blacksmith,
May be pounded into atoms,
Twixt the anvil and the hammer.
"If thou shouldst not heed this order,
Shouldst not leave me to my freedom,
Know I still another kingdom,
Know another spot of resting;
I shall drive thee to the summer,
Lead thy tongue to warmer climates,
There a prisoner to suffer,
Never to obtain thy freedom
Till thy spirit I deliver,
Till I go myself and free thee."
Wicked Frost, the son of Winter,
Saw the magic bird of evil
Hovering above his spirit,
Straightway prayed for Ahti's mercy,
These the words the Frost-fiend uttered:
"Let us now agree together,
Neither one to harm the other,
Never in the course of ages,
Never while the moonlight glimmers
On the snow-capped hills of Northland.

Lönnrot

If thou hearest that I bring thee
Cold to freeze thy feet and fingers,
Hurl me to the fiery furnace,
Hammer me upon the anvil
Of the blacksmith, Ilmarinen;
Lead my tongue to warmer climates,
Banish me to lands of summer,
There a prisoner to suffer,
Nevermore to gain my freedom."
Thereupon wild Lemminkainen
Left his vessel in the ocean,
Frozen in the ice of Northland,
Left his warlike boat forever,
Started on his cheerless journey
To the borders of Pohyola,
And the mighty Tiera followed
In the tracks of his companion.
On the ice they journeyed northward
Briskly walked upon the ice-plain,
Walked one day, and then a second,
Till the closing of the third day,
When the Hunger-land approached them,
When appeared Starvation-island.
Here the hardy Lemminkainen
Hastened forward to the castle,
This the hero's prayer and question;
"Is there food within this castle,
Fish or fowl within its larders,
To refresh us on our journey,
Mighty heroes, cold and weary?
When the hero, Lemminkainen,
Found no food within the castle,
Neither fish, nor fowl, nor bacon,
Thus he cursed it and departed:
"May the fire destroy these chambers,
May the waters flood this dwelling,
Wash it to the seas of Mana!"
Then they hastened onward, onward,
Hastened on through field and forest,
Over by-ways long untrodden,
Over unknown paths and snow-fields;
Here the hardy Lemminkainen,
Reckless hero, Kaukomieli,
Pulled the soft wool from the ledges,
Gathered lichens from the tree-trunks,
Wove them into magic stockings,
Wove them into shoes and mittens,
On the settles of the hoar-frost,
In the stinging cold of Northland.
Then he sought to find some pathway,
That would guide their wayward footsteps,
And the hero spake as follows:
"O thou Tiera, friend beloved,
Shall we reach our destination,
Wandering for days together,
Through these Northland fields and forests?
Kura thus replies to Ahti:
"We, alas! have come for vengeance,
Come for blood and retribution,
To the battle-fields of Northland,
To the dismal Sariola,

The Kalevala
Here to leave our souls and bodies,
Here to starve, and freeze, and perish,
In the dreariest of places,
In this sun-forsaken country!
Never shall we gain the knowledge,
Never learn it, never tell it,
Which the pathway that can guide us
To the forest-beds to suffer,
To the Pohya-plains to perish,
In the home-land of the ravens,
Fitting food for crows and eagles.
Often do the Northland vultures
Hither come to feed their fledgelings;
Hither bring the birds of heaven
Bits of flesh and blood of heroes;
Often do the beaks of ravens
Tear the flesh of kindred corpses,
Often do the eagle's talons
Carry bones and trembling vitals,
Such as ours, to feed their nestlings,
In their rocky homes and ledges.
"Oh! my mother can but wonder,
Never can divine the answer,
Where her reckless son is roaming,
Where her hero's blood is flowing,
Whether in the swamps and lowlands
Whether in the heat of battle,
Or upon the waves of the ocean,
Or upon the hop-feld mountains,
Or along some forest by-way.
Nothing can her mind discover
Of the frailest of her heroes,
Only think that he has perished.
Thus the hoary-headed mother
Weeps and murmurs in her chambers:
'Where is now my son beloved,
In the kingdom of Manala?
Sow thy crops, thou dread Tuoni,
Harrow well the fields of Kalma!
Now the bow receives its respite
From the fingers of my Tiera;
Bow and arrow now are useless,
Now the merry birds can fatten
In the fields, and fens, and forests;
Bears may live in dens of freedom,
On the fields may sport the elk-herds.'"
Spake the reckless Lemminkainen:
"Thus it is, mine aged mother,
Thou that gavest me existence!
Thou hast reared thy broods of chickens,
Hatched and reared thy flights of white-swans
All of them the winds have scattered,
Or the evil Lempo frightened;
One flew hither, and one thither,
And a third one, lost forever!
Think thou of our former pleasures,
Of our better days together,
When I wandered like the flowers,
Like the berry in the meadows.
Many saw my form majestic,
Many thought me well-proportioned.

Lönnrot

Now is not as then with Ahti,
Into evil days have fallen,
Since I see but storms and darkness!
Then my eyes beheld but sunshine,
Then we did not weep and murmur,
Did not fill our hearts with sorrow,
When the maids in joy were singing,
When the virgins twined their tresses;
Then the women joined in joyance,
Whether brides were happy-wedded,
Whether bridegrooms choose discreetly,
Whether they were wise or unwise.
"But we must not grow disheartened,
Let the Island-maidens cheer us;
Here we are not yet enchanted,
Not bewitched by magic singing,
On the paths not left to perish,
Sink and perish on our journey.
Full of youth we should not suffer,
Strong, we should not die unworthy,
Whom the wizards have enchanted,
Have bewitched with songs of magic;
Sorcerers may charm and conquer,
Bury them within their dungeons,
Hide them spell-bound in their cabins.
Let the wizards charm each other,
And bewitch their magic offspring,
Bring their tribes to fell destruction.
Never did my gray-haired father
Bow submission to a wizard,
Offer worship to magicians.
These the words my father uttered,
These the thoughts his son advances:
'Guard us, thou O great Creator,
Shield us, thou O God of mercy,
With thine arms of grace protect us,
Help us with thy strength and wisdom,
Guide the minds of all thy heroes,
Keep aright the thoughts of women,
Keep the old from speaking evil,
Keep the young from sin and folly,
Be to us a help forever,
Be our Guardian and our Father,
That our children may not wander
From the ways of their Creator,
From the path that God has given!'"
Then the hero Lemminkainen,
Made from cares the fleetest racers,
Sable racers from his sorrows,
Reins he made from days of evil,
From his sacred pains made saddles.
To the saddle, quickly springing,
Galloped he away from trouble,
To his dear and aged mother;
And his comrade, faithful Tiera,
Galloped to his Island-dwelling.

The Kalevala
Now departs wild Lemminkainen,
Brave and reckless Kaukomieli,
From these ancient songs and legends;
Only guides his faithful Kura
To his waiting bride and kindred,
While these lays and incantations
Shall be turned to other heroes.

RUNE XXXI
KULLERWOINEN SON OF EVIL.

In the ancient times a mother
Hatched and raised some swans and chickens,
Placed the chickens in the brushwood,
Placed her swans upon the river;
Came an eagle, hawk, and falcon,
Scattered all her swans and chickens,
One was carried to Karyala,
And a second into Ehstland,
Left a third at home in Pohya.
And the one to Ehstland taken
Soon became a thriving merchant;
He that journeyed to Karyala
Flourished and was called Kalervo;
He that hid away in Pohya
Took the name of Untamoinen,
Flourished to his father's sorrow,
To the heart-pain of his mother.
Untamoinen sets his fish-nets
In the waters of Kalervo;
Kullerwoinen sees the fish-nets,
Takes the fish home in his basket.
Then Untamo, evil-minded,
Angry grew and sighed for vengeance,
Clutched his fingers for the combat,
Bared his mighty arms for battle,
For the stealing of his salmon,
For the robbing of his fish-nets.
Long they battled, fierce the struggle,
Neither one could prove the victor;
Should one beat the other fiercely,
He himself was fiercely beaten.
Then arose a second trouble;
On the second and the third days,
Kalerwoinen sowed some barley
Near the barns of Untamoinen;
Untamoinen's sheep in hunger
Ate the crop of Kullerwoinen;
Kullerwoinen's dog in malice
Tore Untamo's sheep in pieces;
Then Untamo sorely threatened
To annihilate the people
Of his brother, Kalerwoinen,
To exterminate his tribe-folk,
To destroy the young and aged,
To out-root his race and kingdom;
Conjures men with broadswords girded,
For the war he fashions heroes,
Fashions youth with spears adjusted,
Bearing axes on their shoulders,
Conjures thus a mighty army,
Hastens to begin a battle,
Bring a war upon his brother.
Kalerwoinen's wife in beauty

The Kalevala

Sat beside her chamber-window,
Looking out along the highway,
Spake these words in wonder guessing:
"Do I see some smoke arising,
Or perchance a heavy storm-cloud,
Near the border of the forest,
Near the ending of the prairie?"
It was not some smoke arising,
Nor indeed a heavy storm-cloud,
It was Untamoinen's soldiers
Marching to the place of battle.
Warriors of Untamoinen
Came equipped with spears and arrows,
Killed the people of Kalervo,
Slew his tribe and all his kindred,
Burned to ashes many dwellings,
Levelled many courts and cabins,
Only, left Kalervo's daughter,
With her unborn child, survivors
Of the slaughter of Untamo;
And she led the hostile army
To her father's halls and mansion,
Swept the rooms and made them cheery,
Gave the heroes home-attentions.
Time had gone but little distance,
Ere a boy was born in magic
Of the virgin, Untamala,
Of a mother, trouble-laden,
Him the mother named Kullervo,
"Pearl of Combat," said Untamo.
Then they laid the child of wonder,
Fatherless, the magic infant,
In the cradle of attention,
To be rocked, and fed, and guarded;
But he rocked himself at pleasure,
Rocked until his locks stood endwise;
Rocked one day, and then a second,
Rocked the third from morn till noontide;
But before the third day ended,
Kicks the boy with might of magic,
Forwards, backwards, upwards, downwards,
Kicks in miracles of power,
Bursts with might his swaddling garments
Creeping from beneath his blankets,
Knocks his cradle into fragments,
Tears to tatters all his raiment,
Seemed that he would grow a hero,
And his mother, Untamala,
Thought that be, when full of stature,
When he found his strength and reason,
Would become a great magician,
First among a thousand heroes.
When three months the boy had thriven,
He began to speak as follows:
"When my form is full of stature,
When these arms grow strong and hardy,
Then will I avenge the murder
Of Kalervo and his people!"
Untamoinen bears the saying,
Speaks these words to those about him;
"To my tribe he brings destruction,

Lönnrot

In him grows a new Kalervo!"
Then the heroes well considered,
And the women gave their counsel,
How to kill the magic infant,
That their tribe may live in safety.
It appeared the boy would prosper;
Finally, they all consenting,
He was placed within a basket,
And with willows firmly fastened,
Taken to the reeds and rushes,
Lowered to the deepest waters,
In his basket there to perish.
When three nights had circled over,
Messengers of Untamoinen
Went to see if he had perished
In his basket in the waters;
But the prodigy, was living,
Had not perished in the rushes;
He had left his willow-basket,
Sat in triumph on a billow,
In his hand a rod of copper,
On the rod a golden fish-line,
Fishing for the silver whiting,
Measuring the deeps beneath him;
In the sea was little water,
Scarcely would it fill three measures.
Untamoinen then reflected,
This the language of the wizard:
"Whither shall we take this wonder,
Lay this prodigy of evil,
That destruction may o'ertake him,
Where the boy will sink and perish?"
Then his messengers he ordered
To collect dried poles of brushwood,
Birch-trees with their hundred branches,
Pine-trees full of pitch and resin,
Ordered that a pyre be builded,
That the boy might be cremated,
That Kullervo thus might perish.
High they piled the and branches,
Dried limbs from the sacred birch-tree,
Branches from a hundred fir-trees,
Knots and branches full of resign;
Filled with bark a thousand sledges,
Seasoned oak, a hundred measures;
Piled the brushwood to the tree-tops,
Set the boy upon the summit,
Set on fire the pile of brushwood,
Burned one day, and then a second,
Burned the third from morn till evening.
When Untamo sent his heralds
To inspect the pyre and wizard,
There to learn if young Kullervo
Had been burned to dust and ashes,
There they saw the young boy sitting
On a pyramid of embers,
In his band a rod of copper,
Raking coals of fire about him,
To increase their heat and power;
Not a hair was burned nor injured,
Not a ringlet singed nor shrivelled.

The Kalevala

Then Untamo, evil-humored,
Thus addressed his trusted heralds:
"Whither shall the boy be taken,
To what place this thing of evil,
That destruction may o'ertake him,
That the boy may sink and perish?"
Then they hung him to an oak-tree,
Crucified him in the branches,
That the wizard there might perish.
When three days and nights had ended,
Untamoinen spake as follows:
"It is time to send my heralds
To inspect the mighty oak-tree,
There to learn if young Kullervo
Lives or dies among the branches."
Thereupon he sent his servants,
And the heralds brought this message:
"Young Kullervo has not perished,
Has not died among the branches
Of the oak-tree where we hung him.
In the oak he maketh pictures
With a wand between his fingers;
Pictures hang from all the branches,
Carved and painted by Kullervo;
And the heroes, thick as acorns,
With their swords and spears adjusted,
Fill the branches of the oak-tree,
Every leaf becomes a soldier."
Who can help the grave Untamo
Kill the boy that threatens evil
To Untamo's tribe and country,
Since he will not die by water,
Nor by fire, nor crucifixion?
Finally it was decided
That his body was immortal,
Could not suffer death nor torture.
In despair grave Untamoinen
Thus addressed the boy, Kullervo:
"Wilt thou live a life becoming,
Always do my people honor,
Should I keep thee in my dwelling?
Shouldst thou render servant's duty,
Then thou wilt receive thy wages,
Reaping whatsoe'er thou sowest;
Thou canst wear the golden girdle,
Or endure the tongue of censure."
When the boy had grown a little,
Had increased in strength and stature,
He was given occupation,
He was made to tend an infant,
Made to rock the infant's cradle.
These the words of Untamoinen:
"Often look upon the young child,
Feed him well and guard from danger,
Wash his linen in the river,
Give the infant good attention."
Young Kullervo, wicked wizard,
Nurses one day then a second;
On the morning of the third day,
Gives the infant cruel treatment,
Blinds its eyes and breaks its fingers;

Lönnrot

And when evening shadows gather,
Kills the young child while it slumbers,
Throws its body to the waters,
Breaks and burns the infant's cradle.
Untamoinen thus reflected:
"Never will this fell Kullervo
Be a worthy nurse for children,
Cannot rock a babe in safety;
Do not know how I can use him,
What employment I can give him!"
Then he told the young magician
He must fell the standing forest,
And Kullervo gave this answer:
"Only will I be a hero,
When I wield the magic hatchet;
I am young, and fair, and mighty,
Far more beautiful than others,
Have the skill of six magicians."
Thereupon he sought the blacksmith,
This the order of Kullervo:
"Listen, O thou metal-artist,
Forge for me an axe of copper,
Forge the mighty axe of heroes,
Wherewith I may fell the forest,
Fell the birch, and oak, and aspen."
This behest the blacksmith honors,
Forges him an axe of copper,
Wonderful the blade he forges.
Kullerwoinen grinds his hatchet,
Grinds his blade from morn till evening,
And the next day makes the handle;
Then he hastens to the forest,
To the upward-sloping mountain,
To the tallest of the birches,
To the mightiest of oak-trees;
There he swings his axe of copper,
Swings his blade with might of magic,
Cuts with sharpened edge the aspen,
With one blow he fells the oak-tree,
With a second blow, the linden;
Many trees have quickly fallen,
By the hatchet of Kullervo.
Then the wizard spake as follows:
"This the proper work of Lempo,
Let dire Hisi fell the forest!"
In the birch he sank his hatchet,
Made an uproar in the woodlands,
Called aloud in tones, of thunder,
Whistled to the distant mountains,
Till they echoed to his calling,
When Kullervo spake as follows:
"May the forest, in the circle
Where my voice rings, fall and perish,
In the earth be lost forever!
May no tree remain unlevelled,
May no saplings grow in spring-time,
Never while the moonlight glimmers,
Where Kullervo's voice has echoed,
Where the forest hears my calling;
Where the ground with seed is planted,
And the grain shall sprout and flourish,

The Kalevala
May it never come to ripeness,
Mar the ears of corn be blasted!"
When the strong man, Untamoinen,
Went to look at early evening,
How Kullervo was progressing,
In his labors in the forest;
Little was the work accomplished,
Was not worthy of a here;
Untamoinen thus reflected:
"Young Kullervo is not fitted
For the work of clearing forests,
Wastes the best of all the timber,
To my lands he brings destruction;
I shall set him making fences."
Then the youth began the building
Of a fence for Untamoinen;
Took the trunks of stately fir-trees,
Trimmed them with his blade for fence-posts,
Cut the tallest in the woodlands,
For the railing of his fences;
Made the smaller poles and cross-bars
From the longest of the lindens;
Made the fence without a pass-way,
Made no wicket in his fences,
And Kullervo spake these measures.
"He that does not rise as eagles,
Does not sail on wings through ether,
Cannot cross Kullervo's pickets,
Nor the fences he has builded."
Untamoinen left his mansion
To inspect the young boy's labors,
View the fences of Kullervo;
Saw the fence without a pass-way,
Not a wicket in his fences;
From the earth the fence extended
To the highest clouds of heaven.
These the words of Untamoinen:
"For this work he is not fitted,
Useless is the fence thus builded;
Is so high that none can cross it,
And there is no passage through it:
He shall thresh the rye and barley."
Young Kullervo, quick preparing
Made an oaken flail for threshing,
Threshed the rye to finest powder,
Threshed the barley into atoms,
And the straw to worthless fragments.
Untamoinen went at evening,
Went to see Kullervo's threshing,
View the work of Kullerwoinen;
Found the rye was ground to powder,
Grains of barley crushed to atoms,
And the straw to worthless rubbish.
Untamoinen then grew angry,
Spake these words in bitter accents:
"Kullerwoinen as a workman
Is a miserable failure;
Whatsoever work he touches
Is but ruined by his witchcraft;
I shall carry him to Ehstland,
In Karyala I shall sell him

Lönnrot

To the blacksmith, Ilmarinen,
There to swing the heavy hammer."
Untamoinen sells Kullervo,
Trades him off in far Karyala,
To the blacksmith, Ilmarinen,
To the master of the metals,
This the sum received in payment:
Seven worn and worthless sickles,
Three old caldrons worse than useless,
Three old scythes, and hoes, and axes,
Recompense, indeed, sufficient
For a boy that will not labor
For the good of his employer.

RUNE XXXII
KULLERVO AS A SHEPHERD.

Kullerwoinen, wizard-servant
Of the blacksmith, Ilmarinen,
Purchased slave from Untamoinen,
Magic son with sky-blue stockings,
With a head of golden ringlets,
In his shoes of marten-leather,
Waiting little, asked the blacksmith,
Asked the host for work at morning,
In the evening asked the hostess,
These the words of Kullerwoinen:
"Give me work at early morning,
In the evening, occupation,
Labor worthy of thy servant."
Then the wife of Ilmarinen,
Once the Maiden of the Rainbow,
Thinking long, and long debating,
How to give the youth employment,
How the purchased slave could labor;
Finally a shepherd made him,
Made him keeper of her pastures;
But the over-scornful hostess,
Baked a biscuit for the herdsman,
Baked a loaf of wondrous thickness,
Baked the lower-half of oat-meal,
And the upper-half of barley,
Baked a flint-stone in the centre,
Poured around it liquid butter,
Then she gave it to the shepherd,
Food to still the herdsman's hunger;
Thus she gave the youth instructions:
"Do not eat the bread in hunger,
Till the herd is in the woodlands!"
Then the wife of Ilmarinen
Sent her cattle to the pasture,
Thus addressing Kullerwoinen:
"Drive the cows to yonder bowers,
To the birch-trees and the aspens,
That they there may feed and fatten,
Fill themselves with milk and butter,
In the open forest-pastures,
On the distant hills and mountains,
In the glens among the birch-trees,
In the lowlands with the aspens,
In the golden pine-tree forests,
In the thickets silver-laden.
"Guard them, thou O kind Creator,
Shield them, omnipresent Ukko,
Shelter them from every danger,
And protect them from all evil,
That they may not want, nor wander
From the paths of peace and plenty.
As at home Thou didst protect them
In the shelters and the hurdles,

Lönnrot

Guard them now beneath the heavens,
Shelter them in woodland pastures,
That the herds may live and prosper
To the joy of Northland's hostess,
And against the will of Lempo.
"If my herdsman prove unworthy,
If the shepherd-maids seem evil,
Let the pastures be their shepherds,
Let the alders guard the cattle,
Make the birch-tree their protector,
Let the willow drive them homeward,
Ere the hostess go to seek them,
Ere the milkmaids wait and worry.
Should the birch-tree not protect them,
Nor the aspen lend assistance,
Nor the linden be their keeper,
Nor the willow drive them homeward,
Wilt thou give them better herdsmen,
Let Creation's beauteous daughters
Be their kindly shepherdesses.
Thou hast many lovely maidens,
Many hundreds that obey thee,
In the Ether's spacious circles,
Beauteous daughters of creation.
"Summer-daughter, magic maiden,
Southern mother of the woodlands,
Pine-tree daughter, Kateyatar,
Pihlayatar, of the aspen,
Alder-maiden, Tapio's daughter,
Daughter of the glen, Millikki,
And the mountain-maid, Tellervo,
Of my herds be ye protectors,
Keep them from the evil-minded,
Keep them safe in days of summer,
In the times of fragrant flowers,
While the tender leaves are whispering,
While the Earth is verdure-laden.
"Summer-daughter, charming maiden,
Southern mother of the woodlands,
Spread abroad thy robes of safety,
Spread thine apron o'er the forest,
Let it cover all my cattle,
And protect the unprotected,
That no evil winds may harm them,
May not suffer from the storm-clouds.
Guard my flocks from every danger,
Keep them from the hands of wild-beasts,
From the swamps with sinking pathways,
From the springs that bubble trouble,
From the swiftly running waters,
From the bottom of the whirlpool,
That they may not find misfortune,
May not wander to destruction,
In the marshes sink and perish,
Though against God's best intentions,
Though against the will of Ukko.
"From a distance bring a bugle,
Bring a shepherd's horn from heaven,
Bring the honey-flute of Ukko,
Play the music of creation,
Blow the pipes of the magician,

The Kalevala
Play the flowers on the highlands,
Charm the hills, and dales, and mount
Charm the borders of the forest,
Fill the forest-trees with honey,
Fill with spice the fountain-borders.
"For my herds give food and shelter,
Feed them all on honeyed pastures,
Give them drink at honeyed fountains
Feed them on thy golden grasses,
On the leaves of silver saplings,
From the springs of life and beauty,
From the crystal-waters flowing,
From the waterfalls of Rutya,
From the uplands green and golden,
From the glens enriched in silver.
Dig thou also golden fountains
On the four sides of the willow,
That the cows may drink in sweetness,
And their udders swell with honey,
That their milk may flow in streamlets;
Let the milk be caught in vessels,
Let the cow's gift be not wasted,
Be not given to Manala.
"Many are the sons of evil,
That to Mana take their milkings,
Give their milk to evil-doers,
Waste it in Tuoni's empire;
Few there are, and they the worthy,
That can get the milk from Mana;
Never did my ancient mother
Ask for counsel in the village,
Never in the courts for wisdom;
She obtained her milk from Mana,
Took the sour-milk from the dealers,
Sweet-milk from the greater distance,
From the kingdom of Manala,
From Tuoni's fields and pastures;
Brought it in the dusk of evening,
Through the by-ways in the darkness,
That the wicked should not know it,
That it should not find destruction.
"This the language of my mother,
And these words I also echo:
Whither does the cow's gift wander,
Whither has the milk departed?
Has it gone to feed the strangers,
Banished to the distant village,
Gone to feed the hamlet-lover,
Or perchance to feed the forest,
Disappeared within the woodlands,
Scattered o'er the hills and mountains,
Mingled with the lakes and rivers?
It shall never go to Mana,
Never go to feed the stranger,
Never to the village-lover;
Neither shall it feed the forest,
Nor be lost upon the mountains,
Neither sprinkled in the woodlands,
Nor be mingled with the waters;
It is needed for our tables,
Worthy food for all our children.'

Lönnrot

Summer-daughter, maid of beauty,
Southern daughter of Creation,
Give Suotikki tender fodder,
To Watikki, give pure water,
To Hermikki milk abundant,
Fresh provisions to Tuorikki,
From Mairikki let the milk flow,
Fresh milk from my cows in plenty,
Coming from the tips of grasses,
From the tender herbs and leaflets,
From the meadows rich in honey,
From the mother of the forest,
From the meadows sweetly dripping,
From the berry-laden branches,
From the heath of flower-maidens,
From the verdure, maiden bowers,
From the clouds of milk-providers,
From the virgin of the heavens,
That the milk may flow abundant
From the cows that I have given
To the keeping of Kullervo.
"Rise thou virgin of the valley,
From the springs arise in beauty,
Rise thou maiden of the fountain,
Beautiful, arise in ether,
Take the waters from the cloudlets,
And my roaming herds besprinkle,
That my cows may drink and flourish,
May be ready for the coming
Of the shepherdess of evening.
"O Millikki, forest-hostess,
Mother of the herds at pasture,
Send the tallest of thy servants,
Send the best of thine assistants,
That my herds may well be guarded,
Through the pleasant days of summer,
Given us by our Creator.
"Beauteous virgin of the woodlands,
Tapio's most charming daughter,
Fair Tellervo, forest-maiden,
Softly clad in silken raiment,
Beautiful in golden ringlets,
Do thou give my herds protection,
In the Metsola dominions,
On the hills of Tapiola;
Shield them with thy hands of beauty,
Stroke them gently with thy fingers,
Give to them a golden lustre,
Make them shine like fins of salmon,
Grow them robes as soft as ermine.
"When the evening star brings darkness,
When appears the hour of twilight,
Send my lowing cattle homeward,
Milk within their vessels coursing,
Water on their backs in lakelets.
When the Sun has set in ocean,
When the evening-bird is singing,
Thus address my herds of cattle:
"Ye that carry horns, now hasten
To the sheds of Ilmarinen;
Ye enriched in milk go homeward,

The Kalevala
To the hostess now in waiting,
Home, the better place for sleeping,
Forest-beds are full of danger;
When the evening comes in darkness,
Straightway journey to the milkmaids
Building fires to light the pathway
On the turf enriched in honey,
In the pastures berry-laden!
"Thou, O Tapio's son, Nyrikki,
Forest-son, enrobed in purple,
Cut the fir-trees on the mountains,
Cut the pines with cones of beauty,
Lay them o'er the streams for bridges,
Cover well the sloughs of quicksand,
In the swamps and in the lowlands,
That my herd may pass in safety,
On their long and dismal journey,
To the clouds of smoke may hasten,
Where the milkmaids wait their coming.
If the cows heed not this order,
Do not hasten home at evening,
Then, O service-berry maiden,
Cut a birch-rod from the glenwood,
From the juniper, a whip-stick,
Near to Tapio's spacious mansion,
Standing on the ash-tree mountain,
Drive my wayward, lowing cattle,
Into Metsola's wide milk-yards,
When the evening-star is rising.
"Thou, O Otso, forest-apple,
Woodland bear, with honeyed fingers,
Let us make a lasting treaty,
Make a vow for future ages,
That thou wilt not kill my cattle,
Wilt not eat my milk-providers;
That I will not send my hunters
To destroy thee and thy kindred,
Never in the days of summer,
The Creator's warmest season.
"Dost thou hear the tones of cow-bells,
Hear the calling of the bugles,
Ride thyself within the meadow,
Sink upon the turf in slumber,
Bury both thine ears in clover,
Crouch within some alder-thicket
Climb between the mossy ledges,
Visit thou some rocky cavern,
Flee away to other mountains,
Till thou canst not hear the cow-bells,
Nor the calling of the herdsmen.
"Listen, Otso of the woodlands,
Sacred bear with honeyed fingers,
To approach the herd of cattle
Thou thyself art not forbidden,
But thy tongue, and teeth, and fingers,
Must not touch my herd in summer,
Must not harm my harmless creatures.
Go around the scented meadows,
Amble through the milky pastures,
From the tones of bells and shepherds.
should the herd be on the mountain,

Lönnrot

Go thou quickly to the marshes;
Should my cattle browse the lowlands,
Sleep thou then within the thicket;
Should they feed upon the uplands,
Thou must hasten to the valley;
Should the herd graze at the bottom,
Thou must feed upon the summit.
"Wander like the golden cuckoo,
Like the dove of silver brightness,
Like a little fish in ocean;
Ride thy claws within thy hair-foot,
Shut thy wicked teeth in darkness,
That my herd may not be frightened,
May not think themselves in danger.
Leave my cows in peace and plenty,
Let them journey home in order,
Through the vales and mountain by-ways,
Over plains and through the forest,
Harming not my harmless creatures.
"Call to mind our former pledges,
At the river of Tuoni,
Near the waterfall and whirlpool,
In the ears of our Creator.
Thrice to Otso was it granted,
In the circuit of the summer,
 To approach the land of cow-bells,
Where the herdsmen's voices echo;
But to thee it was not granted,
Otso never had permission
To attempt a wicked action,
To begin a work of evil.
Should the blinding thing of malice
Come upon thee in thy roamings,
Should thy bloody teeth feel hunger,
Throw thy malice to the mountains,
And thy hunger to the pine-trees,
Sink thy teeth within the aspens,
In the dead limbs of the birches,
Prune the dry stalks from the willows.
Should thy hunger still impel thee,
Go thou to the berry-mountain,
Eat the fungus of the forest,
Feed thy hunger on the ant-hills,
Eat the red roots of the bear-tree,
Metsola's rich cakes of honey,
Not the grass my herd would feed on.
Or if Metsola's rich honey
Should ferment before the eating,
On the hills of golden color,
On the mountains filled with silver,
There is other food for hunger,
Other drink for thirsting Otso,
Everlasting will the food be,
And the drink be never wanting.
"Let us now agree in honor,
And conclude a lasting treaty
That our lives may end in pleasure,
May be, merry in the summer,
Both enjoy the woods in common,
Though our food must be distinctive
Shouldst thou still desire to fight me,

The Kalevala

Let our contests be in winter,
Let our wars be, on the snow-fields.
Swamps will thaw in days of summer,
Warm, the water in the rivers.
Therefore shouldst thou break this treaty,
Shouldst thou come where golden cattle
Roam these woodland hills and valleys,
We will slay thee with our cross-bows;
Should our arrow-men be absent,
We have here some archer-women,
And among them is the hostess,
That can use the fatal weapon,
That can bring thee to destruction,
Thus will end the days of trouble
That thou bringest to our people,
And against the will of Ukko.
"Ukko, ruler in the heavens,
Lend an ear to my entreaty,
Metamorphose all my cattle,
Through the mighty force of magic,
Into stumps and stones convert them,
If the enemy should wander,
Near my herd in days of summer.
"If I had been born an Otso,
I would never stride and amble
At the feet of aged women;
Elsewhere there are hills and valleys,
Farther on are honey-pastures,
Where the lazy bear may wander,
Where the indolent may linger;
Sneak away to yonder mountain,
That thy tender flesh may lessen,
In the blue-glen's deep recesses,
In the bear-dens of the forest,
Thou canst move through fields of acorns,
Through the sand and ocean-pebbles,
There for thee is tracked a pathway,
Through the woodlands on the sea-coast,
To the Northland's farthest limits,
To the dismal plains of Lapland,
There 'tis well for thee to lumber,
There to live will be a pleasure.
Shoeless there to walk in summer,
Stockingless in days of autumn,
On the blue-back of the mountain,
Through the swamps and fertile lowlands.
"If thou canst not journey thither,
Canst not find the Lapland-highway,
Hasten on a little distance,
In the bear-path leading northward.
To the grove of Tuonela,
To the honey-plains of Kalma,
Swamps there are in which to wander,
Heaths in which to roam at pleasure,
There are Kiryos, there are Karyos,
And of beasts a countless number,
With their fetters strong as iron,
Fattening within the forest.
Be ye gracious, groves and mountains,
Full of grace, ye darksome thickets,
Peace and, plenty to my cattle,

Lönnrot

Through the pleasant days of summer,
The Creator's warmest season.
"Knippana, O King of forests,
Thou the gray-beard of the woodlands,
Watch thy dogs in fen and fallow,
Lay a sponge within one nostril,
And an acorn in the other,
That they may not scent my cattle;
Tie their eyes with silken fillets,
That they may not see my herdlings,
May not see my cattle grazing.
"Should all this seem inefficient,
Drive away thy barking children,
Let them run to other forests,
Let them hunt in other marshes,
From these verdant strips of meadow,
From these far outstretching borders,
Hide thy dogs within thy caverns,
Firmly tie thy yelping children,
Tie them with thy golden fetters,
With thy chains adorned with silver,
That they may not do me damage,'
May not do a deed of mischief.
Should all this prove inefficient,
Thou, O Ukko, King of heaven.
Wise director, full of mercy,
Hear the golden words I utter,
Hear a voice that breathes affection,
From the alder make a muzzle,
For each dog, within the kennel;
Should the alder prove too feeble,
Cast a band of purest copper;
Should the copper prove a failure,
Forge a band of ductile iron;
Should the iron snap asunder,
In each nose a small-ring fasten,
Made of molten gold and silver,
Chain thy dogs in forest-caverns,
That my herd may not be injured.
Then the wife of Ilmarinen,
Life-companion of the blacksmith,
Opened all her yards and stables,
Led her herd across the meadow,
Placed them in the herdman's keeping,
In the care of Kullerwoinen.

RUNE XXXIII
KULLERVO AND THE CHEAT-CAKE.

Thereupon the lad, Kullervo,
Laid his luncheon in his basket,
Drove the herd to mountain-pastures,
O'er the hills and through the marshes,
To their grazings in the woodlands,
Speaking as he careless wandered:
"Of the youth am I the poorest,
Hapless lad and full of trouble,
Evil luck to me befallen!
I alas! must idly wander
O'er the hills and through the valleys,
As a watch-dog for the cattle!"
Then she sat upon the greensward,
In a sunny spot selected,
Singing, chanting words as follow:
"Shine, O shine, thou Sun of heaven,
Cast thy rays, thou fire of Ukko,
On the herdsman of the blacksmith,
On the head of Kullerwoinen,
On this poor and luckless shepherd,
Not in Ilmarinen's smithy,
Nor the dwellings of his people;
Good the table of the hostess,
Cuts the best of wheaten biscuit,
Honey-cakes she cuts in slices,
Spreading each with golden butter;
Only dry bread has the herdsman,
Eats with pain the oaten bread-crusts,'
Filled with chaff his and biscuit,
Feeds upon the worst of straw-bread,
Pine-tree bark, the broad he feeds on,
Sipping water from the birch-bark,
Drinking from the tips of grasses I
Go, O Sun, and go, O barley,
Haste away, thou light of Ukko,
Hide within the mountain pine-trees,
Go, O wheat, to yonder thickets,
To the trees of purple berries,
To the junipers and alders,
Safely lead the herdsman homeward
To the biscuit golden-buttered,
To the honeyed cakes and viands!"
While the shepherd lad was singing
Kullerwoinen's song and echo,
Ilmarinen's wife was feasting
On the sweetest bread of Northland,
On the toothsome cakes of barley,
On the richest of provisions;
Only laid aside some cabbage,
For the herdsman, Kullerwoinen;
Set apart some wasted fragments,
Leavings of the dogs at dinner,
For the shepherd, home returning.

Lönnrot

From the woods a bird came flying,
Sang this song to Kullerwoinen:
"'Tis the time for forest-dinners,
For the fatherless companion
Of the herds to eat his viands,
Eat the good things from his basket!"
Kullerwoinen heard the songster,
Looked upon the Sun's long shadow,
Straightway spake the words that follow:
"True, the singing of the song-bird,
It is time indeed for feasting,
Time to eat my basket-dinner."
Thereupon young Kullerwoinen
Called his herd to rest in safety,
Sat upon a grassy hillock,
Took his basket from his shoulders,
Took therefrom the and oat-loaf,
Turned it over in his fingers,
Carefully the loaf inspected,
Spake these words of ancient wisdom:
"Many loaves are fine to look on,
On the outside seem delicious,
On the inside, chaff and tan-bark!"
Then the shepherd, Kullerwoinen,
Drew his knife to cut his oat-loaf,
Cut the hard and arid biscuit;
Cuts against a stone imprisoned,
Well imbedded in the centre,
Breaks his ancient knife in pieces;
When the shepherd youth, Kullervo,
Saw his magic knife had broken,
Weeping sore, he spake as follows:
"This, the blade that I bold sacred,
This the one thing that I honor,
Relic of my mother's people!
On the stone within this oat-loaf,
On this cheat-cake of the hostess,
I my precious knife have broken.
How shall I repay this insult,
How avenge this woman's malice,
What the wages for deception?"
From a tree the raven answered:
"O thou little silver buckle,
Only son of old Kalervo,
Why art thou in evil humor,
Wherefore sad in thy demeanor?
Take a young shoot from the thicket,
Take a birch-rod from the valley,
Drive thy herd across the lowlands,
Through the quicksands of the marshes;
To the wolves let one half wander,
To the bear-dens, lead the other;
Sing the forest wolves together,
Sing the bears down from the mountains,
Call the wolves thy little children,
And the bears thy standard-bearers;
Drive them like a cow-herd homeward,
Drive them home like spotted cattle,
Drive them to thy master's milk-yards;
Thus thou wilt repay the hostess
For her malice and derision."

The Kalevala

Thereupon the wizard answered,
These the words of Kullerwoinen:
"Wait, yea wait, thou bride of Hisi!
Do I mourn my mother's relic,
Mourn the keep-sake thou hast broken?
Thou thyself shalt mourn as sorely
When thy, cows come home at evening!"
From the tree he cuts a birch-wand,
From the juniper a whip-stick,
Drives the herd across the lowlands,
Through the quicksands of the marshes,
To the wolves lets one half wander,
To the bear-dens leads the other;
Calls the wolves his little children,
Calls the bears his standard-bearers,
Changes all his herd of cattle
Into wolves and bears by magic.
In the west the Sun is shining,
Telling that the night is coming.
Quick the wizard, Kullerwoinen,
Wanders o'er the pine-tree mountain,
Hastens through the forest homeward,
Drives the wolves and bears before him
Toward the milk-yards of the hostess;
To the herd he speaks as follows,
As they journey on together:
"Tear and kill the wicked hostess,
Tear her guilty flesh in pieces,
When she comes to view her cattle,
When she stoops to do her milking!"
Then the wizard, Kullerwoinen,
From an ox-bone makes a bugle,
Makes it from Tuonikki's cow-horn,
Makes a flute from Kiryo's shin-bone,
Plays a song upon his bugle,
Plays upon his flute of magic,
Thrice upon the home-land hill-tops,
Six times near the coming gate-ways.
Ilmarinen's wife and hostess
Long had waited for the coming
Of her herd with Kullerwoinen,
Waited for the milk at evening,
Waited for the new-made butter,
Heard the footsteps in the cow-path,
On the heath she beard the bustle,
Spake these joyous words of welcome:
"Be thou praised, O gracious Ukko,
That my herd is home returning!
But I hear a bugle sounding,
'Tis the playing of my herdsman,
Playing on a magic cow-horn,
Bursting all our ears with music!"
Kullerwoinen, drawing nearer,
To the hostess spake as follows:
"Found the bugle in the woodlands,
And the flute among the rushes;
All thy herd are in the passage,
All thy cows within the hurdles,
This the time to build the camp-fire,
This the time to do the milking!"
Ilmarinen's wife, the hostess,

Lönnrot

Thus addressed an aged servant:
"Go, thou old one, to the milking,
Have the care of all my cattle,
Do not ask for mine assistance,
Since I have to knead the biscuit."
Kullerwoinen spake as follows:
"Always does the worthy hostess,
Ever does the wisdom-mother
Go herself and do the milking,
Tend the cows within the hurdles!"
Then the wife of Ilmarinen
Built a field-fire in the passage,
Went to milk her cows awaiting,
Looked upon her herd in wonder,
Spake these happy words of greeting:
"Beautiful, my herd of cattle,
Glistening like the skins of lynxes,
Hair as soft as fur of ermine,
Peaceful waiting for the milk-pail!"
On the milk-stool sits the hostess,
Milks one moment, then a second,
Then a third time milks and ceases;
When the bloody wolves disguising,
Quick attack the hostess milking,
And the bears lend their assistance,
Tear and mutilate her body
With their teeth and sharpened fingers.
Kullerwoinen, cruel wizard,
Thus repaid the wicked hostess,
Thus repaid her evil treatment.
Quick the wife of Ilmarinen
Cried aloud in bitter anguish,
Thus addressed the youth, Kullervo:
"Evil son, thou bloody herdsman,
Thou hast brought me wolves in malice,
Driven bears within my hurdles!
These the words of Kullerwoinen:
"Have I evil done as shepherd,
Worse the conduct of the hostess;
Baked a stone inside my oat-cake,
On the inside, rock and tan-bark,
On the stone my knife, was broken,
Treasure of my mother's household,
Broken virtue of my people!"
Ilmarinen's wife made answer:
"Noble herdsman, Kullerwoinen,
Change, I pray thee, thine opinion,
Take away thine incantations,
From the bears and wolves release me,
Save me from this spell of torture
I will give thee better raiment,
Give the best of milk and butter,
Set for thee the sweetest table;
Thou shalt live with me in welcome,
Need not labor for thy keeping.
If thou dost not free me quickly,
Dost not break this spell of magic,
I shall sink into the Death-land,
Shall return to Tuonela."
This is Kullerwoinen's answer:
"It is best that thou shouldst perish,

The Kalevala

Let destruction overtake thee,
There is ample room in Mana,
Room for all the dead in Kalma,
There the worthiest must slumber,
There must rest the good and evil."
Ilmarinen's wife made answer:
"Ukko, thou O God in heaven,
Span the strongest of thy cross-bows,
Test the weapon by thy wisdom,
Lay an arrow forged from copper,
On the cross-bow of thy forging;
Rightly aim thy flaming arrow,
With thy magic hurl the missile,
Shoot this wizard through the vitals,
Pierce the heart of Kullerwoinen
With the lightning of the heavens,
With thine arrows tipped with copper."
Kullerwoinen prays as follows:
"Ukko, God of truth and justice.
Do not slay thy magic servant,
Slay the wife of Ilmarinen,
Kill in her the worst of women,
In these hurdles let her perish,
Lest she wander hence in freedom,
To perform some other mischief,
Do some greater deed of malice!"
Quick as lightning fell the hostess,
Quick the wife of Ilmarinen
Fell and perished in the hurdles,
On the ground before her cottage
Thus the death of Northland's hostess,
Cherished wife of Ilmarinen,
Once the Maiden of the Rainbow,
Wooed and watched for many summers,
Pride and joy of Kalevala!

RUNE XXXIV
KULLERVO FINDS HIS TRIBE-FOLK.

Kullerwoinen, young magician,
In his beauteous, golden ringlets,
In his magic shoes of deer-skin,
Left the home of Ilmarinen
Wandered forth upon his journey,
Ere the blacksmith heard the tidings
Of the cruel death and torture
Of his wife and joy-companion,
Lest a bloody fight should follow.
Kullerwoinen left the smithy,
Blowing on his magic bugle,
Joyful left the lands of Ilma,
Blowing blithely on the heather,
Made the distant hills re-echo,
Made the swamps and mountains tremble,
Made the heather-blossoms answer
To the music of his cow-horn,
In its wild reverberations,
To the magic of his playing.
Songs were heard within the smithy,
And the blacksmith stopped and listened,
Hastened to the door and window,
Hastened to the open court-yard,
If perchance he might discover
What was playing on the heather,
What was sounding through the forest.
Quick he learned the cruel story,
Learned the cause of the rejoicing,
Saw the hostess dead before him,
Knew his beauteous wife had perished,
Saw the lifeless form extended,
In the court-yard of his dwelling.
Thereupon the metal-artist
Fell to bitter tears and wailings,
Wept through all the dreary night-time,
Deep the grief that settled o'er him,
Black as night his darkened future,
Could not stay his tears of sorrow.
Kullerwoinen hastened onward,
Straying, roaming, hither, thither,
Wandered on through field and forest,
O'er the Hisi-plains and woodlands.
When the darkness settled o'er him,
When the bird of night was flitting,
Sat the fatherless at evening,
The forsaken sat and rested
On a hillock of the forest.
Thus he murmured, heavy-hearted:
"Why was I, alas! created,
Why was I so ill-begotten,
Since for months and years I wander,
Lost among the ether-spaces?
Others have their homes to dwell in,

The Kalevala
Others hasten to their firesides
As the evening gathers round them:
But my home is in the forest,
And my bed upon the heather,
And my bath-room is the rain-cloud.
"Never didst thou, God of mercy,
Never in the course of ages,
Give an infant birth unwisely;
Wherefore then was I created,
Fatherless to roam in ether,
Motherless and lone to wander?
Thou, O Ukko, art my father,
Thou hast given me form and feature;
As the sea-gull on the ocean,
As the duck upon the waters,
Shines the Sun upon the swallow,
Shines as bright upon the sparrow,
Gives the joy-birds song and gladness,
Does not shine on me unhappy;
Nevermore will shine the sunlight,
Never will the moonlight glimmer
On this hapless son and orphan;
Do not know my hero-father,
Cannot tell who was my mother;
On the shore, perhaps the gray-duck
Left me in the sand to perish.
Young was I and small of stature,
When my mother left me orphaned;
Dead, my father and my mother,
Dead, my honored tribe of heroes;
Shoes they left me that are icy,
Stockings filled with frosts of ages,
Let me on the freezing ice-plains
Fall to perish in the rushes;
From the giddy heights of mountains
Let me tumble to destruction.
"O, thou wise and good Creator,
Why my birth and what my service?
I shall never fall and perish
On the ice-plains, in the marshes,
Never be a bridge in swamp-land,
Not while I have arms of virtue
That can serve my honored kindred!"
Then Kullervo thought to journey
To the village of Untamo,
To avenge his father's murder,
To avenge his mother's tortures,
And the troubles of his tribe-folk.
These the words of Kullerwoinen:
"Wait, yea wait, thou Untamoinen,
Thou destroyer of my people;
When I meet thee in the combat,
I will slay thee and thy kindred,
I will burn thy homes to ashes!"
Came a woman on the highway,
Dressed in blue, the aged mother,
To Kullervo spake as follows:
"Whither goest, Kullerwoinen,
Whither hastes the wayward hero?
Kullerwoinen gave this answer:
"I have thought that I would journey

Lönnrot

To the far-off land of strangers,
To the village of Untamo,
To avenge my father's murder,
To avenge my mother's tortures,
And the troubles of my tribe-folk."
Thus the gray-haired woman answered:
"Surely thou dost rest in error,
For thy tribe has never perished,
And thy mother still is living
With thy father in the Northland,
Living with the old Kalervo."
"O, thou ancient dame beloved,
Worthy mother of the woodlands,
Tell me where my father liveth,
Where my loving mother lingers!"
"Yonder lives thine aged father,
And thy loving mother with him,
On the farthest shore of Northland,
On the long-point of the fish-lake!"
"Tell me, O thou woodland-mother,
How to journey to my people,
How to find mine honored tribe-folk."
"Easy is the way for strangers:
Thou must journey through the forest,
Hasten to the river-border,
Travel one day, then a second,
And the third from morn till even,
To the north-west, thou must journey.
If a mountain comes to meet thee,
Go around the nearing mountain,
Westward bold thy weary journey,
Till thou comest to a river,
On thy right hand flowing eastward;
Travel to the river border,
Where three water-falls will greet thee;
When thou comest to a headland,
On the point thou'lt see a cottage
Where the fishermen assemble;
In this cottage is thy father,
With thy mother and her daughters,
Beautiful thy maiden sisters."
Kullerwoinen, the magician,
Hastens northward on his journey,
Walks one day, and then a second,
Walks the third from morn till evening;
To the north-west walks Kullervo,
Till a mountain comes to meet him,
Walks around the nearing mountain;
Westward, westward, holds his journey,
Till he sees a river coming;
Hastens to the river border,
Walks along the streams and rapids
Till three waterfalls accost him;
Travels till he meets a headland,
On the point he spies a cottage,
Where the fishermen assemble.
Quick he journeys to the cabin,
Quick he passes through the portals
Of the cottage on the headland,
Where he finds his long-lost kindred;
No one knows the youth, Kullervo,

The Kalevala
No one knows whence comes the stranger,
Where his home, nor where he goeth.
These the words of young Kullervo:
"Dost thou know me not, my mother,
Dost thou know me not, my father?
I am hapless Kullerwoinen
Whom the heroes of Untamo
Carried to their distant country,
When my height was but a hand-breadth."
Quick the hopeful mother answers:
"O my worthy son, beloved,
O my precious silver-buckle,
Hast thou with thy mind of magic,
Wandered through the fields of Northland
Searching for thy home and kindred?
As one dead I long have mourned thee,
Had supposed thee, in Manala.
Once I had two sons and heroes,
Had two good and beauteous daughters,
Two of these have long been absent,
Elder son and elder daughter;
For the wars my son departed,
While my daughter strayed and perished
If my son is home returning,
Yet my daughter still is absent,
Kullerwoinen asked his mother:
"Whither did my sister wander,
What direction did she journey?
This the answer of the mother:
"This the story of thy sister:
Went for berries to the woodlands,
To the mountains went my daughter,
Where the lovely maiden vanished,
Where my pretty berry perished,
Died some death beyond my knowledge,
Nameless is the death she suffered.
Who is mourning for the daughter?
No one mourns her as her mother,
Walks and wanders, Mourns and searches,
For her fairest child and daughter;
Therefore did the mother wander,
Searching for thy lovely sister,
Like the bear she roamed the forest,
Ran the glenways like the adder,
Searched one day and then a second,
Searched the third from morn till even,
Till she reached the mountain-summit,
There she called and called her daughter,
Till the distant mountains answered,
Called to her who had departed:
I Where art thou, my lovely maiden,
Come my daughter to thy mother!'
"Thus I called, and sought thy sister,
 This the answer of the mountains,

Lönnrot

Thus the hills and valleys echoed:
'Call no more, thou weeping mother,
Weep no more for the departed;
Nevermore in all thy lifetime,
Never in the course of ages,
Will she join again her kindred,
At her brother's landing-places,
In her father's humble dwelling.'"

RUNE XXXV
KULLERVO'S EVIL DEEDS.

Kullerwionen, youthful wizard,
In his blue and scarlet stockings,
Henceforth lingered with his parents;
But he could not change his nature,
Could not gain a higher wisdom,
Could not win a better judgment;
As a child he was ill-nurtured,
Early rocked in stupid cradles,
By a nurse of many follies,
By a minister of evil.
To his work went Kullerwoinen,
Strove to make his labors worthy;
First, Kullervo went a-fishing,
Set his fishing-nets in ocean;
With his hands upon the row-locks,
Kullerwoinen spake as follows:
"Shall I pull with all my forces,
Pull with strength of youthful heroes,
Or with weakness of the aged?"
From the stern arose a gray-beard,
And he answered thus Kullervo:
"Pull with all thy youthful vigor;
Shouldst thou row with magic power,
Thou couldst not destroy this vessel,
Couldst not row this boat to fragments."
Thereupon the youth, Kullervo,
Rowed with all his youthful vigor,
With the mighty force of magic,
Rowed the bindings from the vessel,
Ribs of juniper he shattered,
Rowed the aspen-oars to pieces.
When the aged sire, Kalervo,
Saw the work of Kullerwoinen,
He addressed his son as follows:
"Dost not understand the rowing;
Thou hast burst the bands asunder,
Bands of juniper and willow,
Rowed my aspen-boat to pieces;
To the fish-nets drive the salmon,
This, perchance, will suit thee better."
Thereupon the son, Kullervo,
Hastened to his work as bidden,
Drove the salmon to the fish-nets,
Spake in innocence as follows:
"Shall I with my youthful vigor
Scare the salmon to the fish-nets,
Or with little magic vigor
Shall I drive them to their capture?"
Spake the master of the fish-nets:
"That would be but work of women,
Shouldst thou use but little power
In the frighting of the salmon!"
Kullerwoinen does as bidden,

Scares the salmon with the forces
Of his mighty arms and shoulders,
With the strength of youth and magic,
Stirs the water thick with black-earth,
Beats the scare-net into pieces,
Into pulp he beats the salmon.
When the aged sire, Kalervo,
Saw the work of Kullerwoinen,
To his son these words he uttered:
"Dost not understand this labor,
For this work thou art not suited,
Canst not scare the perch and salmon
To the fish-nets of thy father;
Thou hast ruined all my fish-nets,
Torn my scare-net into tatters,
Beaten into pulp the whiting,
Torn my net-props into fragments,
Beaten into bits my wedges.
Leave the fishing to another;
See if thou canst pay the tribute,
Pay my yearly contribution;
See if thou canst better travel,
On the way show better judgment!"
Thereupon the son, Kullervo,
Hapless youth in purple vestments,
In his magic shoes of deer-skin,
In his locks of golden color,
Sallied forth to pay the taxes,
Pay the tribute for his people.
When the youth had paid the tribute,
Paid the yearly contribution,
He returned to join the snow-sledge,
Took his place upon the cross-bench,
Snapped his whip above the courser,
And began his journey homeward;
Rattled on along the highway,
Measured as he galloped onward
Wainamoinen's hills and valleys,
And his fields in cultivation.
Came a golden maid to meet him,
On her snow-shoes came a virgin,
O'er the hills of Wainamoinen,
O'er his cultivated lowlands.
Quick the wizard-son, Kullervo,
Checked the motion of his racer,
Thus addressed the charming maiden
"Come, sweet maiden, to my snow-sledge,
In my fur-robes rest and linger!"
As she ran, the maiden answered:
"Let the Death-maid sit beside thee,
Rest and linger in thy fur-robes!"
Thereupon the youth, Kullervo,
Snapped his whip above the courser;
Fleet as wind he gallops homeward,
Dashes down along the highway;
With the roar of falling waters,
Gallops onward, onward, onward,
O'er the broad-back of the ocean,
O'er the icy plains of Lapland.
Comes a winsome maid to meet him,
Golden-haired, and wearing snow-shoes,

The Kalevala

On the far outstretching ice-plains;
Quick the wizard checks his racer,
Charmingly accosts the maiden,
Chanting carefully these measures:
"Come, thou beauty, to my snow-sledge,
Hither come, and rest, and linger!
Tauntingly the maiden answered:
"Take Tuoni to thy snow-sledge,
At thy side let Manalainen
Sit with thee, and rest, and linger!"
Quick the wizard, Kullerwoinen,
Struck his fiery, prancing racer,
With the birch-whip of his father.
Like the lightning flew the fleet-foot,
Galloped on the highway homeward;
O'er the hills the snow-sledge bounded,
And the coming mountains trembled.
Kullerwoinen, wild magician,
Measures, on his journey homeward,
Northland's far-extending borders,
And the fertile plains of Pohya.
Comes a beauteous maid to meet him,
With a tin-pin on her bosom,
On the heather of Pohyola,
O'er the Pohya-hills and moorlands.
Quick the wizard son, Kullervo,
Holds the bridle of his courser,
Charmingly intones these measures:
"Come, fair maiden, to my snow-sledge,
In these fur-robes rest, and linger;
Eat with me the golden apples,
Eat the hazel-nut in joyance,
Drink with me the beer delicious,
Eat the dainties that I give thee."
This the answer of the maiden
With the tin-pin on her bosom:
I have scorn to give thy snow-sledge,
 Scorn for thee, thou wicked wizard;
Cold is it beneath thy fur-robes,
And thy sledge is chill and cheerless.
Thereupon the youth, Kullervo,
Wicked wizard of the Northland,
Drew the maiden to his snow-sledge,
Drew her to a seat beside him,
Quickly in his furs enwrapped her;
And the tin-adorned made answer,
These the accents of the maiden:
"Loose me from thy magic power,
Let me leave at once thy presence,
Lest I speak in wicked accents,
Lest I say the prayer of evil;
Free me now as I command thee,
Or I'll tear thy sledge to pieces,
Throw these fur-robes to the north-winds."
Straightway wicked Kullerwoinen,
Evil wizard and magician,
Opens all his treasure-boxes,
Shows the maiden gold and silver,
Shows her silken wraps of beauty,
Silken hose with golden borders,
Golden belts with silver buckles,

Lönnrot

Jewelry that dims the vision,
Blunts the conscience of the virgin.
Silver leads one to destruction,
Gold entices from uprightness.
Kullerwoinen, wicked wizard,
Flatters lovingly the maiden,
One hand on the reins of leather,
One upon the maiden's shoulder;
Thus they journey through the evening,
Pass the night in merry-making.
When the day-star led the morning,
When the second day was dawning,
Then the maid addressed Kullervo,
Questioned thus the wicked wizard:
"Of what tribe art thou descended,
Of what race thy hero-father?
Tell thy lineage and kindred.`
This, Kullervo's truthful answer:
"Am not from a mighty nation,
Not the greatest, nor the smallest,
But my lineage is worthy:
Am Kalervo's son of folly,
Am a child of contradictions,
Hapless son of cold misfortune.
Tell me of thy race of heroes,
Tell thine origin and kindred."
This the answer of the maiden:
"Came not from a race primeval,
Not the largest, nor the smallest,
But my lineage is worthy;
Am Kalervo's wretched daughter,
Am his long-lost child of error,
Am a maid of contradictions,
Hapless daughter of misfortune.
"When a child I lived in plenty
In the dwellings of my mother;
To the woods I went for berries,
Went for raspberries to uplands,
Gathered strawberries on mountains,
Gathered one day then a second;
But, alas! upon the third day,
Could not find the pathway homeward,
Forestward the highways led me,
All the footpaths, to the woodlands.
Long I sat in bitter weeping,
Wept one day and then a second,
Wept the third from morn till even.
Then I climbed a. lofty mountain,
There I called in wailing accents,
And the woodlands gave this answer,
Thus the distant hills re-echoed:
'Call no longer, foolish virgin,
All thy calls and tears are useless;
There is none to give thee answer,
Far away, thy home and people.'
"On the third and on the fourth days,
On the fifth, and sixth, and seventh,
Constantly I sought to perish;
But in vain were all my efforts,
Could not die upon the mountains.
If this wretched maid had perished,

The Kalevala

In the summer of the third year,
She had fed earth's vegetation,
She had blossomed as a flower,
Knowing neither pain nor sorrow."
Scarcely had the maiden spoken,
When she bounded from the snow-sledge,
Rushed upon the rolling river,
To the cataract's commotion,
To the fiery stream and whirlpool.
Thus Kullervo's lovely sister
Hastened to her own destruction,
To her death by fire and water,
Found her peace in Tuonela,
In the sacred stream of Mana.
Then the wicked Kullerwoinen
Fell to weeping, sorely troubled,
Wailed, and wept, and heavy-hearted,
Spake these words in bitter sorrow:
"Woe is me, my life hard-fated!
I have slain my virgin-sister,
Shamed the daughter of my mother;
Woe to thee, my ancient father!
Woe to thee, my gray-haired mother!
Wherefore was I born and nurtured,
Why this hapless child's existence?
Better fate to Kullerwoinen,
Had he never seen the daylight,
Or, if born, had never thriven
In these mournful days of evil!
Death has failed to do his duty,
Sickness sinned in passing by me,
Should have slain me in the cradle,
When the seventh day had ended!"
Thereupon he slips the collar
Of his prancing royal racer,
Mounts the silver-headed fleet-foot,
Gallops like the lightning homeward;
Gallops only for a moment,
When he halts his foaming courser
At the cabin of his father.
In the court-yard stood the mother,
Thus the wicked son addressed her:
"Faithful mother, fond and tender,
Hadst thou slain me when an infant,
Smoked my life out in the chamber,
In a winding-sheet hadst thrown me
To the cataract and whirlpool,
In the fire hadst set my cradle,
After seven nights had ended,
Worthy would have been thy service.
Had the village-maidens asked thee:
'Where is now the little cradle,
Wherefore is the bath-room empty?'
This had been a worthy answer:
'I have burned the wizard's cradle,
Cast the infant to the fire-dogs;
In the bath-room corn is sprouting,
From the barley malt is brewing.'"
Thereupon the aged mother
Asks her wizard-son these questions:
"What has happened to my hero,

Lönnrot

What new fate has overcome thee?
Comest thou as from Tuoni,
From the castles of Manala?"
This, Kullervo's frank confession:
"Infamous the tale I bring thee,
My confession is dishonor:
On the way I met a maiden,
Met thy long-lost, wayward daughter,
Did not recognize my sister,
Fatal was the sin committed!
When the taxes had been settled,
When the tribute had been gathered,
Came a matchless maid to meet me,
Whom I witless led to sorrow,
This my mother's long-lost daughter.
When she saw in me her brother,
Quick she bounded from the snow-sledge,
Hastened to the roaring waters,
To the cataract's commotion,
To the fiery stream and whirlpool,
Hastened to her full destruction.
"Now, alas! must I determine,
Now must find a spot befitting,
Where thy sinful son may perish;
Tell me, all-forgiving mother,
Where to end my life of trouble;
Let me stop the black-wolf's howling,
Let me satisfy the hunger
Of the vicious bear of Northland;
Let the shark or hungry sea-dog
Be my dwelling-place hereafter!"
This the answer of the mother:
"Do not go to stop the howling
Of the hungry wolf of Northland;
Do not haste to still the black-bear
Growling in his forest-cavern;
Let not shark, nor vicious sea-dog
Be thy dwelling-place hereafter.
Spacious are the rooms of Suomi,
Limitless the Sawa-borders,
Large enough to hide transgression,
Man's misdeeds to hide for ages,
With his sins and evil actions.
Six long years man's sins lie hidden
In the border-land of Kalma,
Even nine for magic heroes,
Till the years bring consolation,
Till they quiet all his mourning."
Kullerwoinen, wicked wizard,
Answers thus his grieving mother:
"I can never hide from sorrow,
Cannot flee from my misconduct;
To the jaws of death I hasten,
To the open courts of Kalma,
To the hunting-grounds of Pohya,
To the battle-fields of heroes.
Untamoinen still is living,
Unmolested roams the wicked,
Unavenged my father's grievance,
Unavenged my mother's tortures,
Unavenged the wrongs I suffer!"

RUNE XXXVI
KULLERWOINEN'S VICTORY AND DEATH.

Kullerwionen, wicked wizard,
In his purple-colored stockings,
Now prepares himself for battle;
Grinds a long time on his broadsword,
Sharpens well his trusty weapon,
And his mother speaks as follows:
"Do not go, my son beloved,
Go not to the wars, my hero,
Struggle not with hostile spearsmen.
Whoso goes to war for nothing,
Undertakes a fearful combat,
Undertakes a fatal issue;
Those that war without a reason
Will be slaughtered for their folly,
Easy prey to bows and arrows.
Go thou with a goat to battle,
Shouldst thou go to fight the roebuck,
'Tis the goat that will be vanquished,
And the roebuck will be slaughtered;
With a frog thou'lt journey homeward,
Victor, with but little honor!"
These the words of Kullerwoinen:
"Shall not journey through the marshes,
Shall not sink upon the heather,
On the home-land of the raven,
Where the eagles scream at day-break.
When I yield my life forever,
Bravely will I fall in battle,
Fall upon the field of glory,
Beautiful to die in armor,
And the clang and clash of armies,
Beautiful the strife for conquest!
Thus Kullervo soon will hasten
To the kingdom of Tuoni,
To the realm of the departed,
Undeformed by wasting sickness."
This the answer of the mother:
"If thou diest in the conflict,
Who will stay to guard thy father,
Who will give thy sire protection?"
These the words of Kullerwoinen:
"Let him die upon the court-yard,
Sleeping out his life of sorrow!"
"Who then will protect thy mother,
Be her shield in times of danger?"
"Let her die within the stable,
Or the cabin where she lingers!"
"Who then will defend thy brother,
Give him aid in times of trouble?"
"Let him die within the forest,
Sleep his life away unheeded!"
"Who will comfort then thy sister,
Who will aid her in affliction?"

Lönnrot

"Let her sink beneath the waters,
Perish in the crystal fountain,
Where the brook flows on in beauty,
Like a silver serpent winding
Through the valley to the ocean!"
Thereupon the wild Kullervo
Hastens from his home to battle,
To his father speaks, departing:
"Fare thou well, my aged father!
Wilt thou weep for me, thy hero,
When thou hearest I have perished,
Fallen from thy tribe forever,
Perished on the field of glory?"
Thus the father speaks in answer:
"I shall never mourn the downfall
Of my evil son, Kullervo;
Shall not weep when thou hast perished;
Shall beget a second hero
That will do me better service,
That will think and act in wisdom."
Kullerwoinen gives this answer:
"Neither shall I mourn thy downfall,
Shall not weep when thou hast perished;
I shall make a second father,
Make the head from loam and sandstone,
Make the eyes from swamp-land berries,
Make the beard from withered sea-grass,
Make the feet from roots of willow,
Make the form from birch-wood fungus."
Thereupon the youth, Kullervo,
To his brother speaks as follows:
"Fare thou well, beloved brother!
Wilt thou weep for me departed,
Shouldst thou hear that I have perished,
Fallen on the field of battle?"
This the answer of the brother:
"I shall never mourn the downfall
Of my brother, Kullerwoinen,
Shall not weep when thou hast perished;
I shall find a second brother;
Find one worthier and wiser!"
This is Kullerwoinen's answer:
"Neither shall I mourn thy downfall,
Shall not weep when thou hast perished;
I shall form a second brother,
Make the head from dust and ashes,
Make the eyes from pearls of ocean,
Make the beard from withered verdure,
Make the form from pulp of birch-wood."
To his sister speaks Kullervo:
"Fare thou well, beloved sister!
Surely thou wilt mourn my downfall,
Weep for me when I have perished,
When thou hearest I have fallen
In the heat and din of battle,
Fallen from thy race forever!"
But the sister makes this answer:
"Never shall I mourn thy downfall,
Shall not weep when thou hast perished;
I shall seek a second brother,
Seek a brother, purer, better,

The Kalevala

One that will not shame his sister!"
Kullerwoinen thus makes answer:
"Neither shall I mourn thee fallen,
Shall not weep when thou hast perished;
I shall form a second sister,
Make the head from whitened marble,
Make the eyes from golden moonbeams,
Make the tresses from the rainbow,
Make the ears from ocean-flowers,
And her form from gold and silver.
"Fare thou well, beloved mother,
Mother, beautiful and faithful!
Wilt thou weep when I have perished,
Fallen on the field of glory,
Fallen from thy race forever?"
Thus the mother speaks in answer:
"Canst not fathom love maternal,
Canst not smother her affection;
Bitterly I'll mourn thy downfall,
I would weep if thou shouldst perish,
Shouldst thou leave my race forever;
I would weep in court or cabin,
Sprinkle all these fields with tear-drops,
Weep great rivers to the ocean,
Weep to melt the snows of Northland,
Make the hillocks green with weeping,
Weep at morning, weep at evening,
Weep three years in bitter sorrow
O'er the death of Kullerwoinen!"
Thereupon the wicked wizard
Went rejoicing to the combat;
In delight to war he hastened
O'er the fields, and fens, and fallows,
Shouting loudly on the heather,
Singing o'er the hills and mountains,
Rushing through the glens and forests,
Blowing war upon his bugle.
Time had gone but little distance,
When a messenger appearing,
Spake these words to Kullerwoinen:
"Lo! thine aged sire has perished,
Fallen from thy race forever;
Hasten home and do him honor,
Lay him in the lap of Kalma."
Kullerwoinen inade this answer:
"Has my aged father perished,
There is home a sable stallion
That will take him to his slumber,
Lay him in the lap of Kalma."
Then Kullervo journeyed onward,
Calling war upon his bugle,
Till a messenger appearing,
Brought this word to Kullerwoinen:
"Lo! thy brother too has perished,
Dead he lies within the forest,
Manalainen's trumpet called him;
Home return and do him honor,
Lay him in the lap of Kalma."
Kullerwoinen thus replying:
"Has my hero-brother perished,
There is home a sable stallion

Lönnrot

That will take him' to his slumber,
Lay him in the lap of Kalma."
Young Kullervo journeyed onward
Over vale and over mountain,
Playing on his reed of battle,
Till a messenger appearing
Brought the warrior these tidings:
"Lo! thy sister too has perished,
Perished in the crystal fountain,
Where the waters flow in beauty,
Like a silver serpent winding
Through the valley to the ocean;
Home return and do her honor,
Lay her in the lap of Kalma."
These the words of Kullerwoinen:
"Has my beauteous sister perished,
Fallen from my race forever,
There is home a sable filly
That will take her to her resting,
Lay her in the lap of Kalma."
Still Kullervo journeyed onward,
Through the fens he went rejoicing,
Sounding war upon his bugle,
Till a messenger appearing
Brought to him these words of sorrow:
"Lo! thy mother too has perished,
Died in anguish, broken-hearted;
Home return and do her honor,
Lay her in the lap of Kalma."
These the measures of Kullervo:
"Woe is me, my life hard-fated,
That my mother too has perished,
She that nursed me in my cradle,
Made my couch a golden cover,
Twirled for me the spool and spindle!
Lo! Kullervo was not present
When his mother's life departed;
May have died upon the mountains,
Perished there from cold and hunger.
Lave the dead form of my mother
In the crystal waters flowing;
Wrap her in the robes of ermine,
Tie her hands with silken ribbon,
Take her to the grave of ages,
Lay her in the lap of Kalma.
Bury her with songs of mourning,
Let the singers chant my sorrow;
Cannot leave the fields of battle
While Untamo goes unpunished,
Fell destroyer of my people."
Kullerwoinen journeyed onward,
Still rejoicing, to the combat,
Sang these songs in supplication:
"Ukko, mightiest of rulers,
Loan to me thy sword of battle,
Grant to me thy matchless weapon,
And against a thousand armies
I will war and ever conquer."
Ukko, gave the youth his broadsword,
Gave his blade of magic powers
To the wizard, Kullerwoinen.

The Kalevala
Thus equipped, the mighty hero
Slew the people of Untamo,
Burned their villages to ashes;
Only left the stones and ovens,
And the chimneys of their hamlets.
Then the conqueror, Kullervo,
Turned his footsteps to his home-land,
To the cabin of his father;
To his ancient fields and forests.
Empty did he find the cabin,
And the forests were deserted;
No one came to give him greeting,
None to give the hand of welcome;
Laid his fingers on the oven,
But he found it cold and lifeless;
Then he knew to satisfaction
That his mother lived no longer;
Laid his hand upon the fire-place,
Cold and lifeless were the hearth-stones;
Then he knew to satisfaction
That his sister too had perished;
Then he sought the landing-places,
Found no boats upon the rollers;
Then he knew to satisfaction
That his brother too had perished;
Then he looked upon the fish-nets,
And he found them torn and tangled;
And he knew to satisfaction
That his father too had perished.
Bitterly he wept and murmured,
Wept one day, and then a second,
On the third day spake as follows:
"Faithful mother, fond and tender,
Why hast left me here to sorrow
In this wilderness of trouble?
But thou dost not hear my calling,
Though I sing in magic accents,
Though my tear-drops speak lamenting,
Though my heart bemoans thine absence.
From her grave awakes the mother,
To Kullervo speaks these measures:
"Thou has still the dog remaining,
He will lead thee to the forest;
Follow thou the faithful watcher,
Let him lead thee to the woodlands,
To the farthest woodland border,
To the caverns of the wood-nymphs;
Kullerwoinen's Victory and Death
There the forest maidens linger,
They will give thee food and shelter,
Give my hero joyful greetings."
Kullerwoinen, with his watch-dog,
Hastens onward through the forest,
Journeys on through fields and fallows;
Journeys but a little distance,
Till he comes upon the summit
Where he met his long-lost sister;
Finds the turf itself is weeping,
Finds the glen-wood filled with sorrow,
Finds the heather shedding tear-drops,
Weeping are the meadow-flowers,

Lönnrot

O'er the ruin of his sister.
Kullerwoinen, wicked wizard,
Grasps the handle of his broadsword,
Asks the blade this simple question:
"Tell me, O my blade of honor,
Dost thou wish to drink my life-blood,
Drink the blood of Kullerwoinen?"
Thus his trusty sword makes answer,
Well divining his intentions:
Why should I not drink thy life-blood,
Blood of guilty Kullerwoinen,
Since I feast upon the worthy,
Drink the life-blood of the righteous?"
Thereupon the youth, Kullervo,
Wicked wizard of the Northland,
Lifts the mighty sword of Ukko,
Bids adieu to earth and heaven;
Firmly thrusts the hilt in heather,
To his heart he points the weapon,
Throws his weight upon his broadsword,
Pouring out his wicked life-blood,
Ere be journeys to Manala.
Thus the wizard finds destruction,
This the end of Kullerwoinen,
Born in sin, and nursed in folly.
Wainamoinen, ancient minstrel,
As he hears the joyful tidings,
Learns the death of fell Kullervo,
Speaks these words of ancient wisdom:
"O, ye many unborn nations,
Never evil nurse your children,
Never give them out to strangers,
Never trust them to the foolish!
If the child is not well nurtured,
Is not rocked and led uprightly,
Though he grow to years of manhood,
Bear a strong and shapely body,
He will never know discretion,
Never eat. the bread of honor,
Never drink the cup of wisdom."

RUNE XXXVII
ILMARINEN'S BRIDE OF GOLD.

Ilmarinen, metal-worker,
Wept one day, and then a second,
Wept the third from morn till evening,
O'er the death of his companion,
Once the Maiden of the Rainbow;
Did not swing his heavy hammer,
Did not touch its copper handle,
Made no sound within his smithy,
Made no blow upon his anvil,
Till three months had circled over;
Then the blacksmith spake as follows:
"Woe is me, unhappy hero!
Do not know how I can prosper;
Long the days, and cold, and dreary,
Longer still the nights, and colder;
I am weary in the evening,
In the morning still am weary,
Have no longing for the morning,
And the evening is unwelcome;
Have no pleasure in the future,
All my pleasures gone forever,
With my faithful life-companion
Slaughtered by the hand of witchcraft!
Often will my heart-strings quiver
When I rest within my chamber,
When I wake at dreamy midnight,
Half-unconscious, vainly searching
For my noble wife departed."
Wifeless lived the mourning blacksmith,
Altered in his form and features;
Wept one month and then another,
Wept three months in full succession.
Then the magic metal-worker
Gathered gold from deeps of ocean,
Gathered silver from the mountains,
Gathered many heaps of birch-wood.
Filled with faggots thirty sledges,
Burned the birch-wood into ashes,
Put the ashes in the furnace,
Laid the gold upon the embers,
Lengthwise laid a piece of silver
Of the size of lambs in autumn,
Or the fleet-foot hare in winter;
Places servants at the bellows,
Thus to melt the magic metals.
Eagerly the servants labor,
Gloveless, hatless, do the workmen
Fan the flames within the furnace.
Ilmarinen, magic blacksmith,
Works unceasing at his forging,
Thus to mould a golden image,
Mould a bride from gold and silver;
But the workmen fail their master,

Faithless stand they at the bellows.
Wow the artist, Ilmarinen,
Fans the flame with force of magic,
Blows one day, and then a second,
Blows the third from morn till even;
Then he looks within the furnace,
Looks around the oven-border,
Hoping there to see an image
Rising from the molten metals.
Comes a lambkin from the furnace,
Rising from the fire of magic,
Wearing hair of gold and copper,
Laced with many threads of silver;
All rejoice but Ilmarinen
At the beauty of the image.
This the language of the blacksmith:
"May the wolf admire thy graces;
I desire a bride of beauty
Born from molten gold and silver!"
Ilmarinen, the magician,
To the furnace threw the lambkin;
Added gold in great abundance,
And increased the mass of silver,
Added other magic metals,
Set the workmen at the bellows;
Zealously the servants labor,
Gloveless, hatless, do the workmen
Fan the flames within the furnace.
Ilmarinen, wizard-forgeman,
Works unceasing with his metals,
Moulding well a golden image,
Wife of molten gold and silver;
But the workmen fail their master,
Faithless do they ply the bellows.
Now the artist, Ilmarinen,
Fans the flames by force of magic;
Blows one day, and then a second,
Blows a third from morn till evening,
When he looks within the furnace,
Looks around the oven-border,
Hoping there, to see an image
Rising from the molten metals.
From the flames a colt arises,
Golden-maned and silver-headed,
Hoofs are formed of shining copper.
All rejoice but Ilmarinen
At the wonderful creation;
This the language of the blacksmith;
"Let the bears admire thy graces;
I desire a bride of beauty
Born of many magic metals."
Thereupon the wonder-forger
Drives the colt back to the furnace,
Adds a greater mass of silver,
And of gold the rightful measure,
Sets the workmen at the bellows.
Eagerly the servants labor,
Gloveless, hatless, do the workmen
Fan the flames within the furnace.
Ilmarinen, the magician,
Works unceasing at his witchcraft,

The Kalevala
Moulding well a golden maiden,
Bride of molten gold and silver;
But the workmen fail their master,
Faithlessly they ply the bellows.
Now the blacksmith, Ilmarinen,
Fans the flames with magic powers,
Blows one day, and then a second,
Blows a third from morn till even;
Then he looks within his furnace,
Looks around the oven-border,
Trusting there to see a maiden
Coming from the molten metals.
From the fire a virgin rises,
Golden-haired and silver-headed,
Beautiful in form and feature.
All are filled with awe and wonder,
But the artist and magician.
Ilmarinen, metal-worker,
Forges nights and days unceasing,
On the bride of his creation;
Feet he forges for the maiden,
Hands and arms, of gold and silver;
But her feet are not for walking,
Neither can her arms embrace him.
Ears he forges for the virgin,
But her ears are not for hearing;
Forges her a mouth of beauty,
Eyes he forges bright and sparkling;
But the magic mouth is speechless,
And the eyes are not for seeing.
Spake the artist, Ilmarinen:
"This, indeed, a priceless maiden,
Could she only speak in wisdom,
Could she breathe the breath of Ukko!"
Thereupon he lays the virgin
On his silken couch of slumber,
On his downy place of resting.
Ilmarinen heats his bath-room,
Makes it ready for his service,
Binds together silken brushes,
Brings three cans of crystal water,
Wherewithal to lave the image,
Lave the golden maid of beauty.
When this task had been completed,
Ilmarinen, hoping, trusting,
Laid his golden bride to slumber,
On his downy couch of resting;
Ordered many silken wrappings,
Ordered bear-skins, three in number,
Ordered seven lambs-wool blankets,
Thus to keep him warm in slumber,
Sleeping by the golden image
Re had forged from magic metals.
Warm the side of Ilmarinen
That was wrapped in furs and blankets;
Chill the parts beside the maiden,
By his bride of gold and silver;
One side warm, the other lifeless,
Turning into ice from coldness.
Spake the artist, Ilmarinen:
"Not for me was born this virgin

Lönnrot

From the magic molten metals;
I shall take her to Wainola,
Give her to old Wainamoinen,
As a bride and life-companion,
Comfort to him in his dotage."
Ilmarinen, much disheartened,
Takes the virgin to Wainola,
To the plains of Kalevala,
To his brother speaks as follows:
"O, thou ancient Wainamoinen,
Look with favor on this image;
Make the maiden fair and lovely,
Beautiful in form and feature,
Suited to thy years declining!"
Wainamoinen, old and truthful,
Looked in wonder on the virgin,
On the golden bride of beauty,
Spake these words to Ilmarinen:
"Wherefore dost thou bring this maiden,
Wherefore bring to Wainamoinen
Bride of molten gold and silver?
Spake in answer Ilmarinen:
"Wherefore should I bring this image,
But for purposes the noblest?
I have brought her as companion
To thy life in years declining,
As a joy and consolation,
When thy days are full of trouble!"
Spake the good, old Wainamoinen:
"Magic brother, wonder-forger,
Throw the virgin to the furnace,
To the flames, thy golden image,
Forge from her a thousand trinkets.
Take the image into Ehstland,
Take her to the plains of Pohya,
That for her the mighty powers
May engage in deadly contest,
Worthy trophy for the victor;
Not for me this bride of wonder,
Neither for my worthy people.
I shall never wed an image
Born from many magic metals,
Never wed a silver maiden,
Never wed a golden virgin."
Then the hero of the waters
Called together all his people,
Spake these words of ancient wisdom:
"Every child of Northland, listen,
Whether poor, or fortune-favored:
Never bow before an image
Born of molten gold and silver:
Never while the sunlight brightens,
Never while the moonlight glimmers,
Choose a maiden of the metals,
Choose a bride from gold created
Cold the lips of golden maiden,
Silver breathes the breath of sorrow."

RUNE XXXVIII
ILMARINEN'S FRUITLESS WOOING.

Ilmarinen, the magician,
The eternal metal-artist,
Lays aside the golden image,
Beauteous maid of magic metals;
Throws the harness on his courser,
Binds him to his sledge of birch-wood,
Seats himself upon the cross-bench,
Snaps the whip above the racer,
Thinking once again to journey
To the mansions of Pohyola,
There to woo a bride in honor,
Second daughter of the Northland.
On he journeyed, restless, northward,
Journeyed one day, then a second,
So the third from morn till evening,
When he reached a Northland-village
On the plains of Sariola.
Louhi, hostess of Pohyola,
Standing in the open court-yard,
Spied the hero, Ilmarinen,
Thus addressed the metal-worker:
"Tell me how my child is living,
How the Bride of Beauty prospers,
As a daughter to thy mother."
Then the blacksmith, Ilmarinen,
Head bent down and brow dejected,
Thus addressed the Northland hostess:
"O, thou dame of Sariola,
Do not ask me of thy daughter,
Since, alas I in Tuonela
Sleeps the Maiden of the Rainbow,
Sleeps in death the Bride, of Beauty,
Underneath the fragrant heather,
In the kingdom of Manala.
Come I for a second daughter,
For the fairest of thy virgins.
Beauteous hostess of Pohyola,
Give to me thy youngest maiden,
For my former wife's compartments,
For the chambers of her sister."
Louhi, hostess of the Northland,
Spake these words to Ilmarinen:
"Foolish was the Northland-hostess,
When she gave her fairest virgin,
In the bloom of youth and beauty
To the blacksmith of Wainola,
Only to be led to Mana,
Like a lambkin to the slaughter!
I shall never give my daughter,
Shall not give my youngest maiden
Bride of thine to be hereafter,
Life-companion at thy fireside.
Sooner would I give the fair one

Lönnrot

To the cataract and whirlpool,
To the river of Manala,
To the waters of Tuoni!"
Then the blacksmith, Ilmarinen,
Drew away his head, disdainful,
Shook his sable locks in anger,
Entered to the inner court-room,
Where the maiden sat in waiting,
Spake these measures to the daughter:
"Come with me, thou bright-eyed maiden,
To the cottage where thy sister
Lived and lingered in contentment,
Baked for me the toothsome biscuit,
Brewed for me the beer of barley,
Kept my dwelling-place in order."
On the floor a babe was lying,
Thus he sang to Ilmarinen:
"Uninvited, leave this mansion,
Go, thou stranger, from this dwelling;
Once before thou camest hither,
Only bringing pain and trouble,
Filling all our hearts with sorrow.
Fairest daughter of my mother,
Do not give this suitor welcome,
Look not on his eyes with pleasure,
Nor admire his form and features.
In his mouth are only wolf-teeth,
Cunning fox-claws in his mittens,
In his shoes art only bear-claws,
In his belt a hungry dagger;
Weapons these of blood and murder,
Only worn by the unworthy."
Then the daughter spake as follows
To the blacksmith, Ilmarinen:
"Follow thee this maid will never,
Never heed unworthy suitors;
Thou hast slain the Bride of Beauty,
Once the Maiden of the Rainbow,
Thou wouldst also slay her sister.
I deserve a better suitor,
Wish a truer, nobler husband,
Wish to ride in richer sledges,
Have a better home-protection;
Never will I sweep the cottage
And the coal-place of a blacksmith."
Then the hero, Ilmarinen,
The eternal metal-artist,
Turned his head away, disdainful,
Shook his sable locks in anger,
Quickly seized the trembling maiden,
Held her in his grasp of iron,
Hastened from the court of Louhi
To his sledge upon the highway.
In his sleigh he seats the virgin,
Snugly wraps her in his far-robes,
Snaps his whip above the racer,
Gallops on the high-road homeward;
With one hand the reins be tightens,
With the other holds the maiden.
Speaks the virgin-daughter, weeping:
We have reached the lowland-berries,

The Kalevala

Here the herbs of water-borders;
Leave me here to sink and perish
As a child of cold misfortune.
Wicked Ilmarinen, listen!
If thou dost not quickly free me,
I will break thy sledge to pieces,
Throw thy fur-robes to the north-winds."
Ilmarinen makes this answer:
"When the blacksmith builds his snow-sledge,
All the parts are hooped with iron;
Therefore will the beauteous maiden
Never beat my sledge to fragments."
Then the silver-tinselled daughter
Wept and wailed in bitter accents,
Wrung her hands in desperation,
Spake again to Ilmarinen:
"If thou dost not quickly free me,
I shall change to ocean-salmon,
Be a whiting of the waters."
"Thou wilt never thus escape me,
As a pike I'll fleetly follow."
Then the maiden of Pohyola
Wept and wailed in bitter accents,
Wrung her hands in desperation,
Spake again to Ilmarinen;
"If thou dost not quickly free me,
I shall hasten to the forest,
Mid the rocks become an ermine!"
"Thou wilt never thus escape me,
As a serpent I will follow."
Then the beauty of the Northland,
Wailed and wept in bitter accents,
Wrung her hands in desperation,
Spake once more to Ilmarinen:
"Surely, if thou dost not free me,
As a lark I'll fly the ether,
Hide myself within the storm-clouds."
"Neither wilt thou thus escape me,
As an eagle I will follow."
They had gone but little distance,
When the courser shied and halted,
Frighted at some passing object;
And the maiden looked in wonder,
In the snow beheld some foot-prints,
Spake these words to Ilmarinen:
Who has run across our highway?"
"'Tis the timid hare", he answered.
Thereupon the stolen maiden
Sobbed, and moaned, in deeps of sorrow,
Heavy-hearted, spake these measures:
"Woe is me, ill-fated virgin!
Happier far my life hereafter,
If the hare I could but follow
To his burrow in the woodlands!
Crook-leg's fur to me is finer
Than the robes of Ilmarinen."
Ilmarinen, the magician,
Tossed his head in full resentment,
Galloped on the highway homeward,
Travelled but a little distance,
When again his courser halted,

Frighted at some passing stranger.
Quick the maiden looked and wondered,
In the snow beheld some foot-prints,
Spake these measures to the blacksmith:
Who has crossed our snowy pathway?"
"'Tis a fox", replied the minstrel.
Thereupon the beauteous virgin
Moaned again in depths of anguish,
Sang these accents, heavy-hearted:
"Woe is me, ill-fated maiden!
Happier far my life hereafter,
With the cunning fox to wander,
Than with this ill-mannered suitor;
Reynard's fur to me is finer
Than the robes of Ilmarinen."
Thereupon the metal-worker
Shut his lips in sore displeasure,
Hastened on the highway homeward;
Travelled but a little distance,
When again his courser halted.
Quick the maiden looked in wonder,
in the snow beheld some foot-prints,
Spake these words to the magician:
Who again has crossed our pathway?"
"'Tis the wolf", said Ilmarinen.
Thereupon the fated daughter
Fell again to bitter weeping,
And Intoned these words of sorrow:
"Woe is me, a hapless maiden!
Happier far my life hereafter,
Brighter far would be my future,
If these tracks I could but follow;
On the wolf the hair is finer
Than the furs of Ilmarinen,
Faithless suitor of the Northland."
Then the minstrel of Wainola
Closed his lips again in anger,
Shook his sable locks, resentful,
Snapped the whip above the racer,
And the steed flew onward swiftly,
O'er the way to Kalevala,
To the village of the blacksmith.
Sad and weary from his journey,
Ilmarinen, home-returning,
Fell upon his couch in slumber,
And the maiden laughed derision.
In the morning, slowly waking,
Head confused, and locks dishevelled,
Spake the wizard, words as follow:
"Shall I set myself to singing
Magic songs and incantations?
Shall I now enchant this maiden
To a black-wolf on the mountains,
To a salmon of the ocean?
Shall not send her to the woodlands,
All the forest would be frighted;
Shall not send her to the waters,
All the fish would flee in terror;
This my sword shall drink her life-blood,
End her reign of scorn and hatred."
Quick the sword feels his intention,

The Kalevala
Quick divines his evil purpose,
Speaks these words to Ilmarinen:
"Was not born to drink the life-blood
Of a maiden pure and lovely,
Of a fair but helpless virgin."
Thereupon the magic minstrel,
Filled with rage, began his singing;
Sang the very rocks asunder,
Till the distant hills re-echoed;
Sang the maiden to a sea-gull,
Croaking from the ocean-ledges,
Calling from the ocean-islands,
Screeching on the sandy sea-coast,
Flying to the winds opposing.
When his conjuring had ended,
Ilmarinen joined his snow-sledge,
Whipped his steed upon a gallop,
Hastened to his ancient smithy,
To his home in Kalevala.
Wainamoinen, old and truthful,
Comes to meet him on the highway,
Speaks these words to the magician:
"Ilmarinen, worthy brother,
Wherefore comest heavy-hearted
From the dismal Sariola?
Does Pohyola live and prosper?
Spake the minstrel, Ilmarinen:
"Why should not Pohyola prosper?
There the Sampo grinds unceasing,
Noisy rocks the lid in colors;
Grinds one day the flour for eating,
Grinds the second flour for selling,
Grinds the third day flour for keeping;
Thus it is Pohyola prospers.
While the Sampo is in Northland,
There is plowing, there is sowing,
There is growth of every virtue,
There is welfare never-ending."
Spake the ancient Wainamoinen:
"Ilmarinen, artist-brother,
Where then is the Northland-daughter,
Far renowned and beauteous maiden,
For whose hand thou hast been absent?"
These the words of Ilmarinen:
"I have changed the hateful virgin
To a sea-gull on the ocean;
Now she calls above the waters,
Screeches from the ocean-islands;
On the rocks she calls and murmurs
Vainly calling for a suitor."

RUNE XXXIX
WAINAMOINEN'S SAILING.

Wainamoinen, old and faithful,
Spake these words to Ilmarinen:
"O thou wonder-working brother,
Let us go to Sariola,
There to gain the magic Sampo,
There to see the lid in colors."
Ilmarinen gave this answer:
"Hard indeed to seize the Sampo,
Neither can the lid be captured
From the never-pleasant Northland,
From the dismal Sariola.
Louhi took away the Sampo,
Carried off the lid in colors
To the stone-mount of Pohyola;
Hid it in the copper mountain,
Where nine locks secure the treasure.
Many young roots sprout around it,
Grow nine fathoms deep in sand-earth,
One great root beneath the mountain,
In the cataract a second,
And a third beneath the castle
Built upon the mount of ages."
Spake the ancient Wainamoinen:
"Brother mine, and wonder-worker,
Let us go to Sariola,
That we may secure the Sampo;
Let us build a goodly vessel,
Bring the Sampo to Wainola,
Bring away the lid in colors,
From the stone-berg of Pohyola,
From the copper-bearing mountain.
Where the miracle lies anchored."
Ilmarinen thus made answer:
"By the land the way is safer,
Lempo travels on the ocean,
Ghastly Death upon his shoulder;
On the sea the waves will drift us,
And the storm-winds wreck our vessel;
Then our hands must do the rowing,
And our feet must steer us homeward."
Spake the ancient Wainamoinen:
"Safe indeed by land to journey,
But the way is rough and trying,
Long the road and full of turnings;
Lovely is the ship on ocean,
Beautiful to ride the billows,
Journey easy o'er the waters,
Sailing in a trusty vessel;
Should the West-wind cross our pathway,
Will the South-wind drive us northward.
Be that as it may, my brother,
Since thou dost not love the water,
By the land then let us journey.

The Kalevala

Forge me now the sword of battle,
Forge for me the mighty fire-sword,
That I may destroy the wild-beasts,
Frighten all the Northland people,
As we journey for the Sampo
To the cold and dismal village,
To the never-pleasant Northland,
To the dismal Sariola."
Then the blacksmith, Ilmarinen,
The eternal forger-artist,
Laid the metals in the furnace,
In the fire laid steel and iron,
In the hot-coals, gold and silver,
Rightful measure of the metals;
Set the workmen at the furnace,
Lustily they plied the bellows.
Like the wax the iron melted,
Like the dough the hard steel softened,
Like the water ran the silver,
And the liquid gold flowed after.
Then the minstrel, Ilmarinen,
The eternal wonder-forger,
Looks within his magic furnace,
On the border of his oven,
There beholds the fire-sword forming,
Sees the blade with golden handle;
Takes the weapon from the furnace,
Lays it on his heavy anvil
For the falling of the hammer;
Forges well the blade of magic,
Well the heavy sword be tempers,
Ornaments the hero-weapon
With the finest gold and silver.
Wainamoinen, the magician,
Comes to view the blade of conquest,
Lifts admiringly the fire-sword,
Then these words the hero utters:
"Does the weapon match the soldier,
Does the handle suit the bearer?
Yea, the blade and hilt are molded
To the wishes of the minstrel."
On the sword-point gleams the moonlight,
On the blade the sun is shining,
On the hilt the bright stars twinkle,
On the edge a horse is neighing,
On the handle plays a kitten,
On the sheath a dog is barking.
Wainamoinen wields his fire-sword,
Tests it on the iron-mountain,
And these words the hero utters:
"With this broadsword I could quickly
Cleave in twain the mount of Pohya,
Cut the flinty rocks asunder."
Spake the blacksmith, Ilmarinen:
"Wherewith shall I guard from danger,
How protect myself from evil,
From the ills by land and water?
Shall I wear an iron armor,
Belt of steel around my body?
Stronger is a man in armor,
Safer in a mail of copper."

Lönnrot

Now the time has come to journey
To the never-pleasant Northland;
Wainamoinen, ancient minstrel,
And his brother, Ilmarinen,
Hasten to the field and forest,
Searching for their fiery coursers,
In each shining belt a bridle,
With a harness on their shoulders.
In the woods they find a race;
In the glen a steed of battle,
Ready for his master's service.
Wainamoinen, old and trusty,
And the blacksmith, Ilmarinen,
Throw the harness on the courser,
Hitch him to the sledge of conquest,
Hasten on their journey Northward;
Drive along the broad-sea's margin
Till they bear some one lamenting
On the strand hear something wailing
Near the landing-place of vessels.
Wainamoinen, ancient minstrel,
Speaks these words in wonder, guessing,
"This must be some maiden weeping,
Some fair daughter thus lamenting;
Let us journey somewhat nearer,
To discover whence this wailing."
Drew they nearer, nearer, nearer,
Hoping thus to find a maiden
Weeping on the sandy sea-shore.
It was not a maiden weeping,
But a vessel, sad, and lonely,
Waiting on the shore and wailing.
Spake the ancient Wainamoinen:
"Why art weeping, goodly vessel,
What the cause of thy lamenting?
Art thou mourning for thy row-locks,
Is thy rigging ill-adjusted?
Dost thou weep since thou art anchored
On the shore in times of trouble?"
Thus the war-ship spake in answer:
"To the waters would this vessel
Haste upon the well-tarred rollers,
As a happy maiden journeys
To the cottage of her husband.
I, alas! a goodly vessel,
Weep because I lie at anchor,
Weep and wail because no hero
Sets me free upon the waters,
Free to ride the rolling billows.
It was said when I was fashioned,
Often sung when I was building,
That this bark should be for battle,
Should become a mighty war-ship,
Carry in my hull great treasures,
Priceless goods across the ocean.
Never have I sailed to conquest,
Never have I carried booty;
Other vessels not as worthy
To the wars are ever sailing,
Sailing to the songs of battle.
Three times in the summer season

The Kalevala

Come they home with treasures laden,
In their hulls bring gold and silver;
I, alas! a worthy vessel,
Many months have lain at anchor,
I, a war-ship well constructed,
Am decaying in the harbor,
Never having sailed to conquest;
Worms are gnawing at my vitals,
In my hull their dwelling-places,
And ill-omened birds of heaven
Build their nests within my rigging;
Frogs and lizards of the forest
Play about my oars and rudder;
Three times better for this vessel
Were he but a valley birch-tree,
Or an aspen on the heather,
With the squirrels in his branches,
And the dogs beneath them barking!"
Wainamoinen, old and faithfull
Thus addressed the ship at anchor:
"Weep no more, thou goodly vessel,
Man-of-war, no longer murmur;
Thou shalt sail to Sariola,
Sing the war-songs of the Northland,
Sail with us to deadly combat.
Wert thou built by the Creator,
Thou canst sail the roughest waters,
Sidewise journey o'er the ocean;
Dost not need the hand to touch thee,
Dost not need the foot to turn thee,
Needing nothing to propel thee."
Thus the weeping boat made answer:
"Cannot sail without assistance,
Neither can my brother-vessels
Sail unaided o'er the waters,
Sail across the waves undriven."
Spake the ancient Wainamoinen:
"Should I lead thee to the broad-sea,
Wilt thou journey north unaided,
Sail without the help of rowers,
Sail without the aid of south-winds,
Sail without the b elm to guide thee?
Thus the wailing ship replying:
Cannot sail without assistance,
Neither can my brother-vessels
Sail without the aid of rowers
Sail without the help of south-winds,
Nor without the helm to guide them."
These the words of Wainamoinen:
"Wilt thou run with aid of oarsmen
When the south-winds give assistance,
Guided by a skillful pilot?"
This the answer of the war-ship:
"Quickly can I course these waters,
When my oars are manned by rowers,
When my sails are filled with south-winds,
All my goodly brother-vessels
Sail the ocean with assistance,
When the master holds the rudder."
Then the ancient Wainamoinen
Left the racer on the sea-side,

Lönnrot

Tied him to the sacred birch-tree,
Hung the harness on a willow,
Rolled the vessel to the waters,
ang the ship upon the broad-sea,
Asked the boat this simple question:
"O thou vessel, well-appearing
From the mighty oak constructed,
Art thou strong to carry treasures
As in view thou art commanding?
Thus the goodly ship made answer:
"Strong am I to carry treasures,
In my hull a golden cargo;
I can bear a hundred oarsmen,
And of warriors a thousand."
Wainamoinen, the magician,
Then began his wondrous singing.
On one side the magic vessel,
Sang he youth with golden virtues,
Bearded youth with strength of heroes,
Sang them into mail of copper.
On the other side the vessel,
Sang he silver-tinselled maidens,
Girded them with belts of copper,
Golden rings upon their fingers.
Sings again the great magician,
Fills the magic ship with heroes,
Ancient heroes, brave and mighty;
Sings them into narrow limits,
Since the young men came before them.
At the helm himself be seated,
Near the last beam of the vessel,
Steered his goodly boat in joyance,
Thus addressed the willing war-ship:
Glide upon the trackless waters,
Sail away, my ship of magic,
Sail across the waves before thee,
Speed thou like a dancing bubble,
Like a flower upon the billows!"
Then the ancient Wainamoinen
Set the young men to the rowing,
Let the maidens sit in waiting.
Eagerly the youthful heroes
Bend the oars and try the row-locks,
But the distance is not lessened.
Then the minstrel, Wainamoinen,
Set the maidens to the rowing,
Let the young men rest in waiting.
Eagerly the merry maidens
Bend the aspen-oars in rowing,
But the distance is not lessened.
Then the master, Wainamoinen,
Set the old men to the rowing,
Let the youth remain in waiting.
Lustily the aged heroes
Bend and try the oars of aspen,
But the distance is not lessened.
Then the blacksmith, Ilmarinen,
Grasped the oars with master-magic,
And the boat leaped o'er the surges,
Swiftly sped across the billows;
Far and wide the oars resounded,

The Kalevala
Quickly was the distance lessened,
With a rush and roar of waters
Ilmarinen sped his vessel,
Benches, ribs, and row-locks creaking,
Oars of aspen far resounding;
Flap the sails like wings of moor-cocks,
And the prow dips like a white-swan;
In the rear it croaks like ravens,
Loud the oars and rigging rattle.
Straightway ancient Wainamoinen
Sitting by the bending rudder,
Turns his magic vessel landward,
To a jutting promontory,
Where appears a Northland-village.
On the point stands Lemminkainen,
Kaukomieli, black magician,
Ahti, wizard of Wainola,
Wishing for the fish of Pohya,
Weeping for his fated dwelling,
For his perilous adventures,
Hard at work upon a vessel,
On the sail-yards of a fish-boat,
Near the hunger-point and island,
Near the village-home deserted.
Good the ears of the magician,
Good the wizard's eyes for seeing;
Casts his vision to the South-east,
Turns his eyes upon the sunset,
Sees afar a wondrous rainbow,
Farther on, a cloudlet hanging;
But the bow was a deception,
And the cloudlet a delusion;
'Tis a vessel swiftly sailing,
'Tis a war-ship flying northward,
O'er the blue-back of the broad-sea,
On the far-extending waters,
At the helm the master standing,
At the oars a mighty hero.
Spake the reckless Lemminkainen:
"Do not know this wondrous vessel,
Not this well-constructed war-ship,
Coming from the distant Suomi,
Rowing for the hostile Pohya."
Thereupon wild Lemminkainen
Called aloud in tones of thunder
O'er the waters to the vessel;
Made the distant hills re-echo
With the music of his calling:
"Whence this vessel on the waters,
Whose the war-ship sailing hither?"
Spake the master of the vessel
To the reckless Lemminkainen:
"Who art thou from fen or forest,
Senseless wizard from the woodlands,
That thou dost not know this vessel,
Magic war-ship of Wainola?
Dost not know him at the rudder,
Nor the hero at the row-locks?"
Spake the wizard, Lemminkainen:
"Well I know the helm-director,
And I recognize the rower;

Lönnrot

Wainamoinen, old and trusty,
At the helm directs the vessel;
Ilmarinen does the rowing.
Whither is the vessel sailing,
Whither wandering, my heroes?
Spake the ancient Wainamoinen:
"We are sailing to the Northland,
There to gain the magic Sampo,
There to get the lid in colors,
From the stone-berg of Pohyola,
From the copper-bearing mountain."
Spake the evil Lemminkainen:
"O, thou good, old Wainamoinen,
Take me with thee to Pohyola,
Make me third of magic heroes,
Since thou goest for the Sampo,
Goest for the lid in colors;
I shall prove a valiant soldier,
When thy wisdom calls for fighting;
I am skilled in arts of warfare!"
Wainamoinen, ancient minstrel,
Gave assent to Ahti's wishes;
Thereupon wild Lemminkainen
Hastened to Wainola's war-ship,
Bringing floats of aspen-timber,
To the ships of Wainamoinen.
Thus the hero of the Northland
Speaks to reckless Lemminkainen:
"There is aspen on my vessel,
Aspen-floats in great abundance,
And the boat is heavy-laden.
Wherefore dost thou bring the aspen
To the vessel of Wainola?"
Lemminkainen gave this answer:
"Not through caution sinks a vessel,
Nor a hay-stack by its proppings;
Seas abound in hidden dangers,
Heavy storms arise and threaten
Fell destruction to the sailor
That would brave the angry billows."
Spake the good, old Wainamoinen:
"Therefore is this warlike vessel
Built of trusty steel and copper,
Trimmed and bound in toughest iron,
That the winds may, not destroy it,
May not harm my ship of magic."

RUNE XL
BIRTH OF THE HARP.

Wainamoinen, ancient minstrel,
Onward steered his goodly vessel,
From the isle of Lemminkainen,
From the borders of the village;
Steered his war-ship through the waters,
Sang it o'er the ocean-billows,
Joyful steered it to Pohyola.
On the banks were maidens standing,
And the daughters spake these measures:
"List the music on the waters!
What this wonderful rejoicing,
What this singing on the billows?
Far more beautiful this singing,
This rejoicing on the waters,
Than our ears have heard in Northland."
Wainamoinen, the magician,
Steered his wonder-vessel onward,
Steered one day along the sea-shore,
Steered the next through shallow waters,
Steered the third day through the rivers.
Then the reckless Lemminkainen
Suddenly some words remembered,
He had heard along the fire-stream
Near the cataract and whirlpool,
And these words the hero uttered:
"Cease, O cataract, thy roaring,
Cease, O waterfall, thy foaming!
Maidens of the foam and current,
Sitting on the rocks in water,
On the stone-blocks in the river,
Take the foam and white-capped billows
In your arms and still their anger,
That our ships may pass in safety!
Aged dame beneath the eddy,
Thou that livest in the sea-foam,
Swimming, rise above the waters,
Lift thy head above the whirlpool,
Gather well the foam and billows
In thine arms and still their fury,
That our ship may pass in safety!
Ye, O rocks beneath the current,
Underneath the angry waters,
Lower well your heads of danger,
Sink below our magic vessel,
That our ship may pass in safety!
"Should this prayer prove inefficient,
Kimmo, hero son of Kammo,
Bore an outlet with thine auger,
Cut a channel for this vessel
Through the rocks beneath the waters,
That our ship may pass in safety!
Should all this prove unavailing,
Hostess of the running water,

Lönnrot

Change to moss these rocky ledges,
Change this vessel to an air-bag,
That between these rocks and billows
It may float, and pass in safety!
"Virgin of the sacred whirlpool,
Thou whose home is in the river,
Spin from flax of strongest fiber,
Spin a thread of crimson color,
Draw it gently through the water,
That the thread our ship may follow,
And our vessel pass in safety!
Goddess of the helm, thou daughter
Of the ocean-winds and sea-foam,
Take thy helm endowed with mercy,
Guide our vessel through these dangers,
Hasten through these floods enchanted,
Passing by the house of envy,
By the gates of the enchanters,
That our ship may pass in safety!
"Should this prayer prove inefficient,
Ukko, Ruler of creation,
Guide our vessel with thy fire-sword,
Guide it with thy blade of lightning,
Through the dangers of these rapids,
Through the cataract and whirlpool,
That our ship may pass in safety!"
Thereupon old Wainamoinen
Steered his boat through winds and waters,
Through the rocky chinks and channels,
Through the surges wildly tossing;
And the vessel passed in safety
Through the dangers of the current,
Through the sacred stream and whirlpool.
As it gains the open waters,
Gains at length the broad-lake's bosom,
Suddenly its motion ceases,
On some object firmly anchored.
Thereupon young Ilmarinen,
With the aid of Lemminkainen,
Plunges in the lake the rudder,
Struggles with the aid of magic;
But he cannot move the vessel,
Cannot free it from its moorings.
Wainamoinen, old and truthful,
Thus addresses his companion:
"O thou hero, Lemminkainen,
Stoop and look beneath this war-ship,
See on what this boat is anchored,
See on what our craft is banging,
In this broad expanse of water,
In the broad-lake's deepest soundings,
If upon some rock or tree-snag,
Or upon some other hindrance."
Thereupon wild Lemminkainen
Looked beneath the magic vessel,
Peering through the crystal waters,
Spake and these the words be uttered:
"Does not rest upon a sand-bar,
Nor upon a rock, nor tree-snag,
But upon the back and shoulders
Of the mighty pike of Northland,

The Kalevala

On the fin-bones of the monster."
Wainamoinen, old and trusty,
Spake these words to Lemminkainen:
"Many things we find in water,
Rocks, and trees, and fish, and sea-duck;
Are we on the pike's broad shoulders,
On the fin-bones of the monster,
Pierce the waters with thy broadsword,
Cut the monster into pieces."
Thereupon wild Lemminkainen,
Reckless wizard, filled with courage,
Pulls his broadsword from his girdle,
From its sheath, the bone-divider,
Strikes with might of magic hero,
Headlong falls into the water;
And the blacksmith, Ilmarinen,
Lifts the wizard from the river,
Speaks these words to dripping Ahti:
"Accidents will come to mortals,
Accidents will come to heroes,
By the hundreds, by the thousands,
Even to the gods above us!"
Then the blacksmith, Ilmarinen,
Drew his broadsword from his girdle,
From its sheath his blade of honor,
Tried to slay the pike of Northland
With the weapon of his forging;
But he broke his sword in pieces,
Did not harm the water-monster.
Wainamoinen, old and trusty,
Thus addresses his companions
"Poor apologies for heroes!
When occasion calls for victors,
When we need some great magician,
Need a hero filled with valor,
Then the arm that comes is feeble,
And the mind insane or witless,
Strength and reason gone to others!"
Straightway ancient Wainamoinen,
Miracle of strength and wisdom,
Draws his fire-sword from his girdle,
Wields the mighty blade of magic,
Strikes the waters as the lightning,
Strikes the pike beneath the vessel,
And impales, the mighty monster;
Raises him above the surface,
In the air the pike he circles,
Cuts the monster into pieces;
To the water falls the pike-tail,
To the ship the head and body;
Easily the ship moves onward.
Wainamoinen, old and faithful,
To the shore directs his vessel,
On the strand the boat he anchors,
Looks in every nook and corner
For the fragments of the monster;
Gathers well the parts together,
Speaks these words to those about him:
"Let the oldest of the heroes
Slice for me the pike of Northland,
Slice the fish to fitting morsels."

Lönnrot

Answered all the men and heroes,
And the maidens spake, assenting:
"Worthier the catcher's fingers,
Wainamoinen's hands are sacred!"
Thereupon the wise magician
Drew a fish-knife from his girdle,
Sliced the pike to fitting morsels,
Spake again to those about him:
"Let the youngest of the maidens
Cook for me the pike of Northland,
Set for me a goodly dinner!"
All the maidens quick responded,
All the virgins vied in cooking;
Neither could outdo the other,
Thus the pike was rendered toothsome.
Feasted all the old magicians,
Feasted all the younger heroes,
Feasted all the men and maidens;
On the rocks were left the fish-bones,
Only relics of their feasting.
Wainamoinen, ancient minstrel,
Looked upon the pile of fragments,
On the fish-bones looked and pondered,
Spake these words in meditation:
"Wondrous things might be constructed
From the relies of this monster,
Were they in the blacksmith's furnace,
In the hands of the magician,
In the hands of Ilmarinen."
Spake the blacksmith of Wainola:
"Nothing fine can be constructed
From the bones and teeth of fishes
By the skillful forger-artist,
By the hands of the magician."
These the words of Wainamoinen:
"Something wondrous might be builded
From these jaws, and teeth, and fish-bones;
Might a magic harp be fashioned,
Could an artist be discovered
That could shape them to my wishes."
But he found no fish-bone artist
That could shape the harp of joyance
From the relies of their feasting,
From the jaw-bones of the monster,
To the will of the magician.
Thereupon wise Wainamoinen
Set himself at work designing;
Quick became a fish-bone artist,
Made a harp of wondrous beauty,
Lasting joy and pride of Suomi.
Whence the harp's enchanting arches?
From the jaw-bones of the monster.
Whence the necessary harp-pins?
From the pike-teeth firmly fastened.
Whence the sweetly singing harp-strings?
From the tail of Lempo's stallion.
Thus was born the harp of magic
From the mighty pike of Northland,
From the relies from the feasting
Of the heroes of Wainola.
All the young men came to view it,

The Kalevala

All the aged with their children,
Mothers with their beauteous daughters,
Maidens with their golden tresses;
All the people on the islands
Came to view the harp of joyance,
Pride and beauty of the Northland.
Wainamoinen, ancient minstrel,
Let the aged try the harp-strings,
Gave it to the young magicians,
To the dames and to their daughters,
To the maidens, silver-tinselled,
To the singers of Wainola.
When the young men touched the harp-strings,
Then arose the notes of discord;
When the aged played upon it,
Dissonance their only music.
Spake the wizard, Lemminkainen:
"O ye witless, worthless children,
O ye senseless, useless maidens,
O ye wisdom-lacking heroes,
Cannot play this harp of magic,
Cannot touch the notes of concord!
Give to me this thing or beauty,
Hither bring the harp of fish-bones,
Let me try my skillful fingers."
Lemminkainen touched the harp-strings,
Carefully the strings adjusted,
Turned the harp in all directions,
Fingered all the strings in sequence,
Played the instrument of wonder,
But it did not speak in concord,
Did not sing the notes of joyance.
Spake the ancient Wainamoinen:
"There is none among these maidens,
None among these youthful heroes,
None among the old magicians
That can play the harp of magic,
Touch the notes of joy and pleasure.
Let us take the harp to Pohya,
There to find a skillful player
That can touch the strings in concord."
Then they sailed to Sariola,
To Pohyola took the wonder,
There to find the harp a master.
All the heroes of Pohyola,
All the boys and all the maidens,
Ancient dames, and bearded minstrels,
Vainly touched the harp of beauty.
Louhi, hostess of the Northland,
Took the harp-strings in her fingers;
All the youth of Sariola,
Youth of every tribe and station,
Vainly touched the harp of fish-bone;
Could not find the notes of joyance,
Dissonance their only pleasure;
Shrieked the harp-strings like the whirlwinds,
All the tones wore harsh and frightful.
In a corner slept a blind man,
Lay a gray-beard on the oven,
Rousing from his couch of slumber,
Murmured thus within his corner:

Lönnrot

"Cease at once this wretched playing,
Make an end of all this discord;
It benumbs mine ears for hearing,
Racks my brain, despoils my senses,
Robs me of the sweets of sleeping.
If the harp of Suomi's people
True delight cannot engender,
Cannot bring the notes of pleasure,
Cannot sing to sleep the aged,
Cast the thing upon the waters,
Sink it in the deeps of ocean,
Take it back to Kalevala,
To the home of him that made it,
To the bands of its creator."
Thereupon the harp made answer,
To the blind man sang these measures:
"Shall not fall upon the waters,
Shall not sink within the ocean;
I will play for my creator,
Sing in melody and concord
In the fingers of my master."
Carefully the harp was carried
To the artist that had made it
To the hands of its creator,
To the feet of Wainamoinen.

RUNE XLI
WAINAMOINEN'S HARP-SONGS.

Wainamoinen, ancient minstrel,
The eternal wisdom-singer,
Laves his hands to snowy whiteness,
Sits upon the rock of joyance,
On the stone of song be settles,
On the mount of silver clearness,
On the summit, golden colored;
Takes the harp by him created,
In his hands the harp of fish-bone,
With his knee the arch supporting,
Takes the harp-strings in his fingers,
Speaks these words to those assembled:
"Hither come, ye Northland people,
Come and listen to my playing,
To the harp's entrancing measures,
To my songs of joy and gladness."
Then the singer of Wainola
Took the harp of his creation,
Quick adjusting, sweetly tuning,
Deftly plied his skillful fingers
To the strings that he had fashioned.
Now was gladness rolled on gladness,
And the harmony of pleasure
Echoed from the hills and mountains:
Added singing to his playing,
Out of joy did joy come welling,
Now resounded marvelous music,
All of Northland stopped and listened.
Every creature in the forest,
All the beasts that haunt the woodlands,
On their nimble feet came bounding,
Came to listen to his playing,
Came to hear his songs of joyance.
Leaped the squirrels from the branches,
Merrily from birch to aspen;
Climbed the ermines on the fences,
O'er the plains the elk-deer bounded,
And the lynxes purred with pleasure;
Wolves awoke in far-off swamp-lands,
Bounded o'er the marsh and heather,
And the bear his den deserted,
Left his lair within the pine-wood,
Settled by a fence to listen,
Leaned against the listening gate-posts,
But the gate-posts yield beneath him;
Now he climbs the fir-tree branches
That he may enjoy and wonder,
Climbs and listens to the music
Of the harp of Wainamoinen.
Tapiola's wisest senior,
Metsola's most noble landlord,
And of Tapio, the people,
Young and aged, men and maidens,

Lönnrot

Flew like red-deer up the mountains
There to listen to the playing,
To the harp, of Wainamoinen.
Tapiola's wisest mistress,
Hostess of the glen and forest,
Robed herself in blue and scarlet,
Bound her limbs with silken ribbons,
Sat upon the woodland summit,
On the branches of a birch-tree,
There to listen to the playing,
To the high-born hero's harping,
To the songs of Wainamoinen.
All the birds that fly in mid-air
Fell like snow-flakes from the heavens,
Flew to hear the minstrel's playing,
Hear the harp of Wainamoinen.
Eagles in their lofty eyrie
Heard the songs of the enchanter;
Swift they left their unfledged young ones,
Flew and perched around the minstrel.
From the heights the hawks descended,
From the clouds down swooped the falcon,
Ducks arose from inland waters,
Swans came gliding from the marshes;
Tiny finches, green and golden,
Flew in flocks that darkened sunlight,
Came in myriads to listen;
Perched upon the head and shoulders
Of the charming Wainamoinen,
Sweetly singing to the playing
Of the ancient bard and minstrel.
And the daughters of the welkin,
Nature's well-beloved daughters,
Listened all in rapt attention;
Some were seated on the rainbow,
Some upon the crimson cloudlets,
Some upon the dome of heaven.
In their hands the Moon's fair daughters
Held their weaving-combs of silver;
In their hands the Sun's sweet maidens
Grasped the handles of their distaffs,
Weaving with their golden shuttles,
Spinning from their silver spindles,
On the red rims of the cloudlets,
On the bow of many colors.
As they hear the minstrel playing,
Hear the harp of Wainamoinen,
Quick they drop their combs of silver,
Drop the spindles from their fingers,
And the golden threads are broken,
Broken are the threads of silver.
All the fish in Suomi-waters
Heard the songs of the magician,
Came on flying fins to listen
To the harp of Wainamoinen.
Came the trout with graceful motions,
Water-dogs with awkward movements,
From the water-cliffs the salmon,
From the sea-caves came the whiting,
From the deeper caves the bill-fish;
Came the pike from beds of sea-fern,

The Kalevala
Little fish with eyes of scarlet,
Leaning on the reeds and rushes,
With their heads above the surface;
Came to bear the harp of joyance,
Hear the songs of the enchanter.
Ahto, king of all the waters,
Ancient king with beard of sea-grass,
Raised his head above the billows,
In a boat of water-lilies,
Glided to the coast in silence,
Listened to the wondrous singing,
To the harp of Wainamoinen.
These the words the sea-king uttered:
"Never have I heard such playing,
Never heard such strains of music,
Never since the sea was fashioned,
As the songs of this enchanter,
This sweet singer, Wainamoinen."
Satko's daughters from the blue-deep,
Sisters of the wave-washed ledges,
On the colored strands were sitting,
Smoothing out their sea-green tresses
With the combs of molten silver,
With their silver-handled brushes,
Brushes forged with golden bristles.
When they hear the magic playing,
Hear the harp of Wainamoinen,
Fall their brushes on the billows,
Fall their combs with silver handles
To the bottom of the waters,
Unadorned their heads remaining,
And uncombed their sea-green tresses.
Came the hostess of the waters,
Ancient hostess robed in flowers,
Rising from her deep sea-castle,
Swimming to the shore in wonder,
Listened to the minstrel's playing,
To the harp of Wainamoinen.
As the magic tones re-echoed,
As the singer's song out-circled,
Sank the hostess into slumber,
On the rocks of many colors,
On her watery couch of joyance,
Deep the sleep that settled o'er her.
Wainamoinen, ancient minstrel,
Played one day and then a second,
Played the third from morn till even.
There was neither man nor hero,
Neither ancient dame, nor maiden,
Not in Metsola a daughter,
Whom he did not touch to weeping;
Wept the young, and wept the aged,
Wept the mothers, wept the daughters
Wept the warriors and heroes
At the music of his playing,
At the songs of the magician.
Wainamoinen's tears came flowing,
Welling from the master's eyelids,
Pearly tear-drops coursing downward,
Larger than the whortle-berries,
Finer than the pearls of ocean,

Lönnrot

Smoother than the eggs of moor-hens,
Brighter than the eyes of swallows.
From his eves the tear-drops started,
Flowed adown his furrowed visage,
Falling from his beard in streamlets,
Trickled on his heaving bosom,
Streaming o'er his golden girdle,
Coursing to his garment's border,
Then beneath his shoes of ermine,
Flowing on, and flowing ever,
Part to earth for her possession,
Part to water for her portion.
As the tear-drops fall and mingle,
Form they streamlets from the eyelids
Of the minstrel, Wainamoinen,
To the blue-mere's sandy margin,
To the deeps of crystal waters,
Lost among the reeds and rushes.
Spake at last the ancient minstrel:
"Is there one in all this concourse,
One in all this vast assembly
That can gather up my tear-drops
From the deep, pellucid waters?"
Thus the younger heroes answered,
Answered thus the bearded seniors:
"There is none in all this concourse,
None in all this vast assembly,
That can gather up thy tear-drops
From the deep, pellucid waters."
Spake again wise Wainamoinen:
"He that gathers up my tear-drops
From the deeps of crystal waters
Shall receive a beauteous plumage."
Came a raven, flying, croaking,
And the minstrel thus addressed him:
"Bring, O raven, bring my tear-drops
From the crystal lake's abysses;
I will give thee beauteous plumage,
Recompense for golden service."
But the raven failed his master.
Came a duck upon the waters,
And the hero thus addressed him:
"Bring O water-bird, my tear-drops;
Often thou dost dive the deep-sea,
Sink thy bill upon the bottom
Of the waters thou dost travel;
Dive again my tears to gather,
I will give thee beauteous plumage,
Recompense for golden service."
Thereupon the duck departed,
Hither, thither, swam, and circled,
Dived beneath the foam and billow,
Gathered Wainamoinen's tear-drops
From the blue-sea's pebbly bottom,
From the deep, pellucid waters;
Brought them to the great magician,
Beautifully formed and colored,
Glistening in the silver sunshine,

The Kalevala
Glimmering in the golden moonlight,
Many-colored as the rainbow,
Fitting ornaments for heroes,
Jewels for the maids of beauty.
This the origin of sea-pearls,
And the blue-duck's beauteous plumage.

Lönnrot

RUNE XLII
CAPTURE OF THE SAMPO.

Wainamoinen, old and truthful,
With the blacksmith, Ilmarinen,
With the reckless son of Lempo,
Handsome hero, Kaukomieli,
On the sea's smooth plain departed,
On the far-extending waters,
To the village, cold and dreary,
To the never-pleasant Northland,
Where the heroes fall and perish.
Ilmarinen led the rowers
On one side the magic war-ship,
And the reckless Lemminkainen
Led the rowers on the other.
Wainamoinen, old and trusty,
Laid his hand upon the rudder,
Steered his vessel o'er the waters,
Through the foam and angry billows
To Pohyola's place of landing,
To the cylinders of copper,
Where the war-ships lie at anchor.
When they had arrived at Pohya,
When their journey they had ended,
On the land they rolled their vessel,
On the copper-banded rollers,
Straightway journeyed to the village,
Hastened to the halls and hamlets
Of the dismal Sariola.
Louhi, hostess of the Northland,
Thus addressed the stranger-heroes:
Magic heroes of Wainola,
What the tidings ye are bringing
To the people of my village?"
Wainamoinen, ancient minstrel.
Gave this answer to the hostess:
"All the hosts of Kalevala
Are inquiring for the Sampo,
Asking for the lid in colors;
Hither have these heroes journeyed
To divide the priceless treasure.
Thus the hostess spake in answer:
"No one would divide a partridge,
Nor a squirrel, with three heroes;
Wonderful the magic Sampo,
Plenty does it bring to Northland;
And the colored lid re-echoes
From the copper-bearing mountains,
From the stone-berg of Pohyola,
To the joy of its possessors."
Wainamoinen, ancient minstrel,
Thus addressed the ancient Louhi:
"If thou wilt not share the Sampo,
Give to us an equal portion,
We will take it to Wainola,

The Kalevala
With its lid of many colors,
Take by force the hope of Pohya."
Thereupon the Northland hostess
Angry grew and sighed for vengeance;
Called her people into council,
Called the hosts of Sariola,
Heroes with their trusted broadswords,
To destroy old Wainamoinen
With his people of the Northland.
Wainamoinen, wise and ancient,
Hastened to his harp of fish-bone,
And began his magic playing;
All of Pohya stopped and listened,
Every warrior was silenced
By the notes of the magician;
Peaceful-minded grew the soldiers,
All the maidens danced with pleasure,
While the heroes fell to weeping,
And the young men looked in wonder.
Wainamoinen plays unceasing,
Plays the maidens into slumber,
Plays to sleep the young and aged,
All of Northland sleeps and listens.
Wise and wondrous Wainamoinen,
The eternal bard and singer,
Searches in his pouch of leather,
Draws therefrom his slumber-arrows,
Locks the eyelids of the sleepers,
Of the heroes of Pohyola,
Sings and charms to deeper slumber
All the warriors of the Northland.
Then the heroes of Wainola
Hasten to obtain the Sampo,
To procure the lid in colors
From the copper-bearing mountains.
From behind nine locks of copper,
In the stone-berg of Pohyola.
Wainamoinen, ancient minstrel,
Then began his wondrous singing,
Sang in gentle tones of magic,
At the entrance to the mountain,
At the border of the stronghold;
Trembled all the rocky portals,
And the iron-banded pillars
Fell and crumbled at his singing.
Ilmarinen, magic blacksmith,
Well anointed all the hinges,
All the bars and locks anointed,
And the bolts flew back by magic,
All the gates unlocked in silence,
Opened for the great magician.
Spake the minstrel Wainamoinen:
"O thou daring Lemminkainen,
Friend of mine in times of trouble,
Enter thou within the mountain,
Bring away the wondrous Sampo,
Bring away the lid in colors!"
Quick the reckless Lemminkainen,
Handsome hero, Kaukomieli,
Ever ready for a venture,
Hastens to the mountain-caverns,

Lönnrot

There to find the famous Sampo,
There to get the lid in colors;
Strides along with conscious footsteps,
Thus himself he vainly praises:
"Great am I and full of glory,
Wonder-hero, son of Ukko,
I will bring away the Sampo,
Turn about the lid in colors,
Turn it on its magic hinges!"
Lemminkainen finds the wonder,
Finds the Sampo in the mountain,
Labors long with strength heroic,
Tugs with might and main to turn it;
Motionless remains the treasure,
Deeper sinks the lid in colors,
For the roots have grown about it,
Grown nine fathoms deep in sand-earth.
Lived a mighty ox in Northland,
Powerful in bone and sinew,
Beautiful in form and color,
Horns the length of seven fathoms,
Mouth and eyes of wondrous beauty.
Lemminkainen, reckless hero,
Harnesses the ox in pasture,
Takes the master-plow of Pohya,
Plows the roots about the Sampo,
Plows around the lid in colors,
And the sacred Sampo loosens,
Falls the colored lid in silence.
Straightway ancient Wainamoinen
Brings the blacksmith, Ilmarinen,
Brings the daring Lemminkainen,
Lastly brings the magic Sampo,
From the stone-berg of Pohyola,
From the copper-bearing mountain,
Hides it in his waiting vessel,
In the war-ship of Wainola.
Wainamoinen called his people,
Called his crew of men and maidens,
Called together all his heroes,
Rolled his vessel to the water,
Into billowy deeps and dangers.
Spake the blacksmith, Ilmarinen:
"Whither shall we take the Sampo,
Whither take the lid in colors,
From the stone-berg of Pohyola,
From this evil spot of Northland?"
Wainamoinen, wise and faithful,
Gave this answer to the question:
"Thither shall we take the Sampo,
Thither take the lid in colors,
To the fog-point on the waters,
To the island forest-covered;
There the treasure may be hidden,
May remain in peace for ages,
Free from trouble, free from danger,
Where the sword will not molest it."
Then the minstrel, Wainamoinen,
Joyful, left the Pohya borders,
Homeward sailed, and happy-hearted,
Spake these measures on departing:

The Kalevala

"Turn, O man-of-war, from Pohya,
Turn thy back upon the strangers,
Turn thou to my distant country!
Rock, O winds, my magic vessel,
Homeward drive my ship, O billows,
Lend the rowers your assistance,
Give the oarsmen easy labor,
On this vast expanse of waters!
Give me of thine oars, O Ahto,
Lend thine aid, O King of sea-waves,
Guide as with thy helm in safety,
Lay thy hand upon the rudder,
And direct our war-ship homeward;
Let the hooks of metal rattle
O'er the surging of the billows,
On the white-capped waves' commotion."
Then the master, Wainamoinen,
Guided home his willing vessel;
And the blacksmith, Ilmarinen,
With the lively Lemminkainen,
Led the mighty host of rowers,
And the war-ship glided homeward
O'er the sea's unruffled surface,
O'er the mighty waste of waters.
Spake the reckless Lemminkainen:
"Once before I rode these billows,
There were viands for the heroes,
There was singing for the maidens;
But to-day I hear no singing,
Hear no songs upon the vessel,
Hear no music on the waters."
Wainamoinen, wise and ancient,
Answered thus wild Lemminkainen:
"Let none sing upon the blue-sea,
On the waters, no rejoicing;
Singing would prolong our journey,
Songs disturb the host of rowers;
Soon will die the silver sunlight,
Darkness soon will overtake us,
On this evil waste of waters,
On this blue-sea, smooth and level."
These the words of Lemminkainen:
"Time will fly on equal pinions
Whether we have songs or silence;
Soon will disappear the daylight,
And the night as quickly follow,
Whether we be sad or joyous."
Wainamoinen, the magician,
O'er the blue backs of the billows,
Steered one day, and then a second,
Steered the third from morn till even,
When the wizard, Lemminkainen,
Once again addressed the master:
"Why wilt thou, O famous minstrel,
Sing no longer for thy people,
Since the Sampo thou hast captured,
Captured too the lid in colors?"
These the words of Wainamoinen:
"'Tis not well to sing too early!
Time enough for songs of joyance
When we see our home-land mansions,

Lönnrot

When our journeyings have ended!"
Spake the reckless Lemminkainen:
"At the helm, if I were sitting,
I would sing at morn and evening,
Though my voice has little sweetness;
Since thy songs are not forthcoming
Listen to my wondrous singing!"
Thereupon wild Lemminkainen,
Handsome hero, Kaukomieli,
Raised his voice above the waters,
O'er the sea his song resounded;
But his measures were discordant,
And his notes were harsh and frightful.
Sang the wizard, Lemminkainen,
Screeched the reckless Kaukomieli,
Till the mighty war-ship trembled;
Far and wide was heard his singing,
Heard his songs upon the waters,
Heard within the seventh village,
Heard beyond the seven oceans.
Sat a crane within the rushes,
On a hillock clothed in verdure,
And the crane his toes was counting;
Suddenly he heard the singing
Of the wizard, Lemminkainen;
And the bird was justly frightened
At the songs of the magician.
Then with horrid voice, and screeching,
Flew the crane across the broad-sea
To the lakes of Sariola,
O'er Pohyola's hills and hamlets,
Screeching, screaming, over Northland,
Till the people of the darkness
Were awakened from their slumbers.
Louhi hastens to her hurdles,
Hastens to her droves of cattle,
Hastens also to her garners,
Counts her herds, inspects her store-house;
Undisturbed she finds her treasures.
Quick she journeys to the entrance
To the copper-bearing mountain,
Speaks these words as she approaches:
"Woe is me, my life hard-fated,
Woe to Louhi, broken-hearted!
Here the tracks of the destroyers,
All my locks and bolts are broken
By the hands of cruel strangers!
Broken are my iron hinges,
Open stand the mountain-portals
Leading to the Northland-treasure.
Has Pohyola lost her Sampo?"
Then she hastened to the chambers
Where the Sampo had been grinding;
But she found the chambers empty,
Lid and Sampo gone to others,
From the stone-berg of Pohyola,
From behind nine locks of copper,
In the copper-bearing mountain.
Louhi, hostess of the Northland,
Angry grew and cried for vengeance;
As she found her fame departing,

The Kalevala
Found her-strength fast disappearing,
Thus addressed the sea-fog virgin:
"Daughter of the morning-vapors,
Sift thy fogs from distant cloud-land,
Sift the thick air from the heavens,
Sift thy vapors from the ether,
On the blue-back of the broad-sea,
On the far extending waters,
That the ancient Wainamoinen,
Friend of ocean-wave and billow,
May not baffle his pursuers!
"Should this prayer prove unavailing,
Iku-Turso, son of Old-age,
Raise thy head above the billows,
And destroy Wainola's heroes,
Sink them to thy deep sea-castles,
There devour them at thy pleasure;
Bring thou back the golden Sampo
To the people of Pohyola!
"Should these words be ineffective,
Ukko, mightiest of rulers,
Golden king beyond the welkin,
Sitting on a throne of silver,
Fill thy skies with heavy storm-clouds,
Call thy fleetest winds about thee,
Send them o'er the seven broad-seas,
There to find the fleeing vessel,
That the ancient Wainamoinen
May not baffle his pursuers!"
Quick the virgin of the vapors
Breathed a fog upon the waters,
Made it settle on the war-ship
Of the heroes of the Northland,
Held the minstrel, Wainamoinen,
Anchored in the fog and darkness;
Bound him one day, then a second,
Then a third till dawn of morning,
In the middle of the blue-sea,
Whence he could not flee in safety
From the wrath of his pursuers.
When the third night had departed,
Resting in the sea, and helpless,
Wainamoinen spake as follows,
"Not a man of strength and courage,
Not the weakest of the heroes,
Who upon the sea will suffer,
Sink and perish in the vapors,
Perish in the fog and darkness!"
With his sword he smote the billows,
From his magic blade flowed honey;
Quick the vapor breaks, and rises,
Leaves the waters clear for rowing;
Far extend the sky and waters,
Large the ring of the horizon,
And the troubled sea enlarges.
Time had journeyed little distance,
Scarce a moment had passed over,
When they heard a mighty roaring,
Heard a roaring and a rushing
Near the border of the vessel,
Where the foam was shooting skyward

Lönnrot

O'er the boat of Wainamoinen.
Straightway youthful Ilmarinen
Sank in gravest apprehension,
From his cheeks the blood departed;
Pulled his cap down o'er his forehead,
Shook and trembled with emotion.
Wainamoinen, ancient minstrel,
Casts his eyes upon the waters
Near the broad rim of his war-ship;
There perceives an ocean-wonder
With his head above the sea-foam.
Wainamoinen, brave and mighty,
Seizes quick the water-monster,
Lifts him by his ears and questions:
"Iku-Turso, son of Old-age,
Why art rising from the blue-sea?
Wherefore dost thou leave thy castle,
Show thyself to mighty heroes,
To the heroes of Wainola?"
Iku-Turso, son of Old-age,
Ocean monster, manifested
Neither pleasure, nor displeasure,
Was not in the least affrighted,
Did not give the hero answer.
Whereupon the ancient minstrel,
Asked the second time the monster,
Urgently inquired a third time:
"Iku-Turso, son of Old-age,
Why art rising from the waters,
Wherefore dost thou leave the blue-sea?
Iku-Turso gave this answer:
For this cause I left my castle
Underneath the rolling billows:
Came I here with the intention
To destroy the Kalew-heroes,
And return the magic Sampo
To the people of Pohyola.
If thou wilt restore my freedom,
Spare my life, from pain and sorrow,
I will quick retrace my journey,
Nevermore to show my visage
To the people of Wainola,
Never while the moonlight glimmers
On the hills of Kalevala!"
Then the singer, Wainamoinen,
Freed the monster, Iku-Turso,
Sent him to his deep sea-castles,
Spake these words to him departing:
"Iku-Turso, son of Old-age,
Nevermore arise from ocean,
Nevermore let Northland-heroes
See thy face above the waters I
Nevermore has Iku-Turso
Risen to the ocean-level;
Never since have Northland sailors
Seen the head of this sea-monster.
Wainamoinen, old and truthful,
Onward rowed his goodly vessel,
Journeyed but a little distance,
Scarce a moment had passed over,
When the King of all creators,

The Kalevala
Mighty Ukko of the heavens,
Made the winds blow full of power,
Made the storms arise in fury,
Made them rage upon the waters.
From the west the winds came roaring,
From the north-east came in anger,
Winds came howling from the south-west,
Came the winds from all directions,
In their fury, rolling, roaring,
Tearing branches from the lindens,
Hurling needles from the pine-trees,
Blowing flowers from the heather,
Grasses blowing from the meadow,
Tearing up the very bottom
Of the deep and boundless blue-sea.
Roared the winds and lashed the waters
Till the waves were white with fury;
Tossed the war-ship high in ether,
Tossed away the harp of fish-bone,
Magic harp of Wainamoinen,
To the joy of King Wellamo,
To the pleasure of his people,
To the happiness of Ahto,
Ahto, rising from his caverns,
On the floods beheld his people
Carry off the harp of magic
To their home below the billows.
Wainamoinen, ancient minstrel,
Heavy-hearted, spake these measures:
"I have lost what I created,
I have lost the harp of joyance;
Now my strength has gone to others,
All my pleasure too departed,
All my hope and comfort vanished!
Nevermore the harp of fish-bone
Will enchant the hosts of Suomi!"
Then the blacksmith, Ilmarinen,
Sorrow-laden, spake as follows:
"Woe is me, my life hard-fated!
Would that I had never journeyed
On these waters filled with dangers,
On the rolling waste before me,
In this war-ship false and feeble.
Winds and storms have I encountered,
Wretched days of toil and trouble,
I have witnessed in the Northland;
Never have I met such dangers
On the land, nor on the ocean,
Never in my hero life-time!"
Then the ancient Wainamoinen
Spake and these the words he uttered:
"Weep no more, my goodly comrades,
In my bark let no one murmur;
Weeping cannot mend disaster,
Tears can never still misfortune,
Mourning cannot save from evil.
"Sea, command thy warring forces,
Bid thy children cease their fury!
Ahto, still thy surging billows!
Sink, Wellamo, to thy slumber,
That our boat may move in safety.

Lönnrot

Rise, ye storm-winds, to your kingdoms,
Lift your heads above the waters,
To the regions of your kindred,
To your people and dominions;
Cut the trees within the forest,
Bend the lindens of the valley,
Let our vessel sail in safety!"
Then the reckless Lemminkainen,
Handsome wizard, Kaukomieli,
Spake these words in supplication:
"Come, O eagle, Turyalander,
Bring three feathers from thy pinions,
Three, O raven, three, O eagle,
To protect this bark from evil!"
All the heroes of Wainola
Call their forces to the rescue,
And repair the sinking vessel.
By the aid of master-magic,
Wainamoinen saved his war-ship,
Saved his people from destruction,
Well repaired his ship to battle
With the roughest seas of Northland;
Steers his mighty boat in safety
Through the perils of the whirlpool,
Through the watery deeps and dangers.

RUNE XLIII

THE SAMPO LOST IN THE SEA.

Louhi, hostess of Pohyola,
Called her many tribes together,
Gave the archers bows and arrows,
Gave her brave men spears and broadswords;
Fitted out her mightiest war-ship,
In the vessel placed her army,
With their swords a hundred heroes,
With their bows a thousand archers;
Quick erected masts and sail-yards,
On the masts her sails of linen
Hanging like the clouds of heaven,
Like the white-clouds in the ether,
Sailed across the seas of Pohya,
To re-take the wondrous Sampo
From the heroes of Wainola.
Wainamoinen, old and faithful,
Sailed across the deep, blue waters,
Spake these words to Lemminkainen:
"O thou daring son of Lempo,
Best of all my friends and heroes,
Mount the highest of the topmasts,
Look before you into ether,
Look behind you at the heavens,
Well examine the horizon,
Whether clear or filled with trouble."
Climbed the daring Lemminkainen,
Ever ready for a venture,
To the highest of the mastheads;
Looked he eastward, also westward,
Looked he northward, also southward,
Then addressed wise Wainamoinen.
"Clear the sky appears before me,
But behind a dark horizon;
In the north a cloud is rising,
And a longer cloud at north-west."
Wainamoinen thus made answer:
Art thou speaking truth or fiction?
I am fearful that the war-ships
Of Pohyola are pursuing;
Look again with keener vision."
Thereupon wild Lemminkainen
Looked again and spake as follows:
"In the distance seems a forest,
In the south appears an island,
Aspen-groves with falcons laden,
Alders laden with the wood-grouse."
Spake the ancient Wainamoinen:
"Surely thou art speaking falsehood;
'Tis no forest in the distance,
Neither aspen, birch, nor alders,
Laden with the grouse, or falcon;
I am fearful that Pohyola
Follows with her magic armies;

Lönnrot

Look again with keener vision."
Then the daring Lemminkainen
Looked the third time from the topmast,
Spake and these the words be uttered:
"From the north a boat pursues us,
Driven by a hundred rowers,
Carrying a thousand heroes!"
Knew at last old Wainamoinen,
Knew the truth of his inquiry,
Thus addressed his fleeing people:
"Row, O blacksmith, Ilmarinen,
Row, O mighty Lemminkainen,
Row, all ye my noble oarsmen,
That our boat may skim the waters,
May escape from our pursuers!"
Rowed the blacksmith, Ilmarinen,
Rowed the mighty Lemminkainen,
With them rowed the other heroes;
Heavily groaned the helm of birch-wood,
Loudly rattled all the row-locks;
All the vessel shook and trembled,
Like a cataract it thundered
As it plowed the waste of waters,
Tossing sea-foam to the heavens.
Strongly rowed Wainola's forces,
Strongly were their arms united;
But the distance did not widen
Twixt the boat and their pursuers.
Quick the hero, Wainamoinen,
Saw misfortune hanging over,
Saw destruction in the distance
Heavy-hearted, long reflecting,
Trouble-laden, spake as follows:
"Only is there one salvation,
Know one miracle for safety!"
Then he grasped his box of tinder,
From the box he took a flint-stone,
Of the tinder took some fragments,
Cast the fragments on the waters,
Spake these words of master-magic.
"Let from these arise a mountain
From the bottom of the deep-sea,
Let a rock arise in water,
That the war-ship of Pohyola,
With her thousand men and heroes,
May be wrecked upon the summit,
By the aid of surging billows."
Instantly a reef arises,
In the sea springs up a mountain,
Eastward, westward, through the waters.
Came the war-ship of the Northland,
Through the floods the boat came steering,
Sailed against the mountain-ledges,
Fastened on the rocks in water,
Wrecked upon the Mount of Magic.
In the deep-sea fell the topmasts,
Fell the sails upon the billows,
Carried by the winds and waters
O'er the waves of toil and trouble.
Louhi, hostess of Pohyola,
Tries to free her sinking vessel,

The Kalevala
Tries to rescue from destruction;
But she cannot raise the war-ship,
Firmly fixed upon the mountain;
Shattered are the ribs and rudder,
Ruined is the ship of Pohya.
Then the hostess of the Northland,
Much disheartened, spake as follows:
"Where the force, in earth or heaven,
That will help a soul in trouble?"
Quick she changes form and feature,
Makes herself another body;
Takes five sharpened scythes of iron,
Also takes five goodly sickles,
Shapes them into eagle-talons;
Takes the body of the vessel,
Makes the frame-work of an eagle;
Takes the vessel's ribs and flooring
Makes them into wings and breastplate;
For the tail she shapes the rudder;
In the wings she plants a thousand
Seniors with their bows and arrows;
Sets a thousand magic heroes
In the body, armed with broadswords
In the tail a hundred archers,
With their deadly spears and cross-bows,
Thus the bird is hero-feathered.
Quick she spreads her mighty pinions,
Rises as a monster-eagle,
Flies on high, and soars, and circles
With one wing she sweeps the heavens,
While the other sweeps the waters.
Spake the hero's ocean-mother:
"O thou ancient Wainamoinen,
Turn thy vision to the north-east,
Cast thine eyes upon the sunrise,
Look behind thy fleeing vessel,
See the eagle of misfortune!"
Wainamoinen turned as bidden,
Turned his vision to the north-east,
Cast his eyes upon the sunrise,
There beheld the Northland-hostess,
Wicked witch of Sariola,
Flying as a monster-eagle,
Swooping on his mighty war-ship;
Flies and perches on the topmast,
On the sail-yards firmly settles;
Nearly overturns the vessel
Of the heroes of Wainola,
Underneath the weight of envy.
Then the hero, Ilmarinen,
Turned to Ukko as his refuge,
Thus entreated his Creator:
"Ukko, thou O God in heaven,
Thou Creator full of mercy,
Guard us from impending danger,
That thy children may not perish,
May not meet with fell destruction.
Hither bring thy magic fire-cloak,
That thy people, thus protected,
May resist Pohyola's forces,
Well may fight against the hostess

Lönnrot

Of the dismal Sariola,
May not fall before her weapons,
May not in the deep-sea perish!"
Then the ancient Wainamoinen
Thus addressed the ancient Louhi:
"O thou hostess of Pohyola,
Wilt thou now divide the Sampo,
On the fog-point in the water,
On the island forest-covered?
Thus the Northland hostess answered:
"I will not divide the Sampo,
Not with thee, thou evil wizard,
Not with wicked Wainamoinen!"
Quick the mighty eagle, Louhi,
Swoops upon the lid in colors,
Grasps the Sampo in her talons;
But the daring Lemminkainen
Straightway draws his blade of battle,
Draws his broadsword from his girdle,
Cleaves the talons of the eagle,
One toe only is uninjured,
Speaks these magic words of conquest:
"Down, ye spears, and down, ye broadswords,
Down, ye thousand witless heroes,
Down, ye feathered hosts of Louhi!"
Spake the hostess of Pohyola,
Calling, screeching, from the sail-yards:
"O thou faithless Lemminkainen,
Wicked wizard, Kaukomieli,
To deceive thy trusting mother!
Thou didst give to her thy promise,
Not to go to war for ages,
Not to war for sixty summers,
Though desire for gold impels thee,
Though thou wishest gold and silver!
Wainamoinen, ancient hero,
The eternal wisdom-singer,
Thinking he had met destruction,
Snatched the rudder from the waters,
With it smote the monster-eagle,
Smote the eagle's iron talons,
Smote her countless feathered heroes.
From her breast her hosts descended,
Spearmen fell upon the billows,
From the wings descend a thousand,
From the tail, a hundred archers.
Swoops again the bird of Pohya
To the bottom of the vessel,
Like the hawk from birch or aspen,
Like the falcon from the linden;
Grasps the Sampo with one talon,
Drags the treasure to the waters,
Drops the magic lid in colors
From the red rim of the war-ship
To the bottom of the deep-sea,
Where the Sampo breaks in pieces,
Scatters through the Alue-waters,
In the mighty deeps for ages,
To increase the ocean's treasures,
Treasures for the hosts of Ahto.
Nevermore will there be wanting

The Kalevala

Richness for the Ahto-nation,
Never while the moonlight brightens
On the waters of the Northland.
Many fragments of the Sampo
Floated on the purple waters,
On the waters deep and boundless,
Rocked by winds and waves of Suomi,
Carried by the rolling billows
To the sea-sides of Wainola.
Wainamoinen, ancient minstrel,
Saw the fragments of the treasure
Floating on the billows landward,
Fragments of the lid in colors,
Much rejoicing, spake as follows:
"Thence will come the sprouting seed-grain,
The beginning of good fortune,
The unending of resources,
From the plowing and the sowing,
From the glimmer of the moonlight,
From the splendor of the sunshine,
On the fertile plains of Suomi,
On the meads of Kalevala."
Louhi, hostess of Pohyola,
Thus addressed old Wainamoinen:
"Know I other mighty measures,
Know I means that are efficient,
And against thy golden moonlight,
And the splendor of thy sunshine,
And thy plowing, and thy reaping;
In the rocks I'll sink the moonbeams,
Hide the sun within the mountain,
Let the frost destroy thy sowings,
Freeze the crops on all thy corn-fields;
Iron-hail I'll send from heaven,
On the richness of thine acres,
On the barley of thy planting;
I will drive the bear from forests,
Send thee Otso from the thickets,
That he may destroy thy cattle,
May annihilate thy sheep-folds,
May destroy thy steeds at pasture.
I will send thee nine diseases,
Each more fatal than the other,
That will sicken all thy people,
Make thy children sink and perish,
Nevermore to visit Northland,
Never while the moonlight glimmers
On the plains of Kalevala!"
Thus the ancient bard made answer:
"Not a Laplander can banish
Wainamoinen and his people;
Never can a Turyalander
Drive my tribes from Kalevala;
God alone has power to banish,
God controls the fate of nations,
Never trusts the arms of evil,
Never gives His strength to others.
As I trust in my Creator,
Call upon benignant Ukko,
He will guard my crops from danger
Drive the Frost-fiend from my corn-fields,

Lönnrot

Drive great Otso to his caverns.
"Wicked Louhi of Pohyola,
Thou canst banish evil-doers,
In the rocks canst hide the wicked,
In thy mountains lock the guilty;
Thou canst never hide the moonlight,
Never bide the silver sunshine,
In the caverns of thy kingdom.
Freeze the crops of thine own planting,
Freeze the barley of thy sowing,
Send thine iron-hail from heaven
To destroy the Lapland corn-fields,
To annihilate thy people,
To destroy the hosts of Pohya;
Send great Otso from the heather,
Send the sharp-tooth from the forest,
To the fields of Sariola,
On the herds and flocks of Louhi!"
Thus the wicked hostess answered:
"All my power has departed,
All my strength has gone to others,
All my hope is in the deep-sea;
In the waters lies my Sampo!"
Then the hostess of Pohyola
Home departed, weeping, wailing,
To the land of cold and darkness;
Only took some worthless fragments
Of the Sampo to her people;
Carried she the lid to Pohya,
In the blue-sea left the handle;
Hence the poverty of Northland,
And the famines of Pohyola.
Wainamoinen, ancient minstrel,
Hastened to the broad-sea's margin,
Stepped upon the shore in joyance;
Found there fragments of the Sampo,
Fragments of the lid in colors,
On the borders of the waters,
On the curving sands and sea-sides;
Gathered well the Sampo-relics
From the waters near the fog-point,
On the island forest-covered.
Spake the ancient Wainamoinen,
Spake these words in supplication:
"Grant, O Ukko, our Creator,
Grant to us, thy needful children,
Peace, and happiness, and plenty,
That our lives may be successful,
That our days may end in honor,
On the vales and hills of Suomi,
On the prairies of Wainola,
In the homes of Kalevala!
"Ukko, wise and good Creator,
Ukko, God of love and mercy,
Shelter and protect thy people
From the evil-minded heroes,
From the wiles of wicked women,
That our country's plagues may leave us,
That thy faithful tribes may prosper.
Be our friend and strong protector,
Be the helper of thy children,

The Kalevala
In the night a roof above them,
In the day a shield around them,
That the sunshine may not vanish,
That the moonlight may not lessen,
That the killing frosts may leave them,
And destructive hail pass over.
Build a metal wall around us,
rom the valleys to the heavens;
Build of stone a mighty fortress
On the borders of Wainola,
Where thy people live and labor,
As their dwelling-place forever,
Sure protection to thy people,
Where the wicked may not enter,
Nor the thieves break through and pilfer,
Never while the moonlight glistens,
And the Sun brings golden blessings
To the plains of Kalevala."

Lönnrot

RUNE XLIV
BIRTH OF THE SECOND HARP.

Wainamoinen, ancient minstrel,
Long reflecting, sang these measures:
"It is now the time befitting
To awaken joy and gladness,
Time for me to touch the harp-strings,
Time to sing the songs primeval,
In these spacious halls and mansions,
In these homes of Kalevala;
But, alas! my harp lies hidden,
Sunk upon the deep-sea's bottom,
To the salmon's hiding-places,
To the dwellings of the whiting,
To the people of Wellamo,
Where the Northland-pike assemble.
Nevermore will I regain it,
Ahto never will return it,
Joy and music gone forever!
"O thou blacksmith, Ilmarinen,
Forge for me a rake of iron,
Thickly set the teeth of copper,
Many fathoms long the handle;
Make a rake to search the waters,
Search the broad-sea to the bottom,
Rake the weeds and reeds together,
Rake them to the curving sea-shore,
That I may regain my treasure,
May regain my harp of fish-bow
From the whiting's place of resting,
From the caverns of the salmon,
From the castles of Wellamo."
Thereupon young Ilmarinen,
The eternal metal-worker,
Forges well a rake of iron,
Teeth in length a hundred fathoms,
And a thousand long the handle,
Thickly sets the teeth of copper.
Straightway ancient Wainamoinen
Takes the rake of magic metals,
Travels but a little distance,
To the cylinders of oak-wood,
To the copper-banded rollers,
Where he finds two ships awaiting,
One was new, the other ancient.
Wainamoinen, old and faithful,
Thus addressed the new-made vessel:
"Go, thou boat of master-magic,
Hasten to the willing waters,
Speed away upon the blue-sea,
And without the hand to move thee;
Let my will impel thee seaward."
Quick the boat rolled to the billows
On the cylinders of oak-wood,
Quick descended to the waters,

The Kalevala

Willingly obeyed his master.
Wainamoinen, the magician,
Then began to rake the sea-beds,
Raked up all the water-flowers,
Bits of broken reeds and rushes,
Deep-sea shells and colored pebbles,
Did not find his harp of fish-bone,
Lost forever to Wainola!
Thereupon the ancient minstrel
Left the waters, homeward hastened,
Cap pulled clown upon his forehead,
Sang this song with sorrow laden:
"Nevermore shall I awaken
With my harp-strings, joy and gladness!
Nevermore will Wainamoinen
Charm the people of the Northland
With the harp of his creation!
Nevermore my songs will echo
O'er the hills of Kalevala!"
Thereupon the ancient singer
Went lamenting through the forest,
Wandered through the sighing pine-woods,
Heard the wailing of a birch-tree,
Heard a juniper complaining;
Drawing nearer, waits and listens,
Thus the birch-tree he addresses:
"Wherefore, brother, art thou weeping,
Merry birch enrobed in silver,
Silver-leaved and silver-tasselled?
Art thou shedding tears of sorrow,
Since thou art not led to battle,
Not enforced to war with wizards?
Wisely does the birch make answer:
"This the language of the many,
Others speak as thou, unjustly,
That I only live in pleasure,
That my silver leaves and tassels
Only whisper my rejoicings;
That I have no cares, no sorrows,
That I have no hours unhappy,
Knowing neither pain nor trouble.
I am weeping for my smallness,
Am lamenting for my weakness,
Have no sympathy, no pity,
Stand here motionless for ages,
Stand alone in fen and forest,
In these woodlands vast and joyless.
Others hope for coming summers,
For the beauties of the spring-time;
I, alas! a helpless birch-tree,
Dread the changing of the seasons,
I must give my bark to, others,
Lose my leaves and silken tassels.
Men come the Suomi children,
Peel my bark and drink my life-blood;
Wicked shepherds in the summer,
Come and steal my belt of silver,
Of my bark make berry-baskets,
Dishes make, and cups for drinking.
Oftentimes the Northland maidens
Cut my tender limbs for birch-brooms,'

Lönnrot

Bind my twigs and silver tassels
Into brooms to sweep their cabins;
Often have the Northland heroes
Chopped me into chips for burning;
Three times in the summer season,
In the pleasant days of spring-time,
Foresters have ground their axes
On my silver trunk and branches,
Robbed me of my life for ages;
This my spring-time joy and pleasure,
This my happiness in summer,
And my winter days no better!
When I think of former troubles,
Sorrow settles on my visage,
And my face grows white with anguish;
Often do the winds of winter
And the hoar-frost bring me sadness,
Blast my tender leaves and tassels,
Bear my foliage to others,
Rob me of my silver raiment,
Leave me naked on the mountain,
Lone, and helpless, and disheartened!"
Spake the good, old Wainamoinen:
"Weep no longer, sacred birch-tree,
Mourn no more, my friend and brother,
Thou shalt have a better fortune;
I will turn thy grief to joyance,
Make thee laugh and sing with gladness."
Then the ancient Wainamoinen
Made a harp from sacred birch-wood,
Fashioned in the days of summer,
Beautiful the harp of magic,
By the master's hand created
On the fog-point in the Big-Sea,
On the island forest-covered,
Fashioned from the birch the archings,
And the frame-work from the aspen.
These the words of the magician:
"All the archings are completed,
And the frame is fitly finished;
Whence the hooks and pins for tuning,
That the harp may sing in concord?"
Near the way-side grew an oak-tree,
Skyward grew with equal branches,
On each twig an acorn growing,
Golden balls upon each acorn,
On each ball a singing cuckoo.
As each cuckoo's call resounded,
Five the notes of song that issued
From the songster's throat of joyance;
From each throat came liquid music,
Gold and silver for the master,
Flowing to the hills and hillocks,
To the silvery vales and mountains;
Thence he took the merry harp-pins,
That the harp might play in concord.
Spake again wise Wainamoinen:
"I the pins have well completed,
Still the harp is yet unfinished;
Now I need five strings for playing,
Where shall I procure the harp-strings?"

The Kalevala
Then the ancient bard and minstrel
Journeyed through the fen and forest.
On a hillock sat a maiden,
Sat a virgin of the valley;
And the maiden was not weeping,
Joyful was the sylvan daughter,
Singing with the woodland songsters,
That the eventide might hasten,
In the hope that her beloved
Would the sooner sit beside her.
Wainamoinen, old and trusted,
Hastened, tripping to the virgin,
Asked her for her golden ringleta,
These the words of the magician.
"Give me, maiden, of thy tresses,
Give to me thy golden ringlets;
I will weave them into harp-strings,
To the joy of Wainamoinen,
To the pleasure of his people."
Thereupon the forest-maiden
Gave the singer of her tresses,
Gave him of her golden ringlets,
And of these he made the harp-strings.
Sources of eternal pleasure
To the people of Wainola.
Thus the sacred harp is finished,
And the minstrel, Wainamoinen,
Sits upon the rock of joyance,
Takes the harp within his fingers,
Turns the arch up, looking skyward;
With his knee the arch supporting,
Sets the strings in tuneful order,
Runs his fingers o'er the harp-strings,
And the notes of pleasure follow.
Straightway ancient Wainamoinen,
The eternal wisdom-singer,
Plays upon his harp of birch-wood.
Far away is heard the music,
Wide the harp of joy re-echoes;
Mountains dance and valleys listen,
Flinty rocks are tom asunder,
Stones are hurled upon the waters,
Pebbles swim upon the Big-Sea,
Pines and lindens laugh with pleasure,
Alders skip about the heather,
And the aspen sways in concord.
All the daughters of Wainola
Straightway leave their shining needles,
Hasten forward like the current,
Speed along like rapid rivers,
That they may enjoy and wonder.
Laugh the younger men and maidens,
Happy-hearted are the matrons
Flying swift to bear the playing,
To enjoy the common pleasure,
Hear the harp of Wainamoinen.
Aged men and bearded seniors,
Gray-haired mothers with their daughters
Stop in wonderment and listen.
Creeps the babe in full enjoyment
As he hears the magic singing,

Lönnrot

Hears the harp of Wainamoinen.
All of Northland stops in wonder,
Speaks in unison these measures:
"Never have we heard such playing,
Never heard such strains of music,
Never since the earth was fashioned,
As the songs of this magician,
This sweet singer, Wainamoinen!"
Far and wide the sweet tones echo,
Ring throughout the seven hamlets,
O'er the seven islands echo;
Every creature of the Northland
Hastens forth to look and listen,
Listen to the songs of gladness,
To the harp of Wainamoinen.
All the beasts that haunt the woodlands
Fall upon their knees and wonder
At the playing of the minstrel,
At his miracles of concord.
All the songsters of the forests
Perch upon the trembling branches,
Singing to the wondrous playing
Of the harp of Wainamoinen.
All the dwellers of the waters
Leave their beds, and eaves, and grottoes,
Swim against the shore and listen
To the playing of the minstrel,
To the harp of Wainamoinen.
All the little things in nature,
Rise from earth, and fall from ether,
Come and listen to the music,
To the notes of the enchanter,
To the songs of the magician,
To the harp of Wainamoinen.
Plays the singer of the Northland,
Plays in miracles of sweetness,
Plays one day, and then a second,
Plays the third from morn till even;
Plays within the halls and cabins,
In the dwellings of his people,
Till the floors and ceilings echo,
Till resound the roofs of pine-wood,
Till the windows speak and tremble,
Till the portals echo joyance,
And the hearth-stones sing in pleasure.
As he journeys through the forest,
As he wanders through the woodlands,
Pine and sorb-tree bid him welcome,
Birch and willow bend obeisance,
Beech and aspen bow submission;
And the linden waves her branches
To the measure of his playing,
To the notes of the magician.
As the minstrel plays and wanders,
Sings upon the mead and heather,
Glen and hill his songs re-echo,
Ferns and flowers laugh in pleasure,
And the shrubs attune their voices
To the music of the harp-strings,
To the songs of Wainamoinen.

RUNE XLV

BIRTH OF THE NINE DISEASES.

Louhi, hostess of the Northland,
Heard the word in Sariola,
Heard the Dews with ears of envy,
That Wainola lives and prospers,
That Osmoinen's wealth increases,
Through the ruins of the Sampo,
Ruins of the lid in colors.
Thereupon her wrath she kindled,
Well considered, long reflected,
How she might prepare destruction
For the people of Wainola,
For the tribes of Kalevala.
With this prayer she turns to Ukko,
Thus entreats the god of thunder:
"Ukko, thou who art in heaven,
Help me slay Wainola's people
With thine iron-hail of justice,
With thine arrows tipped with lightning,
Or from sickness let them perish,
Let them die the death deserving;
Let the men die in the forest,
And the women in the hurdles!"
The blind daughter of Tuoni,
Old and wicked witch, Lowyatar,
Worst of all the Death-land women,
Ugliest of Mana's children,
Source of all the host of evils,
All the ills and plagues of Northland,
Black in heart, and soul, and visage,
Evil genius of Lappala,
Made her couch along the wayside,
On the fields of sin and sorrow;
Turned her back upon the East-wind,
To the source of stormy weather,
To the chilling winds of morning.
When the winds arose at evening,
Heavy-laden grew Lowyatar,
Through the east-wind's impregnation,
On the sand-plains, vast and barren.
Long she bore her weight of trouble,
Many morns she suffered anguish,
Till at last she leaves the desert,
Makes her couch within the forest,
On a rock upon the mountain;
Labors long to leave her burden
By the mountain-springs and fountains,
By the crystal waters flowing,
By the sacred stream and whirlpool,
By the cataract and fire-stream;
But her burden does not lighten.
Blind Lowyatar, old and ugly,
Knew not where to look for succor,
How to lose her weight of sorrow,

Lönnrot

Where to lay her evil children.
Spake the Highest from the heavens,
These, the words of mighty Ukko:
"Is a triangle in Swamp-field,
Near the border of the ocean,
In the never-pleasant Northland,
In the dismal Sariola;
Thither go and lay thy burden,
In Pohyola leave thine offspring;
There the Laplanders await thee,
There will bid thy children welcome."
Thereupon the blind Lowyatar,
Blackest daughter of Tuoni,
Mana's old and ugly maiden,
Hastened on her journey northward,
To the chambers of Pohyola,
To the ancient halls of Louhi,
There to lay her heavy burdens,
There to leave her evil offspring.
Louhi, hostess of the Northland,
Old and toothless witch of Pohya,
Takes Lowyatar to her mansion;
Silently she leads the stranger
To the bath-rooms of her chamber,
Pours the foaming beer of barley,
Lubricates the bolts and hinges,
That their movements may be secret,
Speaks these measures to Lowyatar:
"Faithful daughter of Creation,
Thou most beautiful of women,
First and last of ancient mothers,
Hasten on thy feet to ocean,
To the ocean's centre hasten,
Take the sea-foam from the waters,
Take the honey of the mermaids,
And anoint thy sacred members,
That thy labors may be lightened.
"Should all this be unavailing,
Ukko, thou who art in heaven,
Hasten hither, thou art needed,
Come thou to thy child in trouble,
Help the helpless and afflicted.
Take thy golden-colored sceptre,
Charm away opposing forces,
Strike the pillars of the stronghold,
Open all resisting portals,
That the great and small may wander
From their ancient hiding-places,
Through the courts and halls of freedom."
Finally the blind Lowyatar,
Wicked witch of Tuonela,
Was delivered of her burden,
Laid her offspring in the cradle,
Underneath the golden covers.
Thus at last were born nine children,
In an evening of the summer,
From Lowyatar, blind and ancient,
Ugly daughter of Tuoni.
Faithfully the virgin-mother
Guards her children in affection,
As an artist loves and nurses

The Kalevala
What his skillful hands have fashioned.
Thus Lowyatar named her offspring,
Colic, Pleurisy, and Fever,
Ulcer, Plague, and dread Consumption,
Gout, Sterility, and Cancer.
And the worst of these nine children
Blind Lowyatar quickly banished,
Drove away as an enchanter,
To bewitch the lowland people,
To engender strife and envy.
Louhi, hostess of Pohyola,
Banished all the other children
To the fog-point in the ocean,
To the island forest-covered;
Banished all the fatal creatures,
Gave these wicked sons of evil
To the people of Wainola,
To the youth of Kalevala,
For the Kalew-tribe's destruction.
Quick Wainola's maidens sicken,
Young and aged, men and heroes,
With the worst of all diseases,
With diseases new and nameless;
Sick and dying is Wainola.
Thereupon old Wainamoinen,
Wise and wonderful enchanter,
Hastens to his people's rescue,
Hastens to a war with Mana,
To a conflict with Tuoni,
To destroy the evil children
Of the evil maid, Lowyatar.
Wainamoinen heats the bath-rooms,
Heats the blocks of healing-sandstone
With the magic wood of Northland,
Gathered by the sacred river;
Water brings in covered buckets
From the cataract and whirlpool;
Brooms he brings enwrapped with ermine,
Well the bath the healer cleanses,
Softens well the brooms of birch-wood;
Then a honey-heat be wakens,
Fills the rooms with healing vapors,
From the virtue of the pebbles
Glowing in the heat of magic,
Thus he speaks in supplication:
"Come, O Ukko, to my rescue,
God of mercy, lend thy presence,
Give these vapor-baths new virtues,
Grant to them the powers of healing,
And restore my dying people;
Drive away these fell diseases,
Banish them to the unworthy,
Let the holy sparks enkindle,
Keep this heat in healing limits,
That it may not harm thy children,
May not injure the afflicted.
When I pour the sacred waters
On the heated blocks of sandstone,
May the water turn to honey
Laden with the balm of healing.
Let the stream of magic virtues

Ceaseless flow to all my children,
From this bath enrolled in sea-moss,
That the guiltless may not suffer,
That my tribe-folk may not perish,
Till the Master gives permission,
Until Ukko sends his minions,
Sends diseases of his choosing,
To destroy my trusting people.
Let the hostess of Pohyola,
Wicked witch that sent these troubles,
Suffer from a gnawing conscience,
Suffer for her evil doings.
Should the Master of Wainola
Lose his magic skill and weaken,
Should he prove of little service
To deliver from misfortune,
To deliver from these evils,
Then may Ukko be our healer,
Be our strength and wise Physician.
"Omnipresent God of mercy,
Thou who livest in the heavens,
Hasten hither, thou art needed,
Hasten to thine ailing children,
To observe their cruel tortures,
To dispel these fell diseases,
Drive destruction from our borders.
Bring with thee thy mighty fire-sword,
Bring to me thy blade of lightning,
That I may subdue these evils,
That these monsters I may banish,
Send these pains, and ills, and tortures,
To the empire of Tuoni,
To the kingdom of the east-winds,
To the islands of the wicked,
To the caverns of the demons,
To the rocks within the mountains,
To the hidden beds of iron,
That the rocks may fall and sicken,
And the beds of iron perish.
Rocks and metals do not murmur
At the hands of the invader.
"Torture-daughter of Tuoni,
Sitting on the mount of anguish,
At the junction of three rivers,
Turning rocks of pain and torture,
Turn away these fell diseases
Through the virtues of the blue-stone;
Lead them to the water-channels,
Sink them in the deeps of ocean,
Where the winds can never find them,
Where the sunlight never enters.
"Should this prayer prove unavailing,
O, Health-virgin, maid of beauty
Come and heal my dying people,
Still their agonies and anguish,
Give them consciousness and comfort,
Give them healthful rest and slumber;
These diseases take and banish,
Take them in thy copper vessel,
To thy caves within the mountains,
To the summit of the Pain-rock,

The Kalevala

Hurl them to thy boiling caldrons.
In the mountain is a touch-stone,
Lucky-stone of ancient story,
With a hole bored through the centre,
Through this pour these pains and tortures,
Wretched feelings, thoughts of evil,
Human ailments, days unlucky,
Tribulations, and misfortunes,
That they may not rise at evening,
May not see the light of morning."
Ending thus, old Wainamoinen,
The eternal, wise enchanter,
Rubbed his sufferers with balsams,
Rubbed the tissues, red and painful,
With the balm of healing flowers,
Balsams made of herbs enchanted,
Sprinkled all with healing vapors,
Spake these words in supplication.
"Ukko, thou who art in heaven,
God of justice, and of mercy,
Send us from the east a rain-cloud,
Send a dark cloud from the North-west,
From the north let fall a third one,
Send us mingled rain and honey,
Balsam from the great Physician,
To remove this plague of Northland.
What I know of healing measures,
Only comes from my Creator;
Lend me, therefore, of thy wisdom,
That I may relieve my people,
Save them from the fell destroyer,
If my hands should fall in virtue,
Let the hands of Ukko follow,
God alone can save from trouble.
Come to us with thine enchantment,
Speak the magic words of healing,
That my people may not perish;
Give to all alleviation
From their sicknesses and sorrows;
In the morning, in the evening,
Let their wasting ailments vanish;
Drive the Death-child from Wainola,
Nevermore to visit Northland,
Never in the course of ages,
Never while the moonlight glimmers
O'er the lakes of Kalevala."
Wainamoinen, the enchanter,
The eternal wisdom-singer,
Thus expelled the nine diseases,
Evil children or Lowyatar,
Healed the tribes of Kalevala,
Saved his people from destruction.

RUNE XLVI
OTSO THE HONEY-EATER.

Came the tidings to Pohyola,
To the village of the Northland,
That Wainola had recovered
From her troubles and misfortunes,
From her sicknesses and sorrows.
Louhi, hostess of the Northland,
Toothless dame of Sariola,
Envy-laden, spake these measures:
"Know I other means of trouble,
I have many more resources;
I will drive the bear before me,
From the heather and the mountain,
Drive him from the fen and forest,
Drive great Otso from the glen-wood
On the cattle of Wainola,
On the flocks of Kalevala."
Thereupon the Northland hostess
Drove the hungry bear of Pohya
From his cavern to the meadows,
To Wainola's plains and pastures.
Wainamoinen, ancient minstrel,
To his brother spake as follows:
"O thou blacksmith, Ilmarinen,
Forge a spear from magic metals,
Forge a lancet triple-pointed,
Forge the handle out of copper,
That I may destroy great Otso,
Slay the mighty bear of Northland,
That he may not eat my horses,
Nor destroy my herds of cattle,
Nor the flocks upon my pastures."
Thereupon the skillful blacksmith
Forged a spear from magic metals,
Forged a lancet triple-pointed,
Not the longest, nor the shortest,
Forged the spear in wondrous beauty.
On one side a bear was sitting,
Sat a wolf upon the other,
On the blade an elk lay sleeping,
On the shaft a colt was running,
Near the hilt a roebuck bounding.
Snows had fallen from the heavens,
Made the flocks as white as ermine
Or the hare, in days of winter,
And the minstrel sang these measures:
"My desire impels me onward
To the Metsola-dominions,
To the homes of forest-maidens,
To the courts of the white virgins;
I will hasten to the forest,
Labor with the woodland-forces.
"Ruler of the Tapio-forests,
Make of me a conquering hero,

The Kalevala

Help me clear these boundless woodlands.
O Mielikki, forest-hostess,
Tapio's wife, thou fair Tellervo,
Call thy dogs and well enchain them,
Set in readiness thy hunters,
Let them wait within their kennels.
"Otso, thou O Forest-apple,
Bear of honey-paws and fur-robes,
Learn that Wainamoinen follows,
That the singer comes to meet thee;
Hide thy claws within thy mittens,
Let thy teeth remain in darkness,
That they may not harm the minstrel,
May be powerless in battle.
Mighty Otso, much beloved,
Honey-eater of the mountains,
Settle on the rocks in slumber,
On the turf and in thy caverns;
Let the aspen wave above thee,
Let the merry birch-tree rustle
O'er thy head for thy protection.
Rest in peace, thou much-loved Otso,
Turn about within thy thickets,
Like the partridge at her brooding,
In the spring-time like the wild-goose."
When the ancient Wainamoinen
Heard his dog bark in the forest,
Heard his hunter's call and echo,
He addressed the words that follow:
"Thought it was the cuckoo calling,
Thought the pretty bird was singing;
It was not the sacred cuckoo,
Not the liquid notes of songsters,
'Twas my dog that called and murmured,
'Twas the echo of my hunter
At the cavern-doors of Otso,
On the border of the woodlands."
Wainamoinen, old and trusty,
Finds the mighty bear in waiting,
Lifts in joy the golden covers,
Well inspects his shining fur-robes;
Lifts his honey-paws in wonder,
Then addresses his Creator:
"Be thou praised, O mighty Ukko,
As thou givest me great Otso,
Givest me the Forest-apple,
Thanks be paid to thee unending."
To the bear he spake these measures:
"Otso, thou my well beloved,
Honey-eater of the woodlands,
Let not anger swell thy bosom;
I have not the force to slay thee,
Willingly thy life thou givest
As a sacrifice to Northland.
Thou hast from the tree descended,
Glided from the aspen branches,
Slippery the trunks in autumn,
In the fog-days, smooth the branches.
Golden friend of fen and forest,
In thy fur-robes rich and beauteous,
Pride of woodlands, famous Light-foot,

Leave thy cold and cheerless dwelling,
Leave thy home within the alders,
Leave thy couch among the willows,
Hasten in thy purple stockings,
Hasten from thy walks restricted,
Come among the haunts of heroes,
Join thy friends in Kalevala.
We shall never treat thee evil,
Thou shalt dwell in peace and plenty,
Thou shalt feed on milk and honey,
Honey is the food of strangers.
Haste away from this thy covert,
From the couch of the unworthy,
To a couch beneath the rafters
Of Wainola's ancient dwellings.
Haste thee onward o'er the snow-plain,
As a leaflet in the autumn;
Skip beneath these birchen branches,
As a squirrel in the summer,
As a cuckoo in the spring-time."
Wainamoinen, the magician,
The eternal wisdom-singer,
O'er the snow-fields hastened homeward,
Singing o'er the hills and mountains,
With his guest, the ancient Otso,
With his friend, the famous Light-foot,
With the Honey-paw of Northland.
Far away was heard the singing,
Heard the playing of the hunter,
Heard the songs of Wainamoinen;
All the people heard and wondered,
Men and maidens, young and aged,
From their cabins spake as follows:
"Hear the echoes from the woodlands,
Hear the bugle from the forest,
Hear the flute-notes of the songsters,
Hear the pipes of forest-maidens!"
Wainamoinen, old and trusty,
Soon appears within the court-yard.
Rush the people from their cabins,
And the heroes ask these questions:
"Has a mine of gold been opened,
Hast thou found a vein of silver,
Precious jewels in thy pathway?
Does the forest yield her treasures,
Give to thee the Honey-eater?
Does the hostess of the woodlands,
Give to thee the lynx and adder,
Since thou comest home rejoicing,
Playing, singing, on thy snow-shoes?"
Wainamoinen, ancient minstrel,
Gave this answer to his people:
"For his songs I caught the adder,
Caught the serpent for his wisdom;
Therefore do I come rejoicing,
Singing, playing, on my snow-shoes.
Not the mountain lynx, nor serpent,
Comes, however, to our dwellings;
The Illustrious is coming,
Pride and beauty of the forest,
'Tis the Master comes among us,

The Kalevala
Covered with his friendly fur-robe.
Welcome, Otso, welcome, Light-foot,
Welcome, Loved-one from the glenwood!
If the mountain guest is welcome,
Open wide the gates of entry;
If the bear is thought unworthy,
Bar the doors against the stranger."
This the answer of the tribe-folk:
"We salute thee, mighty Otso,
Honey-paw, we bid thee welcome,
Welcome to our courts and cabins,
Welcome, Light-foot, to our tables
Decorated for thy coming!
We have wished for thee for ages,
Waiting since the days of childhood,
For the notes of Tapio's bugle,
For the singing of the wood-nymphs,
For the coming of dear Otso,
For the forest gold and silver,
Waiting for the year of plenty,
Longing for it as for summer,
As the shoe waits for the snow-fields,
As the sledge for beaten highways,
As the maiden for her suitor,
And the wife her husband's coming;
Sat at evening by the windows,
At the gates have, sat at morning,
Sat for ages at the portals,
Near the granaries in winter, Vanished,
Till the snow-fields warmed and
Till the sails unfurled in joyance,
Till the earth grew green and blossomed,
Thinking all the while as follows:
"Where is our beloved Otso,
Why delays our forest-treasure?
Has he gone to distant Ehstland,
To the upper glens of Suomi?"
Spake the ancient Wainamoinen:
"Whither shall I lead the stranger,
Whither take the golden Light-foot?
Shall I lead him to the garner,
To the house of straw conduct him?"
This the answer of his tribe-folk:
"To the dining-hall lead Otso,
Greatest hero of the Northland.
Famous Light-foot, Forest-apple,
Pride and glory of the woodlands,
Have no fear before these maidens,
Fear not curly-headed virgins,
Clad in silver-tinselled raiment
Maidens hasten to their chambers
When dear Otso joins their number,
When the hero comes among them."
This the prayer of Wainamoinen:
"Grant, O Ukko, peace and plenty
Underneath these painted rafters,
In this ornamented dwelling;
Thanks be paid to gracious Ukko!"
Spake again the ancient minstrel:
"Whither shall we lead dear Otso,
'Whither take the fur-clad stranger?

Lönnrot

This the answer of his people:
"Hither let the fur-robed Light-foot
Be saluted on his coming;
Let the Honey-paw be welcomed
To the hearth-stone of the penthouse,
Welcomed to the boiling caldrons,
That we may admire his fur-robe,
May behold his cloak with joyance.
Have no care, thou much-loved Otso,
Let not anger swell thy bosom
As thy coat we view with pleasure;
We thy fur shall never injure,
Shall not make it into garments
To protect unworthy people."
Thereupon wise Wainamoinen
Pulled the sacred robe from Otso,
Spread it in the open court-yard,
Cut the members into fragments,
Laid them in the heating caldrons,
In the copper-bottomed vessels--
O'er the fire the crane was hanging,
On the crane were hooks of copper,
On the hooks the broiling-vessels
Filled with bear-steak for the feasting,
Seasoned with the salt of Dwina,
From the Saxon-land imported,
From the distant Dwina-waters,
From the salt-sea brought in shallops.
Ready is the feast of Otso;
From the fire are swung the kettles
On the crane of polished iron;
In the centers of the tables
Is the bear displayed in dishes,
Golden dishes, decorated;
Of the fir-tree and the linden
Were the tables newly fashioned;
Drinking cups were forged from copper,
Knives of gold and spoons of silver;
Filled the vessels to their borders
With the choicest bits of Light-foot,
Fragments of the Forest-apple.
Spake the ancient Wainamoinen
"Ancient one with bosom golden,
Potent voice in Tapio's councils
Metsola's most lovely hostess,
Hostess of the glen and forest,
Hero-son of Tapiola,
Stalwart youth in cap of scarlet,
Tapio's most beauteous virgin,
Fair Tellervo of the woodlands,
Metsola with all her people,
Come, and welcome, to the feasting,
To the marriage-feast of Otso!
All sufficient, the provisions,
Food to eat and drink abundant,
Plenty for the hosts assembled,
Plenty more to give the village."
This the question of the people:
"Tell us of the birth of Otso!
Was he born within a manger,
Was he nurtured in the bath-room

The Kalevala

Was his origin ignoble?"
This is Wainamoinen's answer:
"Otso was not born a beggar,
Was not born among the rushes,
Was not cradled in a manger;
Honey-paw was born in ether,
In the regions of the Moon-land,
On the shoulders of Otava,
With the daughters of creation.
"Through the ether walked a maiden,
On the red rims of the cloudlets,
On the border of the heavens,
In her stockings purple-tinted,
In her golden-colored sandals.
In her hand she held a wool-box,
With a hair-box on her shoulder;
Threw the wool upon the ocean,
And the hair upon the rivers;
These are rocked by winds and waters,
Water-currents bear them onward,
Bear them to the sandy sea-shore,
Land them near the Woods of honey,
On an island forest-covered.
"Fair Mielikki, woodland hostess,
Tapio's most cunning daughter,
Took the fragments from the sea-side,
Took the white wool from the waters,
Sewed the hair and wool together,
Laid the bundle in her basket,
Basket made from bark of birch-wood,
Bound with cords the magic bundle;
With the chains of gold she bound it
To the pine-tree's topmost branches.
There she rocked the thing of magic,
Rocked to life the tender baby,
Mid the blossoms of the pine-tree,
On the fir-top set with needles;
Thus the young bear well was nurtured,
Thus was sacred Otso cradled
On the honey-tree of Northland,
In the middle of the forest.
"Sacred Otso grew and flourished,
Quickly grew with graceful movements,
Short of feet, with crooked ankles,
Wide of mouth and broad of forehead,
Short his nose, his fur-robe velvet;
But his claws were not well fashioned,
Neither were his teeth implanted.
Fair Mielikki, forest hostess,
Spake these words in meditation:
'Claws I should be pleased to give him,
And with teeth endow the wonder,
Would he not abuse the favor.'
"Swore the bear a promise sacred,
On his knees before Mielikki,
Hostess of the glen and forest,
And before omniscient Ukko,
First and last of all creators,
That he would not harm the worthy,
Never do a deed of evil.
Then Mielikki, woodland hostess,

Lönnrot

Wisest maid of Tapiola,
Sought for teeth and claws to give him,
From the stoutest mountain-ashes,
From the juniper and oak tree,
From the dry knots of the alder.
Teeth and claws of these were worthless,
Would not render goodly service.
"Grew a fir-tree on the mountain,
Grew a stately pine in Northland,
And the fir had silver branches,
Bearing golden cones abundant;
These the sylvan maiden gathered,
Teeth and claws of these she fashioned
In the jaws and feet of Otso,
Set them for the best of uses.
Then she freed her new-made creature,
Let the Light-foot walk and wander,
Let him lumber through the marshes,
Let him amble through the forest,
Roll upon the plains and pastures;
Taught him how to walk a hero,
How to move with graceful motion,
How to live in ease and pleasure,
How to rest in full contentment,
In the moors and in the marshes,
On the borders of the woodlands;
How unshod to walk in summer,
Stockingless to run in autumn;
How to rest and sleep in winter
In the clumps of alder-bushes
Underneath the sheltering fir-tree,
Underneath the pine's protection,
Wrapped securely in his fur-robes,
With the juniper and willow.
This the origin of Otso,
Honey-eater of the Northlands,
Whence the sacred booty cometh.
Thus again the people questioned:
Why became the woods so gracious,
Why so generous and friendly?
Why is Tapio so humored,
That he gave his dearest treasure,
Gave to thee his Forest-apple,
Honey-eater of his kingdom?
Was he startled with thine arrows,
Frightened with the spear and broadsword?"
Wainamoinen, the magician,
Gave this answer to the question:
"Filled with kindness was the forest,
Glen and woodland full of greetings,
Tapio showing greatest favor.
Fair Mielikki, forest hostess,
Metsola's bewitching daughter,
Beauteous woodland maid, Tellervo,
Gladly led me on my journey,
Smoothed my pathway through the glen-wood.
Marked the trees upon the mountains,
Pointing me to Otso's caverns,
To the Great Bear's golden island.
"When my journeyings had ended,
When the bear had been discovered,

The Kalevala

Had no need to launch my javelins,
Did not need to aim the arrow;
Otso tumbled in his vaulting,
Lost his balance in his cradle,
In the fir-tree where he slumbered;
Tore his breast upon the branches,
Freely gave his life to others.
"Mighty Otso, my beloved,
Thou my golden friend and hero,
Take thy fur-cap from thy forehead,
Lay aside thy teeth forever,
Hide thy fingers in the darkness,
Close thy mouth and still thine anger,
While thy sacred skull is breaking.
"Now I take the eyes of Otso,
Lest he lose the sense of seeing,
Lest their former powers shall weaken;
Though I take not all his members,
Not alone must these be taken.
"Now I take the ears of Otso,
Lest he lose the sense of hearing,
Lest their former powers shall weaken;
Though I take not all his members,
Not alone must these be taken.
"Now I take the nose of Otso,
Lest he lose the sense of smelling,
Lest its former powers shall weaken;
Though I take not all his members,
Not alone must this be taken.
"Now I take the tongue of Otso,
Lest he lose the sense of tasting
Lest its former powers shall weaken;
Though I take not all his members,
Not alone must this be taken.
"Now I take the brain of Otso,
Lest he lose the means of thinking,
Lest his consciousness should fail him,
Lest his former instincts weaken;
Though I take not all his members,
Not alone must this be taken.
"I will reckon him a hero,
That will count the teeth of Light-foot,
That will loosen Otso's fingers
From their settings firmly fastened."
None he finds with strength sufficient
To perform the task demanded.
Therefore ancient Wainamoinen
Counts the teeth of sacred Otso;
Loosens all the claws of Light-foot,
With his fingers strong as copper,
Slips them from their firm foundations,
Speaking to the bear these measures:
"Otso, thou my Honey-eater,
Thou my Fur-ball of the woodlands,
Onward, onward, must thou journey
From thy low and lonely dwelling,
To the court-rooms of the village.
Go, my treasure, through the pathway
Near the herds of swine and cattle,
To the hill-tops forest covered,
To the high and rising mountains,

Lönnrot

To the spruce-trees filled with needles,
To the branches of the pine-tree;
There remain, my Forest-apple,
Linger there in lasting slumber,
Where the silver bells are ringing,
To the pleasure of the shepherd."
Thus beginning, and thus ending,
Wainamoinen, old and truthful,
Hastened from his emptied tables,
And the children thus addressed him:
"Whither hast thou led thy booty,
Where hast left thy Forest-apple,
Sacred Otso of the woodlands?
Hast thou left him on the iceberg,
Buried him upon the snow-field?
Hast thou sunk him in the quicksand,
Laid him low beneath the heather?"
Wainamoinen spake in answer:
"Have not left him on the iceberg,
Have not buried him in snow-fields;
There the dogs would soon devour him,
Birds of prey would feast upon him;
Have not hidden him in Swamp-land,
Have not buried him in heather;
There the worms would live upon him,
Insects feed upon his body.
Thither I have taken Otso,
To the summit of the Gold-hill,
To the copper-bearing mountain,
Laid him in his silken cradle
In the summit of a pine-tree,
Where the winds and sacred branches
Rock him to his lasting slumber,
To the pleasure of the hunter,
To the joy of man and hero.
To the east his lips are pointing,
While his eyes are northward looking;
But dear Otso looks not upward,
For the fierceness of the storm-winds
Would destroy his sense of vision."
Wainamoinen, ancient minstrel,
Touched again his harp of joyance,
Sang again his songs enchanting,
To the pleasure of the evening,
To the joy of morn arising.
Spake the singer of Wainola:
"Light for me a torch of pine-wood,
For the darkness is appearing,
That my playing may be joyous
And my wisdom-songs find welcome."
Then the ancient sage and singer,
Wise and worthy Wainamoinen,
Sweetly sang and played, and chanted,
Through the long and dreary evening,
Ending thus his incantation:
"Grant, O Ukko, my Creator,
That the people of Wainola
May enjoy another banquet
In the company of Light-foot;
Grant that we may long remember
Kalevala's feast with Otso!

The Kalevala
"Grant, O Ukko, my Creator,
That the signs may guide our footsteps,
That the notches in the pine-tree
May direct my faithful people
To the bear-dens of the woodlands;
That great Tapio's sacred bugle
May resound through glen and forest;
That the wood-nymph's call may echo,
May be heard in field and hamlet,
To the joy of all that listen!
Let great Tapio's horn for ages
Ring throughout the fen and forest,
Through the hills and dales of Northland
O'er the meadows and the mountains,
To awaken song and gladness
In the forests of Wainola,
On the snowy plains of Suomi,
On the meads of Kalevala,
For the coming generations."

RUNE XLVII
LOUHI STEALS SUN, MOON, AND FIRE.

Wainamoinen, ancient minstrel,
Touched again his magic harp-strings,
Sang in miracles of concord,
Filled the north with joy and gladness.
Melodies arose to heaven,
Songs arose to Luna's chambers,
Echoed through the Sun's bright windows
And the Moon has left her station,
Drops and settles in the birch-tree;
And the Sun comes from his castle,
Settles in the fir-tree branches,
Comes to share the common pleasure,
Comes to listen to the singing,
To the harp of Wainamoinen.
Louhi, hostess of Pohyola,
Northland's old and toothless wizard,
Makes the Sun and Moon her captives;
In her arms she takes fair Luna
From her cradle in the birch-tree,
Calls the Sun down from his station,
From the fir-tree's bending branches,
Carries them to upper Northland,
To the darksome Sariola;
Hides the Moon, no more to glimmer,
In a rock of many colors;
Hides the Sun, to shine no longer,
In the iron-banded mountain;
Thereupon these words she utters:
"Moon of gold and Sun of silver,
Hide your faces in the caverns
Of Pohyola's dismal mountain;
Shine no more to gladden Northland,
Till I come to give ye freedom,
Drawn by coursers nine in number,
Sable coursers of one mother!"
When the golden Moon had vanished,
And the silver Sun had hidden
In the iron-banded caverns,
Louhi stole the fire from Northland,
From the regions of Wainola,
Left the mansions cold and cheerless,
And the cabins full of darkness.
Night was king and reigned unbroken,
Darkness ruled in Kalevala,
Darkness in the home of Ukko.
Hard to live without the moonlight,
Harder still without the sunshine;
Ukko's life is dark and dismal,
When the Sun and Moon desert him.
Ukko, first of all creators,
Lived in wonder at the darkness;
Long reflected, well considered,
Why this miracle in heaven,

The Kalevala
What this accident in nature
To the Moon upon her journey;
Why the Sun no more is shining,
Why has disappeared the moonlight.
Then great Ukko walked the heavens,
To the border of the cloudlets,
In his purple-colored vestments,
In his silver-tinselled sandals,
Seeking for the golden moonlight,
Looking for the silver sunshine.
Lightning Ukko struck in darkness
From the edges of his fire-sword;
Shot the flames in all directions,
From his blade of golden color,
Into heaven's upper spaces,
Into Ether's starry pastures.
When a little fire had kindled,
Ukko hid it in the cloud-space,
In a box of gold and silver,
In a case adorned with silver,
Gave it to the ether-maidens,
Called a virgin then to rock it,
That it might become a new-moon,
That a second sun might follow.
On the long-cloud rocked the virgin,
On the blue-edge of the ether,
Rocked the fire of the Creator,
In her copper-colored cradle,
With her ribbons silver-studded.
Lowly bend the bands of silver,
Loud the golden cradle echoes,
And the clouds of Northland thunder,
Low descends the dome of heaven,
At the rocking of the lightning,
Rocking of the fire of Ukko.
Thus the flame was gently cradled
By the virgin of the ether.
Long the fair and faithful maiden
Stroked the Fire-child with her fingers,
Tended it with care and pleasure,
Till in an unguarded moment
It escaped the Ether-virgin,
Slipped the hands of her that nursed it.
Quick the heavens are burst asunder,
Quick the vault of Ukko opens,
Downward drops the wayward Fire-child,
Downward quick the red-ball rushes,
Shoots across the arch of heaven,
Hisses through the startled cloudlets,
Flashes through the troubled welkin,
Through nine starry vaults of ether.
Then the ancient Wainamoinen
Spake and these the words he uttered:
"Blacksmith brother, Ilmarinen,
Let us haste and look together,
What the kind of fire that falleth,
What the form of light that shineth
From the upper vault of heaven,
From the lower earth and ocean.
Has a second moon arisen,
Can it be a ball of sunlight?

Thereupon the heroes wandered,
Onward journeyed and reflected,
How to gain the spot illumined,
How to find the sacred Fire-child.
Came a river rushing by them,
Broad and stately as an ocean.
Straightway ancient Wainamoinen
There began to build a vessel,
Build a boat to cross the river.
With the aid of Ilmarinen,
From the oak he cut the row-locks,
From the pine the oars be fashioned,
From the aspen shapes the rudder.
When the vessel they had finished,
Quick they rolled it to the current,
Hard they rowed and ever forward,
On the Nawa-stream and waters,
At the head of Nawa-river.
Ilmatar, the ether-daughter,
Foremost daughter of creation,
Came to meet them on their journey,
Thus addressed the coming strangers:
"Who are ye of Northland heroes,
Rowing on the Nawa-waters?"
Wainamoinen gave this answer:
"This the blacksmith, Ilmarinen,
I the ancient Wainamoinen.
Tell us now thy name and station,
Whither going, whence thou comest,
Where thy tribe-folk live and linger?
Spake the daughter of the Ether:
"I the oldest of the women,
Am the first of Ether's daughters,
Am the first of ancient mothers;
Seven times have I been wedded.
To the heroes of creation.
Whither do ye strangers journey?
Answered thus old Wainamoinen:
"Fire has left Wainola's hearth-stones,
Light has disappeared from Northland;
Have been sitting long in darkness,
Cold and darkness our companions;
Now we journey to discover
What the fire that fell from heaven,
Falling from the cloud's red lining,
To the deeps of earth and ocean."
Ilmatar returned this answer:
"Hard the flame is to discover,
Hard indeed to find the Fire-child;
Has committed many mischiefs,
Nothing good has he accomplished;
Quick the fire-ball fell from ether,
From the red rims of the cloudlets,
From the plains of the Creator,
Through the ever-moving heavens,
Through the purple ether-spaces,
Through the blackened flues of Turi,
To Palwoinen's rooms uncovered.
When the fire had reached the chambers
Of Palwoinen, son of evil,
He began his wicked workings,

The Kalevala

He engaged in lawless actions,
Raged against the blushing maidens,
Fired the youth to evil conduct,
Singed the beards of men and heroes.
"Where the mother nursed her baby,
In the cold and cheerless cradle,
Thither flew the wicked Fire-child,
There to perpetrate some mischief;
In the cradle burned the infant,
By the infant burned the mother,
That the babe might visit Mana,
In the kingdom of Tuoni;
Said the child was born for dying,
Only destined for destruction,
Through the tortures of the Fire-child.
Greater knowledge had the mother,
Did not journey to Manala,
Knew the word to check the red-flame,
How to banish the intruder
Through the eyelet of a needle,
Through the death-hole of the hatchet."
Then the ancient Wainamoinen
Questioned Ilmatar as follows:
"Whither did the Fire-child wander,
Whither did the red-flame hasten,
From the border-fields of Turi,
To the woods, or to the waters?
Straightway Ilmatar thus answers:
"When the fire had fled from Turi,
From the castles of Palwoinen,
Through the eyelet of the needle,
Through the death-hole of the hatchet,
First it burned the fields, and forests,
Burned the lowlands, and the heather;
Then it sought the mighty waters,
Sought the Alue-sea and river,
And the waters hissed and sputtered
In their anger at the Fire-child,
Fiery red the boiling Alue!
"Three times in the nights of, summer,
Nine times in the nights of autumn,
Boil the waters to the tree-tops,
Roll and tumble to the mountain,
Through the red-ball's force and fury;
Hurls the pike upon the pastures,
To the mountain-cliffs, the salmon,
Where the ocean-dwellers wonder,
Long reflect and well consider
How to still the angry waters.
Wept the salmon for his grotto,
Mourned the whiting for his cavern,
And the lake-trout for his dwelling,
Quick the crook-necked salmon darted,
Tried to catch the fire-intruder,
But the red-ball quick escaped him;
Darted then the daring whiting,
Swallowed quick the wicked Fire-child,
Swallowed quick the flame of evil.
Quiet grow the Alue-waters,
Slowly settle to their shore-lines,
To their long-accustomed places,

Lönnrot

In the long and dismal evening.
"Time had gone but little distance,
When the whiting grow affrighted,
Fear befel the fire-devourer;
Burning pain and writhing tortures
Seized the eater of the Fire-child;
Swam the fish in all directions,
Called, and moaned, and swam, and circled,
Swam one day, and then a second,
Swam the third from morn till even;
Swam she to the whiting-island,
To the caverns of the salmon,
Where a hundred islands cluster;
And the islands there assembled
Thus addressed the fire-devourer:
'There is none within these waters,
In this narrow Alue-lakelet,
That will eat the fated Fire-fish
That will swallow thee in trouble,
In thine agonies and torture
From the Fire-child thou hast eaten.'
"Hearing this a trout forth darting,
Swallowed quick as light the whiting,
Quickly ate the fire-devourer.
Time had gone but little distance,
When the trout became affrighted,
Fear befel the whiting-eater;
Burning pain and writhing torment
Seized the eater of the Fire-fish.
Swam the trout in all directions,
Called, and moaned, and swam, and circled,
Swam one day, and then a second,
Swain the third from morn till even;
Swam she to the salmon-island,
Swam she to the whiting-grottoes,
Where a thousand islands cluster,
And the islands there assembled
Thus addressed the tortured lake-trout:
'There is none within this river,
In these narrow Alue-waters,
That will eat the wicked Fire-fish,
That will swallow thee in trouble,
In thine agonies and tortures,
From the Fire-fish thou hast eaten."
Hearing this the gray-pike darted,
Swallowed quick as light the lake-trout,
Quickly ate the tortured Fire-fish.
"Time had gone but little distance,
When the gray-pike grew affrighted,
Fear befel the lake-trout-eater;
Burning pain and writhing torment
Seized the reckless trout-devourer;
Swam the pike in all directions,
Called, and moaned, and swam, and circled,
Swam one day, and then a second,
Swam the third from morn till even,
To the cave of ocean-swallows,
To the sand-hills of the sea-gull,
Where a hundred islands cluster;
And the islands there assembled
Thus addressed the fire-devourer:

The Kalevala
'There is none within this lakelet,
In these narrow Alue-waters,
That will eat the fated Fire-fish,
That will swallow thee in trouble,
In thine agonies and tortures,
From the Fire-fish thou hast eaten.'"
Wainamoinen, wise and ancient,
With the aid of Ilmarinen,
Weaves with skill a mighty fish-net
From the juniper and sea-grass;
Dyes the net with alder-water,
Ties it well with thongs of willow.
Straightway ancient Wainamoinen
Called the maidens to the fish-net,
And the sisters came as bidden.
With the netting rowed they onward,
Rowed they to the hundred islands,
To the grottoes of the salmon,
To the caverns of the whiting,
To the reeds of sable color,
Where the gray-pike rests and watches.
On they hasten to the fishing,
Drag the net in all directions,
Drag it lengthwise, sidewise, crosswise,
And diagonally zigzag;
But they did not catch the Fire-fish.
Then the brothers went a-fishing,
Dragged the net in all directions,
Backwards, forwards, lengthwise, sidewise,
Through the homes of ocean-dwellers,
Through the grottoes of the salmon,
Through the dwellings of the whiting,
Through the reed-beds of the lake-trout,
Where the gray-pike lies in ambush;
But the fated Fire-fish came not,
Came not from the lake's abysses,
Came not from the Alue-waters.
Little fish could not be captured
In the large nets of the masters;
Murmured then the deep-sea-dwellers,
Spake the salmon to the lake-trout,
And the lake-trout to the whiting,
And the whiting to the gray-pike:
Have the heroes of Wainola
Died, or have they all departed
From these fertile shores and waters?
Where then are the ancient weavers,
Weavers of the nets of flax-thread,
Those that frighten us with fish-poles,
Drag us from our homes unwilling?"
Hearing this wise Wainamoinen
Answered thus the deep-sea-dwellers:
"Neither have Wainola's heroes
Died, nor have they all departed
From these fertile shores and waters,
Two are born where one has perished;
Longer poles and finer fish-nets
Have the sons of Kalevala!"

RUNE XLVIII
CAPTURE OF THE FIRE-FISH.

Wainamoinen, the enchanter,
The eternal wisdom-singer,
Long reflected, well considered,
How to weave the net of flax-yarn,
Weave the fish-net of the fathers.
Spake the minstrel of Wainola:
"Who will plow the field and fallow,
Sow the flax, and spin the flax-threads,
That I may prepare the fish-net,
Wherewith I may catch the Fire-pike,
May secure the thing of evil?"
Soon they found a fertile island,
Found the fallow soil befitting,
On the border of the heather,
And between two stately oak-trees.
They prepared the soil for sowing.
Searching everywhere for flax-seed,
Found it in Tuoni's kingdom,
In the keeping of an insect.
Then they found a pile of ashes,
Where the fire had burned a vessel;
In the ashes sowed the seedlings
Near the Alue-lake and border,
In the rich and loamy fallow.
There the seed took root and flourished,
Quickly grew to great proportions,
In a single night in summer.
Thus the flax was sowed at evening,
Placed within the earth by moonlight;
Quick it grew, and quickly ripened,
Quick Wainola's heroes pulled it,
Quick they broke it on the hackles,
Hastened with it to the waters,
Dipped it in the lake and washed it;
Quickly brought it borne and dried it.
Quickly broke, and combed, and smoothed it,
Brushed it well at early morning,
Laid it into laps for spinning
Quick the maidens twirl the spindles,
Spin the flaxen threads for weaving,
In a single night in summer.
Quick the sisters wind and reel it,
Make it ready for the needle.
Brothers weave it into fish-nets,
And the fathers twist the cordage,
While the mothers knit the meshes,
Rapidly the mesh-stick circles;
Soon the fish-net is completed,
In a single night in summer.
As the magic net is finished,
And in length a hundred fathoms,
On the rim three hundred fathoms.
Rounded stones are fastened to it,

The Kalevala

Joined thereto are seven float-boards.
Now the young men take the fish-net,
And the old men cheer them onward,
Wish them good-luck at their fishing.
Long they row and drag the flax-seine,
Here and there the net is lowered;
Now they drag it lengthwise, sidewise,
Drag it through the slimy reed-beds;
But they do not catch the Fire-pike,
Only smelts, and luckless red-fish,
Little fish of little value.
Spake the ancient Wainamoinen:
"O thou blacksmith, Ilmarinen,
Let us go ourselves a-fishing,
Let us catch the fish of evil!"
To the fishing went the brothers,
Magic heroes of the Northland,
Pulled the fish-net through the waters,
Toward an island in the deep-sea
Then they turn and drag the fish-net
Toward a meadow jutting seaward;
Now they drag it toward Wainola,
Draw it lengthwise, sidewise, crosswise,
Catching fish of every species,
salmon, trout, and pike, and whiting,
Do not catch the evil Fire-fish.
Then the master, Wainamoinen,
Made additions to its borders,
Made it many fathoms wider,
And a hundred fathoms longer,
Then these words the hero uttered
"Famous blacksmith, Ilmarinen,
Let us go again a-fishing,
Row again the magic fish-net,
Drag it well through all the waters,
That we may obtain the Fire-pike!"
Thereupon the Northland heroes
Go a second time a-fishing,
Drag their nets across the rivers,
Lakelets, seas, and bays, and inlets,
Catching fish of many species,
But the Fire-fish is not taken.
Wainamoinen, ancient singer,
Long reflecting, spake these measures:
"Dear Wellamo, water-hostess,
Ancient mother with the reed-breast,
Come, exchange thy water-raiment,
Change thy coat of reeds and rushes
For the garments I shall give thee,
Light sea-foam, thine inner vesture,
And thine outer, moss and sea-grass,
Fashioned by the wind's fair daughters,
Woven by the flood's sweet maidens;
I will give thee linen vestments
Spun from flax of softest fiber,
Woven by the Moon's white virgins,
Fashioned by the Sun's bright daughters
Fitting raiment for Wellamo!
"Ahto, king of all the waters,
Ruler of a thousand grottoes,
Take a pole of seven fathoms,

Lönnrot

Search with this the deepest waters,
Rummage well the lowest bottoms;
Stir up all the reeds and sea-weeds,
Hither drive a school of gray-pike,
Drive them to our magic fish-net,
From the haunts in pike abounding,
From the caverns, and the trout-holes,
From the whirlpools of the deep-sea,
From the bottomless abysses,
Where the sunshine never enters,
Where the moonlight never visits,
And the sands are never troubled."
Rose a pigmy from the waters,
From the floods a little hero,
Riding on a rolling billow,
And the pigmy spake these measures:
"Dost thou wish a worthy helper,
One to use the pole and frighten
Pike and salmon to thy fish-nets?"
Wainamoinen, old and faithful,
Answered thus the lake-born hero:
"Yea, we need a worthy helper,
One to hold the pole, and frighten
Pike and salmon to our fish-nets."
Thereupon the water-pigmy
Cut a linden from the border,
Spake these words to Wainamoinen:
"Shall I scare with all my powers,
With the forces of my being,
As thou needest shall I scare them?"
Spake the minstrel, Wainamoinen:
"If thou scarest as is needed,
Thou wilt scare with all thy forces,
With the strength of thy dominions."
Then began the pigmy-hero,
To affright the deep-sea-dwellers;
Drove the fish in countless numbers
To the net of the magicians.
Wainamoinen, ancient minstrel,
Drew his net along the waters,
Drew it with his ropes of flax-thread,
Spake these words of magic import:
"Come ye fish of Northland waters
To the regions of my fish-net,
As my hundred meshes lower."
Then the net was drawn and fastened,
Many were the gray-pike taken
By he master and magician.
Wainamoinen, happy-hearted,
Hastened to a neighboring island,
To a blue-point in the waters,
Near a red-bridge on the headland;
Landed there his draught of fishes,
Cast the pike upon the sea-shore,
And the Fire-pike was among them,
Cast the others to the waters.
Spake the ancient Wainamoinen:
"May I touch thee with my fingers,
Using not my gloves of iron,
Using not my blue-stone mittens?
This the Sun-child hears and answers:

The Kalevala
"I should like to carve the Fire-fish,
I should like this pike to handle,
If I had the knife of good-luck."
Quick a knife falls from the heavens,
From the clouds a magic fish-knife,
Silver-edged and golden-headed,
To the girdle of the Sun-child;
Quick he grasps the copper handle,
Quick the hero carves the Fire-pike,
Finds therein the tortured lake-trout;
Carves the lake-trout thus discovered,
Finds therein the fated whiting;
Carves the whiting, finds a blue-ball
In the third cave of his body.
He, the blue-ball quick unwinding,
Finds within a ball of scarlet;
Carefully removes the cover,
Finds the ball of fire within it,
Finds the flame from heaven fallen,
From the heights of the seventh heaven,
Through nine regions of the ether.
Wainamoinen long reflected
How to get the magic fire-ball
To Wainola's fireless hearth-stones,
To his cold and cheerless dwellings.
Quick he snatched the fire of heaven
From the fingers of the Sun-child.
Wainamoinen's beard it singes,
Burns the brow of Ilmarinen,
Burns the fingers of the blacksmith.
Rolling forth it hastens westward,
Hastens to the Alue shore-lines,
Burns the juniper and alder,
Burns the and heath and meadow,
Rises to the lofty linden,
Burns the firs upon the mountains;
Hastens onward, onward, onward,
Burns the islands of the Northland,
Burns the Sawa fields and forests,
Burns the dry lands of Karyala.
Straightway ancient Wainamoinen
Hastens through the fields and fenlands,
Tracks the ranger to the glen-wood,
Finds the Fire-child in an elm-tree,
Sleeping in a bed of fungus.
Thereupon wise Wainamoinen
Wakes the child and speaks these measures:
"Wicked fire that God created,
Flame of Ukko from the heavens,
Thou hast gone in vain to sea-caves,
To the lakes without a reason;
Better go thou to my village,
To the hearth-stones of my people;
Hide thyself within my chimneys,
In mine ashes sleep and linger.
In the day-time I will use thee
To devour the blocks of birch-wood;
In the evening I will hide thee
Underneath the golden circle."
Then he took the willing Panu,
Took the willing fire of Ukko,

Lönnrot

Laid it in a box of tinder,
In the punk-wood of a birch-tree,
In a vessel forged from copper;
Carried it with care and pleasure
To the fog-point in the waters,
To the island forest covered.
Thus returned the fire to Northland,
To the chambers of Wainola,
To the hearths of Kalevala.
Ilmarinen, famous blacksmith,
Hastened to the deep-sea's margin,
Sat upon the rock of torture,
Feeling pain the flame had given,
Laved his wounds with briny water,
Thus to still the Fire-child's fury,
Thus to end his persecutions.
Long reflecting, Ilmarinen
Thus addressed the flame of Ukko:
"Evil Panu from the heavens,
Wicked son of God from ether,
Tell me what has made thee angry,
Made thee burn my weary members,
Burn my beard, and face, and fingers,
Made me suffer death-land tortures?
Spake again young Ilmarinen:
"How can I wild Panu conquer,
How shall I control his conduct,
Make him end his evil doings?
Come, thou daughter from Pohyola,
Come, white virgin of the hoar-frost,
Come on shoes of ice from Lapland,
Icicles upon thy garments,
In one band a cup of white-frost,
In the other hand an ice-spoon;
Sprinkle snow upon my members,
Where the Fire-child has been resting,
Let the hoar-frost fall and settle.
"Should this prayer be unavailing,
Come, thou son of Sariola,
Come, thou child of Frost from Pohya,
Come, thou Long-man from the ice-plains,
Of the height of stately pine-trees,
Slender as the trunks of lindens,
On thy hands the gloves of Hoar-frost,
Cap of ice upon thy forehead,
On thy waist a white-frost girdle;
Bring the ice-dust from Pohyola,
From the cold and sunless village.
Rain is crystallized in Northland,
Ice in Pohya is abundant,
Lakes of ice and ice-bound rivers,
Frozen smooth, the sea of ether.
Bounds the hare in frosted fur-robe,
Climbs the bear in icy raiment,
Ambles o'er the snowy mountains.
Swans of frost descend the rivers,
Ducks of ice in countless numbers
Swim upon thy freezing waters,
Near the cataract and whirlpool.
Bring me frost upon thy snow-sledge,
Snow and ice in great abundance,

The Kalevala
From the summit of the wild-top,
From the borders of the mountains.
With thine ice, and snow, and hoar-frost
Cover well mine injured members
Where wild Panu has been resting,
Where the child of Fire has lingered.
"Should this call be ineffective,
Ukko, God of love and mercy,
First and last of the creators,
From the east send forth a snow-cloud,
From the west despatch a second,
Join their edges well together,
Let there be no vacant places,
Let these clouds bring snow and
Lay the healing balm of Ukko
On my burning, tortured tissues,
Where wild Panu has been resting."
Thus the blacksmith, Ilmarinen,
Stills the pains by fire engendered,
Stills the agonies and tortures
Brought him by the child of evil,
Brought him by the wicked Panu.

RUNE XLIX
RESTORATION OF THE SUN AND MOON.

Thus has Fire returned to Northland
But the gold Moon is not shining,
Neither gleams the silver sunlight
In the chambers of Wainola,
On the plains of Kalevala.
On the crops the white-frost settled,
And the cattle died of hunger,
Even birds grew sick and perished.
Men and maidens, faint and famished,
Perished in the cold and darkness,
From the absence of the sunshine,
From the absence of the moonlight.
Knew the pike his holes and hollows,
And the eagle knew his highway,
Knew the winds the times for sailing;
But the wise men of the Northland
Could not know the dawn of morning,
On the fog-point in the ocean,
On the islands forest-covered.
Young and aged talked and wondered,
Well reflected, long debated,
How to live without the moonlight,
Live without the silver sunshine,
In the cold and cheerless Northland,
In the homes of Kalevala.
Long conjectured all the maidens,
Orphans asked the wise for counsel.
Spake a maid to Ilmarinen,
Running to the blacksmith's furnace:
"Rise, O artist, from thy slumbers,
Hasten from thy couch unworthy;
Forge from gold the Moon for Northland,
Forge anew the Sun from silver
Cannot live without the moonlight,
Nor without the silver sunshine!"
From his couch arose the artist,
From his couch of stone, the blacksmith,
And began his work of forging,
Forging Sun and Moon for Northland.
Came the ancient Wainamoinen,
In the doorway sat and lingered,
Spake, these Words to Ilmarinen:
"Blacksmith, my beloved brother,
Thou the only metal-worker,
Tell me why thy magic hammer
Falls so heavy on thine anvil?"
Spake the youthful Ilmarinen:
"Moon of gold and Sun of silver,
I am forging for Wainola;
I shall swing them into ether,
Plant them in the starry heavens."
Spake the wise, old Wainamoinen:
"Senseless blacksmith of the ages,

The Kalevala

Vainly dost thou swing thy hammer,
Vainly rings thy mighty anvil;
Silver will not gleam as sunshine,
Not of gold is born the moonlight!"
Ilmarinen, little heeding,
Ceases not to ply his hammer,
Sun and Moon the artist forges,
Wings the Moon of Magic upward,
Hurls it to the pine-tree branches;
Does not shine without her master.
Then the silver Sun he stations
In an elm-tree on the mountain.
From his forehead drip the sweat-drops,
Perspiration from his fingers,
Through his labors at the anvil
While the Sun and Moon were forging;
But the Sun shone not at morning
From his station in the elm-tree;
And the Moon shone not at evening
From the pine-tree's topmost branches.
Spake the ancient Wainamoinen:
"Let the Fates be now consulted,
And the oracles examined;
Only thus may we discover
Where the Sun and Moon lie hidden."
Thereupon old Wainamoinen,
Only wise and true magician,
Cut three chips from trunks of alder,
Laid the chips in magic order,
Touched and turned them with his fingers,
Spake these words of master-magic:
"Of my Maker seek I knowledge,
Ask in hope and faith the answer
From the great magician, Ukko:
Tongue of alder, tell me truly,
Symbol of the great Creator,
Where the Sun and Moon are sleeping;
For the Moon shines not in season,
Nor appears the Sun at midday,
From their stations in the sky-vault.
Speak the truth, O magic alder,
Speak not words of man, nor hero,
Hither bring but truthful measures.
Let us form a sacred compact:
If thou speakest me a falsehood,
I will hurl thee to Manala,
Let the nether fires consume thee,
That thine evil signs may perish."
Thereupon the alder answered,
Spake these words of truthful import:
"Verily the Sun lies hidden
And the golden Moon is sleeping
In the stone-berg of Pohyola,
In the copper-bearing mountain."
These the words of Wainamoinen:
"I shall go at once to Northland,
To the cold and dark Pohyola,
Bring the Sun and Moon to gladden
All Wainola's fields and forests."
Forth he hastens on his journey,
To the dismal Sariola,

Lönnrot

To the Northland cold and dreary;
Travels one day, then a second,
So the third from morn till evening,
When appear the gates of Pohya,
With her snow-clad hills and mountains.
Wainamoinen, the magician,
At the river of Pohyola,
Loudly calls the ferry-maiden:
Bring a boat, O Pohya-daughter,
Bring a strong and trusty vessel,
Row me o'er these chilling waters,
O'er this rough and rapid river!"
But the Ferry-maiden heard not,
Did not listen to his calling.
Thereupon old Wainamoinen,
Laid a pile of well-dried brush-wood,
Knots and needles of the fir-tree,
Made a fire beside the river,
Sent the black smoke into heaven
Curling to the home of Ukko.
Louhi, hostess of the Northland,
Hastened to her chamber window,
Looked upon the bay and river,
Spake these words to her attendants:
"Why the fire across the river
Where the current meets the deep-sea,
Smaller than the fires of foemen,
Larger than the flames of hunters?"
Thereupon a Pohyalander
Hastened from the court of Louhi
That the cause he might discover,'
Bring the sought-for information
To the hostess of Pohyola;
Saw upon the river-border
Some great hero from Wainola.
Wainamoinen saw the stranger,
Called again in tones of thunder:
"Bring a skiff; thou son of Northland,
For the minstrel, Wainamoinen!
Thus the Pohyalander answered:
"Here no skiffs are lying idle,
Row thyself across the waters,
Use thine arms, and feet, and fingers,
To propel thee o'er the river,
O'er the sacred stream of Pohya."
Wainamoinen, long reflecting,
Bravely thus soliloquizes:
"I will change my form and features,
Will assume a second body,
Neither man, nor ancient minstrel,
Master of the Northland waters!"
Then the singer, Wainamoinen,
Leaped, a pike, upon the waters,
Quickly swam the rapid river,
Gained the frigid Pohya-border.
There his native form resuming,
Walked he as a mighty hero,
On the dismal isle of Louhi,
Spake the wicked sons of Northland:
Come thou to Pohyola's court-room."
To Pohyola's, court he hastened.

The Kalevala
Spake again the sons of evil:
Come thou to the halls of Louhi!"
To Pohyola's halls he hastened.
On the latch he laid his fingers,
Set his foot within the fore-hall,
Hastened to the inner chamber,
Underneath the painted rafters,
Where the Northland-heroes gather.
There he found the Pohya-masters
Girded with their swords of battle,
With their spears and battle-axes,
With their fatal bows and arrows,
For the death of Wainamoinen,
Ancient bard, Suwantolainen.
Thus they asked the hero-stranger.
"Magic swimmer of the Northland,
Son of evil, what the message
That thou bringest from thy people,
What thy mission to Pohyola?"
Wainamoinen, old and truthful,
Thus addressed the hosts of Louhi:
"For the Sun I come to Northland,
Come to seek the Moon in Pohya;
Tell me where the Sun lies hidden,
Where the golden Moon is sleeping."
Spake the evil sons of Pohya:
"Both the Sun and Moon are hidden
In the rock of many colors,
In the copper-bearing mountain,
In a cavern iron-banded,
In the stone-berg of Pohyola,
Nevermore to gain their freedom,
Nevermore to shine in Northland!"
Spake the hero, Wainamoinen:
"If the Sun be not uncovered,
If the Moon leave not her dungeon,
I will challenge all Pohyola
To the test of spear or broadsword,
Let us now our weapons measure!"
Quick the hero of Wainola
Drew his mighty sword of magic;
On its border shone the moonlight,
On its hilt the Sun was shining,
On its back, a neighing stallion,
On its face a cat was mewing,
Beautiful his magic weapon.
Quick the hero-swords are tested,
And the blades are rightly measured
Wainamoinen's sword is longest
By a single grain of barley,
By a blade of straw, the widest.
To the court-yard rushed the heroes,
Hastened to the deadly combat,
On the plains of Sariola.
Wainamoinen, the magician,
Strikes one blow, and then a second,
Strikes a third time, cuts and conquers.
As the house-maids slice the turnips,
As they lop the heads of cabbage,
As the stalks of flax are broken,
So the heads of Louhi's heroes

Lönnrot

Fall before the magic broadsword
Of the ancient Wainamoinen.
Then victor from Wainola,
Ancient bard and great magician,
Went to find the Sun in slumber,
And the golden Moon discover,
In the copper-bearing Mountains,
In the cavern iron-banded,
In the stone-berg of Pohyola.
He had gone but little distance,
When he found a sea-green island;
On the island stood a birch-tree,
Near the birch-tree stood a pillar
Carved in stone of many colors;
In the pillar, nine large portals
Bolted in a hundred places;
In the rock he found a crevice
Sending forth a gleam of sunlight.
Quick he drew his mighty broadsword,
From the pillar struck three colors,
From the magic of his weapon;
And the pillar fell asunder,
Three the number of the fragments.
Wainamoinen, old and faithful,
Through the crevice looked and wondered.
In the center of the pillar,
From a scarlet-colored basin,
Noxious serpents beer were drinking,
And the adders eating spices.
Spake the ancient Wainamoinen:
"Therefore has Pohyola's hostess
Little drink to give to strangers,
Since her beer is drank by serpents,
And her spices given to adders."
Quick he draws his magic fire-blade,
Cuts the vipers green in pieces,
Lops the heads off all the adders,
Speaks these words of master-magic:
Thus, hereafter, let the serpent
Drink the famous beer of barley,
Feed upon the Northland-spices!"
Wainamoinen, the magician,
The eternal wizard-singer,
Sought to open wide the portals
With the hands and words of magic;
But his hands had lost their cunning,
And his magic gone to others.
Thereupon the ancient minstrel
Quick returning, heavy-hearted,
To his native halls and hamlets,
Thus addressed his brother-heroes:
"Woman, he without his weapons,
With no implements, a weakling!
Sun and Moon have I discovered,
But I could not force the Portals
Leading to their rocky cavern
In the copper bearing mountain.
Spake the reckless Lemminkainen
"O thou ancient Wainamoinen,
Why was I not taken with thee
To become, thy war-companion?

The Kalevala
Would have been of goodly service,
Would have drawn the bolts or broken,
All the portals to the cavern,
Where the Sun and Moon lie hidden
In the copper-bearing mountain!"
Wainamoinen, ancient minstrel,
Thus replied to Lemminkainen:
"Empty Words will break no portals,
Draw no bolts of any moment;
Locks and bolts are never broken.
With the words of little wisdom!
Greater means than thou commandest
Must be used to free the sunshine,
Free the moonlight from her dungeon."
Wainamoinen, not discouraged,
Hastened to the forge and smithy,
Spake these words to Ilmarinen:
"O thou famous metal-artist,
Forge for me a magic trident,
Forge from steel a dozen stout-rings,
Master-keys, a goodly number,
Iron bars and heavy hammers,
That the Sun we may uncover
In the copper-bearing mountain,
In the stone-berg of Pohyola."
Then the blacksmith, Ilmarinen,
The eternal metal-worker,
Forged the needs of Wainamoinen,
Forged for him the magic trident,
Forged from steel a dozen stout-rings,
Master-keys a goodly number,
Iron bars and heavy hammers,
Not the largest, nor the smallest,
Forged them of the right dimensions.
Louhi, hostess of Pohyola,
Northland's old and toothless wizard,
Fastened wings upon her shoulders,
As an eagle, sailed the heavens,
Over field, and fen, and forest,
Over Pohya's many, waters,
To the hamlets of Wainola,
To the forge of Ilmarinen.
Quick the famous metal-worker
Went to see if winds were blowing;
Found the winds at peace and silent,
Found an eagle, sable-colored,
Perched upon his window-casement.
Spake the artist, Ilmarinen:
"Magic bird, whom art thou seeking,
Why art sitting at my window?"
This the answer of the eagle:
"Art thou blacksmith, Ilmarinen,
The eternal iron-forger,
Master of the magic metals,
Northland's wonder-working artist?"
Ilmarinen gave this answer:
"There is nothing here of wonder,
Since I forged the dome of heaven,
Forged the earth a concave cover!"
Spake again the magic eagle:
Why this ringing of thine anvil,

Why this knocking of thy hammer,
Tell me what thy hands are forging?"
This the answer of the blacksmith:
"'Tis a collar I am forging
For the neck of wicked Louhi,
Toothless witch of Sariola,
Stealer of the silver sunshine,
Stealer of the golden moonlight;
With this collar I shall bind her
To the iron-rock of Ehstland!"
Louhi, hostess of Pohyola,
Saw misfortune fast approaching,
Saw destruction flying over,
Saw the signs of bad-luck lower;
Quickly winged her way through ether
To her native halls and chambers,
To the darksome Sariola,
There unlocked the massive portals
Where the Sun and Moon were hidden,
In the rock of many colors,
In the cavern iron-banded,
In the copper-bearing mountain.
Then again the wicked Louhi
Changed her withered form and features,
And became a dove of good-luck;
Straightway winged the starry heavens,
Over field, and fen, and forest,
To the meadows of Wainola,
To the plains of Kalevala,
To the forge of Ilmarinen.
This the question of the blacksmith
"Wherefore comest, dove of good-luck,
What the tidings that thou bringest?"
Thus the magic bird made answer:
"Wherefore come I to thy smithy?
Come to bring the joyful tidings
That the Sun has left his cavern,
Left the rock of many colors,
Left the stone-berg of Pohyola;
That the Moon no more is hidden
In the copper-bearing mountains,
In the caverns iron-banded."
Straightway hastened Ilmarinen
To the threshold of his smithy,
Quickly scanned the far horizon,
Saw again the silver sunshine,
Saw once more the golden moonlight,
Bringing peace, and joy, and plenty,
To the homes of Kalevala.
Thereupon the blacksmith hastened
To his brother, Wainamoinen,
Spake these words to the magician:
"O thou ancient bard and minstrel,
The eternal wizard-singer
See, the Sun again is shining,
And the golden Moon is beaming
From their long-neglected places,
From their stations in the sky-vault!"
Wainamoinen, old and faithful,
Straightway hastened to the court-yard,
Looked upon the far horizon,

The Kalevala
Saw once more the silver sunshine,
Saw again the golden moonlight,
 Bringing peace, and joy, and plenty,
To the people of the Northland,
And the minstrel spake these measures:
"Greetings to thee, Sun of fortune,
Greetings to thee, Moon of good-luck,
Welcome sunshine, welcome moonlight,
Golden is the dawn of morning!
Free art thou, O Sun of silver,
Free again, O Moon beloved,
As the sacred cuckoo's singing,
As the ring-dove's liquid cooings.
"Rise, thou silver Sun, each Morning,
Source of light and life hereafter,
Bring us, daily, joyful greetings,
Fill our homes with peace and plenty,
That our sowing, fishing, hunting,
May be prospered by thy coming.
Travel on thy daily journey,
Let the Moon be ever with thee;
Glide along thy way rejoicing,
End thy journeyings in slumber;
Rest at evening in the ocean,
When the daily cares have ended,
To the good of all thy people,
To the pleasure Of Wainoloa,
To the joy of Kalevala!"

RUNE L
MARIATTA--WAINAMOINEN'S DEPARTURE.

Mariatta, child of beauty,
Grew to maidenhood in Northland,
In the cabin of her father,
In the chambers of her mother,
Golden ringlets, silver girdles,
Worn against the keys paternal,
Glittering upon her bosom;
Wore away the father's threshold
With the long robes of her garments;
Wore away the painted rafters
With her beauteous silken ribbons;
Wore away the gilded pillars
With the touching of her fingers;
Wore away the birchen flooring
With the tramping of her fur-shoes.
Mariatta, child of beauty,
Magic maid of little stature,
Guarded well her sacred virtue,
Her sincerity and honor,
Fed upon the dainty whiting,
On the inner bark of birch-wood,
On the tender flesh of lambkins.
When she hastened in the evening
To her milking in the hurdles,
Spake in innocence as follows:
"Never will the snow-white virgin
Milk the kine of one unworthy!"
When she journeyed over snow-fields,
On the seat beside her father,
Spake in purity as follows:
"Not behind a steed unworthy
Will I ever ride the snow-sledge!"
Mariatta, child of beauty,
Lived a virgin with her mother,
As a maiden highly honored,
Lived in innocence and beauty,
Daily drove her flocks to pasture,
Walking with the gentle lambkins.
When the lambkins climbed the mountains,
When they gamboled on the hill-tops,
Stepped the virgin to the meadow,
Skipping through a grove of lindens,
At the calling of the cuckoo,
To the songster's golden measures.
Mariatta, child of beauty,
Looked about, intently listened,
Sat upon the berry-meadow
Sat awhile, and meditated
On a hillock by the forest,
And soliloquized as follows:
"Call to me, thou golden cuckoo,
Sing, thou sacred bird of Northland,
Sing, thou silver breasted songster,

The Kalevala

Speak, thou strawberry of Ehstland,
Tell bow long must I unmarried,
As a shepherdess neglected,
Wander o'er these bills and mountains,
Through these flowery fens and fallows.
Tell me, cuckoo of the woodlands,
Sing to me how many summers
I must live without a husband,
As a shepherdess neglected!"
Mariatta, child of beauty,
Lived a shepherd-maid for ages,
As a virgin with her mother.
Wretched are the lives of shepherds,
Lives of maidens still more wretched,
Guarding flocks upon the mountains;
Serpents creep in bog and stubble,
On the greensward dart the lizards;
But it was no serpent singing,
Nor a sacred lizard calling,
It was but the mountain-berry
Calling to the lonely maiden:
"Come, O virgin, come and pluck me,
Come and take me to thy bosom,
Take me, tinsel-breasted virgin,
Take me, maiden, copper-belted,
Ere the slimy snail devours me,
Ere the black-worm feeds upon me.
Hundreds pass my way unmindful,
Thousands come within my hearing,
Berry-maidens swarm about me,
Children come in countless numbers,
None of these has come to gather,
Come to pluck this ruddy berry."
Mariatta, child of beauty,
Listened to its gentle pleading,
Ran to pick the berry, calling,
With her fair and dainty fingers,.
Saw it smiling near the meadow,
Like a cranberry in feature,
Like a strawberry in flavor;
But be Virgin, Mariatta,
Could not pluck the woodland-stranger,
Thereupon she cut a charm-stick,
Downward pressed upon the berry,
When it rose as if by magic,
Rose above her shoes of ermine,
Then above her copper girdle,
Darted upward to her bosom,
Leaped upon the maiden's shoulder,
On her dimpled chin it rested,
On her lips it perched a moment,
Hastened to her tongue expectant
To and fro it rocked and lingered,
Thence it hastened on its journey,
Settled in the maiden's bosom.
Mariatta, child of beauty,
Thus became a bride impregnate,
Wedded to the mountain-berry;
Lingered in her room at morning,
Sat at midday in the darkness,
Hastened to her couch at evening.

Lönnrot

Thus the watchful mother wonders:
"What has happened to our Mary,
To our virgin, Mariatta,
That she throws aside her girdle,
Shyly slips through hall and chamber,
Lingers in her room at morning,
Hastens to her couch at evening,
Sits at midday in the darkness?"
On the floor a babe was playing,
And the young child thus made answer:
"This has happened to our Mary,
To our virgin, Mariatta,
This misfortune to the maiden:
She has lingered by the meadows,
Played too long among the lambkins,
Tasted of the mountain-berry."
Long the virgin watched and waited,
Anxiously the days she counted,
Waiting for the dawn of trouble.
Finally she asked her mother,
These the words of Mariatta:
"Faithful mother, fond and tender,
Mother whom I love and cherish,
Make for me a place befitting,
Where my troubles may be lessened,
And my heavy burdens lightened."
This the answer of the mother:
"Woe to thee, thou Hisi-maiden,
Since thou art a bride unworthy,
Wedded only to dishonor!"
Mariatta, child of beauty,
Thus replied in truthful measures:
"I am not a maid of Hisi,
I am not a bride unworthy,
Am not wedded to dishonor;
As a shepherdess I wandered
With the lambkins to the glen-wood,
Wandered to the berry-mountain,
Where the strawberry had ripened;
Quick as thought I plucked the berry,
On my tongue I gently laid it,
To and fro it rocked and lingered,
Settled in my heaving bosom.
This the source of all my trouble,
Only cause of my dishonor!"
As the mother was relentless,
Asked the maiden of her father,
This the virgin-mother's pleading:
O my father, full of pity,
Source of both my good and evil,
Build for me a place befitting,
Where my troubles may be lessened,
And my heavy burdens lightened."
This the answer of the father,
Of the father unforgiving:
"Go, thou evil child of Hisi,
Go, thou child of sin and sorrow,
Wedded only to dishonor,
To the Great Bear's rocky chamber,
To the stone-cave of the growler,
There to lessen all thy troubles,

The Kalevala
There to cast thy heavy burdens!"
Mariatta, child of beauty,
Thus made answer to her father:
"I am not a child of Hisi,
I am not a bride unworthy,
Am not wedded to dishonor;
I shall bear a noble hero,
I shall bear a son immortal,
Who will rule among the mighty,
Rule the ancient Wainamoinen."
Thereupon the virgin-mother
Wandered hither, wandered thither,
Seeking for a place befitting,
Seeking for a worthy birth-place
For her unborn son and hero;
Finally these words she uttered
"Piltti, thou my youngest maiden,
Trustiest of all my servants,
Seek a place within the village,
Ask it of the brook of Sara,
For the troubled Mariatta,
Child of sorrow and misfortune."
Thereupon the little maiden,
Piltti, spake these words in answer:
"Whom shall I entreat for succor,
Who will lend me his assistance?
These the words of Mariatta:
"Go and ask it of Ruotus,
Where the reed-brook pours her waters."
Thereupon the servant, Piltti,
Ever hopeful, ever willing,
Hastened to obey her mistress,
Needing not her exhortation;
Hastened like the rapid river,
Like the flying smoke of battle
To the cabin of Ruotus.
When she walked the hill-tops tottered,
When she ran the mountains trembled;
Shore-reeds danced upon the pasture,
Sandstones skipped about the heather
As the maiden, Piltti, hastened
To the dwelling of Ruotus.
At his table in his cabin
Sat Ruotus, eating, drinking,
In his simple coat of linen.
With his elbows on the table
Spake the wizard in amazement:
"Why hast thou, a maid of evil,
Come to see me in my cavern,
What the message thou art bringing?
Thereupon the servant, Piltti,
Gave this answer to the wizard:
"Seek I for a spot befitting,
Seek I for a worthy birth-place,
For an unborn child and hero;
Seek it near the Sara-streamlet,
Where the reed-brook pours her waters.
Came the wife of old Ruotus,
Walking with her arms akimbo,
Thus addressed the maiden, Piltti:
"Who is she that asks assistance,

Lönnrot

Who the maiden thus dishonored,
What her name, and who her kindred?"
"I have come for Mariatta,
For the worthy virgin-mother."
Spake the wife of old Ruotus,
Evil-minded, cruel-hearted:
"Occupied are all our chambers,
All our bath-rooms near the reed-brook;
in the mount of fire are couches,
is a stable in the forest,
For the flaming horse of Hisi;
In the stable is a manger
Fitting birth-place for the hero
From the wife of cold misfortune,
Worthy couch for Mariatta!"
Thereupon the servant, Piltti,
Hastened to her anxious mistress,
Spake these measures, much regretting.
"There is not a place befitting,
on the silver brook of Sara.
Spake the wife of old Ruotus:
'Occupied are all the chambers,
All the bath-rooms near the reed-brook;
In the mount of fire are couches,
Is a stable, in the forest,
For the flaming horse of Hisi;
In the stable is a manger,
Fitting birth-place for the hero
From the wife of cold misfortune,
Worthy couch for Mariatta.'"
Thereupon the hapless maiden,
Mariatta, virgin-mother,
Fell to bitter tears and murmurs,
Spake these words in depths of sorrow:
"I, alas! must go an outcast,
Wander as a wretched hireling,
Like a servant in dishonor,
Hasten to the burning mountain,
To the stable in the forest,
Make my bed within a manger,
Near the flaming steed of Hisi!"
Quick the hapless virgin-mother,
Outcast from her father's dwelling,
Gathered up her flowing raiment,
Grasped a broom of birchen branches,
Hastened forth in pain and sorrow
To the stable in the woodlands,
On the heights of Tapio's mountains,
Spake these words in supplication:
"Come, I pray thee, my Creator,
Only friend in times of trouble,
Come to me and bring protection
To thy child, the virgin-mother,
To the maiden, Mariatta,
In this hour of sore affliction.
Come to me, benignant Ukko,
Come, thou only hope and refuge,
Lest thy guiltless child should perish,
Die the death of the unworthy!"
When the virgin, Mariatta,
Had arrived within the stable

The Kalevala
Of the flaming horse of Hisi,
She addressed the steed as follows:
"Breathe, O sympathizing fire-horse,
Breathe on me, the virgin-mother,
Let thy heated breath give moisture,
Let thy pleasant warmth surround me,
Like the vapor of the morning;
Let this pure and helpless maiden
Find a refuge in thy manger!"
Thereupon the horse, in pity,
Breathed the moisture of his nostrils
On the body of the virgin,
Wrapped her in a cloud of vapor,
Gave her warmth and needed comforts,
Gave his aid to the afflicted,
To the virgin, Mariatta.
There the babe was born and cradled
Cradled in a woodland-manger,
Of the virgin, Mariatta,
Pure as pearly dews of morning,
Holy as the stars in heaven.
There the mother rocks her infant,
In his swaddling clothes she wraps him,
Lays him in her robes of linen;
Carefully the babe she nurtures,
Well she guards her much-beloved,
Guards her golden child of beauty,
Her beloved gem of silver.
But alas! the child has vanished,
Vanished while the mother slumbered.
Mariatta, lone and wretched,
Fell to weeping, broken-hearted,
Hastened off to seek her infant.
Everywhere the mother sought him,
Sought her golden child of beauty,
Her beloved gem of silver;
Sought him underneath the millstone,
In the sledge she sought him vainly,
Underneath the sieve she sought him,
Underneath the willow-basket,
Touched the trees, the grass she parted,
Long she sought her golden infant,
Sought him on the fir-tree-mountain,
In the vale, and hill, and heather;
Looks within the clumps of flowers,
Well examines every thicket,
Lifts the juniper and willow,
Lifts the branches of the alder.
Lo! a star has come to meet her,
And the star she thus beseeches-.
"O, thou guiding-star of Northland,
Star of hope, by God created,
Dost thou know and wilt thou tell me
Where my darling child has wandered,
Where my holy babe lies hidden?"
Thus the star of Northland answers:
"If I knew, I would not tell thee;
'Tis thy child that me created,
Set me here to watch at evening,
In the cold to shine forever,
Here to twinkle in the darkness."

Comes the golden Moon to meet her,
And the Moon she thus beseeches:
"Golden Moon, by Ukko fashioned,
Hope and joy of Kalevala,
Dost thou know and wilt thou tell me
Where my darling child has wandered,
Where my holy babe lies hidden?
Speaks the golden Moon in answer:
"If I knew I would not tell thee;
'Tis thy child that me created,
Here to wander in the darkness,
All alone at eve to wander
On my cold and cheerless journey,
Sleeping only in the daylight,
Shining for the good of others."
Thereupon the virgin-mother
Falls again to bitter weeping,
Hastens on through fen and forest,
Seeking for her babe departed.
Comes the silver Sun to meet her,
And the Sun she thus addresses:
"Silver Sun by Ukko fashioned,
Source of light and life to Northland,
Dost thou know and wilt thou tell me
Where my darling child has wandered,
Where my holy babe lies hidden?"
Wisely does the Sun make answer:
"Well I know thy babe's dominions,
Where thy holy child is sleeping,
Where Wainola's light lies hidden;
'Tis thy child that me created,
Made me king of earth and ether,
Made the Moon and Stars attend me,
Set me here to shine at midday,
Makes me shine in silver raiment,
Lets me sleep and rest at evening;
Yonder is thy golden infant,
There thy holy babe lies sleeping,
Hidden to his belt in water,
Hidden in the reeds and rushes."
Mariatta, child of beauty,
Virgin-mother of the Northland,
Straightway seeks her babe in Swamp-land,
Finds him in the reeds and rushes;
Takes the young child on her bosom
To the dwelling of her father.
There the infant grew in beauty,
Gathered strength, and light, and wisdom,
All of Suomi saw and wondered.
No one knew what name to give him;
When the mother named him, Flower,
Others named him, Son-of-Sorrow.
When the virgin, Mariatta,
Sought the priesthood to baptize him,
Came an old man, Wirokannas,
With a cup of holy water,
Bringing to the babe his blessing;
And the gray-beard spake as follows:
"I shall not baptize a wizard,
Shall not bless a black-magician
With the drops of holy water;

The Kalevala

Let the young child be examined,
Let us know that he is worthy,
Lest he prove the son of witchcraft."
Thereupon old Wirokannas
Called the ancient Wainamoinen,
The eternal wisdom-singer,
To inspect the infant-wonder,
To report him good or evil.
Wainamoinen, old and faithful,
Carefully the child examined,
Gave this answer to his people:
"Since the child is but an outcast,
Born and cradled in a manger,
Since the berry is his father;
Let him lie upon the heather,
Let him sleep among the rushes,
Let him live upon the mountains;
Take the young child to the marshes,
Dash his head against the birch-tree."
Then the child of Mariatta,
Only two weeks old, made answer:
"O, thou ancient Wainamoinen,
Son of Folly and Injustice,
Senseless hero of the Northland,
Falsely hast thou rendered judgment.
In thy years, for greater follies,
Greater sins and misdemeanors,
Thou wert not unjustly punished.
In thy former years of trouble,
When thou gavest thine own brother,
For thy selfish life a ransom,
Thus to save thee from destruction,
Then thou wert not sent to Swamp-land
To be murdered for thy follies.
In thy former years of sorrow,
When the beauteous Aino perished
In the deep and boundless blue-sea,
To escape thy persecutions,
Then thou wert not evil-treated,
Wert not banished by thy people."
Thereupon old Wirokannas,
Of the wilderness the ruler,
Touched the child with holy water,
Crave the wonder-babe his blessing,
Gave him rights of royal heirship,
Free to live and grow a hero,
To become a mighty ruler,
King and Master of Karyala.
As the years passed Wainamoinen
Recognized his waning powers,
Empty-handed, heavy-hearted,
Sang his farewell song to Northland,
To the people of Wainola;
Sang himself a boat of copper,
Beautiful his bark of magic;
At the helm sat the magician,
Sat the ancient wisdom-singer.
Westward, westward, sailed the hero
O'er the blue-back of the waters,
Singing as he left Wainola,
This his plaintive song and echo:

Lönnrot

"Suns may rise and set in Suomi,
Rise and set for generations,
When the North will learn my teachings,
Will recall my wisdom-sayings,
Hungry for the true religion.
Then will Suomi need my coming,
Watch for me at dawn of morning,
That I may bring back the Sampo,
Bring anew the harp of joyance,
Bring again the golden moonlight,
Bring again the silver sunshine,
Peace and plenty to the Northland."
Thus the ancient Wainamoinen,
In his copper-banded vessel,
Left his tribe in Kalevala,
Sailing o'er the rolling billows,
Sailing through the azure vapors,
Sailing through the dusk of evening,
Sailing to the fiery sunset,
To the higher-landed regions,
To the lower verge of heaven;
Quickly gained the far horizon,
Gained the purple-colored harbor.
There his bark be firmly anchored,
Rested in his boat of copper;
But he left his harp of magic,
Left his songs and wisdom-sayings,
To the lasting joy of Suomi.

EPILOGUE

Now I end my measured singing,
Bid my weary tongue keep silence,
Leave my songs to other singers.
Horses have their times of resting
After many hours of labor;
Even sickles will grow weary
When they have been long at reaping;
Waters seek a quiet haven
After running long in rivers;
Fire subsides and sinks in slumber
At the dawning of the morning
Therefore I should end my singing,
As my song is growing weary,
For the pleasure of the evening,
For the joy of morn arising.
Often I have heard it chanted,
Often heard the words repeated:
"Worthy cataracts and rivers
Never empty all their waters."
Thus the wise and worthy singer
Sings not all his garnered wisdom;
Better leave unsung some sayings
Than to sing them out of season.
Thus beginning, and thus ending,
Do I roll up all my legends,
Roll them in a ball for safety,
In my memory arrange them,
In their narrow place of resting,
Lest the songs escape unheeded,
While the lock is still unopened,
While the teeth remain unparted,
And the weary tongue is silent.
Why should I sing other legends,
Chant them in the glen and forest,
Sing them on the hill and heather?
Cold and still my golden mother
Lies beneath the meadow, sleeping,
Hears my ancient songs no longer,
Cannot listen to my singing;
Only will the forest listen,
Sacred birches, sighing pine-trees,
Junipers endowed with kindness,
Alder-trees that love to bear me,
With the aspens and the willows.
When my loving mother left me,
Young was I, and low of stature;
Like the cuckoo of the forest,
Like the thrush upon the heather,
Like the lark I learned to twitter,
Learned to sing my simple measures,
Guided by a second mother,
Stern and cold, without affection;
Drove me helpless from my chamber
To the wind-side of her dwelling,

Lönnrot

To the north-side of her cottage,
Where the chilling winds in mercy
Carried off the unprotected.
As a lark I learned to wander,
Wander as a lonely song-bird,
Through the forests and the fenlands
Quietly o'er hill and heather;
Walked in pain about the marshes,
Learned the songs of winds and waters,
Learned the music of the ocean,
And the echoes of the woodlands.
Many men that live to murmur,
Many women live to censure,
Many speak with evil motives;
Many they with wretched voices
Curse me for my wretched singing,
Blame my tongue for speaking wisdom,
Call my ancient songs unworthy,
Blame the songs and curse the singer.
Be not thus, my worthy people,
Blame me not for singing badly,
Unpretending as a minstrel.
I have never had the teaching,
Never lived with ancient heroes,
Never learned the tongues of strangers,
Never claimed to know much wisdom.
Others have had language-masters,
Nature was my only teacher,
Woods and waters my instructors.
Homeless, friendless, lone, and needy,
Save in childhood with my mother,
When beneath her painted rafters,
Where she twirled the flying spindle,
By the work-bench of my brother,
By the window of my sister,
In. the cabin of my father,
In my early days of childhood.
Be this as it may, my people,
This may point the way to others,
To the singers better gifted,
For the good of future ages,
For the coming generations,
For the rising folk of Suomi.

The Kalevala

GLOSSARY

Aar'ni (Ar'ni). The guardian of hidden treasures.
A-ha'va. The West-wind; the father of the swift dogs.
Ah'ti. The same as Lemminkainen.
Ah'to. The great god of the waters.
Ah'to-la. The water-castle of Ahto and his people.
Ah'to-lai'set. The inhabitants of Ahtola.
Ai-nik'ki. A sister of Ahti.
Ai'no (i'no). Youkahainen's sister.
An'te-ro. A goddess of the waves.
Ai'ue-lake. The lake into which the Fire-child falls.
An-nik'ki. Ilmarinen's sister.
An'te-ro. Another name for Wipanen, or Antero Wipunen.
Dus'ter-land. The Northland; Pimentola.
Et'e-le'tar. A daugter of the South-wind.
Fire-Child. A synonym of Panu.
Frost. The English for Pakkanen.
Hal'lap-yo'ra. A lake in Finland.
Hal'ti-a (plural Haltiat). The Genius of Finnish mythology.
Het'e-wa'ne. The Finnish name of the Pleiades.
Hi'si (original Hiisi). The Evil Principle; also called Jutas, Lempo, and Piru.
Mon'ja-tar. The daughter of the Pine-tree.
Hor'na. A sacred rock in Finland.
I'ku-Tur'so. An evil giant of the sea.
Il'ma-ri'nem. The worker of the metals; a brother of Wainamoinen.
Il'ma-tar. Daughter of the Air, and mother of Wainamoinen.
Il'po-tar. Believed to be the daughter of the Snow flake; the same as Louhi.
Im-a'tra. A celebrated waterfall near Wiborg.
In'ger-land. The present St. Petersburg.
Ja'men (Ya'men). A river of Finland.
Jor'dan. Curiously, the river of Palestine.
Jou'ka-hai'nen (You-ka-hai'nen). A celebrated minstrel of Pohyola.
Jou-ko'la (You-ko'la). The home or dwelling of Youkahainen.
Ju-ma'la (You-ma'la). Originally the heavens, then the god of the heavens, and finally God.
Ju'tas (yu'tas). The Evil Principle; Hisi, Piru, and Lempo are synonyms,
Kai'to-lai'nen. A son of the god of metals; from his spear came the tongue of the serpent.
Ka-ler'vo. The father of Kullervo.
Ka-le'va (Kalewai'nen). The father of heroes; a hero in general.
Kal'e-va'la (kaleva, hero, and la, the place of). The land of heroes; the name of the epic poem of Finland.
Kal'e-va'tar (Kalewa'tar). Daughter of Kaleva.
Kal-e'vo. The same as Kaleva.
Ka'lew. Often used for Kaleva.
Kal'ma. The god of death.
Kam'mo. The father of Kimmo.
Kan'ka-hat'ta-ret. The goddesses of weaving.
Ka'pe. A synonym of Ilmatar, the mother of Wainamoinen.
Ka'po. A synonym of Osmotar.
Ka-re'len. A province of Finland.
Kar-ja'la, (karya'la). The seat of the waterfall, Kaatrakoski.
Kat'e-ja'tar (kataya'tar). The daughter of the Pine-tree.
Kat'ra-kos'ki (Kaatrakos'ki). A waterfall in Karjala.
Kau'ko. The same as Kaukomieli.
Kau'ko-miel'li. The same as Lemminkainen.
Kaup'pi. The Snowshoe-builder; Lylikki.

Ke'mi. A river of Finland.
Kim'mo. A name for the cow; the daughter of Kammo, the patron of the rocks.
Ki'pu-ki'vi. The name of the rock at Hell-river, beneath which the spirits of all diseases are imprisoned.
Kir'kon-Woe'ki. Church dwarfs living under altars.
Knik'ka-no. Same as Knippana.
Knip'pa-no. Same as Tapio.
Koot'a-moi'nen. The Moon.
Kos'ken-nei'ti. The goddess of the cataract.
Kul-ler'vo. The vicious son of Kalervo.
Kul'ler-woi'nen. The same as Kullervo.
Kul'li. A beautiful daughter of Sahri.
Kun. The Moon, and the Moon-god.
Kun'tar. One of the daughters of the Moon.
Ku'ra (Kuura). The Hoar-frost; also called Tiera, a ball of ice.
Kul-lik'ki (also Kyl'li). The Sahri-maiden whom Lemminkainen kidnapped.
Lak'ka. Mother of Ilmarinen.
Lak-ko. The hostess of Kalevala.
Lem'min-kai'nen. One of the brothers of Wainamoinen; a son of Lempi.
Lem'pi-bay. A bay of Finland.
Lem'po. The Evil Principle; same as Hisi, Piru, and Jutas.
Lin'nun-ra'ta (Bird-way). The Milky-way.
Lou'hi. The hostess of Pohyola.
Low-ya'tar. Tuoni's blind daughter, and the originator of the Plagues.
Lu'on-no'tar. One of the mystic maidens, and the nurse of Wainamoinen.
Lu'o-to'la. A bay of Finland, named with Joukola.
Ly-lik'ki (Lyylik'ki). Maker of the snow-shoe.
Maan-e'mo (man-e'mo). The mother of the Earth.
Ma'hi-set (Maa'hi-set). The invisibly small deities of Finnish mythology.
Mam'me-lai'nen. The goddess of hidden treasures.
Ma'na. A synonym of Tuoni, the god of death.
Man'a-lai'nen. The same as Mana.
Masr'i-at'ta (marja, berry). The Virgin Mary of Finnish mythology.
Mat'ka-Tep'po. The road-god.
Meh'i-lai'nen. The honey-bee.
Mel'a-tar. The goddess of the helm.
Met'so-la. The same as Tapiola, the abode of the god of the forest,
Mie-lik'ki. The hostess of the forest.
Mi-merk'ki. A synonym of Mielikki.
Mosk'va. A province of Suomi.
Mu-rik'ki (Muurik'ki). The name of the cow.
Ne'wa. A river of Finland.
Ny-rik'ki. A son of Tapio.
Os'mo. The same as Osmoinen.
Os-noi'nen. A synonym of Wainola's hero.
Os'mo-tar. The daughter of Osmo; she directs the brewing of the beer for Ilmarinen's wedding-feast.
O-ta'va. The Great Bear of the heavens.
Ot'so. The bear of Finland.
Poe'ivoe. The Sun, and the Sun god.
Pai'va-tar. The goddess of the summer.
Pak'ka-nen. A synonym of Kura.
Pal-woi'nen. A synonym of Turi, and also of Wirokannas.
Pa'nu. The Fire-Child, born from the sword of Ukko.
Pa'ra. A tripod-deity, presiding over milk and cheese.
Pel'ler-woi'nen. The sower of the forests.
Pen'i-tar. A blind witch of Pohyola; and the mother of the dog.
Pik'ku Mies. The water-pigmy that felled the over-spreading oak-tree for Wainamoinen.
Pil'a-ya'tar (Pilaja'tar). The daughter of the Aspen; and the goddess of the Mountain-ash.
Pilt'ti. The maid-servant of Mariatta.
Pi'men-to'la. A province of Finland; another name for Pohyola.
Pi'ru. The same as Lempo, Jutas, and Hisi.
Pi'sa. A mountain of Finland.

Poh'ya (Poh'ja). An abbreviated form for Pohyola.
Poh-yo'la (Poh-jo'la). The Northland; Lapland.
Pok-ka'nen. The Frost, the son of Puhuri; a synonym of Tiera.
Puh-hu'ri. The North-wind; the father of Pokkanen.
Rem'men. The father of the hop-vine.
Re'mu. The same as Remmen.
Ru-o'tus. A persecutor of the Virgin Mariatta.
Rut'ya (Rut'ja). A waterfall of Northland.
Sah'ri (Saari). The home of Kyllikki.
Sam'po. The jewel that Ilmarinen forges from the magic metals; a talisman of success to the possessor; a continual source of strife between the tribes of the North.
Samp'sa. A synonym of Pellerwoinen.
Sa'ra. The same as Sariola.
Sar'i-o'la. The same as Pohyola.
Sat'ka. A goddess of the sea.
Sa'wa (Sa'wo). The eastern part of Finland.
Sim'a Pil'li (Honey-flute). The flute of Sima-suu.
Sim'a-Suu. One of the maidens of Tapio.
Sin'e-tar. The goddess of the blue sky.
Si-net'ta-ret. The goddesses of dyeing.
Suk'ka-mie'li. The goddess of love.
Suo'mi (swo'mi). The ancient abode of the Finns.
Suo'ne-tar (swone-tar). The goddess of the veins.
Suo-wak'ko. An old wizard of Pohyola.
Suo'ya-tar (Syo'jatar). The mother of the serpent.
Su've-tar (Suve, summer). Goddess of the South-wind
Su-wan'to-lai'nen. Another name for Wainamoinen.
Taeh'ti. The Polar Star.
Ta-he'tar. The daughter of the Stars.
Tai'vas. The firmament in general.
Ta-ni'ka. A magic mansion of Pohja.
Ta'pi-o. The god of the forest.
Tel-le'rvo. A daughter of Tapio.
Ter'he-ne'tar. Daughter of the Fog.
Tie'ra. Same as Kura; the Hoar-frost.
Tont'tu. A little house-spirit.
Tu'a-me'tar. Daughter of the Alder-tree.
Tu-le'tar (Tuule'tar). A goddess of the winds.
Tu-lik'ki (Tuullk'ki). One of the daughters of Tapio.
Tu'o-ne'la. The abode of Tuoni.
Tuo'nen Poi'ka. The son of Tuoni.
Tu'o-ne'tar. The hostess of Death-land; a daughter of Tuoni.
Tu-o'ni. The god of death.
Tu'ri (Tuuri). The god of the Honey-land.
Turja (tur'ya). Another name for Pohya.
Tur'ya-lan'der. An epithet for one of the tribe of Louhi.
Tur'ya (Tyrja). A name for the waterfall of Rutya.
Uk'ko. The Great Spirit of Finnish mythology; his abode is in Jumala.
Uk'on-koi'va (Ukko's dog). The messenger of Ukko; the butterfly.
U'lap-pa'la. Another term for the abode of Tuoni.
Un'du-tar. Goddess of the fog.
U'ni. The god of sleep.
Un'ta-ma'la. A synonym for "the dismal Sariola."
Un-ta'mo. The god of dreams; the dreamer; a brother of Kalervo, and his enemy.
Un'tar. The same as Undutar.
Un'to. The same as Untamo.
Utu-tyt'to. The same as Undutar.
Wai'nam-oi'nen (Vainamoinen). The chief hero of the Kalevala; the hero of Wainola, whose mother, Ilmatar, fell from the air into the ocean.
Wai'no (Vai'no). The same as Wainamoinen.
Wai-no'la. The home of Wainamoinen and his people; a synonym of Kalevala.

Lönnrot

Wel-la'mo.   The hostess of the waters.
Wet'e-hi'nen.   An evil god of the sea.
Wi-pu'nen (Vipu'nen).   An old song-giant that swallowed Wainamoinen searching for the "lost words."
Wi'ro-kan'nas (Virokan'nas).   Ruler of the wilderness; the slayer of the huge bull of Suomi; the priest that baptizes the son of Mariatta.
Wo'ya-lan'der (Vuojalan'der).   An epithet for Laplander.
Wuok'sen (Vuo'ksen).   A river in the east of Finland.
Wuok'si.   The same as Wuoksen.

THE END.

Printed in the USA
CPSIA information can be obtained
at www.ICGtesting.com
LVHW010918240224
772718LV00003B/99